TRANSFORMATIVE PLANNING

The *Dialogues in Urban and Regional Planning* series offers a selection of some of the best scholarship in urban and regional planning from around the world with internationally recognized authors taking up urgent and salient issues from theory, education for, and practice of planning.

This 7th volume features contributions on the theme of *Transformative Planning: Smarter, Greener and More Inclusive Practices*. It includes chapters from leading planning scholars and practitioners who critically examine how transformative planning practices seek to reduce inequalities, promote sustained, inclusive and sustainable economic growth, achieve gender equality, improve human health and well-being, foster resilience of urban communities and protect the environment and thereby change urban planning paradigms. Several case studies of emerging transformative planning interventions illustrate practical ways forward.

Transformative Planning offers provocative insights into the global planning community's struggle and contribution to tackle the major challenges to society in the 21st century. It will be of use for advanced undergraduate and graduate courses in the wide-ranging fields encompassed by urban studies, sustainability studies, and urban and regional planning.

The *Dialogues in Urban and Regional Planning* (DURP) series is published in association with the Global Planning Education Association Network (GPEAN) and its member national and transnational planning schools associations.

Andrea I. Frank, PhD, is Senior Lecturer in Urban Planning at the University of Birmingham, UK. Her research interests encompass comparative international planning, sustainable development, public participation, and pedagogy. Throughout her career she has promoted capacity building for and in planning education. She has represented the Association of European Schools of Planning and chaired the Global Planning Education Association Network (GPEAN)

2010–14. She is currently Chair of the Association of European Schools of Planning's (AESOP) Excellence in Teaching Prize Jury and coordinates the AESOP Thematic Group on Planning Education. Her scholarly work includes *Urban Planning Education: Beginnings, Global Movement and Future Prospects* (co-edited with C. Silver, 2018) and *Teaching Urban and Regional Planning: Innovative Pedagogies in Practice* (2021) with Artur da Rosa Pires. She is one of the founders of AESOP's open access, double-blind peer-reviewed journal *Transactions of AESOP*.

Christopher Silver, PhD, FAICP, is Professor of Urban and Regional Planning who joined the faculty at University of Florida in 2006 as Dean of the College of Design, Construction and Planning (until 2016). Previously he served as Head of the Department of Urban and Regional Planning at the University of Illinois, Urbana-Champaign (1998–2006) and as Professor of Planning and Associate Dean at Virginia Commonwealth University. He is a four-time Fulbright Senior Scholar in Indonesia and holds honorary professorships at the University of Indonesia and the Institute of Technology, Bandung. Silver's scholarship includes 8 books (authored, co-authored and edited), 16 book chapters and 18 refereed articles. His initial publications dealt with race, politics, and planning in the United States, including *Twentieth Century Richmond: Planning, Politics and Race* (1984) and (with John Moeser) *The Separate City: Black Communities in Urban South, 1940–1968* (1995). Teaching, consulting, and researching in Indonesia led to *Planning the Megacity: Jakarta in the Twentieth Century* (2008), (with Victoria Beard and Faranak Miraftab), *Decentralization and Planning: Contested Spaces for Public Action in the Global South* (2008) and (with Andrea Frank) *Urban Planning Education: Beginnings, Global Movement and Future Prospects* (2018). His current publications focus on urban flood risk and water management in Jakarta. He is a past co-editor of the *Journal of the American Planning Association* and the founding editor of the *Journal of Planning History*. He served as President of the Society of American City Planning History, Vice President and President of the Association of Collegiate Schools of Planning, Chair of the Global Planning Education Association Network and Executive Secretary of the International Planning History Society.

Dialogues in Urban and Regional Planning

Leading Scholarship from the World's Planning Schools Associations

Transformative Planning: Smarter, Greener and More Inclusive Practices offers a selection of the best urban and regional planning scholarship from the world's planning schools associations. The papers presented here illustrate some of the concerns and discourse of planning scholars and provide a glimpse of planning theory and practice around the world. Everyone with an interest in urban and regional planning will find this collection stimulating in opening avenues for research and debate. The selection of papers for this volume is intended to highlight the complex concerns associated with smarter, greener and more inclusive planning as realized through transformative planning practices.

This book is published in association with the Global Planning Education Association Network (GPEAN) and its eleven member planning schools associations, which have nominated papers through regional competitions. These associations represent over 400 planning schools in nearly fifty countries around the world.

- Association of African Planning Schools (AAPS)
- Association of Collegiate Schools of Planning (ACSP)
- Association of Canadian University Planning Programs (ACUPP)
- Association of European Schools of Planning (AESOP)
- Association of Latin-American Schools of Urbanism and Planning (ALEUP)
- National Association of Urban and Regional Postgraduate and Research Programs (ANPUR)
- Australia and New Zealand Association of Planning Schools (ANZAPS)
- Association for the Promotion of Teaching and Research in Urban Planning and Development (APERAU)
- Asian Planning Schools Association (ASPA)
- Association of Schools of Planning in Indonesia (ASPI)
- The Association of Planning Schools of Turkey (TUPOB)

Editorial Advisory Board

- Sandeep Agrawal, University of Alberta, ACUPP
- Eda Beyazit, Istanbul Technical University, TUPOB
- Daan M. Bossuyt, University of Amsterdam, AESOP
- Ebru Cubukcu, Dokuz Eylul University, TUPOB
- Camila D'Ottaviano, University of São Paulo, ANPUR
- Marc Dumont, University of Lille, APERAU
- Robert Freestone, University of New South Wales, ANZAPS
- Delik Hudalah, Institute of Technology Bandung, ASPI
- Sang-In Jun, Seoul National University, APSA
- Garth Klein, University of Witwatersrand, AAPS
- Kristina L. Nilsson, Luleå University of Technology, AESOP
- Francis Y. Owusu, Iowa State University, ACSP
- Magdalena Vicuna Del Rio, Pontificia Universidad Catolica, ALEUP

TRANSFORMATIVE PLANNING

Smarter, Greener and More
Inclusive Practices

Edited by
Andrea I. Frank and Christopher Silver

First published 2022
by Routledge
605 Third Avenue, New York, NY 10158

and by Routledge
2 Park Square, Milton Park, Abingdon, Oxon, OX14 4RN

Routledge is an imprint of the Taylor & Francis Group, an informa business

© 2022 Taylor & Francis

The right of Andrea I. Frank and Christopher Silver to be identified as the authors of the editorial material, and of the authors for their individual chapters, has been asserted in accordance with sections 77 and 78 of the Copyright, Designs and Patents Act 1988.

All rights reserved. No part of this book may be reprinted or reproduced or utilised in any form or by any electronic, mechanical, or other means, now known or hereafter invented, including photocopying and recording, or in any information storage or retrieval system, without permission in writing from the publishers.

Trademark notice: Product or corporate names may be trademarks or registered trademarks, and are used only for identification and explanation without intent to infringe.

Library of Congress Cataloging-in-Publication Data
A catalog record for this title has been requested

ISBN: 9781032014197 (hbk)
ISBN: 9781032014166 (pbk)
ISBN: 9781003178545 (ebk)

DOI: 10.4324/9781003178545

Typeset in Bembo
by codeMantra

Dedicated to
Dr. Vanessa Watson, AAPS
Co-editor of Volumes 1 and 2,
Dialogues in Urban and Regional Planning

CONTENTS

Acknowledgments	*xiii*
Contributors	*xv*

Introduction   1
Andrea I. Frank and Christopher Silver

Theoretical and Conceptual Frameworks   13

1 Transformative Incrementalism: Implications for Transformative Planning Practice   15
  Robert Buchan and Mark Holland

2 The Privatization of Metropolitan Jakarta's (Jabodetabek) Urban Fringes: The Early Stages of Post-Suburbanization in Indonesia   29
  Tommy Firman and Fikri Zul Fahmi

3 Transforming Transport Planning in the Post-Political Era   47
  Crystal Legacy

4 Local Values and Fairness in Climate Change Adaptation: Insights from Marginal Rural Australian Communities   66
  Sonia Graham, Jon Barnett, Ruth Fincher, Anna Hurlimann, and Colette Mortreux

5 Governance for Resilient Smart Cities 90
Darren Nel and Verna Nel

Educating for Transformative Planning Practices 101

6 De-Colonising Planning Education: Exploring the
Geographies of Urban Planning Education Networks 103
Julia Wesely and Adriana Allen

7 Transforming Planning Education: Practicing
Collaborative Governance and Experiential Learning in a
Graduate Level Planning Studio 121
Imge Akcakaya Waite, Elif Alkay and Sinem Becerik Altindis

8 Planners Moving Toward the New Urban Agenda:
Research Contribution and Training 140
Juan José Gutiérrez-Chaparro

9 Urban Planning in Guadalajara, Mexico: The New Urban
Agenda and Experience of Its Application Locally 154
José Luis Águila Flores and Raúl Agraz Joya

Research and Evaluations of Transformative Policy Initiatives 175

10 Towards Circular Economy Implementation in Urban
Projects: Practices and Assessment Tools 177
*Federica Appendino, Charlotte Roux, Myriam Saadé
and Bruno Peuportier*

11 Living With Water in the Era of Climate Change: Lessons
from the Lafitte Greenway in Post-Katrina New Orleans 195
Billy Fields, Jeffrey J. Thomas, and Jacob A. Wagner

12 The Role of Local Leaders Regarding Environmental
Concerns in Master Plans: An Empirical Study of China's
80 Large Municipalities 216
*Lei Zhang, Rachel M. Tochen, Michael Hibbard,
and Zhenghong Tang*

13 Further Opportunities to Reduce the Energy Use and
   Greenhouse Gas Emissions of Buildings   238
   David Hsu, Ting Meng, Albert T. Han and Daniel Suh

14 Influences of Planning Policies on Community Shaping in
   China: From Past to Present   265
   Jian Liu

Index   *285*

ACKNOWLEDGMENTS

Chapter 3 in this volume by Crystal Legacy was originally published in as Legacy, C, "Transforming transport planning in the post-political era," *Urban Studies* (53, 14) pp. 3108–24. Copyright © 2016 Sage Journals. DOI: 10.1177/0042098015602649 and reused with permission from Sage Publications.

Chapter 4 was first published as Graham, S., Barnett, J., Mortreux, C., Hurlimann, A. and Fincher, R., "Local values and fairness in climate change adaptation: insights from marginal rural Australian communities," *World Development*, 108, 332–43 (2018) and used here with permission granted by Elsevier Publisher. The research was carried out under a project funded by a Linkage Grant (LP100100586) from the Australian Research Council. Research partners on the linkage grant included the Wellington Shire Council, the East Gippsland Shire Council, the Gippsland Coastal Board, the Department of Sustainability and Environment and the Department of Planning and Community Development. The authors would like to acknowledge the support provided by these agencies. Special thanks go to Chandra Jayasuriya for creating the map and a thank you to all the people who took the time to respond to the survey.

A slightly longer version of Chapter 6 "De-Colonising Planning Education? Exploring the Geographies of Urban Planning Education Networks" was first published in 2019 in *Urban Planning*, 4(4), pp. 139–51. doi: 10.17645/up.v4i4.2200. © 2019 by the authors; licensee Cogitatio (Lisbon, Portugal). The original article was licensed under a Creative Commons Attribution 4.0 International License (CC BY). The article is part of the research project "Knowledge in Action for Urban Equality" (KNOW) funded by ESRC under the Global Challenges Research Fund (GCRF). Project number: ES/ P011225/1.

The authors of Chapter 7 wish to thank the cohort of the two studios of the Urban Planning Master's Program at Istanbul Technical University in the

2018–19 academic year for their contributions to this research. They would also extend their thanks to the Sarıyer Municipality administration and its Urban Design Department. The study would not have been as effective without the eager cooperation of both students and the local municipality associates.

Chapters 8 and 9 are included in this volume with the permission of the Associacion Latinamericana de Escuelas de Urbanismo y Planificacion (ALEUP) having previously appeared in their publication, Doumentos de Trabajo del Instituto de Estudios Urbanon y Territoriales.

Chapter 10 presents some of the first results of the PULSE-PARIS research project, currently under progress and funded by the French environmental and energy management agency (ADEME). An earlier and longer version of this paper is published in the *Journal Transactions of AESOP* and appears in Dialogues 7 with their consent.

The Chapter 13 material is based upon work supported by the Consortium for Building Energy Innovation (CBEI), an energy innovation hub sponsored by the U.S. Department of Energy under Award Number DE-EE0004261. This report was prepared as an account of work sponsored by an agency of the United States Government. Neither the United States Government nor any agency thereof, nor any of their employees, makes any warranty, express or implied; or assumes any legal liability or responsibility for the accuracy, completeness or usefulness of any information, apparatus, product or process disclosed; or represents that its use would not infringe privately owned rights. Reference herein to any specific commercial product, process or service by trade name, trademark, manufacturer or otherwise does not necessarily constitute or imply its endorsement, recommendation or favoring by the United States Government or any agency thereof. The views and opinions of authors expressed herein do not necessarily state or reflect those of the United States Government or any agency thereof. Thanks to the editors and reviewers of the *Journal of Planning Education and Research* for their perceptive and thoughtful comments that greatly improved the quality and focus of the argument in its original version. Thanks also to Laurie Actman, Mark Alan Hughes and Cody Taylor for their helpful comments, thinking and advocacy. Thanks to John Lee and Stacy Lee of the City of New York's Office of Long-Term Planning and Sustainability for providing the original benchmarking data.

Chapter 14 was first published in 2019 in *China City Planning Review* 28, 4 (2019: 18–29 and included in this volume with permission from CCPR.

CONTRIBUTORS

Elif Alkay is a Professor at the Department of Urban and Regional Planning at Istanbul Technical University. Her research field is urban economics and housing, and she currently teaches urban economics, housing policy and local economic development modules. The central theme of her recent research is the impact of market-led planning systems on housing supply outcomes. 0000-0001-6030-9219

Adriana Allen is Professor of Development Planning and Urban Sustainability at the Bartlett Development Planning Unit at University College London. She is also the President of the Habitat International Coalition (2019–23), a global network for the right to habitat and social justice, and the Bartlett's Vice-Dean International. Adriana has over 30 years of experience in research, postgraduate teaching and consultancy in over 25 countries across the Global South. Her work explores the interfaces between everyday city-making practices and planned interventions and their capacity to generate transformative spaces, places and social relations. 0000-0001-6215-5962

Sinem Becerik Altindis is an architect and urban designer working as a Research Assistant at the Department of Urban and Regional Planning at Bursa Technical University. She earned an MS degree from Istanbul Technical University in urban design and now is a PhD student in urban and regional planning. Her research interests include urban design, public places and urban history. 0000-0001-8473-6477

Federica Appendino is an Associate Professor in Urban Planning at ESPI Paris and Research Associate at ESPI2R and Lab'URBA Laboratories. She holds a joint PhD in Urban Planning and Heritage Conservation (2017, Sorbonne University and Politecnico of Turin), and her research focuses on sustainable urban planning, circular economy and environmental assessment procedures. 0000-0001-6846-2058

Jon Barnett is an Australian Research Council Laureate Fellow and Professor in the School of Geography at the University of Melbourne. He is a political geographer whose research investigates social impacts and responses to environmental change. Jon has 20 years of experience conducting field-based research in Pacific Island Countries, and in Australia, China and Timor-Leste. 0000-0002-0862-0808

Robert Buchan, PhD, FCIP, is an instructor at the University of Victoria and the Principal of iPlan Planning and Development Services. His professional work in official community plans, affordable housing, revitalization, trail planning, food system planning and interface fire hazard planning has won 19 awards of excellence including induction into the Canadian Institute of Planners College of Fellows. In 2017, he completed the doctoral program at the University of Victoria with a focus on sustainable food systems. 0000-0001-7067-0171

Fikri Zul Fahmi is an Assistant Professor of Urban and Regional Planning in the School of Architecture, Planning and Policy Development at Institut Teknologi Bandung. He has published articles in various journals such as *Habitat International*, *Urban Studies*, *Cities*, *Journal of the American Planning Association* and *International Development Planning Review*. He has focused his research on creative industries, rural transformation and socio-economic well-being. 0000-0002-4807-7125

Billy Fields is an Associate Professor in the Department of Political Science at Texas State University, San Marcos. His research focuses on climate resilience in transportation, urban planning and hazard mitigation.

Ruth Fincher is Redmond Barry Distinguished Professor Emeritus at the University of Melbourne. Ruth is an urban geographer with research and teaching interests in the urban outcomes of immigration and multiculturalism, diversity and difference in cities, gender issues, inequality and locational disadvantage. Ruth is a Board Member of the International Social Science Council and a past Vice President of the International Geographical Union.

Tommy Firman is a Professor of regional planning in the School of Architecture, Planning and Policy Development at Institut Teknologi Bandung. He has published numerous articles in reputable academic journals such as *Journal of the American Planning Association*, *Habitat International*, *Urban Studies* and *Asia Population Studies*. His research interests include population mobility and urbanization in Southeast Asia, urban labor market and land development, and decentralization. 0000-0002-9708-0902

José Luis Águila Flores is an Architect and PhD in City, Territory and Sustainability, Academic/Research Fellow of the Centro Universitario de Arte, Arquitectura y Diseño of the Universidad de Guadalajara, and Member of the National Researchers System (México). 0000-0002-8489-6515

Sonia Graham is an Australian Research Council DECRA Fellow in the School of Geography and Sustainable Communities at the University of Wollongong. She is a rural geographer who investigates collective action, environmental justice and lived values in the context of climate adaptation and invasive species management. 0000-0003-4195-4559

Juan José Gutiérrez-Chaparro is Research Professor in the Faculty of Urban and Regional Planning at the Autonomous University of the State of Mexico. He is an active member of the National Association of Educational Institutes for Territorial Planning, Urbanism and Urban Design (ANPUD, México). His research areas include theory, history, and trends of urban planning with a special interest in the case of Mexico and Latin America. 0000-0003-3695-1898

Albert T. Han is an Assistant Professor of Urban and Regional Planning at the University of Texas at San Antonio. His research focuses on land use planning and growth management for sprawl mitigation and land preservation, and environmental planning for pollution mitigation, climate change and environmental justice. 0000-0002-8307-9409

Michael Hibbard is Professor Emeritus at the University of Oregon Department of Planning, Public Policy and Management. His research focuses on community and regional development, with a special interest in the social impacts of economic change on small towns, Indigenous communities and rural regions in the United States and other industrialized nations. 0000-0002-0575-5985

Mark Holland, RPP, is planner, real estate development consultant and Professor in community planning. He was the Founding Manager of the City of Vancouver's sustainability office, built several consulting firms, served as Vice President of Development for several development companies and is the co-author of several books. He was awarded the Queen's Diamond Jubilee Medal for his leadership in sustainable community planning.

David Hsu is an Associate Professor of Urban and Environmental Planning in the Department of Urban Studies and Planning at the Massachusetts Institute of Technology. His research focuses on the design, management and governance of environmental networks at the local level, including buildings and systems for energy and water. 0000-0003-1108-9656

xviii Contributors

Anna Hurlimann is an Associate Professor in Urban Planning at The University of Melbourne. Her teaching and research activities focus on the mitigation of and adaptation to climate change through urban planning. Anna is the Lead Chief Investigator on an Australian Research Discovery Grant 2020–23 "Integrating climate change adaptation and mitigation in built environments." 0000-0001-9110-9340

Raúl Agraz Joya is an Architect and holds an MSc in Sustainable Territorial Development—Erasmus Mundus Joint Master Degree from Università degli Studi di Padova / KU Leuven / Université Paris I Panthéon-Sorbonne.

Crystal Legacy is a Senior Lecturer in Urban Planning at the University of Melbourne, Australia, where she is also the Deputy Director of the Informal Urbanism Research Hub (*InfUr-*). Crystal has published widely on the topics of transport governance, urban politics and citizen participation. She has edited two books *Instruments of Planning: Tensions and Challenges for More Equitable and Sustainable Cities* (Routledge, 2016) and *Building Inclusive Cities: Women's Safety and the Right to the City* (Routledge, 2013). 0000-0002-8687-7297

Jian Liu is tenured Associate Professor of Urban Planning and Design at the School of Architecture at Tsinghua University, Managing Chief-Editor of *China City Planning Review* and a registered city planner in China. She is also a Fulbright Visiting Scholar at Harvard University, US, and Visiting Scholar at l'Observatoire d'Architecture de la Chine Contemporaine, France, and University of British Columbia, Canada. She publishes both domestically and overseas, with particular interests on planning institutions, town and rural planning and design, urban regeneration and international comparative studies.

Ting Meng is an Assistant Professor in College of Economics and Management at China Agricultural University. She is a Research Associate in the Academy of Global Food Economics and Policy (AGFEP) and Beijing Food Safety Policy & Strategy Research Base. Her research interests focus on environmental economics and policy, as well as sustainable agricultural development. 0000-0002-0828-2108

Colette Mortreux is a Research Consultant at The Social Research Centre in Melbourne, Australia. She is a human geographer interested in disaster risk reduction, climate change adaptation and migration.

Darren Nel is an urban planner and spatial analyst. He has experience working in both academia and private sector. Darren is currently busy with his PhD that focuses on urban form and resilience at the School of Design at The Hong Kong Polytechnic University. 0000-0001-5411-997X

Verna Nel is Professor of Urban and Regional planning with over 30 years' experience in local government before moving to the University of the Free State, South Africa. Her research interests include urban/spatial resilience, spatial governance, local economic development and mining communities. 0000-0001-7446-5669

Bruno Peuportier, PhD, is Senior Scientist, teacher at MINES ParisTech and responsible of the Chair "Ecodesign of buildings and infrastructure." He is involved in research on the environmental performance of buildings, particularly the application of life cycle assessment (Building LCA tool EQUER), the study of renewable energies and new technologies, thermal modeling of buildings and design tools (energy simulation tool COMFIE). He has coordinated several European projects. 0000-0002-1085-3280

Charlotte Roux is Lecturer and Researcher at the EIVP (Paris School of urban engineering). Her research focuses mainly on life cycle-based eco-design tools at the urban scale and circular economy. 0000-0002-1085-0434

Myriam Saadé is a Research Fellow at the Université Gustave Eiffel. Her research addresses life cycle assessment of circular practices and infrastructures, as well as the politics of environmental expertise. 0000-0002-2219-792X

Daniel Suh is a Senior Data Scientist at Nike. He builds end-to-end ML models for Personalization and Consumer Segmentation.

Zhenghong Tang is an Associate Professor in the Community and Regional Planning Program at University of Nebraska-Lincoln. His major research interests address environmental planning, environmental modeling, hazard planning and planning for geospatial-enabled society.

Jeffrey J. Thomas is a New Orleans-based attorney and government services consultant with over 15 years of experience advising state and local governments on funding strategies, program designs and regulatory compliance strategies related to crisis and disaster recovery and resiliency. Relevant to this publication, Jeffrey served as Special Assistant to the City of New Orleans' post-Hurricane Katrina Office of Recovery and Development, supervising the use of federal funding for long-term recovery projects such as Lafitte Greenway.

Rachel M. Tochen is PhD candidate at the Renmin University of China, Public Administration and Public Policy. Her research focuses on collaborative planning with a special interest in public participation and capacity building. 0000-0002-7739-9836

Jacob A. Wagner is an Associate Professor of Urban Planning and Design at the University of Missouri-Kansas City. His work focuses on neighborhood planning, equity and sustainability in Kansas City and New Orleans. 0000-0001-7761-5837

Imge Akcakaya Waite is currently a Lecturer at the Department of Urban and Regional Planning at Istanbul Technical University. She earned her PhD in the Urban Planning Department of UCLA with her dissertation "Planning, power, politics: Urban redevelopment in Istanbul." Among her recent fields of research and teaching are decision-making and governance mechanisms, collaborative and participatory planning, and reproduction of urban space. 0000-0002-4550-3811

Julia Wesely is a Postdoctoral Research Fellow at The Bartlett Development Planning Unit at University College London. She has multiple years of experience in researching institutional capacities and organizational learning for addressing urban developmental challenges, particularly in the context of environmental and disaster risk management. Her current research in the program Knowledge in Action for Urban Equality (KNOW) seeks to understand and support critical pedagogies for addressing epistemic injustice and urban inequality in Latin American, African and Asian cities. 0000-0003-1691-9620

Lei Zhang is a Professor at the Renmin University of China, Public Administration and Public Policy. His research focuses on plan evaluation, development control and urban informality. 0000-0002-5705-5753

INTRODUCTION

Andrea I. Frank and Christopher Silver

Recognizing the Need for Fundamental Change

In 2021, as this volume is being compiled, our planet where more than 55% of the human population is believed to live in urbanized areas (UN Department of Economic and Social Affairs, 2019) faces multiple crises in the form of climate change, growing social inequalities, volatile economic systems, environmental pollution, resource scarcities (e.g., Pelling et al. 2011) as well as a global pandemic. The notion that these global challenges of the Anthropocene (Crutzen and Stoermer 2000; Kotchen and Young 2007) cannot be addressed successfully by traditional approaches is gaining considerable traction among a range of scientists and scholars (e.g., Hames 2007; Albrechts et al. 2020). Calls for proactive responses using unconventional and creative interventions have—for a start—initiated a converging of the global planning and development communities resulting in the compilation of the 17 Sustainable Development Goals (SDGs; UN 2015), as well as the complementary New Urban Agenda (NUA) (UN 2017) adopted in 2015 and 2016, respectively. Both initiatives call for a transformation of the structures and forms of human societal systems (political, economic, social), a re-orientation of the human-nature relationship and, given the urbanized nature of the world, substantial changes in the way cities, regions and nations plan.

Essentially, the SDGs bring into focus more than four decades of global efforts to fashion and preserve a healthy and productive environment. This began with the United Nations (UN) Conference on the Human Environment in Stockholm, Sweden, in 1972, followed 20 years later by the UN Conference on Environment and Development in Rio de Janeiro, and culminating in the Rio+20 in 2012 where the idea of the SDGs was initiated and advanced through an ambitious resolution outlining "The Future We Want." The UN created the Open Working Group (OWG) on SDGs in January 2013 that spent the next two years formulating the SDGs to succeed the previous set of global initiatives known as the Millennium Development Goals. Initially, the OWG identified 8 SDGs. Between January and August 2015, negotiations on a final SDG document resulted in an expansion of the SDGs from 8 to 17, including 169 targets and 232 indicators to assess accomplishments and monitor progress. The UN formally adopted the SDGs at the Sustainable Development Summit held in New York City in September 2015. The commitment to guide development work towards the SDGs was the document, "Transforming our world: the 2030 Agenda for Sustainable Development." One notable and hotly debated component of the SDGs was the inclusion of a specific goal focused on the sustainability of cities (SDG 11—Sustainable Cities and Communities). The adopted language of SDG 11 refers to the need for affordable housing and reduction of slums and informal housing given the high incidence of substandard housing available for the poor in cities around the globe. But to many of the advocates of a city SDG, this is a much too narrow perspective of the role played by cities in meeting much more of the SDGs. As critics of the limited scope of SDG 11 have since pointed out, many of the challenges and solutions embedded in the SDGs center on cities. Cities are where the majority of the future world population will reside; they account for the highest levels of energy consumption, and, in turn, production of greenhouse gases (GHGs). Yet, cities also have been most successful in reducing poverty levels, improving global health and reducing and correcting gender inequities just to mention several of the broader objectives of the SDGs. So, as cities cut across many sustainable development issues, their challenges cannot be reduced to the single concern of safe and affordable housing.

Implementation and progression toward these sustainability goals remains an issue, though. General theories on transformation (see Grin et al. 2010) state that change requires leadership, a willingness of people to change the way they behave and manage their lives alongside technological innovation (which actually may trigger behavioral changes). Translated to the urban context this means new policies, legislation, institutions and instruments. Thus, as a follow-up to the adoption of the 2030 SDGs, delegates at the third UN Conference on Housing and Sustainable Development (Habitat III) adopted the NUA (UN 2017) to secure global political support, especially among key actors at the city, town and village levels to serve as drivers behind all 17 SDGs but with a specific emphasis on the urban arena. The NUA offers a way for local, regional and national authorities, as well as non-governmental organizations (NGOs) to flesh out and convert into action plans the urban implications of the SDGs. Because "[p]opulations, economic activities, social and cultural interactions, as well as environmental and humanitarian impacts, are increasingly concentrated in cities," the NUA (2017, p. 3) noted, this makes critical the efforts of local authorities in addressing sustainability challenges specifically in the areas of "housing, infrastructure, basic services, food security, health, education, decent jobs, safety and natural resources, among others" (New Urban Agenda, 2017, p. 3). It was in

Quito in 2004 where the World Social Forum articulated the vision of an urban world where all citizens enjoyed full "rights to the city" (Dialogues 6), and this yet to be accomplished objective is reinforced by the guidance of the NUA.

Transformative Planning Practices

Smarter, greener, more sustainable and improved equities have informed the vocabulary of planners across the globe for many decades, in part to realize higher goals of universal livability but also to mitigate major challenges that threaten communities and the planet at large. Indeed, some might argue that Ebenezer Howard's garden city, articulated over a century ago in his seminal book *Tomorrow: A Peaceful Path to Real Reform*, represents an early transformative vision for urban living with an ecological and alternative settlement concept. At the same time, an abundance of questions surrounds the rhetoric versus the reality of its current manifestation. What is transformative planning? What triggers social or even societal transformations which it is increasingly argued we need (Grin et al. 2010; WGBU 2011), and what role can planning and planners play (Marcuse 2017; Williams 2020)? What makes planning practice transformative, and what characterizes the transformative nature of new planning interventions compared to established modes of operation?

Scholars have conceptualized transformative planning in different ways (Albrechts et al. 2020) by questioning the growth paradigm, or truly seeking to democratize planning. Kennedy (2018), for example, who approaches the topic from the standpoint of community development, contends that it is "a way of working with communities across divisions," that "is participatory planning which empowers the community to act in its own interests." Transformative planning is distinguished from advocacy planning because it is participatory rather than representative. Whereas advocacy planning seeks to institutionalize participation in planning, it does not directly confront "power disparities" so that once participation is enabled, "real decisions are made by those who have always made the decisions." In contrast, transformative planning assumes that successful redistribution of resources follows the power to decide on the use of the resources. Both advocacy and transformative planning recognize the political nature of the planning process, but transformative planning involves a political consciousness and engagement of those within the community. For the planner, this involves recognizing biases brought to the process, and a willingness to assist the community with tools to come up with responses that might not mesh with those of the planner. Kennedy concludes that "to be transformative, a centering of community knowledge within planning is needed." She contends this not just a matter of how planning is *done*, but how it is *taught* within professional education. While claiming that transformative planning practices that differ radically and structurally from the present reality are needed as a prerequisite to affect change, Albrechts et al. (2020, p. 2) also caution that questions of the direction of change and the set of mobilizing triggers are by no means clear, nor well understood.

Aims and Organization of Dialogues 7

As noted earlier, new approaches need to be developed to tackle the intractable crises that are threatening humanity and move the world towards more sustainable futures. Indeed, Beling et al. (2017) imply a need for a comprehensive Polyanian-type *Great Transformation* (see Polyani 1944) that would align global development with ecological boundaries and limits. Aspiring to work towards SDGs and following NUA guidance, planners are among those testing and experimenting with new processes, approaches, technologies and concepts. The aim of this volume is to document nascent efforts from the broad reaches of planning, drawing on the work of leading scholars and practitioners from around the world who critically examine how ideas and actions encapsulated by transformative planning practices, the realization of the 17 global SDGs and advancing the NUA are changing urban planning paradigms and offer new ways to reduce inequalities; promote inclusive and sustainable economic development; achieve (greater) gender equality; improve human health and well-being; foster resilience of urban communities; and protect the environment. This global view and the multiple different perspectives offered here are not only a tradition in this *Dialogues in Urban and Regional Planning* book series. It is also a prerequisite to breaking with past traditions—often labeled as de-colonising planning—a theme picked up by Wesley and Allen in Chapter 6. If we want to find ways to address the global challenges facing us, we must consider all ideas, theories and concepts and collaboratively learn and share our insights. The contributions to this volume offer a critical window into the ways that planning in local communities is seeking to use and develop transformative approaches. Not all of the cases of transformative planning fit precisely with the view expressed by Kennedy and may, in fact, largely constitute some improved level of advocacy. But what is important to keep in mind is whether the actions bring about transformation even if not directly involving successful engagement of the community in final decisions. We need to keep in mind that transformations typically take decades to take hold (Osterhammel 2009). Furthermore, other conceptions such as those on radically transforming resource usages are equally valid and important developments (see Chapters 10 and 13).

The 14 cases and perspectives compiled in this volume are arranged under three broad categories: (I) Theoretical and Conceptual Frameworks, (II) Educating for Transformative Practices and (III) Research and Evaluations of Transformative Policy Initiatives.

Part I: Theoretical and Conceptual Frameworks

The contributions in this section explore, broadly speaking, varying dimensions of governance processes that bring about change in conformity with new global objectives. The concept of "transformative incrementalism" (TI)

> **Box 1. Related Literature**
>
> As a complement to the articles in this volume, Taylor and Francis offers the Sustainable Development Goals Online (SDGO) collection. It is an interdisciplinary collection of digital content, including Taylor & Francis' books and journals across all disciplines, themed around the SDGs. SDGO includes more than 12,000 carefully selected articles and chapters in an online library covering the 17 SDGs, plus teaching and learning materials including presentations, videos, case studies, teaching guides and lesson plans. The collection was created in partnership with UN agencies including the Principles for Responsible Management Education, PRME, and guided by an international Advisory Board of academics, practitioners, policymakers and officers in third sector, government and NGOs. It supports teaching, learning and research in the fields associated with the SDGs. A proportion of the collection will always be free to access, and Taylor & Francis work with agencies globally to ensure material is accessible in low-GDP regions.

discussed by Buchan and Holland in "Transformative Incrementalism: Implications for Transformative Practice" highlights the necessity for planners to exert power to bring about change but at the same time acknowledges that this requires navigating within governance systems where there is shared access to decision with other actors. As Buchan and Holland put it, TI recognizes that

> planners need to shift away from the Westminster model where they remain neutral and objective and move into a more overt advocacy and entrepreneurial role using power more purposefully and self-consciously and taking advantage of opportunities in a principled fashion when policy windows open.

The model was developed from research on food systems planning in five communities in British Columbia (Canada) involving official public stakeholders and planning staff and recognizing what was necessary for the planners to realize a change (or transformation) in a non-crisis situation. TI rests upon an entrepreneurial approach that necessitates a sustained long-term process of change. Buchan and Holland present incrementalism as a slow-, cumulative-, power-driven change journey, but nonetheless one that yields results in practice.

The use of power in a more crisis-driven context, as Legacy's contribution on a case study in Melbourne, Australia, shows, occurred when a government-sponsored six-kilometer inner city road tunnel deemed a "done deal" by the state government was defeated through community-engagement in the political process. This was not a classic case of NIMBYism but one of engaging in the politics of transport and infrastructure policy beyond just consultation. As Legacy notes in "Transforming Transport Planning in the Post-Political Era," transformative change required more than participatory processes but a political struggle to change the top-down decision to position the East-West Link as the number one transport priority without adequately engaging those who would be its recipients.

Two other contributions directly focus on the governance challenges of the changing contexts in cities. Nel and Nel explore how planning for resilient smart cities, particularly in cities in the Global South, needs to move beyond responding to climate change, environmental and economic downturn simply as problems of crisis management but as a further impetus to address inequities so as not to exacerbate regional problems and poorly coordinated public responses. In the case of megacity planning and governance in Jakarta, Firman and Fahmi document the increased privatization of development in the metropolitan regions' expanding peripheral cities. While private investments have fueled modernization and the transformation of previous dormitory communities into independent towns, and that process has been beneficial for some, this represents challenges to planning to ensure that private dominance of development decisions does not perpetuate historic inequities and these private developments conform to regional land use, environmental, economic and social priorities. Finally, Graham, Barnett, Mortreux, Hurlimann and Fincher enable us to understand how communities vulnerable to climate change risks in Australia confront the prospects of being displaced and the difficulties faced toward adaptation given differing values of attachment to place versus adequate compensation for loss.

Part II: Educating for Transformative Practices

Understanding the new challenges covered in Part I, such as rapid urbanization, climate change, decisions about alterations in urban transport and how planning engages with governance and political power, it transpires new approaches to train planners are needed. This education section comprises four contributions that explore if and how the recommendations encapsulated in the NUA (UN 2017) are incorporated and promoted in the education for planners. Associated with the NUA, several of the SDGs, in particular SDG 11 on sustainable cities and communities and SDG 4 pertaining to quality education, are considered. A common underlying assumption is that to transform planning practices—the socialization of future professionals—their education and training also requires a substantial overhaul. Albeit coming from vastly different contexts and conceptions of planning from countries in different urbanization and development stages, all authors agree on one matter. Without changing planning education curricula in terms of both content and pedagogy it will be impossible to effectively transform planning practice. This is in line with theories of transformations that suggest that major changes in the past, i.e., profound change stemming from an interaction and co-evolution of factors (WBGU 2011) produce change via (a) technological innovation, (b) crises (e.g., war, economic crash), (c) knowledge advancement and (d) vision (new narratives such as communism, or collaboration/coalition, etc.) (Grin et al. 2010). As such it is consistent and logical to argue that embedding new knowledge and visions in planning education is a prerequisite for a wholesale transformation of planning practice.

Wesely and Allen, in "De-colonising Pedagogies: Exploring the Geographies of Urban Planning Education Networks," argue that urban planning education or education for planning is of considerable importance for achieving SDG 11 "making cities and human settlements inclusive, safe, resilient and sustainable." Yet, in order to do this and also to fulfill SDG 4, i.e., "ensuring inclusive and equitable quality education and promoting lifelong learning" opportunities for all, a process of transformation needs to continue on how and by whom planning education is delivered and what it entails. Planning education networks can play a role in that transformation but that may not be sufficient. The preoccupation in widening geographic distribution of planning education is not enough and must be accompanied by a thorough revision of curricula, appropriate pedagogies and content. In addition, pathways into the profession need to be diversified through different options of delivery (e.g. online, blended and non-higher education-focused routes), and collaboration with different partners including NGOs, practitioners and government will be required to enhance inclusivity of perspectives, and broaden participation and access.

Shifting from the global to a more localized view, Waite, Alkay and Altindis advocate an upgrade/transformation of how planning is taught in Turkey, moving away from the "traditional studio" taught within the confines of the university classroom to a new format where students interact with people in the neighborhood and do field surveys and observation. There is no mention of de-colonising here but an acknowledgement that Turkish planning educational practice would benefit from engaging students with the communities that they seek to help transform.

Gutierez-Chaparro contends that an expanded role of history and theory in the education for planning and planners is critical to enabling the NUA to be understood and accepted. As he discusses in "Planners Moving Towards the New Urban Agenda" these two curricular components, ubiquitous in curricula based in the Global North, are not provided for sufficiently in curricula in Mexico. In his institution, the Autonomous University of the State of Mexico, they recently instituted this curricular change. How successful this will be depends upon how it impacts practice.

The case study by Flores and Joya discusses how an innovative role for educators in Guadalajara led to implementing a new way of translating the NUA into local planning practice. As in the Turkish case, a university-city partnership enabled faculty and graduated students to work directly with residents and local officials to update planning instruments for the city based upon new national legislation. The Guadalajara experience demonstrates how another Mexican planning program embraced the NUA but more in step with the model of the Turkish planning studio. While not in direct contradiction to the contribution of Gutierrez-Chaparro, indeed his scholarly work influenced the Guadalajara educators, it offers a parallel pathway of promoting educational and training changes.

Part III: Research and Evaluations of Transformative Policy Initiatives

One of the essential challenges facing planners as they seek to bring about transformative change is how to assess impacts. The contributions in this part address this. One of the most innovative strategies, known as the circular economy (CE), seeks to increase positive environmental impacts by transforming waste into useful economic products, or as Appendino, Roux, Saadé and Peuportier put it, "to overcome the contradiction between economic and environmental prosperity." They note that the CE strategy has been studied at the city level throughout Europe, in cities such as Berlin, Rotterdam, Paris, London, Milan and Amsterdam, and led to adopted strategic plans and specific actions to make their economies more circular. Their focus is on how the CE strategy is being applied at the neighborhood scale, thereby linking the critical role of the building scale with the larger challenge of sustaining CE practices at the city scale. They examine four neighborhood-scale CE projects, all currently underway, one in Amsterdam, one in Espoo (Finland) and two in Paris. In all of these cases, the goal is regeneration of depressed areas by making full use of existing materials or, if necessary, ensuring recycling and repurposing to limit waste and preserve the energy that went into making the materials. The study also examines how the projects utilize different tools to design their interventions to ensure success in achieving their objectives while also providing a means to assess how well the objectives are being realized.

Repurposing existing resources to enable cities to be more resilient in the face of natural disasters is evidenced in the study of a greenway project in post-Katrina, New Orleans, by Fields, Thomas and Wagner. Drawing upon the Dutch model of flood mitigation that allows rivers to flow where they need to during high water events, the New Orleans project represented a shift in the conventional strategy of using hard infrastructure to protect flood-prone areas. The LaFitte Greenway project transformed a three-mile underused public area along flood-prone neighborhoods to a linear park to provide protection from flooding. The coalition of stakeholders that pushed through the park project was not able to secure funding for infrastructure to help deal with storm water management because of the need to demonstrate such a high-cost investment would be justified in future high water events. Nonetheless, the LaFitte Greenway project represented an important innovation in flood risk management drawing upon the Dutch model and demonstrating the importance of multi-stakeholder collaborations to achieve new forms of resilience planning.

China's 80 largest municipalities, all of which boast master plans, are shaped by national statutory requirements along with the influence of powerful local leaders. Environmental concerns are addressed alongside other mandatory components covering economic development and social equality, thereby affirming a commitment to sustainability objectives. How these goals are translated into actions and the priority given to them in cities is influenced by the views of these local leaders. The Zhang, Tochen, Hibbard and Tang study, "The Role of Local Leaders regarding Environmental Concerns in Master Plans," seeks to explain why the serious problems of environmental degradation are treated differently in the plans of these cities. Explaining the unique process that these cities utilize in preparation of the plans is a key contribution of this study and an important starting point for assessing variations in efforts to address environmental priorities. The authors acknowledge that the language used in the plans can mask important local views on the priority given to environmental. Local leaders empowered by the decentralization process that has been implemented in China are influential in how the language of plans is translated into practice. In addition to analyzing the language in the plans using the word frequency method, the study utilizes a new research approach that focuses on the role of the local leaders in prioritizing environmental concerns depending upon performance factors such as duration in office, education, age and working experience. Their analysis determined that well-educated local leaders embraced a more collaborative planning approach. Work experience and compliance with state mandates were less relevant factors. The study also suggests that there are some city-specific context issues at play that help to differentiate where environmental concerns receive higher priority in local plans.

Local governments in large US cities share with their counterparts in China the power to influence environmental mitigation within a national statutory framework but drawing upon local innovations. Addressing reductions in GHG emissions through reduced energy use of buildings recognizes that climate change mitigation strategy requires understanding the role of the built environment. Drawing upon data covering energy use in buildings in New York City of 50,000 square feet or greater, including office buildings and multifamily structures, "Further Opportunities to Reduce Energy Use and Greenhouse Gas Emissions of Buildings" by Hsu, Meng, Han and Suh provides a new multilayered methodology to determine where interventions could have significant impact. Examining the energy use and emissions from the structure and systems of building, how they are occupied and their relations to surroundings constrains opportunities for interventions, especially in the high proportion of older structures where the building characteristics are already set. Given this condition, their analysis suggests that energy-saving policies proven to affect operations and occupancy of existing buildings should be studied further to reduce GHG emissions. "For the other half of buildings in 2030 that are expected to be relatively new construction," they conclude, "interpreting the meaning of these results requires a more complex discussion of how planning policies can be used to achieve lower energy use and GHG emissions."

Chinese cities have been shaped throughout history by various forces, typically related to the governance system in place and how this system regarded the role of cities in broader societal objective. Jian Liu, in "Influences of Planning Policies on Community Shaping in China," identifies four distinct eras of city development since 1900 that connect with the planning approaches dominant during each of these periods. First, there is the pre-modernization era covering the long imperial period prior to 1900 (and extending through the establishment of the People's Republic in 1950) characterized by the hierarchical *Li-Fang* communities. These were shaped by traditional city building principles which guided city and village development to facilitate the state's regime. From the 1950s through the 1970s, city planning was guided by the objectives of industrial development or what Liu refers to as a *Danwei* community, a self-contained economic and social unit which indirectly borrowed from Western planning ideas. The shift to a market-influenced economy beginning in the 1980s and more recent efforts to elevate Chinese cities to global city status by what Liu refers to as community improvement shaped by quality-oriented planning recognizes how cities have become now central to life in China.

Start of a Journey

The articles and case studies in this volume cannot purport to explore thoroughly the meaning and promise of transformative planning. What they do suggest is that there is a continuum within the process of planning for change, and often this is tied to the issue at stake and the context within which it is being advanced. There is a recognition in many of the cases covered here that planning must engage with power and politics at some level, that policy changes are most effectively achieved when based upon sound research and beneficiaries of engagement include a full complement of stakeholders who will be touched in some way by the intervention. The perspective offered by Kennedy (2018) earlier seems to ring true in so many of the cases, which is that transformative planning requires not just consultation and advocacy but all participants expressing through the exercise of their own form of power (whether it is in the form of education, research, or direct political engagement) to bring about desired outcomes. The volume also features nascent developments to rethink substantively economic and socio-technical paradigms that for a long time have dominated the urban development discourse. The deconstruction of the socio-economic model (Beling et al. 2017) that has dominated urban development in the Global North is vital to a true socio-ecological transformation that respects planetary boundaries and limits. To realize the vision of greener, smarter and more inclusive cities, these efforts seem essential. It is hoped that the global perspectives offered in these selections help to make the necessity of transformative planning better understood and more widely practiced.

References

Albrechts, L., Brabanente, A. and Monno, V. (2020), "Practicing transformative planning: the territory-landscape plan as a catalyst for change," *City, Territory and Architecture* 7 (1): 1–13. https://doi.org/10.1186/s40410-019-0111-2

Beling, A.E., Vanhulst, J., Demaria, F. Rabi, V. Carballo, A.E. and Pelenc J. (2017), "Discursive synergies for a 'Great Transformation' towards sustainability: pragmatic contributions to a necessary dialogue between human development, Degrowth, and Buen Vivir," *Ecological economics* 11. https://doi.org/10.1016/j.ecolecon.2017.08.025

Crutzen, P.J. and Stoermer, E.F. (2000), "The 'anthropocene'," *IGBP Newsletter* 41: 17–18.

Grin, J., Rotmans, J. and Schot, J. (2010), *Transitions to Sustainable Development. New Directions in the Study of Long-Term Transformative Change*. London: Routledge.

Hames, R. (2007), *The Five Literacies of Global Leadership*. San Francisco: Jossey-Bass.

Kennedy, M. (2018), "Transformative planning for community development, part one: moving from advocacy planning to transformative planning," *Planners Network*, November 5, 2018. Retrieved from: https://www.plannersnetwork.org/2018/11/transformative-planning-for-community-development-part-one-moving-from-advocacy-planning-to-transformative-planning/Kotchen, M.J. and Young, O.R. (2007), "Meeting the challenges of the anthropocene: Towards a science of coupled human–biophysical systems," *Global Environmental Change* 17: 149–51.

Marcuse, P. (2017), "From Utopian and realistic to transformative planning," in B. Haselsberger ed. *Encounters in Planning Thought: 16 Autobiographical Essays from Key Thinkers in Spatial Planning*. New York: Routledge, pp. 35–50.

Osterhammel, J. (2009), *Die Verwandlung der Welt. Eine Geschichte des 19.Jahrhunderts*. München: Beck.

Pelling, M., Manuel-Navarrete, D. and Redclift, M. eds. (2011), *Climate Change and the Crisis of Capitalism. A Chance to Reclaim, Self, Society and Nature*. London: Routledge.

Polanyi, K. (1944), *The Great Transformation*. New York: Farrar & Rinehart.

UN. (2015), *Sustainable Development Goals*. New York: United Nations. Retrieved from https://www.un.org/sustainabledevelopment/sustainabledevelopment-goals

UN Department of Economic and Social Affairs. (2019), *World Urbanization Prospects. The 2018 Revision*. New York: United Nations.

UN Habitat. (2017), *New Urban Agenda*. New York: United Nations. Retrieved from http://habitat3.org/wp-content/uploads/NUA-English.pdf

WBGU. (2011), World in transition: a social contract for sustainability. Deutschland. Wissenschaftlicher Beirat Globale Umweltveränderungen, Berlin. Retrieved from https://www.wbgu.de/fileadmin/user_upload/wbgu/publikationen/hauptgutachten/hg2011/pdf/wbgu_jg2011.pdf (accessed June 25, 2020).

Williams, J. (2020), "The role of spatial planning in transitioning to circular urban development," *Urban Geography* 41(6): 915–9. https://doi.org/10.1080/02723638.2020.1796042

Theoretical and Conceptual Frameworks

Chapter 1

TRANSFORMATIVE INCREMENTALISM

Implications for Transformative Planning Practice

Robert Buchan and Mark Holland

Introduction

Much of planning practice is implicitly grounded in the objective to effect a different state than the one existing at the time of the planning exercise. Efforts to implement sustainable development goals highlight the need to transform our city systems and how we plan for them. Curious, though, is the paucity of change theory in the planning literature. Transformative Incrementalism (TI) (Buchan, 2017) is a theory that squarely addresses the change process. Although TI was first developed by analysing local food system planning, it has been recognized by 'change masters' (Buchan, Cloutier and Friedman 2019) as relevant to planning processes focused on effecting change (Beasley, 2019; Holland, 2019). A strong understanding of change processes would enable planning processes to be more effective.

This chapter seeks to contribute to the development of effective transformative planning practice efforts by suggesting TI planning practice approaches and their implications. TI suggests that planning for transformative change is characterized by a long, incremental and deeply social change process driven by power within the political, bureaucratic, industry and public spheres.

Research Approach for Developing TI

TI was the product of a dissertation that used Classic Grounded Theory (CGT) to explore food system planning (Buchan, 2017). CGT is regarded as an effective method for developing theory especially for areas where there is limited scholarship (Griffin, 2011), such as how significant change in the food systems can be effectively planned.

DOI: 10.4324/9781003178545-3

The data for this research project were drawn from interviews with 29 elected officials, public stakeholders and planning staff participants in five communities (Vancouver, Victoria, Kelowna, North Saanich and the Capital Regional District (CRD)) in British Columbia, Canada, with local food system initiatives plus ten additional member checking interviews. Interviews were designed to glean the insights, values, perspectives and experiences of participants in exemplary planning initiatives to identify main variables and their interrelationships.

Transformative Incrementalism

TI is a theory that was first developed to explain how efforts to achieve significant and transformative change in the food system occur during times when change is not responding to a crisis. It explains the interconnected roles of values, practice and the outcomes of practice in the process of change. TI reveals and describes the principal role and modalities of power (influence) in the recursive and multidirectional paths of transformative change initiatives. The change process is driven by power in long-term efforts to respond to and influence values towards states of convergence within the public, bureaucratic, industry and political spheres of actors through practice and outcomes. Once there are convergences of values, windows of opportunity open for effective, incremental change initiatives that contribute to achieving a transformative change. Convergence refers to the point where there is sufficient alignment between all spheres of actors such that there is agreement to undertake action towards transformative change.

None of the initiatives that were included in this research project occurred at a time or in response to a crisis but were generally described as intending to build resilience and sustainability into their communities. Transformative change would be the result of incremental actions and events that are each purposefully working towards a desired system change. This change dynamic involves the public, political and bureaucratic spheres of actors and is characterized by a process of actions and discourse which attempts to move the actors in each sphere from a condition of divergence in values to one of convergences.

The research that produced TI described participants in planning as active agents pushing change through actions such as raising awareness and education, building relationships and engagement. These actions were intended to change how people value local food system planning and develop an alignment of values and support for food planning initiatives. As Saha and Paterson (2008) found, local government staff can be the biggest barriers to sustainability initiatives due to a lack of knowledge. Raising awareness and education is a critical measure for staff as well.

Figure 1.1 illustrates zones of divergence and convergence, the existence of subgroups within each sphere and the fact that there may be differences between these groups in alignment or agreement. Within each sphere, there can be some that are in a convergent state while others are in a divergent state. Change efforts, therefore, would need to address each sphere, including their subgroups.

Transformative Incrementalism 17

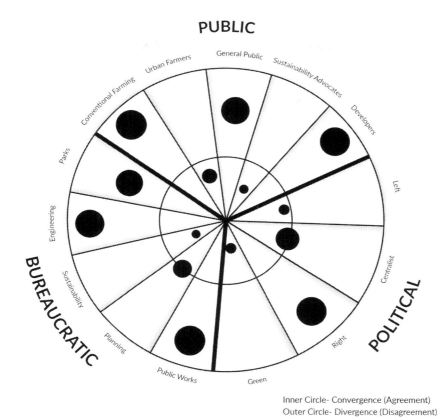

Inner Circle- Convergence (Agreement)
Outer Circle- Divergence (Disagreement)

FIGURE 1.1 Divergence and convergence between and within spheres of actors.

Analysis

The data analysis produced three principal categories of codes (values, practice and outcomes) and one core or master category (power). Power is considered to be the core variable as it manifests in and affects each of the three principal variables. It is about how people influence or are influenced. Values guide and motivate people's behaviour. Practice includes activities designed to create, use and maintain power, such as building relationships with other people that will give ongoing support for planning initiatives. Outcomes can build and reinforce support if the actions are seen to be positive and conversely can erode support if the activities are seen to be negative. The variability of outcomes and the disposition of actors to compete for power also underscores the unstable nature of power. The relationships between the variables describe an incremental, power-laden process intended to lead to transformative change.

Power

The production, maintenance and exercise of power (the ability to influence) is a fundamental dynamic in TI. In this sense, power is viewed as the ability to influence outcomes, not as dictatorial power, or as based exclusively on authority (Siegel, 2015). It is created and used by the public, bureaucracy and politicians in different ways. Power determines which values get privileged. Planners were shown to develop support from the public or external agencies to influence actors within the bureaucracy or those outside of it like politicians. Power is produced through documents and by building supportive relationships and having engaged partners. It is facilitated through knowledge of, and skills in, processes such as decision-making in government, knowledge of food system commercial processes and the ability to empower and motivate people. Leaders and champions are people that are effective in producing and using power. Motivated by their own values, they seek to influence others within and outside of their own groups to move forward on their policy initiatives. Siegel (2015) identified two roles for leaders: leaders by authority and leaders by influence, and he suggests that local government administrators exercise both types of leadership and power, but this is typically done in the 'shadows.' This positioning of local government staff leaders is consistent with the Westminster view that staff are not seen to be leading, whereas TI sees staff leading and exercising considerable influence in less visible ways.

Assche, Duineveld and Beunen (2014) see power as an important concept in planning as it speaks to the possibility of planners being able to make a difference in society. Their view that power is produced and reproduced recursively from one event to the next is consistent with the notion of a recursive and incremental change process in TI theory where the direction of change depends on who has the most power and this direction changes with changes in power. Aarts and Leeuwis (2010) see power instrumentally in planning as the ability to secure outcomes that are dependent on the agency of other participants.

Friedmann (2011) argues that the implementation of visions "requires an acknowledgement of power as a central issue" (p. 137). Deacon (1998) notes that Foucault sees power relations as unstable and in constant struggle. This account of power is consistent with the research finding of power being the central variable in the process of local food system planning. Accounts from the research participants describe actions to influence values and build support and engagement strategies designed to change how people understand local food systems and develop a base of power to support change efforts in food systems.

Allmendinger (2009) suggests that power is hidden and surreptitious in modern societies. He references Foucault's view that power is "found at all levels of society and social existence. It is invisible and flows throughout the complex web of networks that make up modern life" (p. 16). In this view, power is found not only in the dominant social class and economic power; it is found in civil society, and in the bureaucratic and political spheres. Rather than being unidirectional, power is multidirectional and relational. Those, for example, "inside the state who are trying to make cities more livable depend on the existence of mobilized communities just as much as communities and social movements depend on allies within the state" (Evans, 2012).

Participants expressed strong views that leaders and champions are critical and effective agents of change that, while challenged by regimes of power, work with success in changing regimes of power.

PLANNER PARTICIPANT: I think actually having key people in positions of influence [power] is a very critical piece, actually.
INTERVIEWER: Can you elaborate on that for me?
PLANNER PARTICIPANT: Well, I mean having somebody in the organization like I would call it institutional entrepreneur or intra-entrepreneur I guess they call it now. Somebody who understands the system—understands how—you know to make decisions or be—be able to read when there's—you know some of the political situation—be able to stick handle it through all the kind of hoops that it goes through is really powerful.

TI recognizes the omnipresent and unstable quality of power within the public, political and bureaucratic spheres, and it explains how actions in each of these spheres interact to produce and use power incrementally towards transformative change. These actions are often driven by leaders and champions who work hard to develop and maintain relationships through engagement and education.

Values

Transformative change actions are influenced by values which are often highly variable between and within communities as well as between and within community groups and organizations like political bodies, bureaucracies and civic society. Values may be in conflict; they influence other groups; they motivate actors; and when they are aligned within and between groups, they can enable significant change. They are guiding principles and the first link in a chain that leads to behaviour and action (Howell, 2013). Because values are seen as key motivations and can influence the behaviours of actors belonging to other groups (e.g., public values influence politicians), participants in transformative change processes are often focused on influencing shifts in those values to be more supportive of the transformative change goals, e.g., the importance of education and raising awareness in 'value-changing' discourse (Forester, 2012).

Practice

TI sees practice as a way to influence the public and stakeholders in order to build support (e.g., planners in a bureaucracy using education practices to raise awareness). In addition to raising awareness and increasing education, the roles of community engagement, action and effectiveness are not only practices focused on achieving change on the ground, they also influence and reinforce values and the ability to further policy initiatives through building relationships, trust and momentum. The practice of responding to public values implies a power relationship, in that if the public strongly express certain values, politicians and staff feel compelled to respond. For example, local government's interest in local food systems has been associated with shifts in grass roots public opinion, especially in Australia, Europe and North America (Mason and Knowd, 2010).

Raising awareness and education, and building relationships and engagement develop support and the power and capacity to influence and undertake policy initiatives. However, this process of working towards transformative change is slow and incremental, and is consistent in this regard with Friedmann's Transactive Planning (Healey, 2012). Change being slow because it takes time to undertake dialogue, and to build trust through initial actions and relationships through positive engagement. It is also related to staff and political leadership, and it is not unidirectional. Initiatives can be delayed or even retreat under changes in political leadership. TI is more about the slow steps to build relationships, trust and power, rather than choosing between the incremental differences in policy choices characteristic of Lindblom's 'branch method' (2012). Further, action that occurs within the bureaucratic, public and political spheres places planners in the position of measuring, assessing and developing power with other actors to advance transformative change. While building understanding through genuine and meaningful communications (Friedmann, 2011) is a critical part of the transformative change process, that process is also about building power through effective dialogue and engagement within the bureaucracy in order to drive change within public and political spheres.

A key element in practice is the capacity to identify opportunities where certain actions might find support. Being able to facilitate the emergence of an opportunity and to initiate an action within a window of opportunity are important qualities in TI. Contrary to the Foucauldian perspective, effective leaders are seen as essential to the success of a transformative change process and are found in the public, political and bureaucratic spheres. They are people that excel at communicating, listening, empowering other people, enabling and doing.

Outcomes

The outcomes of an initiative can advance or impede the viability and health of a system. Outcomes can be project specific, such as the number of community gardens established by an initiative or the quantity of food produced by a program. Outcomes can also be broader in nature relating to the policy environment in which policy initiatives are determined. For example, one of the research participants said that the policy context in which an initiative is undertaken is central, a critical consideration and an evolving state. Another participant suggested that a successful initiative can provide evidence for future initiatives, whereas a failed initiative may reduce that support. The current policy context in any organization can be seen as the outcome of preceding dialogues; policy works; and values of the politicians, bureaucracy and public. Another participant stated that it is the basis from which further work must begin and moderates the policies and actions that may be the most viable under the existing environment. A policy environment for any particular policy topic may range from under-developed to well-developed.

Moving from an under-developed to a well-developed policy environment is a slow and incremental evolutionary process mediated by champions, values, resources and efforts to build support, as well as opponents with differing values and agendas. Policy initiatives are seen to evolve, and they are vulnerable to changes in power such as a new council, a new city manager and the loss of important leaders within each of the groups. Well-developed policy environments have effectively institutionalized policy programs and have developed power to continue with the programs; for example, the City of Vancouver's food policy initiative arguably occurred within the most well-developed policy context, and that was the result of two decades of preceding work. The stated goal of the initiative for some participants was to institutionalize food system values in policy in order to enable it to persist and influence the actions of others.

The outcome of successful policy work among the bureaucracy, public and politicians over time leads to significant policy opportunities where there is a convergence or alignment of values between and within these groups sufficient enough to enable a major policy initiative to be undertaken and implemented. This process was described by the Vancouver politicians, staff and stakeholders: 20 years of discourse and activity eventually lead to a broad base of support and the ability to undertake a comprehensive food system planning initiative. The greater the degree of alignment between values (agreement), the greater the chance of successfully undertaking an initiative. Such agreement also results in the ability to compete for and receive necessary resources to do the work. Without that agreement and the resources, progress is in part dependent on the existence of effective leaders and champions to work with limited resources, influence other potential partners and develop awareness and support within their and other groups.

Applying TI

TI identifies considerations and approaches for those considering engaging in transformative planning. Further, because TI is an emergent theory, it is expected that it will evolve to become even more useful and effective framework as planners discuss and engage with it. To assist in this discussion, we discuss considerations for undertaking a TI process as well as identify key skills and roles.

Process Considerations

Applying TI should be guided by a process that is informed by the key variables. Accordingly we suggest five process steps: (1) Assessing the policy environment;

(2) Assessing the divergence/convergence of values in the key participant groups; (3) Assessing the power context; (4) Developing a long-term engagement (advocacy, education, encouragement) strategy; and (5) Developing an incremental progress strategy.

1. Policy Environment Assessment

   Policy environment assessment begins by understanding the policies have already been developed or attempted. In other words, it assesses the *outcomes* of preceding initiatives. This recognizes the evolutionary nature of transformative change. This step identifies supportive precedent policies and programs, and reveals barriers posed by existing policies and policy advocates, and it identifies where the community is situated in the incremental evolution towards transformative change.

2. Divergence/Convergence Assessment

   The divergence/convergence assessment step determines the state of agreement or disagreement of *values* regarding the policy and programs being considered. This is similar to the policy environment assessment, but it specifically moves beyond identifying previous work to assessing values within the political, bureaucratic and public spheres. We would note that the initial conception of TI was developed from data that did not include industry participants. Subsequent work has resulted in the recognition of a fourth and critical group of actors—those in industry. Within each sphere are subgroups with values in a convergent state while others are in a divergent state (see Figure 1.1). Change efforts would need to address each sphere, including subgroups within a bureaucracy. The divergence/convergence assessment enables the practitioner to assess where engagement and advocacy work needs to be targeted, and it will indicate in relative terms how close the community is to being ready to undertake more comprehensive and aggressive strategies with a greater likelihood of ongoing support.

3. Power Assessment

   The assessment of power builds on the divergence/convergence assessment step by assessing the sources of power in the political, bureaucratic and public spheres. This step would include, for example, identifying stakeholders, leaders or potential leaders, leadership voids, supporters and opponents.

4. Long-Term Advocacy Strategy Development

   In this step, efforts to engage can be identified in a long-term engagement plan designed to advocate, educate and build support. This can involve finding allies and identifying opportunities and barriers to overcome. From the Westminster model of public service perspective, this may sound like inappropriate behaviour for planning practitioners because it is neither neutral nor objective behaviour. However, as our data indicate, planning staff do and must engage in educational efforts to be effective in achieving change through raising awareness, engagement and building relationships.

TI challenges the appropriateness of the Westminster model as the model for professional planning behaviour.

The alternative of not engaging in a long-term engagement plan designed to advocate, educate and build support within all spheres of actors/participants would be like going to sea in a rudderless ship. The planning practitioner's actions would be directed by the winds and currents generated by others, rather than effectively navigating towards a goal by powering the ship forward using those winds and currents and resources provided from supportive actors within the bureaucratic, political, industry and public spheres of actors. To not recognize the powers affecting the policy environment would also be naive and likely reduce the potential effectiveness of the practitioner. Key elements of a long-term engagement plan would be actions to build relationships and trust (including, for example, quick win projects); develop momentum, support (power), leaders and champions; develop capacity in other groups to lever staff capacity; and provide ongoing advocacy and education.

5   Incremental Strategy Development

The final step is to develop an ongoing, incremental progress strategy. Such a strategy is different from the comprehensive strategy/plan documents normally produced by planners. The latter typically lay out a strategy that is focused on concrete actions and specific policies designed to achieve a planning goal. This approach assumes that with the successful completion of all the actions, the intended goal will be achieved as a function of the completed actions. In contrast, an incremental progress strategy would be more focused on addressing steps 1–4 recursively until the level of convergence of values has been attained so that the more traditional comprehensive strategy and plans can be undertaken. Further, it would also look beyond the preparation of a traditional comprehensive strategy and plan and continue to revisit steps 1–4 until the transformative change has been achieved.

Ongoing monitoring of outcomes would be an essential part of the progress strategy as that would assess shifts in values towards a convergence, growth or diminishment of influence held by key actors/influencers, identification of new opportunities and partners and availability of critical resources for undertaking ongoing change efforts.

Roles and Skills

TI contemplates a different role for planners from that traditionally associated with the public service. The Westminster model sees appropriate civil servant behaviour as being politically neutral, loyal, anonymous and impartial (Vakil, 2009). To be effective change agents, planners may find themselves advocating for policies and initiatives contrary to some local political views. Loyalty in the traditional view of the civil service sees staff as being loyal to the system as a whole (Vakil, 2009). In TI, a planner may explicitly have the goal of changing the current system; engages with the public, forming relationships and partnerships and advocating for change and programs; and, consequently, is highly visible and vocal. Finally, the TI planner is clear about desired changes and therefore partial to those values, and engages in practice to encourage others to support those values. The data also see the TI civil servant as a 'principled opportunist,' undertaking projects when conditions are supportive and favourable, and focused on the need for those projects to be successful in order to maintain support and power.

It would serve planners to better understand the need for alignment of values with the public and politicians. Plans for change that do not align with the public and have only marginal alignment with politicians may have limited success and may be vulnerable to public and political backlash. Similarly, planners should be aware of the need to create external partnerships that build support and capacity for change initiatives. As a result of successful incremental actions with developing partnerships, relationships and trust, more ambitious future initiatives are sustained and built.

TI emphasizes the importance of engagement, relationship building and working with others to develop understanding and support, all with a view to creating, using and maintaining power. This emphasis should be of interest to planning educators so they can provide the training and education to develop appropriate skills that are required for undertaking change-oriented planning. These skills would include engagement strategies, interpersonal communication, relationship building, network management, policy formulation, facilitation, education, advocacy, negotiation, diplomacy and monitoring.

TI also highlights the importance of interdependent relationships with public, politicians and other parts of the bureaucracy. The success of planning initiatives depends on those relationships. In preparing new planners to undertake transformative planning efforts, planning curriculums should demonstrate TI processes, identify common challenges and discuss ethical issues, like the degree to which arguments in support of initiatives can be pushed, and the degree to which radical initiatives can be pursued within the bureaucracy and with the political decision-makers while respecting democratic values and employer/employee relationships.

Conclusions

To be effective in transformative planning efforts, planners need to understand change processes. Transformative change is a long, incremental and recursive process involving values/beliefs, practice and outcomes and, more importantly, recognizes the power and basis of power within the political, bureaucratic, industry and public spheres.

TI builds on the premises of a number of existing planning theories and addresses the lack of attention to the role of power (Aarts and Leeuwis, 2010;

Friedmann, 2011; Assche et al., 2014). While Lindblom (2012) has described a form of incrementalism in choosing between policy options based on their perceived differences in quality (the branch method), TI presents incrementalism as a slow-, cumulative-, power-driven change journey. This view of incrementalism is closer to Friedmann's view of incremental and cumulative actions. However, in Friedmann's characterization of the change process, he did not incorporate power beyond that achieved through the 'authentic' communication between client and planner. Similarly, Forester's (1980; 2012) attempt to address the role of power was also limited to communication. He saw a role for the planner to challenge power with information. TI has a broader view of power. For example, the research participants demonstrated that power can be created and maintained by planners through engagement, building relationships and working with others. Friedmann, however, is clear in his assertion that planning theorists need to address the question of power in planning theory more explicitly and thoroughly. TI responds positively to this call and highlights its ubiquitous and central role in the change process.

TI positions leaders as having a key role as active agents in the change process. It is consistent with Bevir's (1999) reformulated Foucauldian approach which provides for agency in changing power regimes. The research participants suggest that not only are leaders active agents, but they are indispensable agents and changes in leadership can significantly affect the trajectory of change. Planning staff leaders, however, tend to operate in less publicly visible ways, consistent with Siegel's (2015) view of local government leadership. They can be adept at working with others that can operate more publicly. The five-step change process presents one-way TI may be used by planners to undertake long-term planning efforts to achieve change in local food systems. Using TI would require planners to assess power structures, negotiate relationships and advocate and educate to help shift values to build power. Taking this approach will more openly shift the stance of planners from that of neutral civil servant to that of advocate, and agent of change.

There are several implications of the research including the role for planners to more effectively undertake actions to achieve significant change, and in doing so how they should explicitly consider the use of and response to power. Another implication is the need to understand transformative change strategies within a broader context that explicitly addresses the public, political, industry and bureaucratic spheres of actors.

One of TI's revelations for the planning profession is the need to address alignment efforts within the various staff and departments within a bureaucracy. Understanding that individual actors and separate departments can hold different, even conflicting values, and understanding the need for internal alignment between actors and departments suggests that senior leaders should be aware of where values are and are not aligned. With internal alignment, there is a greater likelihood that the goals and objectives of the organization can be achieved more efficiently and effectively since the members within a bureaucracy would be working together rather than being in conflict over work plan items. Where there is a lack of alignment, the senior leaders need to have strategies that would be effective in achieving that alignment.

TI contemplates a different role for planners than that traditionally associated with public service. The Westminster model sees appropriate civil servant behaviour as being politically neutral, being loyal, being anonymous and being impartial (Vakil, 2009). To be effective change agents, staff champions and leaders may find themselves advocating for policies and initiatives contrary to some local political views. In TI, the planner is engaged with the public, forming relationships and partnerships and advocating for change and programs, and is consequently highly visible and vocal, and is decisively not anonymous. Finally, through TI the planner is clear about desired changes and is therefore partial to the values embodied in the change objectives and engages in practice to encourage others to support those values. The TI planner is also a 'principled opportunist' undertaking projects when conditions are supportive and is focused on the need for those projects to be successful in order to maintain support and power.

TI emphasizes leadership, engagement, relationship building and working with others to develop understanding and support, all with a view to creating, using and maintaining power. This emphasis should be of interest to planning educators if they want to facilitate success by providing the training and education that develops those skills. Based on the results from the interviews, these skills would include leadership skills, engagement strategies, interpersonal communication, relationship building, network management, policy formulation, facilitation, education, advocacy, negotiation, diplomacy and monitoring. Educators would highlight the importance of interdependent relationships with the public, politicians and other parts of the bureaucracy. The success of planning initiatives depends on those relationships. Curricula would demonstrate change processes, and discuss ethical issues like the degree to which arguments in support of initiatives can be pushed, and the degree to which initiatives that work outside the normal boundaries of acceptance within the bureaucracy.

If we do not understand where power is and how to use it, we will not be as effective as we could be. It would be like trying to sail a boat blind and without sails in a regatta. If we do not understand how change occurs, our initiatives may be limited in their potential to effect change. We need to understand and anticipate the timeline, to anticipate next steps, and to defend and support a long-term strategic TI process. Arguably we have not been very effective in bringing about the host of changes we need to become more sustainable. Perhaps this is in part because we have not grounded our approaches in a solid understanding of how change occurs. We understand how planning occurs but now is the time to understand its interface and relationship to change processes. With a deep understanding of the change process, we anticipate that our engagement with the public and stakeholders will become more purposive—focusing on value assessment, value shifting, agreement and partner making dialogues rather than simply acting as pollsters of public opinion.

As a closing note we address what some are surely to raise as an important question. Is the long timeframe for achieving transformative change going to address the urgency of climate change? Further, since TI describes our efforts at achieving change prior to the onset of crisis and climate change is being increasingly seen as a current crisis, how can TI assist in this particular challenge? We suggest that the full impact and crisis resulting from climate change has yet to manifest, and indeed, there are strong pockets of population and prominent leaders still denying climate change as recently evidenced by the discourse in the USA and Canada. TI tells us that we have to still achieve more convergence in values and develop and maintain greater influence in moving progressive and responsive transformative planning forward. Without that convergence and influence, sustained and effective climate change responses may not occur or be maintained.

References

AARTS, N. and Leeuwis, C. (2010). "Participation and Power: Reflections on the Role of Government in Land Use Planning and Rural Development," *The Journal of Agricultural Education and Extension* 16 (2): 131–45. doi:10.1080/13892241003651381.

Allmendinger, P. (2009). *Planning Theory*. Palgrave Macmillan.

Assche, K., Duineveld, M., and Beunen, R. (2014). "Power and Contingency in Planning," *Environment and Planning A*, 46: 2385–400. doi:10.1068/a130080p.

Beasley, L. (2019). "A Case Study of Downtown Vancouver," in R. Buchan, ed. *Transformative Incrementalism: A Journey to Sustainability* (pp. 53–82). Municipal World.

Bevir, M. (1999). *Foucault, Power, and Institutions*. Political Studies, XLVII.

Buchan, R. (2017). *Transformative Incrementalism: A Grounded Theory for Planning Transformative Change in Local Food Systems*. University of Victoria.

Buchan, R. (2019). *Transformative Incrementalism: A Journey to Sustainability*. Municipal World.

Buchan, R., Cloutier, D., and Friedman, A. (2019). "Transformative Incrementalism: Planning for Transformative Change in Local Food Systems," *Progress in Planning* 134 (November): 1–27.

Buchan, R., (2017). *Transformative Incrementalism: A Grounded Theory for Planning Transformative Change in Local Food Systems*. University of Victoria.

Deacon, R. (1998)., "Strategies of Governance Michel Foucault on Power," *Theoria: A Journal of Social and Political Theory* 92: 113–149.

Evans, P. (2012). "Political Strategies for More Livable Cities; Lessons from Six Cases of Development and Political Transition," in S. Fainstein and S. Campbell, eds. *Readings in Planning Theory* (pp. 499–518). Wiley-Blackwell, Third Edition.

Forester, J. (1980). *Planning in the Face of Power*. University of California Press.

Forester, J. (2012). "Challenges of Deliberation and Participation," in S. Fainstein and S. Campbell, eds. *Readings in Planning Theory* (pp 206–213). Wiley-Blackwell, Third Edition.

Friedmann, J. (2011). *Insurgencies: Essays in Planning Theory*. Routledge.

Griffin, S. (2011). *Negotiating Duality: A Framework for Understanding the Lives of Street-involved Youth*. University of Victoria.

Healey, P. (2012). "Traditions of Planning Thought," in S. Fainstein and S. Campbell, eds. *Readings in Planning Theory* (pp. 214–223). Wiley-Blackwell, Third Edition.

Holland, M. (2019). "TI and the Real Estate Development Process," in R. Buchan, ed. *Transformative Incrementalism: A Journey to Sustainability* (pp. 23–34). Municipal World.

Howell, R. (2013). "It's Not (Just) "the environment, stupid!" Values, Motivations, and Routes to Engagement of People Adopting Lower-Carbon Lifestyles," *Global Environmental Change* 23: 281–90.

Lindblom, C. (2012). "The Science of 'Muddling Through," in S. Fainstein and S. Campbell, eds. *Readings in Planning Theory* (pp. 176–190). Wiley-Blackwell, Third Edition.

Mason, D. and Knowd, I. (2010). "The Emergence of Urban Agriculture: Sydney, Australia," *International Journal of Agricultural Sustainability* 8 (1): 62–71. doi:10.3763/ijas.2009.0474.

Saha, D. and Paterson, R. G. (2008). "Local Government Efforts to Promote the "Three Es" of Sustainable Development: Survey in Medium to Large Cities in the United States," *Journal of Planning Education and Research* 28 (1): 21–37. doi:10.1177/0739456X08321803.

Siegel, D. (2015). *Leaders in the Shadows: The Leadership qualities of Municipal Chief Administrative Officers*. University of Toronto Press.

Vakil, T. (2009). *Changing Public Service Values: Limits of Fundamental Reform and Rhetoric*. University of Victoria.

Chapter 2
THE PRIVATIZATION OF METROPOLITAN JAKARTA'S (JABODETABEK) URBAN FRINGES

The Early Stage of 'Post-Suburbanization' in Indonesia

Tommy Firman and Fikri Zul Fahmi

Introduction

Recent metropolitan development in developed countries exhibits post-suburbia, or a decline in population in the former central city and the growth and even dominance of polycentric structures outside the traditional core (Borsdorf, 2004; Soja, 2000; Walks, 2013). This pattern is also known as the "edgeless city" (Lang, 2003; Lang & Knox, 2009), and "technoburbia," because technologically advanced industries have made the new city form possible because they do not depend on the older urban core (see Fishman, 2002; Phelps, 2012). Post-suburbanization has also taken place in the developing world; recent Chinese urban development to some extent illustrates an early stage of the "post-suburbia" phenomenon seen in Western countries (Wu & Lu, 2008; Wu & Phelps, 2008). This development is partially triggered by economic globalization which facilitates capital inflows from overseas (see Shatkin, 2008).

The role of the private sector has been central in suburbanization in many Asian countries. Recent urban development in Asia, such as in Indonesia, is associated with extensive metropolitan regions, characterized by a mixture of economic activities and residential land uses in the fringe areas of large cities with built-up areas expanding from urban centers in all directions (Firman, 2009; Jones, 2006; McGee & Robinson, 1995). This phenomenon, often referred to as *mega-urbanization*, accentuates the shift from mono-centric to multi-centric metropolitan regions (Douglass, 2000; Douglass & Jones, 2008; McGee & Robinson, 1995). The private sector has contributed to these patterns through investments in suburban industrial, commercial and residential real estate developments (Firman, 2009; Jones, 2006; McGee & Robinson, 1995). Post-suburbanization in Asia appears to be a continuation of private sector investment patterns with the private sector playing a stronger role than in previous suburban developments: various elements of the

DOI: 10.4324/9781003178545-4

private sector have assumed significant power to make land development and management decisions (Shatkin, 2008). The growing influence of various elements of the private sector constitutes a redistribution of policymaking powers, competencies and responsibilities from the public to the private sectors (Shatkin, 2008; Swyngedouw, Moulaert, & Rodriguez, 2002).

This study examines the extent to which recent development in metropolitan Jakarta, Indonesia—or Jabodetabek—reflects the "post-suburban" phenomenon first seen in the developed world. This chapter goes beyond our previous work on this question (Firman, 2011, 2014b) by providing an update on development in the region, focusing on the key role played by the private sector, facilitated by the growing importance of local government. We discuss the changes and continuity in the development of the fringe areas of the Jakarta metropolitan region over the last four decades. We show that recent development in Jabodetabek does represent an early phase of "post-suburbia," driven by privatization of land management in fringe areas, most notably industrial estates—centers for industrial activities in peripheral areas—and new towns—residential areas built on land previously used for agriculture or forestry and generally geared to middle- and upper-income Indonesians. Privatization in the metropolitan Jakarta region involves both a more aggressive role for the private sector in developing suburban real estate projects, and the redistribution of power and authority from the public to the private sector in land development decisions. This shift is possible due to the national government's pro-growth economic policies and the local autonomy that local governments have in land development decisions; these factors together have given the private sector the power to largely control land in fringe areas. The private sector is now able to actually direct the development of land while often providing municipal services in new developments, services traditionally performed by local governments, removing the need for local governments to do so to facilitate growth. These patterns have important implications for planning scholarship and planning practice: how can planners work to ensure that post-suburban development patterns in developing nations do not lead to the same problems being experienced in North America?

This chapter has three major sections. The first provides a theoretical context for our work by critically assessing "post-suburbanization" as a global phenomenon of urban development. In the second major section we examine recent urban development in Jabodetabek focusing on population growth, land use change and new town and industrial-estate development. In the third major section we reflect on relationship between the changing role of the private sector and central and local government policies that have stimulated post-suburban development in the Jakarta metropolitan region.

Post-Suburbanization as a World-Wide Phenomenon of Urban Development

Suburbanization in the developed world has been characterized for decades by residential development in the outskirts and population redistribution from the urban center to peripheral areas, followed by decentralization of economic activities. Large shopping centers, manufacturing and back office facilities have then moved to these fringe areas as peripheral locations became more appealing. Central cities meanwhile increasingly became unattractive for industry (see Bontje & Burdack, 2011; Champion, 2001).

Post-suburbia is a change in the current process of suburbanization in the developed world, that is, away from the concentric and radial patterns of earlier decades towards new spatial patterns or a "patchwork structure" (Kraemer, 2005 p. 4 as cited in Wu & Phelps, 2008, pp. 465–6). Borsdorf (2004, p. 13) argues that post-suburbia is clearly reflected in the reality that "some new areas are much more independent than the former suburbs, but they are not as multifunctional as the traditional center, resulting in an emerging fragmented structure of specialized outskirts" (p. 13). Post-suburbia now exists in many multi-core regions formed by growth corridors which can extend more than 100 miles from the traditional core; thus, suburbs are part of a complex outer city, which includes jobs as well as residences (Fishman, 2002, pp. 29–30). Post-suburbia in the US, for instance, is characterized by "what was once central…becoming peripheral and what was periphery… becoming central" (Soja, 2000, p. 152).

In post-suburbia, the suburbs have loosened their ties to the central or "mother" city, and are transformed into independent outer cities with many specialized activities in addition to residential areas, including shopping centers, high-tech industrial centers and educational facilities, weakening the centrality of the core city (Fishman, 2002; Soja, 2000). The exodus of shopping malls, offices and manufacturing plants from the core city has resulted in a multi-centered suburban, which in turn blurs the distinction between urban and suburban areas (Feng, Zhou, & Wu, 2008). Governments in developed countries have both directly and indirectly facilitated these growth patterns, for example, the UK's new town programs that began in the 1940s, the US public sector highway development programs (Cochrane, 2011; Feng et al., 2008, p. 85; Phelps & Wood, 2011) and the US mortgage guarantee programs which originally would only fund the purchase of new homes and not the rehabilitation of older homes in core cities.[1]

Post-suburbia differs greatly from the traditional suburban phenomenon in developed countries in several ways (Phelps et al., 2010; Wu & Phelps, 2008):

1   Suburbs lose population and household income declines relative to regional income;
2   Service employment decentralizes away from the urban centers; and
3   Land uses become more mixed with decided polycentric development.

Wu and Phelps (2011, p. 467) contend that the term post-suburbia may capture the important elements of new trends of suburbanization in the developing world, such as in Beijing and Shanghai. Suburbanization in these Chinese cities has now become more market oriented due to the growing role of market forces in those economies. Strategic investments and infrastructures in the economic development zones of China have triggered the formation of metropolitan and suburban economic development in China that fits the post-suburban pattern seen in developed countries (Pan, Guo, Zhang, & Liang, 2015; Wu & Lu, 2008).

There are clearly similarities between Beijing's suburbanization and North American suburbanization, but they are not identical. First, Beijing's suburbanization is still at an early phase of post-suburbanization unlike North America; suburban areas in Beijing have not loosened their ties completely to the core city. Suburbanization in Beijing has indeed resulted in the dispersal of the metropolitan population, changing population density. The majority of employees, however, have remained in the city center even as enterprises move to the outskirts, creating a reverse commute pattern, extending commuting distance and creating more traffic congestion (Wu & Phelps, 2011). The second important aspect of Chinese suburbanization is the shift of power and authority from the public to the private sector. In China as well as in many other Asian countries, the government possesses strong control over land development unlike North America. The private sector, nevertheless, has recently gained more power in the decision-making of land development in China.

The Chinese situation reflects an ongoing process of "privatization," a change in the spectrum of governance structures and power relations between the government and the private sector (see Shatkin, 2008; Swyngedouw et al., 2002). In China, the public sector still plays a strong role in land development, but the private sector has gained more power so that it can influence decision-making about land development (Feng et al., 2008). This process may correspond to economic devolution which empowers local governments; the central government cannot prevent local developments, while local governments play an entrepreneurial role in local development by transferring part of their traditional authority, such as the management of industrial parks, to the private sector (Wu & Phelps, 2008).

Urban Development in Jabodetabek: Post-Suburbanization

The Jakarta region is located in the northern area of West Java, covering a total area of more than 9,000 square kilometers (Hudalah, Viantari, Firman, & Woltjer, 2013). Jabodetabek plays an important role in the national economy, producing about 25% of Indonesia's non-oil and gas GDP (Firman, 2014b). The Jakarta Metropolitan Region has several administrative units at different levels: the Jakarta Special Region (DKI Jakarta) which is the government for the entire province and eight municipalities (kota) and districts (kabupaten) as Figure 2.1 shows—the municipalities of Bogor, Depok, Tangerang, South Tangerang and Bekasi, and the districts of Bogor, Tangerang and Bekasi.

Suburbanization in metropolitan Jakarta is the result of both planned and unplanned activities. In the early 19th century the Dutch colonial government developed Batavia (now Jakarta City), with airy large estates (Leaf, 1994). Since Indonesia proclaimed its independence in 1945, as Silver (2008) describes,

Privatization of Metro Jakarta's Urban Fringes   33

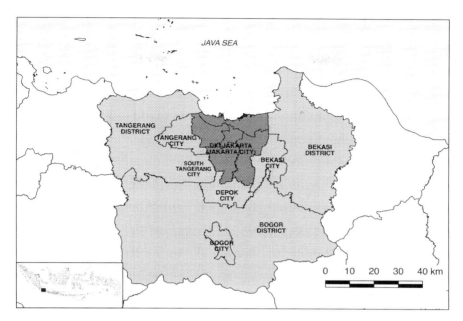

FIGURE 2.1 Jabodetabek.

planning for Jakarta has evolved. In the 1950s the urban administration created a plan for Jakarta using a combination of the Dutch planning legacy, global ideas of an ideal city and local expectations. The plan was strongly focused on beautifying and improving the physical quality of Jakarta City, following President Sukarno's wish to create a beautiful national capital. The central government also developed the Kebayoran Baru new dormitory town, south of Jakarta City, in the 1950s. The 1965 masterplan proposed that Jakarta should be developed based on regional considerations. The masterplan suggested the creation of an administrative body for what came to be Jabotabek.[2]

Spatial planning continued in the New Order period (1966–98), under the leadership of President Suharto; the government's economic policy focused on increasing industrialization. In this period, the central government still had a strong influence on directing plans and developments in Jakarta. The provincial government of DKI Jakarta adopted several spatial plans between the 1960s and 1980s, and the central government strongly influenced the making of these plans. In the 1980s planning for Greater Jakarta was coordinated by a team dominated by central government ministries, which were assigned to manage land development in fringe areas and to administer infrastructure improvement programs, especially transportation. One of the most important development decisions that the central government made in this period was to use tolling as a way to create and finance a network of highways that improved the connectivity of the fringes to the core city and triggered additional development in the periphery. These toll roads were built and financed by private companies, coordinated by the state-owned toll authority, PT Jasamarga.

Planning for the Jakarta region in the New Order regime was characterized by the practice of "clientelism," that is, patronage relationships between the government and key nongovernmental actors that served to exclude others (see Kusno, 2014; Lane, 2003). Spatial plans in the New Order period were just "state of the art products"; local governments often made development decisions and issued building permits without referring to these spatial plans (Silver, 2008, p. 123). Local governments and the private sector viewed local spatial (municipality/district) plans as flexible, to be interpreted "creatively" (Cowherd, 2005). Thus, land conversion, which in the Indonesian context means using agricultural land or forests for residential, commercial and industrial activities, as a result often violated the objectives of the spatial plans for the area.

Development authority today has been devolved to local governments, and the central government is no longer able to strongly direct local development. Decentralization and its associated reforms, as Suharto stepped down from his presidency in 1998, have important implications for how land development is planned and executed. With decentralization authority and responsibility for various functions have been transferred from the central government to local governments. These patterns have led local governments to think that they have "kingdoms" in their own territories (Beard, Miraftab, & Silver, 2008; Rukmana, 2015). Decentralization has also cultivated "urban entrepreneurialism" among local governments: they are motivated to enhance their competitiveness by promoting economic development in their localities and exploiting local resources more intensively (Cowherd, 2005).

Many local governments in municipalities/districts adjacent to DKI Jakarta, which used to be dormitory towns, have been able to develop beyond residential communities by strengthening their economic base. Today, these towns have become independent from Jakarta. Bogor City, south of Jakarta City with a current population of about a million, has now become a center of agricultural higher education and research; Bogor Agricultural University, one of the largest state universities in Indonesia, is housed there. The city has also become an international venue for meetings, conventions and congresses. Depok City, another town south of Jakarta City, the home of the main campus of the University of Indonesia, is now growing rapidly as one of the largest centers of higher education in Indonesia. Serpong City in Tangerang west of Jakarta City has been designated as a research and technology development center (Puspitek) in Indonesia (see Firman, 2011).

The development of multi-functional towns in the Jakarta suburbs has also been facilitated by the toll roads built in the 1980s and 1990s. Today there are privately built toll roads connecting Jakarta City with Tangerang and beyond in the west, Bogor in the south and Bekasi and beyond in the west (Mamas & Komalasari, 2008, p. 123). The suburbs are directly connected to the core of Jakarta; millions of people travel each day from new towns in fringe areas of

Jabodetabek to Jakarta City by trains, buses and personal cars. A number of those living in Jakarta City also commute between the city and the industrial and commercial sites in small and new towns in the outskirts, including Bogor, Tangerang, Bekasi, Depok and Jababeka (Firman, 2011). A 2013 study found that Cikarang, an area on the fringe of the Jakarta metropolitan area where most industrial parks are located, attracted daily commuters from the core of the region as well as from other smaller cities throughout Jabodetabek (Permatasri & Hudalah, 2013), demonstrating how socioeconomic activities have shifted from Jakarta to other centers in the region, such as Cikarang.

Many fringe areas have become increasingly independent from the core city due to a combination of private developer activity and the policies of both central and local governments that explicitly support economic growth. Large-scale residential areas, industrial estates, shopping centers and retails have been developed in the fringes of Jabodetabek. The developers of industrial estates and residential communities located at the fringe built their own utilities and continue to offer the services that local governments normally provide. International and domestic financial institutions, moreover, have made investment funds readily available to developers building in these fringe areas (Firman, 2004a). The development of residential areas in the fringe areas has also been stimulated by a high demand for housing both by people who work in Jakarta and those who work in the suburban or fringe areas. The central government sponsored low-cost housing projects built by private developers in the peripheral areas that have also induced a large number of low and low-middle income groups in Jakarta City to move to those areas. At the same time, local governments easily granted building permits for the private developers that wished to build luxury houses in fringe areas, "exclusive new towns" which provide their own utilities and municipal services.

Below we elaborate on post-suburbanization in Greater Jakarta focusing on three factors: population growth and converting agricultural and forest land to other uses, residential new town development, and planning policies and how they relate to the changing role of the private sector in residential and commercial development at the fringe.

Population Growth and Land Use Conversion in Jabodetabek

In 2014 the population of Jabodetabek was nearly 30 million people; the region had an annual growth rate of 3.6% between 2000 and 2010. Indonesia currently has 12 cities with at least 1 million people, 6 of which are located in Jabodetabek (Jakarta, Bekasi, Tangerang, South Tangerang, Depok and Bogor) which indicates the primacy of the Jakarta region (Firman, 2014a, 2014b). The City of Jakarta, the core of Jabodetabek, had a population of 9.6 million in 2010. Two million people commute for work from the surrounding areas into Jakarta (see Hata, 2003).

The population density of Jabodetabek increased tremendously from 2000 to 2010: there were 37.6 persons per hectare[3] in 2000 but 44.6 in 2010. The population density of Jakarta City, the core of Jabodetabek, increased from 128.0 people per hectare in 2000 to 145.9 in 2010 (Salim, 2013), or a 1.5 annual percent change between 2000 and 2010. The entire Jabodetabek region, however, experienced much more rapid population growth. For example, the populations of Tangerang City and Bekasi City grew 3.2% and 3.4% per year, respectively, over the ten-year period (Firman, 2014b).

Jakarta's share of the population of Jabodetabek, the greater metropolitan area, decreased significantly from 54.6% in 1990 to only 35.5% in 2010, indicating the suburbanization of the peripheral areas. The annual population growth of Jakarta City has slowed from 3.1% between 1980 and 1990 to only 0.4% between 1990 and 2000, although growth rose to 1.5% annually between 2000 and 2010. The fringe areas of Jabodetabek, in contrast, are experiencing much more rapid population growth, nearly 3% per year (Firman, 2014a, 2014b; Firman, Kombaitan, & Pradono, 2007). Many former residents in neighborhoods within Jakarta City have moved to the fringe areas of Jabodetabek, reflecting a functional and spatial integration of these areas into the metropolitan economy (Browder, Bohland, & Scarpaci, 1995). This situation reflects the process of *metropolitan turnaround*, the transformation of the fringes into urban areas, coupled with the deceleration of population growth in the core of the urban metropolitan area (Jones, Tsay, & Bajracharya, 1999).

BPS (2001), the Indonesian statistics agency, estimates that during 1995–2000 about 160,000 Jakarta residents moved to the City and District of Bogor at the fringes of Jakarta City. Moreover, about 190,000 Jakarta City residents moved to the District and City of Bekasi and to the District and the City of Tangerang in the fringe areas, respectively.

The development of economic activities at the fringes of Jabodetabek over the past 40 years has resulted in extensive conversion of prime farmland into non-agricultural uses, including industrial estates, residential new towns and large-scale residential areas, golf courses and recreation areas. These patterns are fueled by both foreign direct and domestic investments (Dharmapatni, Firman, McGee, & Robinson, 1995; Firman, 2000, 2014b; Firman & Dharmapatni, 1995). About 4,000 hectares of paddy fields and 8,000 hectares of primary forest had been converted into industrial and residential areas in south Jabodetabek between 1994 and 2001. In Jakarta City, as a result, many former residential areas have been converted into business spaces, offices, entertainment and both residential and commercial condominium developments.

In the Bogor area, in southern Jakarta, the land area of both old growth and second growth forests, gardens, estates and paddy fields declined substantially from 1994 to 2001, while the land area for settlements increased significantly (Firman, 2011, 2014a). Converting land from rural uses like agricultural and forestry to more urban uses like residential, commercial and industrial is also occurring in the area of South Bogor (Bogor-Puncak-Cianjur), upstream of Jakarta City. This is very problematic because South Bogor has been designated as a conservation area, designed to function as a water recharge zone. The conversion of land in this area away from agriculture and open space is thought to be one of the main causes of floods in Jakarta City in almost every rainy season.

The pace of the conversion of non-urban to urban land uses in Jabodetabek has been much faster in the fringe areas than in Jakarta City. A study employing remote sensing techniques and GIS (Carolita, Zain, Rustiadi, & Trisasongko, 2002) found that built-up areas (those converted from rural to more urban uses) increased from 12% to 24% of the total land area in Jabodetabek between 1992 and 2001 while land devoted to agriculture shrank from 37% to 31% in the same period. A more recent study (Salim, 2013) found that urban or built-up areas at the periphery of Jabodetabek, including Bogor, Tangerang, Bekasi and Depok, expanded from 544 to 850 square kilometers over the period 2000–10, or 4.6% per year, while those in Jakarta City increased from 560 to 594 square kilometer during the same period, or 0.6% per annum.

The development in the fringe areas of Jabodetabek reflects an early but ongoing process of post-suburbanization. The fringe areas now are growing more quickly than the core city and gradually become independent towns. This development is triggered by growing economic activities in the fringe and the increasing role of the private sector in the region.

Industrial Estate Development

Suburbanization in metropolitan Jakarta has also been triggered by the peripheral development of industrial activities and industrial estates. This development is driven by the behavior of private developers who respond to industrialization processes as well as the supportive pro-growth economic policies of both the central and local governments.

The central government's goal, as with most industrial parks or estates, is to encourage additional economic development by making investment in such activities easier and cheaper. Presidential Decree 41/1996 has greatly encouraged the development of these industrial estates by designating them as centers for the development of industrial activities which the government will support by subsidizing the provision of infrastructure and other facilities built and operated by licensed companies (Hudalah et al., 2013).[4]

Companies licensed by the (national or local) government have the exclusive right to develop and manage specific industrial areas and clearly play a significant role in fringe area development.[5] These licensed companies are also authorized to provide and manage ongoing utilities and facilities exclusively for the firms that locate in these areas, removing any barriers to development posed by insufficient local government resources. Companies that wish to develop industrial parks must obtain a license from the local government where the potential industrial estates will be located. When a potential industrial park extends into two or more municipalities/districts, the private developer must acquire additional permits from the provincial government. If the industrial park is located in an area that extends over two or more bordering provinces, or if it is to be managed by a foreign company, the developer must acquire additional permits from the *central* government.

Other companies that wish to start businesses in industrial estates can only buy land directly from the licensed companies, after acquiring several permits from the local government. Foreign companies must also acquire permits and the approval of their direct investments from the central government Investment Coordinating Board (Badan Koordinasi Penanaman Modal: BKPM).

The central government clearly plays a role in the development of industrial estates through laws, policies and regulations that support privatization of these areas. Nonetheless, local governments interact and cooperate directly with private firms seeking potential areas for new development as well as those wishing to extending existing areas for industrial estates.

Many companies have intensively built industrial estates at the fringes of Jabodetabek because of a strong market demand as well as the easy access and proximity to Jakarta City. In 2013 there were 35 industrial estates in the fringes of Jabodetabek, ranging from 50 to 1,800 hectares in size, about one-fourth of which are located in Bekasi District. Another 400 hectares of industrial estates were added to the region in 2013–14, mainly for automotive industries (Firman, 2014b).

Most of the industrial estates in Bekasi District are concentrated in the Cikarang area, about 35 kilometer east of Jakarta (i.e., subdistricts of Cikarang Pusat, Cikarang Barat, Cikarang Utara and Cikarang Timur), including those established as a joint venture with foreign investors. The Hyundai Industrial Estate, for example, is a cooperative venture between the Korean Hyundai company with Lippo Cikarang, a national corporation, while the MM2100 Industrial Estate is a joint venture with Marubeni Group, a Japanese investor (Hudalah & Firman, 2014). As a result of these joint ventures, there are more than 9,000 expatriates working and living in Bekasi City and District. The industrial estates in Cikarang had a potential export value of US$30.56 billion by the mid-2000s, which was almost half of the national non-oil gas export, or US$66.43 billion at the same time (Hudalah & Firman, 2012).

The largest industrial estate in Cikarang is Jababeka, developed and managed by the PT Jababeka Industrial Estate company. The company has developed Jababeka as a self-contained city and a center of manufacturing activities in Indonesia. At present there are more than 1,500 multinational and national companies from over 35 countries operating in the Jababeka industrial estates alone, including those from the USA, UK, France, Germany, Australia, the Netherlands, Japan, South Korea, Taiwan and China (PT Jababeka, 2010). In 2011 the PT Jababeka Industrial Estate company allocated nearly US$434.7 million, about 46.5% of its total capital expenditure, for land acquisition alone. Most of the companies that buy industrial land from the PT Jababeka Industrial Estate company are foreign enterprises from Japan, Korea, Malaysia and Europe seeking to expand their businesses in automotive production, pharmaceuticals, electronics and consumer goods (Yulisman, 2011). The Jababeka industrial estate company has also developed a US$30 million power plant to generate electricity for new manufacturing industries in the area. Jababeka also has houses, hotels, apartments, higher education institutions and malls and shopping centers. Nearly 1 million people, including about 2,500 expatriates, will live in the area by the end of the 21st century (Hudalah & Firman, 2012, p. 45). The total land area of the industrial estates in the Jakarta fringes increased substantially due to the Jababeka developments, from only 11,000 hectares in 2005 to 18,000 hectares in 2012 (Colliers International, 2005, 2012a; Hudalah et al., 2013).

The Jababeka industrial estate company is now building the island Cikarang Dry Port on a 200 hectare lot, which is expected to accommodate up to 2 million twenty-foot equivalent unit (TEUs) container vessels in 2020, with a total investment of US$20 million (Yulisman, 2011).

The demand for industrial land in Jabodetabek has greatly increased as a result of both direct domestic and foreign investments in the region. The cumulative-approved direct foreign investment in Jabodetabek reached US$37 million in the mid-2000s, which is nearly 60% of the total non-oil foreign direct investment in Indonesia (BPS, 2006). The cumulative-approved domestic investment in Jabodetabek, meanwhile, amounted to IDR 82,342 million (US$6.34 million), or approximately 33% of total Indonesia's domestic investment at the time (BPS, 2006).

The massive industrial development in the Jakarta fringes has resulted in high land prices in industrial estates in the region, ranging from US$106 per square meter in Bogor to US$175 per square meter in Bekasi (Colliers International, 2012b). The development of industrial estates has extended into adjacent districts, most notably the District of Serang in the west and District of Karawang in the west.

New Town Residential Development

Suburbanization in metropolitan Jakarta has also been stimulated by the development of residential "new towns." In the Indonesian context a new town is a residential area built on land that is used to be preserved for agricultural or forestry uses (Firman, 2004b). The development of new towns in Jabodetabek was for decades basically a response to the demand of many middle- and upper-income Indonesians for a secure, modern and quiet living environment (Leisch, 2000). Local governments now play a significant role in this continued development, because they have the authority to grant building permits to private developers. Private developers often negotiate with local governments over what the adopted spatial plans allow, especially when a proposed housing project is not located in an area planned for residential and/or commercial uses. Local governments in search of new economic development often approve private development requests and modify officially adopted spatial plans so new town development projects can proceed (Firman, 2004b; Rukmana, 2015).

The original new towns were traditional dormitory communities largely dependent on Jakarta City for employment, shopping and recreation. Today, they have become independent towns with a strong economic base. The nature of recent new towns is very different, however; the new towns of Lippo-Karawaci in Tangerang and Lippo-Cikarang City in Bekasi (Arai, 2015; Hogan & Houston, 2002) were explicitly developed by the Lippo Group to include social, educational and economic activities as well as residential uses. One non-residential facility is the private Pelita Harapan University which operates facilities similar to the best universities in Western countries (Firman, 2004b), the Siloam Hospital, the Matahari Department Store and the Times bookstore.

Another new town, Jababeka City, has 24,000 homes and is also the largest manufacturing cluster in Indonesia with an area of 5,600 hectares and a population of nearly 1 million people (Hudalah & Firman, 2012). Jababeka City hosts over 1,500 companies, including Medical City Health Care and the Movie Land Film industry (Kartajaya & Taufik, 2009; PT Jababeka, 2010). Beginning in 2015 two private property developers, PT Plaza Indonesia Realty and PT Jababeka, collaborated to build a *superblock* in Jababeka, that is, a highly dense, compact area with mixed land uses, containing about 200,000 square meters at a cost of US$1 billion. The development features a five-star hotel, retail areas, serviced apartments and offices (The Jakarta Post, 2014).

Many new towns have become independent because the market now demands for more differentiated but also more protected new towns which private firms are happy to create. PT Bumi Serpong Damai (BSD), one of Indonesia's largest property companies, for instance, doubled its annual profit from 1.48 trillion (US$113.96 million) in 2012 to 2.9 trillion Rupiahs (US$256.28 million) in 2013 (Lubis, 2014) by responding to this more focused demand. They have developed large shopping centers in the outskirts of Jabodetabek as well as in Jakarta City, such as in Bekasi Square and Teraskota in Tangerang. To attract consumers, the developers often hire expatriate architects, urban planners and property specialists, with little knowledge of local architecture and city planning. The physical design of these new towns, as a result, very much resembles gated suburban communities and wealthier residential areas in developed countries (Dick & Rimmer, 1998); moreover, they are neither socially nor culturally mixed responding to the demands of middle- and higher-income residents (Firman, 2014b; Leisch, 2000). Recent new towns have been designed as gated communities, surrounded by walls and separated from nearby local communities (Leisch, 2002), to maintain the security and quality of life that residents seek.

Private developers have long been required by law to provide basic infrastructure when constructing new residential developments[6] but developers now go beyond providing basic utilities; they now administer municipal services as if they were the "government" in the communities they build, appointing their own town managers who ensure service delivery. In the Lippo Karawaci new town, for instance, the town manager is an expatriate employed by the development company, and not appointed by the local government (Arai, 2015). Inside these gated communities the private developers provide and manage utilities exclusive to the inhabitants, such as roads, clean water, waste water disposal, landscaping and gardening, security services and shuttle bus transportation to Jakarta City (Arai, 2015).

The Changing Role of Public and Private Sectors

Over the last four decades the private sector has played a significant role in suburbanization in Jabodetabek. Today, it plays an even stronger role, having taken over from the public sector the power to acquire and develop land, as well as to provide and manage municipal services in fringe areas. This shift of power is strongly facilitated by the central government's pro-growth economic policies and promotion of foreign direct investment, which has encouraged capital inflows from overseas for development in fringe areas. Decentralization has also given local governments the ability to work closely with the private sector in pursuit of local economic growth and development.

The central government today actually has less power to intervene in land development in Jabodetabek than it did in the 1980s and 1990s. The central government does develop national and spatial plans that apply to metropolitan Jakarta,[7] but local governments now have substantial autonomy and stronger powers to develop their own spatial plans and govern development within their jurisdictions. Local governments tend to focus only on their own plans and rarely pay much attention to the spatial plans of the national government or neighboring regions (see Kusno, 2014). This autonomy has, however, strengthened patronage relationships between the local government and the private sector (Rukmana, 2015). Local governments often prepare or alter spatial plans to accommodate the interest of developers (Firman, 2004b; Rukmana, 2015) although both sides have power in the development process (Arai, 2015; Cowherd, 2005).

Privatization of the Urban Fringes and Post-Suburbanization in Jabodetabek

We have sought to identify the extent to which the post-suburbia phenomenon first seen in the developed world is reflected in the current situation in metropolitan Jakarta, Indonesia. We first analyzed the current patterns of suburbanization in the fringe areas of Jakarta: patterns of population growth, land use changes, promotion of industrial estates and new town developments.

The peripheral areas of Jabodetabek today are experiencing a rapid urban transformation, fueled by significant population growth in suburban areas. Jakarta City—the core of the region—in contrast is experiencing low population growth, due to substantial population spillover to fringe areas. Jabodetabek, the entire region, is seeing massive conversion of prime agricultural land into urban land uses in fringe areas, characterized by industrial estates, more mixed-use new towns and large-scale residential areas, and shopping centers. Historic dormitory towns on the fringes have been transformed into independent communities with a full range of opportunities and a strong economic base.

Recent Jabodetabek development, as a result, shows some signs of the early stages of post-suburbanization.

Post-suburbanization in Jabodetabek, as in China, is physically characterized by a mixed pattern of both traditional and new suburban residential developments, occurring as a result of the heavy flow of foreign direct investments drawn by central government economic policies. Post-suburban development in Jakarta, however, is unlikely to fully resemble that of Western cities (Feng et al., 2008) in part because so many people choose to continue to live in the traditional core and commute out to suburban developments for work, as well as other activities.

We find that these patterns strongly correspond to the rapidly increasing role of the private sector, and a shift of power from the public to the private sector in land development, substantially accelerated by central government policies that allow privatization of land development. We believe these findings have important implications for planning practice in the era of post-suburban development. The Jabodetabek example shows that the private sector can help the government to respond to regional needs for housing, jobs, shopping and educational opportunities and infrastructure. The private sector, focused on making profits, however, rarely pays attention to formally adopted plans and public policy objectives unless required to do so; moreover, local governments may act in ways that create regional problems. Land use planning in this context assumes a different meaning and is increasingly fragmented and conflicting. The current situation also highlights, however, the key role that planning can and should play in ensuring that localized and private sector actions in Jakarta and growing regions in other developing nations do not end up exacerbating regional problems and leading to sub-optimal solutions.

Notes

1. See http://www.rd.usda.gov/programs-services/single-family-housing-guaranteed-loan-program
2. Since 1999 it has been called Jabodetabek, when the city of Depok was formed.
3. 259 hectares equal 1 square mile.
4. Law 3/2014 on Industry and Government Regulation 142/2015 on Industrial Estates requires industrial activities in Indonesia to be located within industrial estates.
5. Government Regulation 142/2015 defines licensed industrial park companies as those holding permits from the government to manage industrial parks.
6. Law 4/1992 on Housing and Settlement, now amended by Law 1/2011.
7. The central government still develops spatial plans for the areas that have national interests or strategic values (kawasan strategis nasional), including the plan for Greater Jakarta ("Jabodetabekpunjur") (President Regulation 54/2008).

References

Arai, K. (2015). "Jakarta Since Yesterday': The Making of the Post-New Order Regime in an Indonesian Metropolis," *Southeast Asian Studies*, 4(3): 445–86.

Badan Pusat Statistik. (2001). *Population of Indonesia: Results of the 2000 Population Census*. Jakarta: Badan Pusat Statistik-Statistics Indonesia.

Badan Pusat Statistik. (2006). *Economic Indicators: Monthly Statistical Bulletin.* Jakarta: Badan Pusat Statistik Indonesia.

Beard, V. A., Miraftab, F., and Silver, C. (2008). *Planning and Decentralization: Contested Spaces for Public Action in the Global South.* London and New York: Routledge.

Bontje, M., and Burdack, J. (2011). "Post-Suburbia in Continental Europe," in N. A. Phelps and F. Wu, eds. *International Perspectives on Suburbanization a Post-Suburban World?* (pp. 143–62). New York: Palgrave Macmillan.

Borsdorf, A. (2004). "On the Way to Post-Suburbia?: Changing Structures in the Outskirts of European Cities," in A. Borsdorf and P. Zembri, eds. *European Cities. Insights on Outskirts: Structures* (pp. 7–30). Brussels: Blanchard Printing.

Browder, J., Bohland, J., and Scarpaci, J. (1995). "Patterns of Development on the Metropolitan Fringe: Urban Fringe Expansion in Bangkok, Jakarta, and Santiago," *Journal of the American Planning Association,* 61(3): 310–27.

Carolita, I. A., Zain, A. M., Rustiadi, E., and Trisasongko, B. (2002). "The Land Use Pattern of Jabodetabek Region," *Presented at the 4th Indonesian Regional Science Association International Conference,* Bali, Indonesia.

Champion, T. (2001). "Urbanization, Suburbanization, Counterurbanization and Reurbanization," in R. Paddison, ed. *Handbook of Urban Studies* (pp. 143–61). London: SAGE Publications.

Cochrane, A. (2011). "Post-Suburbia in the Context of Urban Containment: The Case of the South East of England," in N. A. Phelps and F. Wu, eds. *International Perspectives on Suburbanization: A Post-Suburban World?* (pp. 163–76). New York: Palgrave Macmillan.

Colliers International. (2005). *Jakarta Property Market Overview.* Jakarta: Collier International.

Colliers International. (2012a). *Jakarta Property Market.* Jakarta: Colliers International.

Colliers International. (2012b). *Research and Forecast Report: Jakarta Industrial Market, 2nd Quarter 2012.* Jakarta: Collier International.

Cowherd, R. (2005). "Does Planning Culture Matter? Dutch and American Models in Indonesian Urban Transformations," in B. Sanyal, ed. *Comparative Planning Cultures* (pp. 465–92). New York: Routledge.

Dharmapatni, I., Firman, T., McGee, T. G., and Robinson, I. M. (1995). "Problems and Challenges of Mega-Urban Regions in Indonesia," in T. G. McGee and I. M. Robinson, eds. *The Mega-Urban Regions of Southeast Asia* (pp. 296–314). Vancouver: The University of British Columbia Press.

Dick, H. W., and Rimmer, P. J. (1998). "Beyond the Third World City: The New Urban Geography of South-east Asia," *Urban Studies,* 35(12): 2303–21.

Douglass, M. (2000). "Mega-urban Regions and World City Formation: Globalisation, the Economic Crisis and Urban Policy Issues in Pacific Asia," *Urban Studies,* 37(12): 2315–35.

Douglass, M., and Jones, G. W. (2008). "The Morphology of Mega-Urban Regions Expansion," in G. W. Jones and M. Douglass, eds. *Mega-Urban Regions in Pacific Asia: Urban Dynamics in a Global Era* (pp. 19–37). Singapore: NUS Press.

Feng, J., Zhou, Y., and Wu, F. (2008). "New Trends of Suburbanization in Beijing since 1990: From Government-led to Market-oriented," *Regional Studies,* 42(1): 83–99.

Firman, T. (2000). "Rural to Urban Land Conversion in Indonesia during Boom and Bust Periods," *Land Use Policy,* 17(1): 13–20.

Firman, T. (2004a). "Major Issues in Indonesia's Urban Land Development," *Land Use Policy,* 21(4): 347–55.

Firman, T. (2004b). "New Town Development in Jakarta Metropolitan Region: A Perspective of Spatial Segregation," *Habitat International,* 28(3): 349–68.

Firman, T. (2008). "In Search of a Governance Institution Model for Jakarta Metropolitan Area (JMA) under Indonesia's New Decentralisation Policy: Old Problems, New Challenges," *Public Administration and Development*, 28(4): 280–90.

Firman, T. (2009). "Decentralization Reform and Local-Government Proliferation in Indonesia: Towards a Fragmentation of Regional Development," *Review of Urban & Regional Development Studies*, 21(2–3): 143–57.

Firman, T. (2011). "Post-Suburban Elements in an Asian Extended Metropolitan Region: The Case of Jabodetabek (Jakarta Metropolitan Area)," in N. A. Phelps and F. Wu, eds. *International Perspectives on Suburbanization a Post-Suburban World?* (pp. 195–209). New York: Palgrave Macmillan.

Firman, T. (2014a). *Demographic Patterns of Indonesia's Urbanization, 2000–2010: Continuity and Change at the Macro Level*. Unpublished paper, School of Architecture, Planning and Policy Development, Institute of Technology, Bandung, Indonesia.

Firman, T. (2014b). "The Dynamics of Jabodetabek Development: The Challenge of Urban Governance," in H. Hill, ed. *Regional Dynamics in A Decentralized Indonesia* (pp. 368–87). Singapore: Institute of Southeast Asian Studies.

Firman, T., and Dharmapatni, I. A. I. (1995). "The Emergence of Extended Metropolitan Regions in Indonesia: Jabodetabek and Bandung Metropolitan Area," *Review of Urban and Regional Development Studies*, 7(2): 167–88.

Firman, T., Kombaitan, B., and Pradono, P. (2007). "The Dynamics of Indonesia's Urbanisation, 1980–2006," *Urban Policy and Research*, 25(4): 433–54.

Fishman, R. (2002). "Bourgeois Utopias: Vision of Suburbia," in S. Fainstein and S. Campbell, eds. *Readings in Urban Theory* (2nd edition, pp. 21–31). Oxford and Malden, MA: Blackwell Publishers.

Hata, T. (2003). "Improvement of Railway System in Jakarta Metropolitan Area," *Japan Railway & Transportation*, 35: 36–44.

Hogan, T., and Houston, C. (2002). "Corporate Cities—Urban Gateways or Gated Communities against the City? The Case of Lippo, Jakarta," in T. Bunnell, L. B. W. Drummond and K-C. Ho, eds. *Critical Reflections on Cities in Southeast Asia* (pp. 243–64). Singapore: Times Academic Press.

Hudalah, D., and Firman, T. (2012). "Beyond Property: Industrial Estates and Post-Suburban Transformation in Jakarta Metropolitan Region," *Cities*, 29(1): 40–48.

Hudalah, D., and Firman, T. (2014). *Suburban Politics and the Building of Industrial Town in Jakarta Mega-Urban Region*. Unpublished paper, School of Architecture, Planning, and Policy Development—Institute of Technology, Bandung, Indonesia.

Hudalah, D., Viantari, D., Firman, T., and Woltjer, J. (2013). "Industrial Land Development and Manufacturing Deconcentration in Greater Jakarta," *Urban Geography*, 34(7): 950–71.

Hudalah, D., and Woltjer, J. (2007). "Spatial Planning System in Transitional Indonesia," *International Planning Studies*, 12(3): 291–303.

Jones, G. W. (2006). "Urbanization in Southeast Asia," in T.-C. Wong, B. J. Shaw and K. C. Goh, eds. *Challenging Sustainability: Urban Development and Change in Southeast Asia* (pp. 247–67). Singapore: Marshall Cavendish Academic.

Jones, G. W., Tsay, C., and Bajracharya, B. (1999). *'Demography and Employment Change in Megacities of South-east and East Asia*. Working Paper in Demography no. 80, Research School of Social Sciences, Australian National University, Canberra.

Kartajaya, H., and Taufik, T. (2009). "Jababeka Industrial Estate: A Transforming City Developer," (in Indonesian), *Kompas*, April 25 p. i.

Kraemer, C. (2005). "Commuter Belt Turbulence in a Dynamic Region: The Case of the Munich City-Region. In K. Hoggart (Ed.), The City's Hinterland: Dynamism and Divergence in Europe's Peri-Urban Territories (pp. 41–68), Aldershot, UK: Ashgate.

Kusno, A. (2014). *After the New Order: Space, Politics and Jakarta*. Honolulu: University of Hawai'i Press.

Lane, M. B. (2003). "Participation, Decentralization, and Civil Society: Indigenous Rights and Democracy in Environmental Planning," *Journal of Planning Education and Research*, 22(4): 360–73.

Lang, R. (2003). *Edgeless Cities: Exploring the Elusive Metropolis*. Washington, DC: Brookings Institution Press.

Lang, R., and Knox, P. K. (2009). "The New Metropolis: Rethinking Megalopolis," *Regional Studies*, 43(6): 789–802.

Leaf, M. (1994). "The Suburbanization of Jakarta: A Concurrence of Economics and Ideoglogy." *Third World Planning Review*, 16 (4): 341–356.

Leisch, H. (2000). "Structures and Functions of New Towns in Jabotabek," *Presented at the Workshop of Indonesian Town Revisited*, The University of Leiden.

Leisch, H. (2002). "Gated Communities in Indonesia," *Cities*, 19(5): 341–50.

Lubis, A. M. (2014, March 20). BSD Doubles Profits on Rising Sales. *The Jakarta Post*. Retrieved from https://www.thejakartapost.com/news/2014/03/20/bsd-doubles-profits-rising-sales.html

Mamas, S. G. M., and Komalasari, R. (2008). "The Growth of Jakarta Mega Urban Region: An Analysis of Demographic, Educational and Employment Change," *Presented at the Conference on Growth Dynamic of Mega Urban Regions in Asia*, Singapore.

McGee, T. G., and Robinson, I. M., eds. (1995). *The Mega-Urban Regions of Southeast Asia*. Vancouver: UBC Press.

Pan, F., Guo, J., Zhang, H., and Liang, J. (2015). "Building a 'Headquarters Economy': The Geography of Headquarters within Beijing and Its Implications for Urban Restructuring," *Cities*, 42: 1–12.

Phelps, N. A. (2012). "The Growth Machine Stops? Urban Politics and the Making and Remaking of an Edge City," *Urban Affairs Review*, 48(5): 670–700.

Phelps, N. A., and Wood, A. M. (2011). "The New Post-suburban Politics?," *Urban Studies*, 48(12): 2591–610.

Phelps, N. A., Wood, A. M., and Valer, D. C. (2010). "A Post-Suburban World? An Outline of Research Agenda," *Environment & Planning A*, 42(2): 366–83.

Permatasri, P. S. and Hudalah, D. (2013). Mobility Patterns and Job Deconcentration in a Metropoliutan Area: The Case of Cikarang City, Bekasi. Unpublished Paper, Department of Regional and City Planning, Institute of Technology, Bandung. (In Indonesian).

PT Jababeka. (2010). *Annual Report: Ready to Capitalize, Ready to Growth*. Jakarta: PT Jababeka.

Rukmana, D. (2015). "The Change and Transformation of Indonesian Spatial Planning after Suharto's New Order Regime: The Case of the Jakarta Metropolitan Area," *International Planning Studies*, 20(4): 350–70.

Salim, W. (2013, March). *Urban Development and Spatial Planning of Greater Jakarta*. Power Point Presentation presented at the Forum Komunikasi Pembangunan Indonesia.

Shatkin, G. (2008). "The City and the Bottom Line: Urban Megaprojects and the Privatization of Planning in Southeast Asia," *Environment and Planning A*, 40(2): 383–401.

Silaen, L., Watanabe, S., and Nugroho, B. (2015, January 14). Indonesia Simplifies Permit Process to Spur Domestic Investment Linda Silaen, Sadachika Watanabe and Bobby Nugroho. *Asia Nikkei*. Retrieved from http://asia.nikkei.com/Politics-Economy/Policy-Politics/Indonesia-simplifies-permit-process-to-spur-domestic-investment

Silver, C. (2008). *Planning the Megacity: Jakarta in the Twentieth Century*. London: New York: Routledge.

Soja, E. W. (2000). *Postmetropolis: Critical Studies of Cities and Regions*. Malden, MA: Blackwell Publishers.

Swyngedouw, E., Moulaert, F., and Rodriguez, A. (2002). "Neoliberal Urbanization in Europe: Large-Scale Urban Development Projects and the New Urban Policy," *Antipode*, *34*(3): 542–77.

The Jakarta Post. (2014, October 13). Building of $1 billion Superblock to begin in Jababeka. *The Jakarta Post*. Retrieved from http://www.thejakartapost.com/news/2014/10/13/building-1-billion-superblock-begin-jababeka.html

Walks, A. (2013). "Suburbanism as a Way of Life, Slight Return," *Urban Studies*, *50*(8): 1471–88.

Wu, F., and Lu, D. (2008). "The Transition of Chinese Cities," *Built Environment*, *34*(4): 385–91.

Wu, F., and Phelps, N. A. (2008). "From Suburbia to Post-Suburbia in China? Aspects of the Transformation of the Beijing and Shanghai Global City Regions," *Built Environment*, *34*(4): 464–81.

Wu, F., and Phelps, N. A. (2011). "(Post)Suburban Development and State Entrepreneurialism in Beijing's Outer Suburbs," *Environment and Planning A*, *43*(2): 410–30.

Yulisman, L. (2011, June 24). Jababeka Plans Expansion as Demand Surges. *The Jakarta Post*. Retrieved from https://www.thejakartapost.com/news/2011/06/24/jababeka-plans-expansion-demand-surges.html

Chapter 3
TRANSFORMING TRANSPORT PLANNING IN THE POST-POLITICAL ERA

Crystal Legacy

Introduction

Urban scholars have long argued that planning is a political and contested process (Forester, 1989; Sandercock, 1995; Flyvbjerg, 1998). Within the specific context of transport planning, Walks (2014) has, for example, described the tensions that transpire in relation to the prioritization of freeway construction that continues in some North American and Australian cities as a 'politics of automobility' (see also Urry, 2004; Boudreau et al, 2009; Stone & Mees, 2010). Urban transport planning is however inherently political, always involving priority setting and investment decision-making that will ultimately serve some needs better than others, yet entrenched within the orthodoxy of road construction is a depolitization of transport decision-making through the ascendency of new public management systems that rely on centralized executive decision-making powers (McGuirk, 2005). In other words, the spaces where political decisions are made are shielded from outside public interrogation where challenges could be lodged and bigger questions could be asked about the social distribution of benefits.

Limiting civic participation in transport decision-making sets up a 'democratic deficit' (Marres, 2005) inhibiting citizens from challenging dominant urban transport discourses. New platforms are created elsewhere, but beyond the formal processes and institutions of the state. This is where the political is shifted, a phenomenon described within the urban studies literature as a post-political condition (Oosterlynck and Swyngedouw, 2010; Blühdorn, 2013). The concept of the post-political can be traced to post-foundational political theory and to the work of Mouffe (2005), Žižek (1999) and Rancière (1999) on the displacement of politics. In this work dissensus is central to a functioning democracy; it is the displacement of politics into locations beyond the state apparatus that is creating multiple sites of democratic practice (Marres, 2005). However as Bylund (2012) points out,

DOI: 10.4324/9781003178545-5

the displacement of the rather informal (citizen-driven) political from the formal (government-led) post-political introduces an unhelpful binary. This binary fails to consider the multiple ways in which the two—government-led interventionist decision-making and citizen action—intersect and where political and counter-hegemonic pursuits may arise. This chapter uses the terminology of binaries and intersections as a conceptual tool to engage with the post-political/political aspects of transport planning (Cloke and Johnston, 2005). While binaries can provide a powerful description of difference, there is value in also understanding how these differences interact—and intersect—through a dialectical relationship creating opportunities for change (Harvey, 1996: 19). It is in these spaces of intersection, as Purcell (2013: 572) posits, that a process of 'perpetual democratisation' occurs.

Bridging the post-political and urban transport literatures invites a reconceptualization of the politics of transport planning (and of strategic planning more generally) within a post-political context (Olesen, 2013: 298). Thinking about how a reconceptualisation could transpire, the question guiding this chapter is, in what ways can the political provide a platform for a redemocratization of transport planning? To answer this question, this chapter focuses on a single case study of an urban transport infrastructure decision-making process in Melbourne, Australia. Although the controversial inner city road tunnel was deemed a 'done deal' by elected officials in the lead up to the November 2014 state election, the decision to expedite the signing of the project's contracts before the plebiscite was an extraordinary step by elected officials to remove the project from the formal political process. This only provoked a direct politicization of the project. In addition, the government's decision to withhold the release of the business case for this project and to accelerate contract signing for a public-private partnership delivery arrangement to weeks before a state election was met with significant distress from concerned residents.

The sections that follow draw on the Melbourne case study to illustrate how affected and concerned citizens and community-based groups respond to the inherently political, yet not always democratic, aspects of setting transport investment priorities. The next section explores the tenuous link between transport infrastructure and citizen participation. Here the notion of a post-political decision-making environment illustrates the implications that post-political governance frameworks have on broader notions of democratic process. Then I turn to a discussion on the post-political binary before offering an illustrative example of how this binary presents a reimagining of an alternative transport future. This chapter concludes by discussing how the intersections that exist between the political and the post-political spaces enable a redemocratization of transport planning.

The Tenuous Link between Transport Infrastructure Planning and Participation

Urban transport planning is weakly linked to progressive conceptions of participatory planning. Within urban scholarship, the spaces dedicated to theorizing the role of citizen participation in transport implementation are limited (Molina

Costa, 2014). This absence stands in contrast to the expansive body of theoretical and empirical research within the strategic planning literature that examines the relationship between citizen participation and policy decision-making (Healey, 1997; Innes and Booher, 2010; Albrechts, 2012). Instead, the engagement of citizens at the implementation stage is typically reduced to narrow consultation briefs and rarely associated with broader discussions about transport problems and possible solutions (Sturup, 2016). Under a neoliberal political regime, governments will seek to create a more certain investment environment to attract private sector participation. In a post-political context, governance aligns with a 'managerial logic' that concentrates decisions into the hands of experts situated in non-state or quasi-state agencies (Swyngedouw, 2010: 225). Under these conditions the relationship between inclusive citizen participation and infrastructure delivery remains partial if existing at all.

But this is not to suggest that citizen participation at these latter stages in the transport planning process is entirely absent. Some planning jurisdictions impose legal requirements to undertake a form of citizen consultation. This may include a call for resident submissions and, in some planning jurisdictions, opportunities to appeal decisions. In those jurisdictions that have embraced deliberative forms of engagement and despite these advances recent research has shown that innovation in participation—such as deliberative decision-making seen in citizens juries—has been embraced, but in very limited ways for the purpose of political experiment and grandstanding (Legacy et al., 2014), and to promote a kind of 'consensus politics' (Rancière, 2000: 119). To establish an inclusive process of transport planning and implementation would require repositioning of citizens as key stakeholders towards a renewal of democracy (Bickerstaff and Walker, 2005), as well as recasting the relationship between infrastructure implementation and citizen participation.

Participation under a neoliberal political regime severely limits the democratic reach of participatory and deliberative planning. For instance, de Souza (2006: 334) argues that where participation exists formal processes of citizen participation provide an illustrative example of 'structural co-optation.' The political dimension that deliberation in participation introduces remains absent. Rancière (1999: 102) calls this condition postdemocracy defining it as,

> the government practice and conceptual legitimization of a democracy *after* the demos, a democracy that has eliminated the appearance, miscount, and dispute of the people and is thereby reducible to the sole interplay of state mechanisms and combinations of social energies and interests.

The post-political represents that shift away from a purely social characterization of politics to what Žižek (1999: 248) calls a "perverse mode of administering social affairs." Yet Rancière (1999) and Mouffe (2005) challenge the provocation that politics can be eliminated; they describe politics as the passions and interests of individuals, and eliminating politics is to support a kind of democracy that narrowly focuses on 'reason, moderation and consensus' and evades conflict (Mouffe, 2005: 28).

The use of the word 'democracy' in this post-political neoliberal context is used in association with a form of governance that seeks to eliminate politics (Oosterlynck and Swyngedouw, 2010: 1581). Oosterlynck and Swyngedouw (2010: 1591) posit that under a post-political context, "politics is identified as 'good governance,' based on achieving a stakeholder-based negotiated consensus." Hendriks (2014) describes 'good urban governance' as a set of underlying values and principles driving conduct, but separates it from what could be described as 'good urban politics.' Good urban governance provides the platform to which input legitimacy and output legitimacy for a proposed project can be exercised, but it fails to facilitate or provide an opportunity for political interventions to shape a new urban transport paradigm. Citizen participation as a component of urban democracy is restricted to serving the implementation of infrastructure and economic development (Sturup, 2010). Therefore, bigger questions about what kind of urban transport infrastructure should be built, who will be served by it and when and where should it be built could be addressed in policy and planning strategies but are rarely put forward by governments for discussion and rigorous evaluation (Legacy, 2014). But it is within these opaque structures of urban good governance, aligned with the post-political condition, that provokes an opening up of a new urban transport politics beyond the state if you will. As has been seen in the environmental sustainability movement (Blühdorn, 2013), the binary created between the post-political condition and the political invites a dialectic relationship that paradoxically acts to redemocratize and politicize urban transport planning. The new political game is being played out at these intersections.

Political Binaries

The post-political condition (Rancière, 1999; Žižek, 1999; Mouffe, 2005) has reshaped the way the political is constituted in urban scholarship (Oosterlynck and Swyngedouw, 2010; Bylund, 2012; Metzger et al., 2015). However, as Davidson and Iveson (2014: 4) posits, "Labelling cities 'post-political' risks treating depoliticization as a condition that has been realized, rather than a tendency that has taken hold." This fails to consider the dialectic nature of the political/post-political relationship. Critical appraisals of citizen engagement exercises that intercept a plan-making effort have uncovered a consensual practice that does not present hard choices for careful open scrutiny (Purcell, 2009; Albrechts, 2015). In the context of urban transport, deliberative planning in such settings offers an insufficient democratic experience to residents seeking to transform urban transport decision-making. When engagement does persist, these processes are characterized by bounded deliberative engagement that corrals citizens into formulaic objection settings that impose very strict and limiting procedural settings. It is in these settings where citizen opposition—often framed as 'NIMBY' opposition—is framed as non-rational and beyond the scope of the project and process for decision-makers to consider.

Yet, it is the action taken by citizens beyond the state that is both redefining state-civil society interrelationships and forging an interactive setting that is driving socio-political innovation (Swyngedouw, 2005). Newman (2013: 9) argues that the post-political turn in urban planning is prompting new social movements embracing rather unique ways of 'performing politics' but doing so in a manner that focuses efforts on the intersections created between the formal government rationalities of urban transport planning and the rationalities that exist beyond the state. Citizen opposition can prompt engaged residents and community-based groups to create informal spaces to devise transport strategies to counteract propositions by the government. There are many different theorizations that describe the act of opposing. These alternative planning spaces have come to be known by a range of different terminology. Insurgent planning, radical planning, grassroots planning and 'direct action' planning, to name a few, form a body of planning scholarship examining citizen activity made in response to and even in spite of the state (de Souza, 2006; Iveson, 2013). Considerably more informal and plural undertakings now represent the arenas where policy influence may arise. The post-political literature has used case studies to illustrate the displacement of the political to places outside of government (Mouffe, 2005). This creates a binary between the post-political mode of governing and the political reaction some communities have to closing the door completely; when the door is open, the reaction is directed at heavily stage managed consultation environments.

Purcell (2013) describes the political as pluralistic consisting of a connected set of autonomous movements. This is more than another example of radical democracy or everyday pluralism (Laclau & Mouffe, 1985). It is a movement that is also aware of the constraining effects of current institutions and is thus willing to seek transformational change through political struggle to reform and achieve structural change (e.g. introducing new funding regimes). In the case study that follows, I examine the counterhegemonic movement that transpired with the announcement of a 6-kilometre inner city road tunnel project in Melbourne, Australia. Specific attention is given to exploring the political/post-political binary that formed in response to the announcement of the proposed project. I will also focus on the opposition that mounted at the intersection between the political and post-political and which forged political, institutional, cultural change within the deeply political spaces of transport planning.

Research Methods

This study draws upon an ethnographic study of 15 community-based campaigners in Melbourne, Australia, that both engaged with the government's formal consultation process and also actively pursued alternative forums to mobilize a broader effort to protest against a proposed 6-kilometre inner city East-West Link road tunnel. The ethnographic research was conducted over a six-month period of public engagement between October 2013 and June 2014, which was marked by the release of the project's Comprehensive Impact Statement (CIS) and concluded with the approval of the proposed road tunnel in June 2014 by the Planning Minister. As an interested observer of the relationship between urban democracy and planning, I embedded myself within the campaign to stop the East-West Link. I did so by attending street protests, community meetings and public forums as well as following Twitter feeds and Facebook posts where I observed the strategies to protest against the projects and how the various groups coordinated their efforts with other groups. I also conducted interviews with 15 community campaigners. A cross section of campaigners was determined to capture different campaigning styles. There were those groups that embraced direct forms of action such as on-street protests, as well as politically savvy strategists that worked to position the East-West Link project on the political agenda in advance of the state election, and neighbourhood-based interest groups and broader-interest groups (e.g. pro-public transport groups). During this six-month period of observation the 15 campaigners mounted a coordinated and collective effort to oppose this project. Semi-structured interviews with the campaigners were undertaken producing narratives about the campaigner's efforts to oppose the East-West Link project. Interview questions prompted interviewees to speak candidly about their motivations to oppose the project, including reflections on their specific role and contribution to the broader anti-East-West Link movement. The interview questions also invited campaigners to reflect upon their choice of strategies, and how these strategies helped (if at all) to forge relationships with other community groups to assert the political into transport infrastructure planning.

To capture the formal government engagement with affected residents, analysis was also undertaken of media releases, commercial media and policy documents. Also considered were participant observations from a 30-day public panel hearing where resident, local government and the authority responsible for the project—the Linking Melbourne Authority (LMA)—discussed and debated their respective cases for and against the proposed project. Analysis from these observations and media stories provided an account of how the state government interacted with and responded to opposition. The focus of this research was on the active citizens and community-based group's engagement with a formal (post-political) CIS process and the (political) informal campaigns and protests that occurred beyond the government's formal process. It is important to note here that the positioning of the formal and informal engagement strategies as a political and post-political binary in some ways overly simplifies the relationship between the state and residents in opposition. To begin to understand the nuances of this relationship, I examine the dialectical relationship that this binary introduces and to reveal the ways in which transport politics is played out within a post-political context.

Case Study: Melbourne's East-West Link

Over the past six decades, Melbourne has suffered from a lack of investment in urban public transport (Victorian Government, 2014). In 2010, a new government was elected in the State of Victoria on an election platform to build public transport. Labor's time in power (between 1999 and 2010) resulted in no substantial expansion in public transport infrastructure within the metropolis. Instead, the Labor Government successfully produced five transport plans over an 11-year period but it was their inability to implement those plans which commentators prescribed as the primary factor that led to their election defeat in 2010 (Davidson, 2010).

In the lead up to the 2010 election, the opposition party pledged to 'Fix the problems. Build the future' (Austin, 2010). The Liberal-National Coalition was elected to government on November 27, 2010, with public transport forming its key platform issue. Its centrepiece was a $1.55 billion transport policy pledging improved train, tram and bus services and the construction of rail links to Victoria's two airports. A newly formed independent Public Transport Authority would also oversee the development of regional rail links, a cross-country passenger rail route and new stations in the middle suburbs (Austin, 2010).

Following the election, surfacing to the top of this project priority list was an inner city East-West Link road tunnel. In December 2012 the East-West Link was declared a major transport project of state significance under the *Major Transport Projects Facilitation Act 2009*. A year later, a Bill was introduced into State Parliament in June 2013 to amend this Act to "reduc[e] procedural delays and red tape" for all large urban transport projects, including the East-West Link (Parliament of Victoria, 2013). At the second reading of the Bill, Opposition Planning Minister Brian Tee stated his concerns arguing that the proposed amendment would "exclude[] local communities from the process" and give "the minister power to .... decide which matters will be considered at a public hearing. The minister, not the public, will decide what is important" (Tee, 2013). What Tee did not note in his speech to the State Parliament in September 2013 was that the Minister for Planning would also be given 'overarching approval decision' for this project (DTPLI, 2013: 11).

The elevation of the East-West Link as a major transport priority in 2012 occurred in the absence of community engagement, and was quickly positioned in the wider media and political discourse as a 'done deal.' Initially, a unilateral decision by the state government positioned the road tunnel as the state government's number one transport priority. This positioning was further crystallized when the newly elected federal government committed $1.5 billion of federal money exclusively to fund the controversial inner city road tunnel project (Wright, 2014). With this investment pledge in place, and following the release of the state and federal budgets in early 2014, both the Australian government and the state government firmly committed to building this road above all other alternative public transport projects in Victoria.

Subverting the Political in Transport Planning

In July 2010, Victoria's Minister for Roads established the statutory agency the LMA under the Transport Integration Act 2010 to manage complex road projects on behalf of the state (LMA, 2014). The state government announced that, through a process called a Comprehensive Impact Statement, it would examine the anticipatory impacts from the proposed project. The process involved a public exhibition of the CIS report, a public submission process and a 30-day panel hearing (LMA, 2014). In May 2013, the Planning Minister published the scoping directions for the CIS (DTPLI, 2013: 9). At this time, affected residents and the broader public were invited through local newspaper and government websites to prepare written submissions to a Minister appointed Independent Assessment Committee (IAC). The IAC would then respond directly to citizen concerns as they related to a predetermined set of evaluation objectives and a 'reference design' (DPTLI, 2013: 12); the former was prepared by the Minister and the latter prepared by the LMA (The Act, 2009: 26; DTPLI, 2013: 9–10). As was made clear in the CIS statement, firms tendering for the project could "offer variations to its design or route alignment that deliver better value for money or that incorporate innovative approaches to design, technology or operations that have not been considered specifically as part of the assessment of the Reference Project" (DTPLI, 2013: 11). Over 1,500 individual submissions were lodged in that period from across metropolitan Melbourne and the state of Victoria. Following the submission period, a public hearing was held between March and April 2014. Submitters, including special interest groups (local government and community-based organizations), as well as individuals were invited to present their concerns to the IAC.

Following public and media scrutiny directed at the state government for refusing to release the business case for the project, citizen opposition leading into the CIS process was already fierce. Thus, when the state government announced the two-stage CIS process in October 2013 at the same time as a call to tender for the construction and operation of the tunnel project, cynicism was directed at the government's formal consultation process. There was a degradation of trust, as indicated in the following CIS submission:

> The CIS assumes that effective mitigation of impacts will be achieved because of effective community consultation and engagement and yet the

community consultation on this project to date has been very unsatisfactory. Where information should have been provided in a meaningful way, far too often we have been given promotional material.
  (Residents Against the Tunnel CIS Public Submission, 2013: 3)

The process was linear and top-down and did not invite an interactive or reflexive engagement between citizens, project proponents and the multiple tiers of government, which could have enabled scrutiny of the project's scope as well as finer details revealed as the project's design matured. Instead, the CIS process was designed in a manner that subverted the political, sidelined contestation and disavowed the engaged citizen as a political subject (Rancière, 1999) worthy of and able to engage thoughtfully with the project selection process.

The announcement to commit to a major road project in their first term of government occurred in parallel to an 18-month extensive public engagement process to produce a new planning strategy for the state. October 2013—which marked the start of the CIS process—also marked the release of the draft planning strategy. This plan proposed a number of other priority transport projects for the state including a number of large public transport projects. Examination of the 18-month plan-making process revealed that the East-West Link project was not put forward to the citizens of Victoria. This engagement platform offered few opportunities to citizens to question the efficacy of the project or consider if the public dollars could be spent elsewhere.

At the end of 2013, and following the decline of the automotive industry in the state of Victoria the proposed road tunnel was positioned by the state government as part of a broader economic crisis management strategy (Lucas and Hawthorne, 2014)—the construction of the tunnel would produce a forecasted 3,500 construction jobs and would help to boost the local economy (ABC News, 2014). A move to fast-track the delivery of the road tunnel under the Act 2009 was initiated by state politicians to deliver key infrastructure for Victorians. However, the move to push the signing of the contracts to just weeks before the November state election was widely held by civil and professional interest groups to be an assault on the democratic process (see below). There was a growing discord that the political will to see the East-West Link to fruition was effectively working to suppress opportunities to openly discuss and debate the merits of the project.

Reaction, Action and Intersections

Positioning the East-West Link tunnel as the state's top transport priority prompted several groups, including political, professional and civil bodies to emerge in opposition to the East-West Link. The government's top-down intervention to position the East-West Link as the state's number one transport and infrastructure priority occurred in a vacuum of critical debate over transport projects in the state. One campaigner expressed a concern about a growing vacuum of honest and informed scrutiny directed at the government over their transport decisions. Pointing fingers at a lack of critical engagement on the part of academics, the major opposition party and senior government transport bureaucrats, this perceived absence of critical debate catalyzed some citizens to play a more active and political role:

> I think maybe it's up to the community now. We are not going to get it from the Government; politicians follow they don't lead. We're not going to get it from the Department because the Department is only going to do what the Government tells them. We can't get a lot of academics because one way or another they are financially compromised too through grants. But someone has to be able to stand up.
> (Interviewee 6)

Long-standing transport advocacy groups, local government councils located within the inner city and even smaller neighbourhood associations took it upon themselves to change the rhetoric around transport in the state. Their focus was on presenting transport infrastructure planning as a grassroots political issue. Critically, their efforts would be directed at (1) shaping the Opposition Party's transport policy and (2) positioning the East-West Link as a key election issue in the forthcoming state election. Mounting a grassroots campaign, long-standing public transport advocacy groups organized activities ranging from door-knocking and letter-writing campaigns, public rallies and street protests, to holding public forums and conducting surveys and polls in marginal seats. Other groups adopted direct action strategies aiming to stop preliminary drilling at sites along the project's corridor, while other resident groups took to writing letters into the state newspapers and sought expert and legal advice on how to stop the project.

One tactic the community pursued was to delay the signing of the contracts until after the election. Doing so would position the project as an election issue:

> The most realistic thing for us and our primary aim is to delay the signing of the contracts… And if it goes to an election then let Victorians decide. Everyone is impacted by this… and we think it should be an election issue. This is really starting to come out now.
> (Interviewee 12)

Another strategy considered by residents and public transport advocacy groups was to establish a community-wide coalition called the Victorian Integrated Transport Alliance (VITAL). As an observer at that first meeting, it was noted that a narrow focus on organizational details quickly shifted focus away from mobilizing action both to oppose the project and to delay the signing of the contracts. Following this failed attempt to establish a coalition, one of the long-standing public transport advocacy groups mounted the Public Transport Not Traffic (PTNT) campaign, which quickly became the umbrella campaign from which all other groups sought to align. Interest in a non-hierarchical community-based structure was superseded by a more top-down and aggressive coalition form that could actively engage in two primary ways: by responding to frequent and mostly unpredictable government announcements and timelines for community engagement and contract signing, and by providing strong leadership that could strategically oppose the East-West Link project, without co-opting groups into a unified structure. One campaigner interviewed for this research remarked that the PTNT campaign offered leadership and direction to respond to very tight timeframes available to influence policy and outcomes, and also allowed groups to remain autonomous to pursue their own lobbying efforts.

> Public Transport Not Traffic. That group is now moving very quickly and it's a completely different model of organisation. It's not consensus based. It's a loose coalition in the sense that it includes 30 or so groups from across Melbourne—and really truly from across Melbourne—that support what PTNT stands for.
> *(Interviewee 14)*

The PTNT campaign represents a significant shift away from consensus politics that have come to be associated with neoliberal governance frameworks. More specifically, the campaign reveals cracks between the post-political and political binary. For example, the campaign departs from a common model of citizen, grassroots activism that sometimes evolves into a network of groups who come to share a similar objective—be that a more sustainable future or a shared pursuit of the common good. In the case of the PTNT, each group could remain autonomous within this loose structure, but still collectively engage in a broader political movement. In most cases the strategies associated both with the campaign and with the individual groups were necessarily reactive to effectively respond to government decisions and media releases. Several groups felt that they were forced into this reactive position with little time to mobilize a proper fight. One campaigner described the reasons for such a reactive disposition:

> We're operating on a timeline and we're operating to an election not because we want to but because that's the agenda that [the Premier] set. He said he wants to get all this up and running before the State election, well you're setting the timeline then, we're going to play those cards. Whatever cards we have we'll play, because of the tight timeline you're giving us.
> *(Interviewee 16)*

Community-based groups launched reactionary campaigns to the media commentary that sometimes painted these inner city residents and groups as "The ratbag gang of unionists, unwashed hippies, NIMBY greenies, bellicose socialists, confused pensioners and progress-hating layabouts" (Panahi, 2013). In response, campaigners found it critical to maintain morale and confidence that change is possible in the context of 'done deal' politics. The interview data revealed a strong sense of purpose amongst the groups to contribute.

There is also evidence of self-awareness exhibited by campaigners that their efforts against the tunnel are perceived by some as an inner city NIMBY battle. Transcending beyond the NIMBY framing of an inner city elite preserving their existing liveability, campaigners aimed to transform the discussion to appeal to residents and groups living beyond the immediately affected corridor. This led some inner city groups to adjust their campaign strategies accordingly to form broader, spatially diverse, anti-East-West Link and pro-public transport alternative movements.

> I don't even want to bother in the Collingwood/Fitzroy space because it's literally flooded. The people in that area are well informed, they are already campaigning and that's great....Instead we really need to go to the outer suburbs and have more conversations with them. These are the people who actually have shit public transport. Collingwood and Fitzroy, public transport is alright, they could do with a train line, but they're OK.
> *(Interviewee 16)*

The sentiment expressed from this interviewee reveals the nuance of the political/post-political binary. There is a spatial dimension associated with the binary as illustrated by the case that reveals subjectivity linked with the politicization of the transport issue. For many of the long-standing public transport advocacy groups implicated in this movement campaigns were focused on inviting the broader community to imagine an alternative future. Examining the strategies employed by these 15 campaigners, their individual and collective efforts were undertaken in a pragmatic way. Citizens and established community-based groups organized public panels and workshops, and commissioned transport planning academics from the local universities to share their expert knowledge. What is also evident by the breadth and content presented across the range of campaigns and events is a broad engagement with the transport 'problem' that is affecting metropolitan Melbourne. Groups also gave their attention to demonstrating how funding the East-West Link tunnel would result in other public transport projects not being funded. Those groups advocating 'a positive alternative' to the controversial East-West Link project remain engaged in the anti-East-West Link movement. However, these groups sought to reposition public transport as the unfunded number two priority to the funded priority number one project.

Intersections and Interceptions

The government-led CIS process framed the proposed road tunnel as a 'done deal.' This meant that the government-designed CIS process would focus narrowly upon anticipatory negative effects and their management. Opponents of this project mobilized grassroots campaigns to slow down the signing of the contracts as it was hoped that by preventing the contracts from being signed before the election, the East-West Link tunnel would emerge as a primary election issue opening this project to public scrutiny. At the start of this study the main opposition party—the Labor Government—stated that they would not proceed with the project if contracts were not signed before the election. It was in the context of this statement that slowing contract signing emerged as the primary goal for citizens, and if successful, their attention would then turn to the election. One campaigner commented upon the party-political nature of the East-West Link project siting the need to engage with the upcoming election cycle:

> Realistically it will be very difficult…a political decision has been made, it's a political issue. The only way we are going to change it is politically. I don't think we are going to change [the Premier's] mind. He's locked in, he locked himself in a long time ago and he continues to lock himself in.
> *(Interviewee 12)*

Slowing down the signing of the contracts until after the state election meant that for some groups and individuals their primary focus was on engaging with the CIS. The selection of an IAC offered initial hope to residents and those community-based groups who believed that if enough compelling evidence was presented, the project as it was initially conceived would need to be rescoped, which would warrant a review of the CIS brief, and therefore delay the contract signing. A former Labor Government advisor and long-time transport advocate proved to be a valuable resource to the community groups during the CIS process. Drawing from his experience in government he believed that the process was so tightly structured to meet the looming deadline that if any suggestion that the project reference should be reconsidered, the project would be inevitably delayed:

> I don't think it's wasted time …If all the community groups did [was advocate for no East West Link tunnel] they wouldn't be likely to get a result. I mean, this project will fall over if it stumbles. If it's held up for three months it will never go ahead. So the government is relying on momentum and momentum solely.
> *(Interviewee 13)*

Cynicism around this process however propelled some groups to consider a formal legal challenge against the government directed at the CIS process. Two inner city local councils would also lead legal challenges. Other groups chose to focus on the chance that the project would form a key election issue in the lead up to the 2014 November state election. This included placing significant pressure onto the opposition party to oppose the road tunnel and commit to tearing up the contracts (once they are signed). A position such as this, taken up by the primary opposition party, would situate the East-West Link as an election issue. Other groups sought support to oppose this project by engaging in a debate about the relationship between infrastructure and job creation. Their proposal was not anti-development or anti-neoliberalism. Rather, campaigners were prepared to engage in a debate about alternative avenues to promote job growth and economic stimulus. Policy and politically savvy campaigners—people that have held senior advisory positions in government, or are seasoned campaigners—prepared economic arguments to oppose the project. In one particular instance, effort was made to show how the construction and long-term operation of an urban train line offered higher economic rewards (including jobs creation) than a road. Analysing US federal spending into transport the PTNT campaign reported on their website that:

> investment in public transportation produced almost twice as many jobs per dollar as investments in roads. Every one billion dollars (USD) spent on public transportation produced 19,299 jobs, compared with only 10,493 jobs if the same was spent on highway road works.
>
> *(PTNT, 2014)*

Following months of pressure, in September, two months before the state election, the opposition party declared that if signed before the election, they would destroy the contracts upon being elected if the court case lodged by the inner city local governments ruled in favour of these local governments. It was at this point that the East-West Link project was no longer framed as a done deal. Rather, the project could now be contested at the ballot box. Indeed, on November 29, 2014, the Labor Party was elected into government with a commanding majority and the East-West Link tunnel was removed from the state transport agenda to much fanfare from the community campaigners.

Conclusions

This chapter examined the binaries that are introduced when post-political governance provokes political contestation from beyond the state and the intersections this binary forges. Bylund (2012) suggests that framing recent political contestation through a post-political/political binary fails to consider the dialectic potential of this contested landscape to both transform the transport planning agenda and transform how that agenda is set. The ascendency of neoliberal governance settings within transport planning and infrastructure implementation more broadly has allowed consensus-driven politics to continue to nurture a culture of automobility (Walks, 2014). Without a public discussion that challenges the positioning of the automobility discourse, a paradigm shift will be difficult to achieve. The binary setup by the post-political/political does not go far enough as a theoretical framework to offer a basis to inspire long-term institutional, political and cultural change.

The Melbourne case study offers an extreme case (Flyvbjerg, 2006) of the kind of colonization of the decision-making space that restricts debate and avoids conflict. In the case of the East-West Link road tunnel, both the Australian and Victorian Governments embraced a post-political positioning. This is evidenced by the state government's efforts to restrict public discussion and scrutiny of the East-West Link tunnel project by keeping the business case confidential, fast-tracking the signing of the contracts and avoiding a public discussion around transport alternatives. Few efforts were taken to actually construct a process where public legitimacy for this project could be sought (Oosterlynck and Swyngedouw, 2010). Instead, the decision to avoid a discussion around alternative ways to address the transport problems facing Melbourne, as well as offer a clear articulation of what those challenges actually are, aimed to evade (albeit unsuccessfully) any challenges to the dominant discourses around automobility. In this case, the post-political position embraced by the government resulted in a decision to avoid public scrutiny and contestation of this road project. Such a decision was inherently a political one, and as a result of advocacy groups engaging at the intersections of the post-political/political binary, their actions repoliticized the political action taken by the government. The decision to avoid public scrutiny and contestation of this road project was inherently a political action (by government asserting an automobile vision of mobility), which was ultimately addressed in a political event: the state election.

On a practical level, despite all efforts to depoliticize infrastructure prioritization, decision-makers still confront a political landscape of resistance and dissent, be that from the development industry, interest groups and/or citizens. It is not possible to separate the politics from infrastructure implementation. New urban governance settings that respond to the politics are needed. These settings would invite debate and public deliberation and would not disavow this process of its politics. In cities like Melbourne, the absence of formal deliberation at this critical stage in planning forces concerned and politically engaged citizens and community groups to create their own informal deliberative and democratic spaces—whether they are public forums where knowledge and information can be exchanged, preparing economic arguments in favour of alternative transport projects, or appearing on local television and radio programs to present the case against the East-West Link. The politicization of transport to the spaces beyond the formal government processes (e.g. the CIS two-stage process) is shaping a redemocratization of transport planning that is occurring at the intersections between post-political formal government processes and political grassroots activism.

At a theoretical level, as Inch (2012) has argued recently, the implementation stage of planning is the point in the planning process when negative impacts are more clearly known and when citizens are most likely to actively engage agonistically. But unlike the NIMBY conflicts, citizens may also embark at this stage in planning through their own directed process of deliberation and coalition forming to counterhegemonic policy settings. The post-political turn has not rendered urban transport planning non-political, but rather the opposite; the political has emerged elsewhere and is forming a redemocratization of city making through emergent accountability and deliberative spheres of engagement, led by citizens. The case of citizen opposition to the proposed road tunnel in Melbourne illustrates how transport politics is performed. It illustrates what Marres (2005: 135) describes as the 'modifications of democratic spaces' challenging the view that all politics is to occur within the formal spaces of planning. Drawing inspiration from the work of Dewey (1927[2012]) on the role politics plays in constituting the public, Marres (2005) and others writing in the space of science and technology studies such as Callon et al. (2009) argue that the displacement of politics supports the creation of a political (or rather a dialectical) democracy and an active public that can continue to engage with critical urban issues; in the case of Melbourne, that issue was alternative transport priorities. The extent to which citizens influence decisions, depends on their actions beyond the formal state processes. In these informal spaces, citizen action groups are seeking ways to not only dictate an alternative urban transport policy agenda, they are also advocating for ways to reinstate democratic practice into planning by reasserting themselves into decisions that affect their lives. For some, there is a need to 'work[] together better' (Brownhill & Parker, 2010: 281) across all actors groups both to change the urban policy debate and to inspire urban politics that speaks to the reality of climate change and oil vulnerability, and not be constrained by the limits of the institutional and post-political dispositions embraced by some governments.

References

ABC News (2014), PM committed to second phase of East West Link as job creation initiative, ABC News, Canberra May 14, 2014, accessed 16 December, http://www.abc.net.au/news/2014-03-14/pm-committed-to-east-west-link-as-job-creation-initiative/5320636

Albrechts, L. (2012), "Reframing strategic spatial planning by using a coproduction perspective," *Planning Theory* 12(1): 46–63.

Albrechts, L. (2015), "Ingredients for a more radical strategic spatial planning," *Environment and Planning B: Planning and Design* 42: 000–000.

Austin, P. (2010), "Labor's forward focus designed to make voters forget failures," *Sydney Morning Herald*, accessed 15 December, http://www.smh.com.au/federal-politics/political-opinion/labors-forward-focus-designed-to-make-voters-forget-failures-20101103-17dz5.html

Bickerstaff, K. and Walker, G. (2005), "Shared visions, unholy alliances: Power, governance and deliberative processes in local transport planning," *Urban Studies* 42(12): 2123–44.

Blühdorn, I. (2013), "The governance of unsustainability: Ecology and democracy after the post-democratic turn," *Environmental Politics* 22(1): 16–36.

Boudreau, J-A, Keil, R. and Young, D. (2009), *Changing Toronto: Governing urban neoliberalism*. Toronto: University of Toronto Press.

Brownhill, S. and Parker, G. (2010), "Why bother with good works? The relevance of public participation(s) in planning in a post-collaborative era," *Planning Practice and Research* 25(3): 275–82.

Bylund, J. (2012), "Post-political correctness?," *Planning Theory* 11(3): 319–27.

Callon, M., Lascoumes, P. and Barthe, Y. (2009). *Acting in an uncertain world: An essay on technical democracy.* Cambridge, MA: MIT Press.

Cloke, P. and Johnston, R. (2005), "Deconstructing human geography's binaries," in P. Cloke and R. Johnston eds., *Spaces of geographical thought: Deconstructing human geography's binaries.* London: SAGE Publications, pp. 1–20.

Davidson, K. (2010), "Labor's loss is explained by the rail politics," *Sydney Morning Herald,* 30 November 2010, http://www.smh.com.au/federal-politics/political-opinion/labors-loss-is-explained-by-the-rail-politic-20101129-18dwp.html

Davidson, M. and Iveson, K. (2014), "Recovering the politics of the city: From the 'post-political city' to a 'method of equality' for critical geography," *Progress in Human Geography* 39(5): 543–59.

de Souza, M. L. (2006), "Together *with* the state, *despite* the state, *against* the state: Social movements as 'critical urban planning' agents," *City* 10(3): 327–42.

Dewey, J. (1927 [2012]), *The public and its problems: An essay in political inquiry.* Pennsylvania: Penn State Press.

DTPLI (2013), 'East West Link (Eastern Section)—Comprehensive Impact Statement,' Department of Transport, Planning and Local Infrastructure, State Government of Victoria, Australia.

Flyvbjerg, B. (1998), *Rationality and power: Democracy in practice.* Chicago, IL: The University of Chicago Press.

Flyvbjerg, B. (2006), "Five misunderstandings about case-study research," *Qualitative Inquiry,* 12(2): 219–45.

Forester, J. (1989), *Planning in the face of power.* Berkeley: University of California Press.

Harvey, D. (1996). *Justice, nature and the geography of difference.* Cornwall: Blackwell Publishers.

Healey, P. (1997). *Collaborative planning: Shaping places in fragmented societies.* London: MacMillan Press Ltd.

Hendriks, F. (2014), "Understanding good urban governance: Essentials, shifts, and values," *Urban Affairs Review* 50(4): 553–76.

Inch, A. (2012), "Creating 'a generation of NIMBYs'? Interpreting the role of the state in managing the politics of urban development," *Environment and Planning C: Government and Policy* 30: 520–35.

Innes, J. E. and Booher, D. E. (2010), *Planning with complexity: An introduction to collaborative rationality for public policy.* New York: Routledge.

Iveson, K. (2013), "Building a city for 'The People': The politics of alliance-building in the Sydney Green Ban Movement," *Antipode* 46(4): 992–1013.

Laclau, E. and Mouffe, C. (1985), *Hegemony and socialist strategy: Towards a radical democratic politics.* London: Verso.

Legacy, C. (2014), "Public plan-making: A deliberative approach," in B. Gleeson and B. Beza, eds. *The Public City: Essays in honour of Paul Mees.* Melbourne: Melbourne University Press, pp. 74–88.

Legacy, C., Curtis, C. and Neuman, M. (2014), "Adapting the deliberative democracy 'template' for planning practice," *Town Planning Review* 85(3): 319–40.

LMA (2014), *About Us,* Linking Melbourne Authority, Melbourne, Australia, accessed December 13, http://www.linkingmelbourne.vic.gov.au/about-us

Lucas, C. and Hawthorne, M. (2014), "Road to recession: End of car industry may cost 50,000 jobs," *The Age,* February 11, 2014, accessed December 18, http://www.smh.com.au/federal-politics/political-news/road-to-recession-end-of-car-industry-may-cost-50000-jobs-20140210-32d3g.html

Marres, N. S. (2005), No issue, no public: Democratic deficits after the displacement of politics. PhD thesis, University of Amsterdam.

McGuirk, P. (2005), "Neoliberalist planning? Re-thinking and re-casting Sydney's metropolitan planning," *Geographical Research* 43(1): 59–70.

Metzger, J., Allmendinger, P. and Oosterlynck, S., eds. (2015). *Planning against the political: Democratic deficits in European territorial governance.* New York: Routledge.

Molina Costa, P. (2014), "From plan to reality: Implementing a community vision in Jackson Square, Boston," *Planning Theory and Practice* 15(3): 293–310.

Mouffe, C. (2005). *On the political.* London: Routledge.

Newman, J. (2013), "Governing the present: Activism, neoliberalism, and the problem of power and consent," *Critical Policy Studies* 8(2): 133–47.

Olesen, K. (2013), "The neoliberalisation of strategic spatial planning," *Planning Theory* 13(3): 288–303.

Oosterlynck, S. and Swyngedouw, E. (2010), "Noise reduction: The post-political quandary of night flights at Brussels airport," *Environment and Planning A* 42: 1577–94.

Panahi, R. (2013), "Protesters' arrogance undermines their cause over East West Link," *The Herald Sun* November 11, 2013, accessed December 16, 2014 http://www.heraldsun.com.au/news/opinion/protesters-arrogance-undermines-their-cause-over-east-west-link/story-fni0fhh1-1226756866171

Parliament of Victoria (2013), Major Transport Projects Facilitation Amendment (East West Link and Other Projects) Bill 2013. Victorian Bills, http://www.austlii.edu.au/au/legis/vic/bill/mtpfawlaopb2013821/

PTNT (2014), Does public transport infrastructure create more jobs than roads? Public Transport Not Traffic website, Melbourne, accessed December 16, 2014, http://www.publictransportnottraffic.org/jobs

Purcell, M. (2009), "Hegemony and difference in political movements: Articulating networks of equivalence," *New Political Science* 31(3): 291–317.

Purcell, M. (2013), "To inhabit well: Counterhegemonic movements and the right to the city," *Urban Geography* 34(4): 560–74.

Rancière, J. (1999), *Dis-agreement: Politics and philosophy.* London: University of Minnesota Press.

Rancière, J. (2000), "Dissenting words. A conversation with Jacques Ranciere (with Davide Panagia)," *Diacritics* 30(2): 113–26.

Residents Against the Tunnel (2013), *Comprehensive impact statement, residents against the tunnel (RAT) response.* Submission to Comprehensive Impact Statement review process, Melbourne, Australia

Sandercock, L. (1995), "Voices from the Borderlands: A meditation on a metaphor," *Journal of Planning Education and Research* 14(2): 77–88.

Stone, J. and Mees, P. (2010), "Planning public transport networks in the post-petroleum era," *Australian Planner* 47(4): 263–71.

Sturup, S. (2010), Managing mentalities of mega projects: The art of government of mega urban transport projects. PhD thesis, The University of Melbourne, Melbourne.

Sturup, S. (2016), "The problem/solution nexus and its effects on public consultation," in R. Leshinsky and C. Legacy, eds. *Instruments of planning: Tensions and challenges for more equitable and sustainable cities.* New York: Routledge.

Swyngedouw, E. (2005), "Governance innovation and the citizen: The Janus Face of Governance-beyond-the-State," *Urban Studies* 42(11): 1991–2006.

Swyngedouw, E. (2010), "Apocalypse forever?: Post-political populism and the spectre of climate change," *Theory, Culture & Society* 27(2–3): 213–32.

Tee, B (2013). Major Transport Projects Facilitation Amendment (East West Link and Other Projects) Bill 2013—Second Reading). Parliament of Victoria, September 3, 2013.

The Act (2009) *Major Transport Projects Facilitation Act 2009*, No. 56 of 2009, Government of Victoria, Melbourne, Australia.

Urry, J. (2004), "The 'system' of automobility," *Theory, Culture & Society* 21(4–5): 25–39.

Victorian Government (2014) *Plan Melbourne: Metropolitan planning strategy*, Department of Transport, Planning and Local Infrastructure, Melbourne.

Walks, A. (2014), "Stopping the 'War on the Car': Neoliberalism, Fordism, and the politics of automobility in Toronto," *Mobilities* 10(3): 402–22.

Whatmore, S. J. and Landstrom, C. (2011), "Flood apprentices: An exercise in making things public," *Economy and Society* 40(4): 582–610.

Wright, J. (2014), "Tony Abbott says he doesn't need to see the east-west link's full business case," *The Age*, September 27, 2013, accessed December 18 http://www.theage.com.au/victoria/tony-abbott-says-he-doesnt-need-to-see-the-eastwest-links-full-business-case-20130927-2uih8.html

Žižek, S. (1999), *The ticklish subject: The absent centre of political ontology.* New York: Verso.

Chapter 4
LOCAL VALUES AND FAIRNESS IN CLIMATE CHANGE ADAPTATION
Insights from Marginal Rural Australia Communities

Sonia Graham, Jon Barnett, Ruth Fincher, Anna Hurlimann, and Colette Mortreux

Introduction

Governments worldwide are preparing for climate change through the development of national adaptation strategies and plans (e.g. the 39 National Action Plans for Adaptation in least developed countries). There is also a proliferation of local adaptation plans being developed by municipalities (Baker et al., 2012). The concept of fairness pervades adaptation plans, with many aspiring to achieve fair adaptation by prioritizing the needs of those 'most at risk,' 'most at need' or the 'most vulnerable,' particularly the poor, homeless, elderly, children, people with disabilities and the mentally ill (Collins, 2016). However, it is unclear how such people are identified and considered, how their needs and interests are identified and accommodated (Hamin and Gurran, 2015) and how controls are put in place to ensure adaptation efforts reduce vulnerability (Holland, 2017) and do not overlook or exacerbate existing inequalities or create new inequalities (Barnett and O'Neill, 2010; Forsyth, 2014; Mikulewicz, 2018). Thus, despite the widespread recognition of the principle, it is unclear if and how fair adaptation is being pursued in practice at local scales in developing and/or developed countries.

In the last decade three emerging bodies of social science research have sought to understand how fair adaptation can be achieved (Figure 4.1). This has involved: elaborating what fair adaptation is and how this relates to climate justice more broadly, identifying the challenges that governments face in developing and implementing (fair) local adaptation plans and developing processes for democratizing adaptation to ensure local values are incorporated into adaptation plans. While there is considerable scope for these three bodies of literature to inform one another and government policies to enhance adaptation outcomes in practice, there is little research at the nexus of these three domains—a contribution which this chapter aims to make.

DOI: 10.4324/9781003178545-6

Local Values in Climate Change Adaptation 67

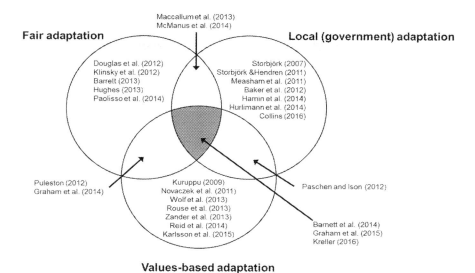

FIGURE 4.1 Examples of empirical research conducted on fair adaptation, local government adaptation and value-based adaptation in Australia and internationally.

The aim of this chapter is to consider how an understanding of lived values can inform fairer local adaptation plans. We do this through a study of values in four small coastal communities in a regional local government area in the state of Victoria, Australia, whose physical and social geography renders them highly vulnerable to sea-level rise. The large land area of the local government area (10,924 km^2) and long coastline (approximately 100 km) compared to the small population (41,355 residents) means the municipality has limited resources to protect its eight coastal settlements from sea-level rise. The residents are also among the most socially disadvantaged in Australia: their lack of political voice (Hurlimann et al., 2014) and little access to markets and services means their experiences and capacity to adapt are limited compared to their wealthier and more politically powerful counterparts in urban coastal Australia.

This chapter begins with a discussion about fairness, the challenges governments face in developing and implementing local adaptation to climate change and the ways in which a values-based approach can assist governments to achieve fair local adaptation. Background information is then provided about four coastal communities at risk of sea-level rise in eastern Victoria, Australia, as well as the mixed-method approach adopted. The results describe five types of residents who live in the four communities and how they may be differentially affected by sea-level rise, challenging and expanding traditional notions of vulnerability. Finally, we elaborate the issues that these diverse values raise for fair adaptation policies and programmes in these four communities, and more broadly.

This study builds on past adaptation research undertaken in eastern Victoria which has sought to understand how fairness is understood by people in marginal coastal regional communities (Graham et al., 2015) and local governments (Graham and Barnett, 2017), how local communities understand sea-level rise in relation to their everyday lives (Fincher et al., 2014) and how regional governments can better plan for adaptation (Barnett et al., 2014; Hurlimann et al., 2014). Previous research has sought to understand the values of different types of residents who live within a larger community along the same coastline in an adjoining jurisdiction, and that has a wider range of adaptation options available to it (Graham et al., 2014). Here we seek to understand how residents in four remote and small communities (fewer than 300 residents in each) with few resources and adaptation options value their everyday lives to help the local government prepare for sea-level rise. This study also builds on past research in developing countries that has sought to understand the values of small island and remote coastal communities in the context of climate adaptation (e.g. Karlsson and Hovelsrud, 2015; Kuruppu, 2009; Mortreux and Barnett, 2009).

Fairness, Values and Local Government Adaptation Effort

Climate change invokes questions of fairness, blame and responsibility. It raises questions about who causes, benefits and loses from climate change impacts and who is required to pay to mitigate or adapt (Adger, 2016). These questions are at the heart of climate justice scholarship, which seeks to find solutions to the perceived inequities in who has caused climate change and who is most affected by its impacts (Barrett, 2013). To date, the majority of research on climate justice has focused on the international politics of mitigation and the developed/developing and present/future generational divides (Caney, 2005; Schlosberg and Collins, 2014). More recently, the concept of fair adaptation has received increased attention in recognition of the formidable justice challenges that climate adaptation creates, especially at local scales (Adger, 2016; Paavola and Adger, 2006). We seek to add to the latter body of research, which highlights the importance of fairness to local communities regardless of their level of development.

Research on climate justice, including fair adaptation, has focused on two main dimensions of fairness: distributive and procedural (Forsyth, 2014). In the context of adaptation, distributive fairness involves ensuring that *outcomes* are equitable (Adger, 2013). It involves asking questions such as "who bears the costs of adaptation?" and "what kinds of change are acceptable?" (Adger, 2013, p. 71). Procedurally fair adaptation involves *decision-making* that is democratic, participatory and inclusive (Mikulewicz, 2018; Paolisso et al., 2012), by asking questions about "how do we define, as well as distribute, these objectives fairly" (Forsyth, 2014, p. 232); "whether vulnerable populations have the political power—or political capability—to influence adaptation decisions" (Holland, 2017, p. 2); and "who takes action?" (Adger, 2013, p. 71). Such questions of fairness are most visible and acute at local levels (Paavola and Adger, 2002), yet there is little empirical research that investigates how governments perceive fairness when developing and implementing local adaptation policies (Graham and Barnett, 2017).

Much of the research on governments' experiences with developing and implementing local climate adaptation plans focuses on identifying the barriers that governments face (Hamin et al., 2014; Measham et al., 2011; Pasquini et al., 2015). There is considerable attention given to institutional constraints, such as competing priorities within local governments, resources, access to information, decision-making processes and interactions with other levels of government (Hamin et al., 2014; Karlsson and Hovelsrud, 2015; Pasquini et al., 2015). Some attention is also given to the ways in which community values and beliefs intersect with institutional adaptation decision-making (Paschen and Ison, 2012). Where values and beliefs are discussed, attention is often given to the ways that beliefs about climate change constrain climate adaptation for local governments (Hamin et al., 2014; Moser and Ekstrom, 2010) or how material values, such as property and infrastructure, can be protected (Ishaya and Abaje, 2008).

Most of this research is philosophical in nature, which means the difficult task of determining measures of fairness for evaluating and monitoring outcomes is avoided, or assumed to be encompassed in standard metrics of social vulnerability which, at their most sophisticated, rely on sustainable livelihoods-based criteria: natural, social, financial, physical and human capital (Hahn et al., 2009). Yet when considering outcomes of climate change or climate change institutions universal metrics are unsatisfying (Nielsen and Reenberg, 2010). Much of that which constitutes 'loss,' or 'insecurity,' or 'success' depends on personal and local contexts, and so demands measures derived from more situated forms of knowledge (Kuruppu, 2009; Tschakert et al., 2013). Some adverse outcomes—such as losses of health and life—can be said to be universal and so measured across diverse populations, but many—such as the loss of social cohesion or occupational identities—are far more culturally specific and less amenable to standard measures (Barnett et al., 2016). Understanding local perspectives of fairness in outcomes therefore requires knowledge of what people value about their lives and what people see as urgent (Forsyth, 2014), which demands more context-specific and democratic community-driven assessments and measures (Mikulewicz, 2018). It is this new knowledge that we seek to advance in this chapter.

In their review of the research on the role of human values in public engagement with climate change, Corner et al. (2014) found that many studies conceptualize values in a way that is consistent with social psychologists understanding of values as a guiding principle. Graham et al. (2013) argue that in the context of understanding the impacts of climate change, it is useful to understand the things people value about their everyday lives, i.e. their lived values, which is consistent with a human geography understanding of values. These values are not general attitudes that people hold but rather are practices lived by people in places (Graham et al., 2013). Graham et al. (2013, p. 49) proposed that there are five types of lived values that are likely to be affected by sea-level rise: health, safety, belonging, esteem and self-actualization.

Empirical studies conducted since then in developing and developed countries have identified various social values at risk of climate change and sea-level rise that are consistent with this definition and categorization of values (e.g. Karlsson et al., 2015; Kreller, 2021; Reid et al., 2014). Further, Karlsson et al. (2015) found that studying valued objects at risk is useful for understanding different groups in the community and the trade-offs they are willing to make to safeguard their community's future. Thus, lived values exist beyond the context of climate adaptation and vulnerability, but are useful for understanding whose everyday lives are vulnerable to climate change and provide a social metric for evaluating the relative fairness of local adaptation options.

While social researchers in developing and developed countries argue that local values need to be incorporated into climate adaptation to achieve fairer processes and outcomes, few studies explore lived values and fairness together in the context of climate adaptation. For example, Graham et al. (2014) explored the values of residents in Lakes Entrance, a coastal town in Victoria, Australia, and found that understanding community values can help to identify who is vulnerable and how adaptation options may benefit some groups at the expense of others. We seek to extend this research at the interface between local values and fairness by going beyond examining a single community to considering multiple small communities within the one local government jurisdiction. This is important because different communities and different people within a community prioritize different adaptation options (Paolisso et al., 2012), and this challenges the ability of local governments to achieve fair adaptation.

The aim of this study is to use a quantitative approach to identify the values at risk in four marginal rural communities in Wellington Shire, situated in the Gippsland East region of the state of Victoria, Australia. It explores how the local government that spans these four communities can use this information on lived values to ensure that adaptation plans are fair within and across communities, while working within the constraints of limited finances and adaptation options.

Case Study Locations

We examined the lived values and fairness of adaptation to sea-level rise in four small coastal communities—Port Albert, Manns Beach, McLoughlins Beach and Seaspray—in Wellington Shire on the Gippsland East coast (Figure 4.2), of the state of Victoria. The Gippsland East coast is an ideal place to study local adaptation to sea-level rise because it is considered to be highly vulnerable to flooding and sea-level rise (Department of Climate Change, 2009), already experiences coastal flooding and has been the site of controversial decisions about adaptation through the imposition of planning restrictions (Hurlimann et al., 2014; Macintosh, 2013). Most settlements in the region are small and experience relational remoteness (Fincher et al., 2015); they lack the political and socio-economic connections that characterize marginal communities the world over, and similarly struggle to maintain investment, growth, wealth and populations (Bock, 2016). In these communities there is limited capacity for governmental institutions to manage the risks posed by sea-level rise. In addition, there is a declining youth population, who are moving to the capital cities for education and employment opportunities (ABS, 2011; Edwards et al., 2011).

FIGURE 4.2 Location of four case study sites on the Gippsland East Coast.

There are few coastal environments in the world that have been as intensively researched as the Gippsland East coast. Since 1995 numerous studies have investigated the effects of sea-level rise, changes in wind and waves and subsidence on extreme sea levels in Gippsland East (e.g. McInnes et al., 2005, 2006; Wheeler et al., 2009). The effect of these studies has been to build awareness among the local, state and national governments about the physical problem of sea-level rise in Gippsland East.

There is little urban infrastructure in the four communities. Port Albert and Seaspray have a general store with postal services, community hall and café. Seaspray has a Surf Life Saving club, caravan park and a primary school. Port Albert has a pub, a museum, a restaurant and some accommodation. There are no shops, eateries or accommodation available in McLoughlins Beach or Manns Beach. All four towns have at least one park, boat ramp and jetty/pontoon. Almost all the urban infrastructure in the four communities is located within 1 m of current mean sea levels. The nearest towns with amenities are Yarram for Port Albert, Manns Beach and McLoughlins Beach, and Sale for Seaspray (Figure 4.1).

All four communities are relatively disadvantaged socio-economically, ranking in the lowest quintile in the Australian Bureau of Statistics Socio-Economic Index (ABS, 2011; Table 1). The populations are also considerably older than the Victorian population, with median ages 11–20 years higher than the state median of 37. This indicates that the four communities are physically and socially vulnerable to sea-level rise.

Seaspray and Port Albert have been the focus of some controversial decisions associated with the urban planning system's response to future sea-level rise (Macintosh, 2013). The planning system has been driven by higher (state) level policies. Local residents and developers are already being required to incorporate predictions regarding sea-level rise (20 cm by 2040) into their land use planning permit applications. Macintosh (2013) describes the adaptation approach used in the state as inequitable and 'maladaptive' because it involves deterministic decision-making, fails to promote robust responses and increases the social costs of climate change. In these communities the main adaptation options of protection—using hard and soft structural options—and accommodation—changes to building codes and emergency planning—are only short-term options that are likely to be too expensive in the long term. This means that retreat is the only viable long-term strategy for many of these communities.

Recognizing the limited options, both the local government and local residents are concerned about the fairness of adaptation processes and outcomes. Council staff and local residents have expressed concerns about the ways local values will be impacted by sea-level rise and climate change more broadly (Graham and Barnett, 2017). However, the concerns raised by local residents are not always consistent with those identified by the local government. For example, residents expressed concerns that the local government's understanding of what residents needed was inconsistent with residents' needs (Graham et al., 2015). Therefore, there is a need to understand the differences and similarities in lived values that exist in these four communities and the ways in which these values can be equitably incorporated into future planning decisions. This will help ensure that decision-makers do not make assumptions about community values or local conceptions of fairness and provides a way in for communities to take greater ownership of the adaptation process (Holland, 2017; Mikulewicz, 2018).

Methods

The method used was based on the theory of lived values and associated framework, explained in Graham et al. (2013). Graham et al. (2014) provide one method for operationalizing the framework that involves conducting semi-structured interviews to tailor the design of a quantitative survey, the data of which is then analysed using cluster analysis. We followed the method described in Graham et al. (2014), although here we used a mail-out survey instead of a phone survey because there are a large number of second home-owners who occasionally live in the towns. Additionally, publicly accessible phone numbers for the residences are not widely available.

Scoping Interviews

In April 2012 we conducted 17 semi-structured interviews with residents and second home-owners of the four communities (four interviews each in Port Albert, Manns Beach and McLoughlins Beach, and five in Seaspray). We purposively sought to interview a diverse group of community members to identify as many lived values as possible. A total of 113 lived values were identified, although each interviewee only held a subset of these and only 32 were consistently identified across all four communities. The lived values most frequently mentioned during the interviews were used as the final list of 31 lived values included in the mail-out survey, ensuring that there were lived values from each of the five categories identified in Graham et al. (2013).

Analysis of the interviews indicated that some of the intra- and inter-community variability in interviewees' lived values was related to life circumstances, in particular, their employment status (e.g. working, studying or retirement), level of involvement in the local community (community group membership, number of close friends and residence status—permanent or part-time), where they moved from (city or regional area) and history of association with the Gippsland East region (family connection). Analysis of the interviews informed the survey design as well as selection of variables for the cluster analysis.

Mail-out Survey

A mail-out survey was used to determine whether the lived values identified in the interviews were held by the wider communities, the relative importance attached to these values and the distribution of these values across and within the communities, and whether there were other lived values that were important but that had not yet been identified. There were five parts to the survey: (1) introduction, (2) lived values, (3) everyday activities, (4) social networks and (5) socio-economic information. A combination of open- and closed-ended questions were used to ensure that as many lived values as possible were captured (not just those previously identified) while also measuring the relative importance of the 31 lived values.

During August 2012 surveys were hand delivered to every residence in Manns Beach, McLoughlins Beach and Seaspray because many of these residences do not have letterboxes. The post office in Port Albert agreed to place a survey in every post office box for the town as well as provide surveys to residents who came into the general store who do not own post office boxes. Follow-up reminder postcards (recommended by Dillman, 2007) were also distributed in this way. Wellington Shire Council mailed the survey to residents whose primary residence was listed as an address outside of the four communities.

One hundred and thirty-four respondents answered the survey, representing almost half of all households in the four communities (Table 4.1). Respondents were slightly older than their respective populations, with the exception of Port Albert. The number of people per household was slightly smaller than the respective populations for Seaspray and McLoughlins, but slightly larger for Port Albert and Manns Beach (Table 4.1).

Cluster analysis was used to explore the commonalities and differences in lived values within and across the four communities. The method used followed

TABLE 4.1 Socio-demographic information for the four study sites in Wellington Shire Council

Towns	Number of occupied dwellings	Survey sample	Median household income (weekly)	Median age Population	Median age Survey sample	Number of people per household Population	Number of people per household Survey sample
Port Albert	119	51	$608	57	55–64	1.9	2.2
Seaspray	112	52	$933	48	55–64	2.4	1.9
McLoughlins Beach[a]	62	20	$773	51	55–64	2.2	1.5
Manns Beach[a]		11	$635	53	55–64	2.1	2.5
Victoria	5 354 042		$1216	37		2.6	

[a] McLoughlins Beach and Manns Beach are contained within larger collection districts, and therefore, the numbers presented here may not accurately reflect the populations of these small communities.

Graham et al. (2014). The variables selected for inclusion (employment status, business ownership, family connection, community group membership, social network, residence status and previous location of residence) were categorical and were standardized by transforming them into dummy variables. Each variable was examined to determine whether any categories should be collapsed (e.g. merging those employed full-time and part-time). Correlations were run to ensure that there were no redundant variables among those selected. The only selected variables with high correlations were 'working' and 'retired.' The correlation coefficient was 0.71 (the correlation coefficients among the other variables were all less than 0.47) and so 'retired' was removed from the analysis. The study used hierarchical followed by k-means clustering with pairwise deletion of missing values. The k-means cluster analysis was run with up to seven cluster solutions because the interview analysis indicated there may be up to seven types of residents across these four communities based on their life characteristics.

Results

Overall, survey respondents identified 101 things that they value about the four communities, with 72 lived values identified in Port Albert, 62 in Seaspray, 41 in McLoughlins Beach and 37 in Manns Beach. Nineteen of these lived values were consistent across all four communities, 16 were identified in three communities and 22 were identified in two communities. Twenty-two lived values mentioned in the survey responses were not identified in the interviews.

The most commonly identified lived value within each community and across all communities was the peace and quiet, identified by 62 respondents (46.3% of the sample). Other lived values frequently identified in all four communities were the fishing (23.9%) and being close to the water (23.1%). The lived values most frequently mentioned in each community were the friendly people (15/51) and good eateries (7/51) in Port Albert, the walking opportunities in Manns Beach (4/11) and the beach in Seaspray (18/52) and McLoughlins Beach (7/20).

The four lived values that respondents most frequently and consistently rated as being 'very important' across the four communities were the slow pace of life, peacefulness, being close to water and the natural environment (Figure 4.3). The least agreement across the communities in terms of what was highly valued was affordability of housing, to start a business, the climate and feeling well respected.

Cluster analysis was used to understand variation that existed in the lived values within and across communities and understand whether particular groups of residents are more likely to be affected by sea-level rise with respect to their non-material values. The five cluster solution produced clearly distinguishable groups of residents who had distinct sets of lived values. Table 4.2 shows how residents were distributed among the groups and the characteristics of each group

76 Sonia Graham et al.

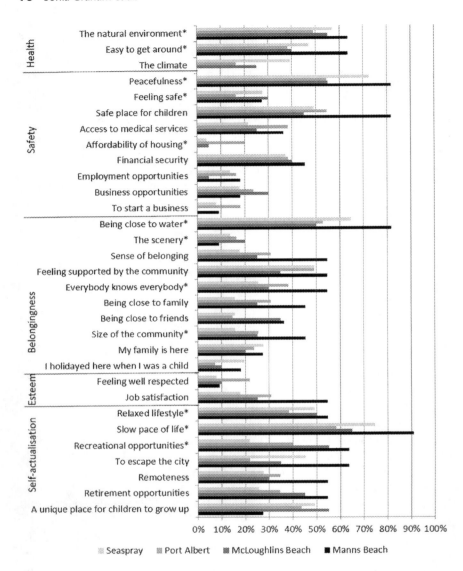

FIGURE 4.3 Proportion of respondents from each community who rated each lived value as 'very important.' Asterisks indicate lived values that were mentioned by respondents in all four.

according to the clustering variables. Table 4.3 shows a selection of lived values that were different across the clusters. Table 4.4 identifies the proportions of respondents from each community that belonged to each cluster. Tables 4.2 and 4.3 underpin the descriptions of each resident group that follows, including the lived values that are most important to each group.

TABLE 4.2 Cluster analysis results. Cluster characteristics as per the selected variables

Selected variables	Group 1	Group 2	Group 3	Group 4	Group 5
	Self-sufficient middle-aged primary residents	Community-minded business owners	Socially networked circumstantial seachangers	Regional retirees	Coastal-hamlet loving second home-owners
N	17	24	43	30	20
Cluster (%)	12.7	17.9	32.1	22.4	14.9
Working (%)	64.7	**100.0**	11.62	*0*	**100.0**
Business owner (%)	*0*	**83.3**	4.7	*0*	15.0
Long-term family connection (%)	*0*	8.3	16.2	76.7	**80**
Seachanger (%)	58.8	25.0	**72.1**	*23.3*	50.0
None or one close friend (%)	**82.4**	*4.2*	20.9	10.0	25.0
Member of at least one community organization (%)	*23.5*	**95.8**	90.7	43.3	55.0
Primary resident (%)	64.7	79.2	**100.0**	60.0	*25.0*

Bold and italics indicate the highest and lowest proportion of all the clusters, respectively.

TABLE 4.3 Selection of demographics, lived values and interactions that were different across the clusters

Non-selected variables	Group 1	Group 2	Group 3	Group 4	Group 5
	Self-sufficient middle-aged primary residents	Community-minded business owners	Socially networked circumstantial seachangers	Regional retirees	Coastal-hamlet loving second home-owners
Demographics					
Education (University or TAFE)	58.8	**75.0**	39.5	*33.3*	55.0
Income (Less than $400/week)	29.4	*4.2*	39.4	**43.3**	5.0
Residence length (Less than 20 years)	**82.4**	75.0	72.1	43.3	*35.0*
Lived values					
Safe for children	*17.6*	58.3	34.9	30.0	**60.0**
Remoteness	*23.5*	33.3	25.6	40.0	**70.0**

(*Continued*)

Non-selected variables	Group 1	Group 2	Group 3	Group 4	Group 5
	Self-sufficient middle-aged primary residents	Community-minded business owners	Socially networked circumstantial seachangers	Regional retirees	Coastal-hamlet loving second home-owners
Natural environment	*41.2*	66.7	44.2	53.3	**80.0**
Close to water	52.9	75.0	*46.5*	60.0	**80.0**
Easy to get around	*29.4*	**67.0**	30.2	43.3	65.0
Peacefulness	58.8	75.0	*51.2*	66.7	**85.0**
Slow pace of life	47.1	54.2	*30.2*	46.7	**70.0**
Feeling safe	*41.2*	**75.0**	44.2	50.0	70.0
Sense of belonging	*11.8*	**50.0**	30.2	33.3	45.0
Everybody knows everybody	*5.9*	25.0	20.9	33.3	**45.0**
Feeling like a well-respected member of the community	*5.9*	20.8	23.3	36.7	**50.0**
Interactions					
Family	35.3	**62.5**	*32.6*	53.3	60.0

Bold and italics indicate the highest and lowest proportion of all the clusters, respectively.

TABLE 4.4 Proportion of respondents from each of the four communities who belonged to each of the five types of residents identified in the cluster analysis

	Group 1	Group 2	Group 3	Group 4	Group 5
	Self-sufficient middle-aged primary residents (%)	Community-minded business owners (%)	Socially networked circumstantial seachangers (%)	Regional retirees (%)	Coastal-hamlet loving second home-owners (%)
Seaspray	19.2	7.7	25	26.9	21.2
Port Albert	7.8	27.5	37.3	15.7	11.8
Manns Beach	9.1	36.4	0	27.3	27.3
McLoughlins Beach	10	10	55	25	0

Group 1: Self-Sufficient, Middle-Aged Primary Residents (12.7%)

This group was the youngest, had the second highest incomes and the second highest levels of educational attainment (Table 4.3). Two-thirds of this group were working (full- or part-time), and none had a long-term family connection to the places in which they lived or owned a second home. This group was considered to be 'middle-aged' because three-quarters (76.4%) of the group were between 45 and 64 years of age. The group was considered to be 'self-sufficient' because they were the least likely to rely on others for their enjoyment of life; they were the least likely to rate 'sense of belonging,' 'being close to friends,' 'everybody knows everybody,' 'feeling supported by the community' and 'feeling like a well-respected member of the community' as very important. This group was also considered to be self-sufficient because four-fifths (82.4%) of the group had few, if any, close friends (Table 4.2) and were less likely to spend time interacting with friends, neighbours and other members of the community than all the other groups. The things that were more important to this group than almost all the other groups were retirement opportunities and escaping the city.

Group 2: Community-Minded Business Owners (17.9%)

All members of this group were employed in full- or part-time work (Table 4.2), and five-sixths (83.3%) of the group were business owners. The importance of running a business and having a job was reflected in their lived values; they were the most likely to rate 'to start a business,' 'business opportunities,' 'employment opportunities' and 'job satisfaction' as very important to them. This group was considered to be 'community-minded' for three reasons. First, they undertake a lot of volunteer work. Almost all (95.8%) were members of at least one community organization, and four-fifths (79.2%) were members of at least two community organizations. Members of this group were the most likely to participate in volunteer work on a weekly or more frequent basis. Second, this group was socially active. Members of this group interacted with family, neighbours, work colleagues, group members and other members of the community more frequently than all the other groups. They were also the most likely to go out for a meal or coffee. Third, members of this group were the most likely to identify 'sense of belonging' as being very important to them.

Group 3: Socially Networked Circumstantial Seachangers (32.1%)

Almost three-quarters (72.1%) of this group have moved to the small communities from a capital city, i.e. they are seachangers (Table 4.2). The ongoing ties to the city from which they came are evident in their lived values; they were the least likely to rate 'slow pace of life,' 'relaxed lifestyle' and 'peacefulness' as being very important to them (Table 4.3). These seachangers are carers, students, workers and retirees. The group is considered to be 'socially networked' because four-fifths (79.1%) of the group have at least a few close friends and nine-tenths (90.7%) are members of at least one community organization. This group was the least wealthy of all the groups; it is estimated that almost half (47.4%) live below the poverty line (the equivalent of 50% of median household incomes; ACOSS, 2014). Given the low income of this group and the lack of enthusiasm for the lived values offered by these small communities, it seems likely that these seachangers are 'circumstantial'; they have moved to these communities because of affordability issues rather than because they wanted to be seachangers. This is consistent with their lived values; this group was more likely than almost all the other groups to rank 'financial security' as being very important to them.

Group 4: Regional Retirees (22.4%)

Nine-tenths (90%) of this group were over 55 years of age, and three-quarters (76.7%) were retired or semi-retired. This group was considered to be 'regional' retirees because only a small proportion (23.3%) of the group had moved from a capital city, three-quarters (76.7%) had a long-term family connection to the area (Table 4.2) and almost half (46.7%) had lived in their community or the surrounding areas for more than 30 years. The lived values that this group rated as more important than the other groups were 'retirement opportunities,' 'affordability of housing,' 'remoteness' and 'feeling supported by the community.' They were more likely to go for a walk or read a newspaper than the other groups. This group was the oldest and the second poorest. It also had the lowest levels of educational attainment; four-tenths (40%) of the group had finished school at year ten or below or had not gone to school, reflecting in part their age.

Group 5: Coastal-Hamlet Loving, Working, Second Home-Owners (14.9%)

Three-quarters (75%) of this group are second home-owners, four-fifths (80%) have a long-term family connection to the small communities and almost two-thirds (65%) have had homes in the communities or surrounding areas for more than 20 years (Table 4.3). All the members of this group are employed in full- or part-time work, hence the inclusion of 'working' in the title. They also have the highest incomes of all the groups; seven-tenths (70%) of this group earned more than the median weekly incomes for their respective communities (Table 4.1). This group is considered to be 'coastal-hamlet loving' because they were consistently more likely than the other groups to rate the lived values of these communities as being very important to them. The values of particular importance to this group pertained to those that make these places coastal-hamlets, such as 'remoteness,' 'peacefulness,' the 'slow pace of life,' 'everybody knows everybody,' 'being close to water' and the 'natural environment.' This group was also the group that reported visiting the beach most often. As second home-owners, this group was the most likely to value being able 'to escape the city' and 'affordability of housing.'

Lived Values and Fairness in Adaptation

The number (135) of lived values identified by interviewees and survey respondents was commensurate with the number of people involved in the research. Seeking to accommodate all these values in adaptation policy would be overwhelming and explains why past research on local responses to climate change has found diverse values to be a barrier to adaptation (e.g. Paschen and Ison, 2012). Yet there are many commonalities among the lived values identified within and across communities; some values are particular to certain places while other values are prioritized by particular types of people across communities. Understanding such spatial and social sharing of lived values can help decision-makers identify how adaptation policies will affect particular places and the people living within them, providing a means of achieving fair adaptation. We now discuss: the range of lived values found to be important in each place; the way in which understanding the values that particular groups of people hold challenges our traditional understanding of vulnerability and how understanding place-specific and people-centric values can inform fair local adaptation.

Region- and Place-Specific Lived Values

There was some agreement among survey participants about what they value about their communities. Residents in all four communities highly value the natural environment, being close to water, the peacefulness and the slow pace of life. They also value the relaxed lifestyle, the ease of getting around and being a safe place for children, although these qualities were ranked less highly (Figure 4.3). Compared to a larger community along the same coastline (Graham et al., 2014), the only lived value that was highly valued across both small and larger communities was the natural environment. Other studies indicate that natural areas were the most highly valued features of urban (Kreller, 2021), remote (Karlsson et al., 2015), indigenous (Reid et al., 2014) and island (Mortreux and Barnett, 2009; Novaczek et al., 2011) coastal communities in developing and developed countries. Yet in these four small communities the value placed on the natural environment went beyond aesthetics (e.g. Graham et al., 2014; Karlsson et al., 2015; Novaczek et al., 2011; Puleston, 2012), as the scenery was valued less highly, and instead was related to its intrinsic, recreation and therapeutic values.

Of particular importance to these small communities was peacefulness. Overall, residents valued the small sizes of the communities they lived in and the associated slow pace of life that comes with living in these relatively remote places. This is consistent with other regional and remote coastal research, where communities that are 'off the beaten track' value the tranquillity of the places in which they live (Karlsson et al., 2015; Puleston, 2012, p. 52). It is also consistent with values of residents in small island states where the 'peaceful' and 'easy' life is highly valued (e.g. Mortreux and Barnett, 2009). As per other small communities in developing countries (Karlsson et al., 2015), the residents here also acknowledge the limitations of living in small communities, such as the limited business and job opportunities.

While the small size of the communities and the proximity to water and natural areas are valued by residents in all four communities, there are some specific qualities valued by residents in each place. The values that were particularly important in Port Albert were those associated with the heritage and history as well as the cafes and restaurants, business opportunities and tourism. Seaspray was valued for its lack of development, such as not having a pub (hotel), and McLoughlins Beach and Manns Beach were valued for the walking opportunities they provide as well as the lack of shops. McLoughlins Beach residents particularly appreciated the walking paths available, and Manns Beach residents appreciated the sense of continuity that Manns Beach provides. These features give each place a sense of uniqueness and make residents feel like there is no other place like where they live (Karlsson et al., 2015).

There were only a small number of lived values that were unique to each place. This shows how identifying commonalities and differences in lived values across communities can readily make a large and diverse list of values small and manageable for decision-makers and help local communities articulate how their needs are different to those of proximate communities. The values that were unique to each place were largely related to the history of each place. Port Albert is one of Victoria's oldest seaports and has a number of historic buildings that not only make it unique among these four communities but to the region more broadly. The lack of development in Seaspray is related to its tenuous history as a settlement, being situated on sandy hummocks at the mouth of Merriman's creek (The Gippsland Times, June 28, 1923, p. 7). Manns Beach has residents whose families have decades-long connections to the place (Fincher et al., 2014). This is consistent with past values-based studies in developing countries, which have highlighted the importance of recognizing historical ties (Karlsson et al., 2015; Mortreux and Barnett, 2009) and historical context (Coulthard, 2008; Nielsen and Reenberg, 2010) in adaptation planning.

While the lived values mentioned here represent a snapshot of what residents currently value, there was evidence that these values are intergenerational. Residents valued the environment, small community size, peacefulness and slow pace of life because it connected them with a way of life of past generations, and a desire that such values could be maintained for future generations (Fincher et al., 2014). The process of documenting and accommodating lived values needs to recognize the extent to which such values grow, persist or decline in importance over time. This is especially important given that policy makers and scientists focus on potential future impacts that are rarely synchronized with local experiences of place and time (Fincher et al., 2015).

People-Centric Lived Values and Vulnerability

Focusing on place-specific values provides decision-makers with one option for tailoring adaptation planning to individual places, yet even within communities there are diverse perspectives on what is valued. The cluster analysis reveals that individuals within a community may have more in common with residents from other communities than their own. Understanding similarities and differences in the types of people who live within and across communities helps decision-makers to understand who is vulnerable and how. It also provides a way of developing regional plans that can be tailored to individual communities while addressing *all* concerns (Forsyth, 2014).

People on low incomes are one of the most commonly identified vulnerable groups in adaptation planning (Collins, 2016). They are usually perceived to be situated in riskier locations, have livelihoods that depend on at-risk natural capital and lack access to resources, which means that they are likely to find it more challenging to adapt to climate change (Collins, 2016). In the small communities here, the socially networked circumstantial seachangers were the poorest of the five groups identified. While they tend to live below the poverty line, this is likely to be because they are on pensions or welfare and therefore do not depend on livelihoods that are likely to be affected by floods, as is the case elsewhere (Kelly and Adger, 2000). This group of residents appears to live in these small communities because of the low cost of living, rather than a particular attachment to the physical place; they did not particularly value the peacefulness, being close to water or the natural environment. Thus, as per research in other at-risk communities in low-lying island states (Mortreux and Barnett, 2009), this poorer group of residents may be the most willing to relocate.

Yet, it is also important to note that this group was socially networked, frequently interacting with friends and volunteering for community organizations. Thus, if this group was to be supported in relocating, consideration would need to be given to their financial security as well as the maintenance of their social relationships. Alternatively, if local governments wished to engage in a community-based approach to adaptation, this group's social networks could provide the cohesion needed for community-based adaptation to be successful (Mikulewicz, 2018).

The elderly are another group who are traditionally considered to be vulnerable to climate change because of their susceptibility to health problems (Schlosberg et al., 2015). In this study the regional retirees were the oldest of the groups in the four communities. It was also the second poorest, indicating that they are vulnerable in more than one way (Collins, 2016). Despite their age, this group did not strongly value having access to medical services. Instead, they valued being part of a small, supportive community where everybody knows everybody. As per other climate adaptation studies, it may be that this group does not perceive themselves to be 'old' or vulnerable and that they believe that their social networks make them more resilient (Quinn and Adger, 2011; Wolf et al., 2010). We concur with Wolf et al. (2010) that adaptation planning for this group should appeal to individuals' sense of independence and explicitly consider social networks in the development of responses. Adaptation plans also need to recognize their residence length (24.9 years on average), which is likely to make them more resistant to relocation (Lewicka, 2011); yet their desire to be part of a supportive community may mean that they can be effective engaged in community-based adaptation efforts (Mikulewicz, 2018).

The community-minded business owners are vulnerable to the impacts of sea-level rise because their lived values are intertwined with their businesses, which are their livelihoods. Past research has recognized that businesses may need to relocate as a result of climate change, yet there is little attention given to the impacts that such relocation would have on communities (Kaján and Saarinen, 2013). In the case of Gippsland East, the community-minded business owners contribute significantly to the social capital of the four communities. If they were to relocate, there would be flow on effects to other residents that value social relationships, such as the socially networked circumstantial seachangers. This suggests that adaptation planning needs to consider the impacts of sea-level rise on business owners, and the flow on effects that may ensue if those businesses chose to relocate in the absence of more strategic, community-based approach.

The self-sufficient, middle-aged primary residents are not poor or elderly, nor do they have livelihoods that are based in these physically vulnerable places. Yet this group may be considered to be vulnerable due to their small or absent social networks. At least one local government within Australia considers 'socially isolated' residents in their adaptation planning because of concerns that such residents may be less likely to adapt or may not have others to provide them with assistance when needed (Collins, 2016). There is limited empirical research into the vulnerabilities to sea-level rise and flooding of those that are socially isolated; however, research into the impacts of temperature on socially isolated individuals suggests that they need measures tailored to them (McGeehin and Mirabelli, 2001). In the case of adaptation to sea-level rise, the self-sufficient, middle-aged primary residents may be more accepting of a relocation policy given their lack of social networks, their relatively short length of residence (their average residence length was 11.3 years, the lowest of all the groups) and their key lived values—recreational opportunities and escaping the city—are qualities that are available elsewhere. This group may also be more challenging to engage in a community-based adaptation solution.

The impacts of climate change on non-permanent residents, like second home-owners, are rarely considered in the academic literature. The finding here that the coastal-hamlet loving second home-owners are strongly attached to the communities is consistent with past research on second home-owners (e.g. Kelly and Hosking, 2008). Indeed, past research has found that the more second home-owners visit a place and the longer their residence (25.2 years on average for this group, the highest of all the groups), the stronger their commitment to those places and the greater the likelihood that they will move permanently to these regions (Kelly and Hosking, 2008). Thus, it is important for local governments to consider the lived values of second home-owners in adaptation planning because they represent potential future permanent residents who will be at risk of sea-level rise and resistant to relocation. Furthermore, second home-owners can halt or reverse rural decline through their contribution to local communities and economy (Connell and McManus, 2011). Thus, adaptation planning needs to consider the possibility that second home-owners may choose not to retire to these communities because of sea-level rise and/or the associated adaptation responses.

Focusing on people at risk reveals that adaptation policy needs to go beyond taking into account the impact of climate change on material things. It especially needs to accommodate the values placed on social networks and community organizations that foster a sense of belonging. Focusing on such people-centric values reveals a risks and hazards approach to vulnerability is not sufficient for understanding how individuals within a community are likely to be affected by and respond to different adaptation policies. Instead, social vulnerability and values need to be considered alongside one another.

Fair Adaptation, Values and Local Governments

The previous sections have explained how understanding place-specific and people-centric lived values can address challenges governments face in reconciling diverse values in local adaptation policy. This section considers how understanding similarities and differences in lived values within and across communities can aid the achievement of fair adaptation beyond rethinking how vulnerability is conceptualized and operationalized.

Distributive fairness in climate adaptation involves ensuring that outcomes are equitable (Adger, 2013). Understanding the diverse lived values within communities provides local governments with a way of evaluating how climate change impacts, such as sea-level rise, as well as adaptation policies are likely to affect different groups of people within a community. For example, retreat may be a more acceptable option to the self-sufficient middle-aged primary residents and the socially networked circumstantial seachangers if retirement opportunities and social relationships are maintained, respectively. If the business owners choose to relocate then this may have flow on effects for the socially networked circumstantial seachangers and coastal-hamlet loving second home-owners. Thus, the lived values approach helps identify trade-offs between different adaptation options, shows where maladaptation may occur and provides ideas on how impacts may be offset to ensure that no particular group is rendered more vulnerable or bears a greater burden as a result of adaptation.

If adaptation is to be procedurally fair, it needs to ensure that all residents are at least represented in adaptation decision-making (Paolisso et al., 2012) or at best have political power to influence adaptation decisions (Holland, 2017; Mikulewicz, 2018). Engaging with community organizations may be an effective means of accommodating the views of socially networked circumstantial seachangers, regional retirees and the community-minded business owners but may be less effective in reaching self-sufficient, middle-aged primary residents and the coastal-hamlet loving second home-owners. While quantitative surveys can help local governments to reach a wider range of residents than may be possible using standard community engagement techniques, it is not sufficient for engaging the community in robust debates about the trade-offs involved or compensation required for various adaptation options. Thus, further research is required to find ways of engaging with people who may be socially isolated or spatially distant from communities at risk.

Conclusion

The lived values approach used here facilitates an understanding of the situated determinants of fair adaptation—fairness has its subjective, spatial, social and temporal dimensions that cannot be captured by assessments based on material and economic circumstances alone. When viewed from the perspective of distributional fairness, a lived values approach goes beyond just measuring the socio-economic characteristics of people (e.g. their incomes, age, dependence) and assuming certain groups are more vulnerable than others on that basis. It allows us to understand what people's practices and resources, including social networks, are in places. From the perspective of procedural fairness, a lived values approach draws attention to the local and the opportunities of shared governance. It enables a more socially nuanced guide to the local politics of adaptation, identifying winners and losers from potential adaptation processes, the diverse needs of constituencies in terms of engagement processes and outcomes and bundles of adaptation responses that may satisfy some—if not all—members of communities. This approach will be particularly important to consider in communities that face some level of disadvantage, located in both developed and developing nations.

References

ABS (2011), *Census of Population and Housing*. Canberra: Australian Bureau of Statistics.
ACOSS (2014) *Poverty in Australia 2014*. Strawberry Hills, NSW: Australian Council of Social Service.
Adger, W. N. (2013), "Emerging dimensions of fair process for adaptation decision-making," in J. Palutikof, et al., eds. *Climate Adaptation Futures*. Chichester, UK: John Wiley & Sons, pp. 69–74.
Adger, W. N. (2016), "Place, well-being, and fairness shape priorities for adaptation to climate change," *Global Environmental Change* 38: A1–A3.
Baker, I., Peterson, A., Brown, G. and McAlpine, C. (2012), "Local government response to the impacts of climate change: An evaluation of local climate adaptation plans," *Landscape and Urban Planning* 107: 127–36.
Barnett, J., Graham, S., Mortreux, C., Fincher, R., Waters, E. and Hurlimann, A. (2014), "A local coastal adaptation pathway," *Nature Climate Change* 4: 1103–8.
Barnett, J. and O'Neill, S. (2010), "Maladaptation," *Global Environmental Change* 2: 211–13.
Barnett, J., Tschakert, P., Head, L. and Adger, W. (2016), "A socially engaged science of loss," *Nature Climate Change* 6(11): 976–8.
Bock, B. B. (2016), "Rural marginalisation and the role of social innovation; a turn towards nexogenous development and rural reconnection," *Sociologia Ruralis* 56(4): 552–73.
Caney, S. (2005), "Cosmopolitan justice, responsibility, and global climate change," *Leiden Journal of International Law* 18: 747–75.
Collins, L. B. (2016), *Confronting the Inconvenient Truth: The Politics and Policies of Australian Climate Change Adaptation Planning*. PhD, University of Sydney.

Connell, J. and McManus, P. (2011), *Rural Revival?: Place Marketing, Tree Change and Regional Migration in Australia*. New York: Routledge.

Corner, A., Markowitz, E. and Pidgeon, N. (2014), "Public engagement with climate change: The role of human values," *Wiley Interdisciplinary Reviews: Climate Change* 5: 411–22.

Coulthard, S. (2008), "Adapting to environmental change in artisanal fisheries—Insights from a South Indian lagoon," *Global Environmental Change* 18: 479–89.

Department of Climate Change (2009), *Climate Change Risks to Australia's Coast*. Canberra: Australia Department of Climate Change.

Dillman, D. A. (2007), *Mail and Internet Surveys: The Tailored Design Method*. Hoboken, NJ: John Wiley & Sons.

Edwards, D., Weldon, P. R. and Friedman, T. (2011), *Industry, Employment, and Population Profile. Supporting Analysis: Gippsland Tertiary Education Plan SV31032011*. Melbourne, Victoria: Australian Council for Educational Research.

Fincher, R., Barnett, J. and Graham, S. (2015), "Temporalities in adaptation to sea-level rise," *Annals of the Association of American Geographers* 105: 263–73.

Fincher, R., Barnett, J., Graham, S. and Hurlimann, A. (2014), "Time stories: Making sense of futures in anticipation of sea-level rise," *Geoforum* 56: 201–10.

Forsyth, T. (2014), "Climate justice is not just ice," *Geoforum* 54: 230–32.

Graham, S. and Barnett, J. (2017), "Accounting for justice in local government responses to sea-level rise: Evidence from two local councils in Victoria, Australia," in A. Lukasiewicz, et al., eds. *Natural Resources and Environmental Justice: Australian Perspectives*. Melbourne, Australia: CSIRO Publishing, pp. 91–104.

Graham, S., Barnett, J., Fincher, R., Hurlimann, A. and Mortreux, C. (2014), "Local values for fairer adaptation to sea-level rise: A typology of residents and their lived values in Lakes Entrance, Australia," *Global Environmental Change* 29: 41–52.

Graham, S., Barnett, J., Fincher, R., Hurlimann, A., Mortreux, C. and Waters, E. (2013), "The social values at risk from sea-level rise," *Environmental Impact Assessment Review* 41: 45–52.

Graham, S., Barnett, J., Fincher, R., Mortreux, C. and Hurlimann, A. (2015), "Towards fair local outcomes in adaptation to sea-level rise," *Climatic Change* 130: 411–24.

Hahn, M. B., Riederer, A. M. and Foster, S. O. (2009), "The livelihood vulnerability index: A pragmatic approach to assessing risks from climate variability and change—A case study in Mozambique," *Global Environmental Change* 19: 74–88.

Hamin, E. and Gurran, N. (2015), "Climbing the adaptation planning ladder: Barriers and enablers in municipal planning," in W. L. Filho, ed. *Handbook of Climate Change Adaptation*. Berlin: Springer-Verlag.

Hamin, E., Gurran, N. and Emlinger, A. M. (2014), "Barriers to municipal climate adaptation: Examples from Coastal Massachusetts' smaller cities and towns," *Journal of the American Planning Association* 80: 110–22.

Holland, B. (2017), "Procedural justice in local climate adaptation: Political capabilities and transformational change," *Environmental Politics* 26: 391–412.

Hurlimann, A., Barnett, J., Fincher, R., Osbaldiston, N., Mortreux, C. and Graham, S. (2014), "Urban planning and sustainable adaptation to sea level rise," *Landscape and Urban Planning* 126: 84–93.

Ishaya, S. and Abaje, I. B. (2008), "Indigenous people's perception on climate change and adaptation strategies in Jema'a local government area of Kaduna State, Nigeria," *Journal of Geography and Regional Planning* 1: 138–43.

Kaján, E. and Saarinen, J. (2013), "Tourism, climate change and adaptation: A review," *Current Issues in Tourism* 16: 167–95.

Karlsson, M. and Hovelsrud, G. K. (2015), "Local collective action: Adaptation to coastal erosion in the Monkey River Village, Belize," *Global Environmental Change* 32: 96–107.

Karlsson, M., Van Oort, B. and Romstad, B. (2015), "What we have lost and cannot become: Societal outcomes of coastal erosion in southern Belize," *Ecology & Society* 20: 237–50.

Kelly, G. and Hosking, K. (2008), "Nonpermanent residents, place attachment, and "Sea Change" communities," *Environment and Behavior* 40: 575–94.

Kelly, P. M. and Adger, W. N. (2000), "Theory and practice in assessing vulnerability to climate change and facilitating adaptation," *Climatic Change* 47: 325–52.

Kreller, A. (2021), "Transforming fair decision-making about sea-level rise in cities: the values and beliefs of residents in Botany Bay, Australia," *Environmental Values* 30(1): 7–42.

Kuruppu, N. (2009), "Adapting water resources to climate change in Kiribati: The importance of cultural values and meanings," *Environmental Science and Policy* 12: 799–809.

Lewicka, M. (2011), "Place attachment: How far have we come in the last 40 years?," *Journal of Environmental Psychology* 31: 207–30.

Macintosh, A. (2013), "Coastal climate hazards and urban planning: How planning responses can lead to maladaptation," *Mitigation and Adaptation Strategies for Global Change* 18: 1035–55.

McGeehin, M. A. and Mairabelli, M. (2001), "The potential impacts of climate variability and change on temperature-related morbidity and mortality in the United States," *Environmental Health Perspectives* 109: 185–9.

McInnes, K. L., Macadam, I. and Hubbert, G. D. (2006), *Climate Change in Eastern Victoria—Stage Three Report: The Effect of Climate Change on Extreme Sea-Levels in Corner Inlet and the Gippsland Lakes*. Melbourne: CSIRO.

McInnes, K. L., Macadam, I., Hubbert, G. D., Abbs, D. J. and Bathols, J. A. (2005), *Climate Change in Eastern Victoria—Stage Two Report: The Effect of Climate Change on Storm Surges*. Melbourne: CSIRO.

Measham, T. G., Preston, B. L., Smith, T. F., Brooke, C., Gorddard, R., Withycombe, G. and Morrison, C. (2011), "Adapting to climate change through local municipal planning: Barriers and challenges," *Mitigation and Adaptation Strategies for Global Change* 16: 889–909.

Mikulewicz, M. (2018), "Politicizing vulnerability and adaptation: On the need to democratize local responses to climate impacts in developing countries," *Climate and Development* 10: 18–34.

Mortreux, C. and Barnett, J. (2009), "Climate change, migration and adaptation in Funafuti, Tuvalu," *Global Environmental Change* 19: 105–12.

Moser, S. C. and Ekstrom, J. A. (2010), "A framework to diagnose barriers to climate change adaptation," *Proceedings of the National Academy of Sciences* 107: 22026–31.

Nielsen, J. Ø. and Reenberg, A. (2010), "Cultural barriers to climate change adaptation: A case study from Northern Burkina Faso," *Global Environmental Change* 20: 142–52.

Novaczek, I., Macfadyen, J., Bardati, D. and Maceachern, K. (2011), *Social and Cultural Values Mapping as a Decision-Support Tool for Climate Change Adaptation*. Charlottetown: The Institute of Island Studies, University of Prince Edward Island.

Paavola, J. and Adger, N. (2002), *Justice and Adaptation to Climate Change*. Norwich: Tyndall Centre for Climate Change Research.

Paavola, J. and Adger, N. (2006), "Fair adaptation to climate change," *Ecological Economics* 56: 594–609.

Paolisso, M., Douglas, E., Enrici, A., Kirshen, P., Watson, C. and Ruth, M. (2012), "Climate change, justice, and adaptation among African American communities in the Chesapeake Bay region," *Weather, Climate, and Society* 4: 34–47.

Paschen, J. and Ison, R. (2012), *Exploring Local Narratives of Environmental Change and Adaptation.* Melbourne: Victorian Centre for Climate Change Adaptation Research.

Pasquini, L., Ziervogel, G., Cowling, R. M. and Shearing, C. (2015), "What enables local governments to mainstream climate change adaptation? Lessons learned from two municipal case studies in the Western Cape, South Africa," *Climate and Development* 7: 60–70.

Puleston, A. (2012), *Adapting to Sea-Level Rise: What's Missing and What Will Be Missed?* Honours, The University of Melbourne.

Quinn, T. and Adger, W. N. (2011), "Climate change when you are getting on in life," *Environment and Planning A* 43: 2257–60.

Reid, M. G., Hamilton, C., Reid, S. K., Trousdale, W., Hill, C., Turner, N., Picard, C. R., Lamontagne, C. and Matthews, H. D. (2014), "Indigenous climate change adaptation planning using a values-focused approach: A case study with the Gitga'at Nation," *Journal of Ethnobiology* 34: 401–24.

Schlosberg, D. and Collins, L. B. (2014), "From environmental to climate justice: Climate change and the discourse of environmental justice," *Wiley Interdisciplinary Reviews: Climate Change* 5: 359–74.

Schlosberg, D., Niemeyer, S. and Collins, L. B. (2015), *Adaptation Deliberation Case Study: City of Sydney.* Sydney: University of Sydney.

Tschakert, P., Tutu, R. and Alcaro, A. (2013), "Embodied experiences of environmental and climatic changes in landscapes of everyday life in Ghana," *Emotion, Space and Society* 7: 13–25.

Wheeler, P. J., Kunapo, J., Coller, M. L. F., Peterson, J. A. and McMahon, M. (2009), "Real-time validation of a digital flood-inundation model: A case-study from Lakes Entrance, Victoria, Australia," in W. Allsop, P. Samuels, J. Harrop and S. Huntington, eds. *Flood Risk Management: Research and Practice.* London: Taylor & Francis Group, pp. 185–94.

Wolf, J., Adger, N., Lorenzoni, I., Abrahamson, V. and Raine, R. (2010), "Social capital, individual responses to heat waves and climate change adaptation: An empirical study of two UK cities," *Global Environmental Change* 20: 44–52.

Chapter 5
GOVERNANCE FOR RESILIENT SMART CITIES

Darren Nel and Verna Nel

Introduction

Cities are complex socio-ecological systems (SES) comprising multiple interacting systems. These include social (people, governance and political), economic, infrastructure (transport, information and communication technology (ICT), water, electricity, sanitation) and environmental systems. The entire SES contains networks of energy and material flows linking people, processes and infrastructure. All complex systems are non-linear and dynamic. The numerous interactions allow information to move through the SES, enabling both change and stability. SES operate at multiple spatial and temporal scales, with smaller systems moving more quickly within smaller spaces compared to larger systems. Complex systems are built from the bottom upwards, enabling them to respond to their environments, adapting and self-organising, a process dubbed emergence. Unlike complicated systems (such as a computer), SES are not easy to control, and if control is exerted, it tends to stifle the adaptability of the system (Gunderson and Holling, 2002).

While complex systems can adapt, the adaption need not be to a desired state if the system's resources are eroded. 'Slow burn' or stress events may tip a system into an impoverished state from which it is difficult to recover (Coaffee & Lee, 2016). Urban SES are under immense pressure, facing social, economic and environmental challenges. Rapid urbanisation has exacerbated problems of pollution, land degradation, social inequality and stressed infrastructure (Bibri & Krogstie, 2017). Smart cities are both a response to these challenges and a means to manage the complexity.

There are many definitions of smart cities, each with a different focus; however, they fall into two broad groups, one with a technological perspective and the other focusing on people (Albino, Berardi, & Dangelico, 2015; Kummitha

DOI: 10.4324/9781003178545-7

& Crutzen, 2017; Mora, Bolici, & Deakin, 2017). The former views a smart city as "one that can be monitored, managed and regulated in real-time using ICT infrastructure and ubiquitous computing" (Kitchin, 2015: 131). Smart cities use "smart urban technology solutions to improve liveability of communities and sustainability of cities—these technologies also include infrastructural ICTs that serve as the backbone such as internet and world wide web" (Yigitcanlar & Kamruzzaman, 2018: 50).

While noting the role of technology, other authors emphasise the human dimension. For Kummitha and Crutzen (2017), well-educated citizens (smart people) are essential. Smart governance has a robust technological foundation which supports participatory governance and improves the quality of life and liveability of the city (Baron, 2012). A holistic concept of smart cities includes ICT and related technologies but also a "balanced combination of human, social, cultural, environmental, economic, and technological aspects" (Mora et al., 2017: 20). Social inclusion and equity as well as environmental sustainability are key elements and goals of smart cities (Ahvenniemi et al., 2017; Bibri and Krogstie, 2017; Mora et al., 2017; Yigitcanlar and Kamruzzaman, 2018). Smart cities thus seek to be equitable and socially just, environmentally sustainable, economically prosperous, innovative and safe, and are supported by ICT and related technologies. A city must be able to survive crises and endure disruptions yet continue serving its citizens and remain competitive. Smart cities must be resilient!

As there is limited literature on the resilience of smart cities, we explore this gap by applying the concepts of resilience to smart cities. In the next section, we discuss the concept of resilience and how social and ecological capital and technology can contribute to resilience. Thereafter, we suggest some principles for the governance of smart and resilient cities that extends beyond disaster risk management, followed by some concluding remarks.

Unpacking Resilience

There are multiple definitions of the concept of resilience. Initial definitions saw (engineering) resilience as the ability of a system to withstand a disturbance and which used the speed of the recovery back to the system's equilibrium as the measure of its resilience (Holling, 1986). This perspective was replaced by 'ecological resilience' that defined resilience as the amount of disturbance that a system could absorb before collapsing or moving into another stability domain (Folke, 2006). The more recent 'evolutionary' (or social-ecological) resilience perspective views the resilience of a system as its ability to recover or adapt and maintain its function despite stresses and disturbances (Carpenter et al., 2001).

The evolutionary resilience perspective emphasises several essential elements. First, a system must be able to absorb a disturbance. Second, a system can self-organise (as opposed to organisation forced upon by external factors, or complete lack of any organisation), adapt to change and if needed, transform in the face of a disturbance. Third, resilient SES can learn from the past and plan for the future (Walker & Salt, 2012; Coaffee & Lee, 2016). Hence, resilience is more than merely anticipating and minimising risk or potential disasters; resilience concerns seeing opportunities in crises, while actively seeking to improve the system (Peres, 2016). Finally, evolutionary resilience acknowledges that all complex systems are comprised of sub-systems which interact with each other across different spatial-temporal scales. Due to the non-linear interactions within systems, small changes can have large and unexpected effects across all scales (Gunderson & Holling, 2001).

With the increasing popularity of resilience in recent years (Elmqvist, Barnett, and Wilkinson, 2014; Zhang & Li, 2018) some scholars are concerned that resilience will be used interchangeably with sustainability. However, it should be noted that resilience and sustainability are not the same things. Unlike suitability, resilience is a value-neutral concept, meaning that resilience can imply both 'good' and 'bad' system states (Barnes & Nel, 2017). For example, an authoritarian regime maintaining power through fear could be considered resilient, even more so than a liberal society embracing democracy and freedom of speech (Elmqvist et al., 2014). Resilience, as a non-normative concept, can be better understood as an emergent characteristic of a complex system which reinforces and maintains some behaviours, whether desired or not. Therefore, to fully leverage the potential that resilience thinking offers cities, resilience must be framed within a normative position such as sustainable development (Peres, Landman, and du Plessis, 2016). If framed within sustainable development, then resilience offers a theoretical framework to identify those aspects of the city-system whose resilience needs to be eroded while simultaneously identifying characteristics and behaviours which should be reinforced to further enhance the sustainable, resilient development of a city (ibid).

If resilience is approached from a normative sustainability position, what then is the role of smart city planning in creating smart resilient cities? Cities, like all complex systems, exhibit a set of common characteristics, which, when studied through a resilience perspective, become a means to both assess and foster resilience. The system characteristics that have the greatest potential to build the resilience of cities are described below.

Diversity

Diversity is critical for resilience as it generates complexity while providing the system with multiple options (Salat, 2011). Diversity can be a variation between types (e.g. land uses), within types (as different forms of residential use) or in the arrangement of types. Ferreira (2016) distinguishes between functional and response diversity. Functional (or structural) diversity pertains to the various functions that different elements of a system perform (e.g. shelter, commerce, transport). Response diversity is the variation within each function and can be considered as the scope of reactions to change within a system (Page, 2010).

Spatial diversity considers the size and spatial distribution of functions and corresponding response (Salat & Bourdic, 2012). More diverse systems have more ways to deal with stresses; for example, a more diverse economy will fare better than one with a narrow economic base. Additionally, if there are acceptable public transport options, people will be more willing to use them instead of private cars, this can also relate to energy options.

Redundancy

Redundancy is the extent to which different system elements can perform the same or similar functions, either through duplication, backups or different elements performing the same function (Page, 2010; United Nations and Asian Development Bank, 2012). Redundancy is routinely built into ICT systems to ensure that the system can function even if one part fails. Diversity, specifically response diversity, can also generate redundancy (Cumming et al., 2008) as the duplication of a function enhances its responsive capacity. Diversity further supports redundancy, as places with a range of alternative transport systems and routes, or sources of water can cope under stress. In contrast, dependence on a single option makes a place vulnerable. Redundancy includes stores and capitals, such as social and human capital. A smart city ensures that there is redundancy in its critical urban services such as water, electricity and increasingly, ICT. For example, South Africa has been experiencing regular blackouts over the past five years due to a lack of capacity to generate sufficient electricity to meet the country's needs (Eskom, n.d.). Clearly, the electricity generation system has neither redundancy nor resilience.

Modularity

Modularity occurs when a system has sub-units that are weakly connected externally but has strong internal connections which enable the sub-units to function semi-independently. For example, if part of a power grid is knocked out, other parts of the system can continue to provide power without disruption. Furthermore, because the sub-systems are still connected, it would still be possible to reroute power to the affected areas, provided there was spare capacity. Together with redundancy, modularity provides the means to mitigate and respond to disasters. However, both redundancy and modularity reduce efficiency; thus, a balance between safeguards and efficiency is required.

Connectivity

Cities create complex networks which facilitate the flow of goods and interaction between people (Batty, 2013). Through the strength and structure of the network, new locations are able to emerge (Salat, 2017). Moreover, poor connectivity can exacerbate a crisis after a shock (Ahern, 2011), such as in Haiti after the

2010 earthquake, when the harbour, airport and other transport infrastructure was damaged. High degrees of connectivity allow the system to quickly access, reorganise and redistribute resources and information after a shock. Furthermore, the structure of the connections is also important. Networks whose structures are 'tree-like' tend to be very efficient, but are also vulnerable should their capacity be exceeded or essential connections damaged. In contrast, 'leaf-like' network structures tend to have many connections, providing a greater degree of network redundancy. Networks that combine these structures are both efficient and resilient (Salat & Bourdic, 2012). Connectivity in the form of social media has been critical in helping people in disasters (Gao et al., 2011).

Foresight and Learning

Evolutionary resilience emphasises the ability of SES to learn from the past—their own and other cities—while also planning for possible future scenarios, enabling them to better plan for similar circumstances (Hassler & Kohler, 2014; Barnes & Nel, 2017). Advances in technology, including sensors, communication technology and remote sensing, can provide cities with real-time data. Other advances, such as artificial intelligence and machine learning, can aid cities in making sense of all the information as well as providing deeper insights into the functioning of the city. Overall, smart cities build resilience as they enable more informed decisions to be made by studying past information, understanding the current situation and helping to plan with the information at hand.

Adaptability

Adaptability—a defining characteristic of a resilient system—is the ability to adjust to changes, and arises from the capability of the components to change their behaviour or structural characteristics in response to changes in other system components or the environment (Holland, 1996). The system's response can vary greatly and is largely dependent on the initial stimulus. Adaptive capacity is, therefore, the ease with which the system's components can respond to an event or even anticipate possible events (Folke et al., 2010; Coaffee & Lee, 2016). For example, some cities are slowly adapting their existing building stock to better manage the impact of climate change or seismic events. Through incentives to accelerate the adaption, governments are improving cities' adaptive capacity. Smart cities can use advanced sensors to aid in identifying which areas need what type of adaption or develop buildings that are more responsive to the real-time needs of the inhabitants. However, caution is required to avoid over-adaption to one specific threat as this can reduce the system's overall capacity to respond to unknown threats (Walker & Salt, 2012). Because the focus of resilience is on adaption, it shifts the attention away from an 'end state' to focus on possible futures which are built on principles and not pragmatism (Eraydin & Taşan-Kok, 2013, p. 6). Such principles are discussed in the next section.

Principles of Resilient Governance in Smart Cities

While 'government' pertains to formal institutions and their right to use force, the concept of governance includes stakeholders from business, communities and other organisations (Healey, 2004; Stoker, 2008). While governance includes authority and constraint, it can be generative and creative (Healey, 2004). Pierre (2005: 452) defines urban governance as "the pursuit of collective goals through an inclusive strategy of resource mobilisation." Governance also includes the norms and standards of a society that inform and determine how decisions are made and resources are allocated. Consequently, value judgements and their impacts on investment decisions, social justice and the environment are critical and raise issues of accountability, participation and representation (Kemp, Parto, and Gibson, 2005; Lebel et al., 2006; Galaz et al., 2010; Goodspeed, 2015). Consequently, appropriate institutions are required, particularly those that can uphold the long-term commitment to resilience and regeneration by using appropriate technologies to achieve these goals. Moreover, strengthening the ability of all stakeholders to adapt and innovate and build their resilience is an essential role of governance. Five policy principles are suggested in the next section to move governance towards enabling more resilient smart cities.

Smart Cities Are for People

Cities are created by people for people: technology is a tool to ensure health, safety and liveability of citizens. Consequently, technology should be used to enhance the quality of life of all residents. Connectivity cannot necessarily be equated with inclusion, particularly where many residents are illiterate or cannot afford the hardware or data required to access a city's e-services (Odendaal, 2003). Furthermore, private companies cannot be expected to meet the needs of all, as they may not have the necessary local knowledge, or it may not be profitable for them. Hence, the onus is on local government to find innovative ways of serving poor and marginalised citizens.

Smart, sustainable and resilient cities involve their residents in participatory planning and inclusive decision-making. This promotes commitment to the proposals as well as enriching their experiences and encouraging participants to creatively solve their problems (Kemp et al., 2005; Lebel et al., 2006; Kummitha & Crutzen, 2017). Technology can, therefore, support collaborative planning, through, for example, social media and improved methods of data sharing (Brabham, 2009; Goodspeed, 2015).

Social Inclusion

Smart cities include smart people and those who have not had the opportunity to learn the skills and knowledge valued in technically advanced cities. Research conducted in the Global South by Baud et al. (2014) indicates that the application of ICT and knowledge management focused more on the middle class but excluded the poor. "The ICT-based perspective, before it is adopted more universally, needs to address questions about how ICTs negotiate between social realities and the utopian promises of achieving an inclusive social order" (Kummitha & Crutzen, 2017: 46). Thus, smart, resilient cities must acknowledge crucial social issues such as housing and essential services and negotiate between the needs of business, government and communities to avoid becoming a more unequal society.

Sustainability and Regenerative Development

An unsustainable city cannot be smart; hence, smart, resilient cities should strive to be sustainable and regenerative (Kemp et al., 2005; Du Plessis, 2012). Smart technology can contribute to conserving resources, reducing greenhouse gasses and increasing efficiency. The innovation and creativity associated with smart cities can invent novel solutions to challenges (De Jong et al., 2015; Bibri & Krogstie, 2017). Critically, sustainable development includes social issues of equity and economic opportunity (Jabareen, 2008).

Learning, Foresight and Planning in the Context of Complexity

Innovation and learning contribute to resilience, while systems are at their most resilient where there is flexibility and creativity (Holling, 2001; Trembaczowski, 2012). Acknowledging uncertainty and the reality of change is crucial, given the nature of urban challenges, the volatility of financial markets and unpredictability of climate change (Jabareen, 2013). Knowledge systems and artificial intelligence can contribute to prediction and appropriate planning to enhance sustainability, improve resilience and prevent disasters.

Accepting complexity and uncertainty implies new ways of planning and governance, where the focus of control should only be on the critical aspects while permitting the emergence of new social and governance structures. Where possible, self-regulation should be encouraged. Control must be balanced with flexibility, adaptability and transformation towards goals (Meerow, Newell, and Stults, 2016).

Managing Vulnerabilities

Smart cities need to manage their vulnerabilities through foresight and contingency planning. Besides natural disasters, economic vagaries and social disruptions, there are risks pertaining to smart cities. Hyper-efficiencies may erode redundancy and thus resilience. Heavy reliance on ITC and connectivity rather than paper-based information (e.g. transport time-tables, maps and books) can leave people stranded if the system is unavailable for any reason (Yigitcanlar & Kamruzzaman, 2018). Moreover, the ability to rapidly restore infrastructure and services after disruptions is critical in a smart city. The fear of "surveillance, technocratic and corporate forms of governance, technological lock-ins, profiling and social sorting, anticipatory governance, control creep, the hollowing out of state" (Kitchin, 2015: 132) must be managed, ideally through collaborative planning and accountable governance.

Conclusion

Although there is significant literature on smart cities, sustainable cities and sustainable smart cities, there is very little available on resilient, smart cities. This chapter has made a small contribution in this area. Having described resilience, its building blocks and their relationship to it to smart cities, this chapter has proposed five principles which contribute to the sound governance of resilient smart cities. However, there are still many avenues of research open around the building of resilience in smart cities. These include the urban form, neighbourhood design, the infrastructure and buildings for robustness, and the ability to restore ecological infrastructure, support greater inclusion and equity of access to the city as well as a prosperous and healthy economy.

References

Ahern, J. (2011), "From fail-safe to safe-to-fail: Sustainability and resilience in the new urban world," *Landscape and Urban Planning* 100(4): 341–3.

Ahvenniemi, H., Huovila, A., Pinto-Seppä, I., and Airaksinen, M. (2017), "What are the differences between sustainable and smart cities?," *Cities* 60: 234–45.

Albino, V., Berardi, U., and Dangelico, R. M. (2015), "Smart cities: Definitions, dimensions, performance, and initiatives," *Journal of Urban Technology* 22(1): 3–21. https://doi.org/10/gcv8xx

Barnes, A., and Nel, V. (2017), "Putting spatial resilience into practice," *Urban Forum* 28(2): 219–32.

Baron, M. (2012), "Do we need smart cities for resilience?," *Journal of Economics and Management* 10: 32–46.

Batty, M. (2013). *The new science of cities*. Cambridge, MA: MIT Press.

Baud, I., Scott, D., Pfeffer, K., Sydenstricker-Neto, J., and Denis, E. (2014), "Digital and spatial knowledge management in urban governance: Emerging issues in India, Brazil, South Africa, and Peru," *Habitat International* 44: 501–9.

Bibri, S. E., and Krogstie, J. (2017), "Smart sustainable cities of the future: An extensive interdisciplinary literature review," *Sustainable Cities and Society* 31: 183–212.

Brabham, D. C. (2009), "Crowdsourcing the public participation process for planning projects," *Planning Theory* 8(3): 242–62. https://doi.org/10.1177/1473095209104824

Carpenter, S., Walker, B., Anderies, J. M., and Abel, N. (2001), "From metaphor to measurement: Resilience of what to what?," *Ecosystems* 4(8): 765–81.

Coaffee, J., and Lee, P. (2016), *Urban resilience: Planning for risk, crisis and uncertainty*. London/New York: Palgrave.

Cumming, G. S., Wilson, J., Walker, B., and Ostrom, E. (2008), "Diversity and resilience of social- ecological systems," in J. Norberg and G. S. Cumming, eds. *Complexity theory for a sustainable future* (pp. 46–80). New York: Columbia University Press.

De Jong, M., Joss, S., Schraven, D., Zhan, C., and Weijnen, M. (2015), "Sustainable–smart–resilient–low carbon–eco–knowledge cities; Making sense of a multitude of concepts promoting sustainable urbanisation," *Journal of Cleaner Production* 109: 25–38.

Du Plessis, C. (2012), "Towards a regenerative paradigm for the built environment," *Building Research and Information* 40(1): 7–22.

Elmqvist, T., Barnett, G., and Wilkinson, C. (2014), "Exploring urban sustainability and resilience," in L. Pearson, P. Newton and P. Roberts, eds. *Resilient sustainable cities* (pp. 19–28). New York: Routledge.

Eraydin, A., and Taşan-Kok, T., eds. (2013), *Resilience thinking in urban planning*. Dordrecht: Springer.

Ferreira, A. (2016), Exploring the meaning of functional and response diversity in the urban context (Masters Dissertation). University of Pretoria, Pretoria.

Folke, C. (2006), "Resilience: The emergence of a perspective for social–ecological systems analyses," *Global Environmental Change* 16(3): 253–67. https://doi.org/10.1016/j.gloenvcha.2006.04.002

Folke, C., Carpenter, S., Walker, B., Scheffer, M., Chapin, T., and Rockström, J. (2010), "Resilience thinking: Integrating resilience, adaptability and transformability," *Ecology and Society* 15(4). Accessed http://www.ecologyandsociety.org/vol15/iss4/art20/ http://www.ecologyandsociety.org/vol15/iss4/art20/

Galaz, V., Duit, A., Eckerberg, K., and Ebbesson, J. (2010), "Special issue: Governance, complexity and resilience," *Global Environmental Change* 20(3): 363–422.

Gao, H., Barbier, G., Goolsby, R., and Zeng, D. (2011). *Harnessing the crowdsourcing power of social media for disaster relief*. Tempe: Arizona State University.

Goodspeed, R. (2015), "Smart cities: Moving beyond urban cybernetics to tackle wicked problems," *Cambridge Journal of Regions, Economy and Society* 8(1): 79–92. https://doi.org/10.1093/cjres/rsu013

Gunderson, L. H., and Holling, C. S. (2002), *Panarchy: Understanding transformations in human and natural systems*. Washington, DC: Island Press.

Hassler, U., and Kohler, N. (2014), "Resilience in the built environment," *Building Research and Information* 42(2): 119–29. https://doi.org/10/gd9bct

Healey, P. (2004), "Creativity and urban governance," *Policy Studies* 25(2): 87–102. https://doi.org/10.1080/0144287042000262189

Holland, J. (1996), *Hidden order: How adaptation builds complexity*. Basic Books. Retrieved from http://books.google.co.za/books?id=3eDOuA5pHDoC

Holling, C. S. (1986), "The resilience of terrestrial ecosystems: Local surprise and global change," in W. C. Clark and R. E. Munn, eds. *Sustainable development of the biosphere* (pp. 292–317). Cambridge: Cambridge University Press.

Holling, C. S. (2001), "Understanding the complexity of economic, ecological, and social systems," *Ecosystems* 4(5): 390–405.

Jabareen, Y. (2008), "A new conceptual framework for sustainable development," *Environment, Development and Sustainability* 10(2): 179–92.

Jabareen, Y. (2013), "Planning the resilient city: Concepts and strategies for coping with climate change and environmental risk," *Cities* 31: 220–29.

Kemp, R., Parto, S., and Gibson, R. B. (2005), "Governance for sustainable development: Moving from theory to practice," *International Journal of Sustainable Development* 8(1–2): 12–30.

Kitchin, R. (2015), "Making sense of smart cities: Addressing present shortcomings," *Cambridge Journal of Regions, Economy and Society* 8(1): 131–6.

Kummitha, R. K. R., and Crutzen, N. (2017), "How do we understand smart cities? An evolutionary perspective," *Cities* 67: 43–52.

Lebel, L., Anderies, J. M., Campbell, B., Folke, C., Hatfield-Dodds, S., Hughes, T. P., and Wilson, J. (2006), "Governance and the capacity to manage resilience in regional social-ecological systems," *Ecology and Society* 11(1): 19. http://www.ecologyandsociety.org/vol11/iss1/art19

Meerow, S., Newell, J. P., and Stults, M. (2016), "Defining urban resilience: A review," *Landscape and Urban Planning* 147: 38–49.

Mora, L., Bolici, R., and Deakin, M. (2017), "The first two decades of smart-city research: A bibliometric analysis," *Journal of Urban Technology* 24(1): 3–27. https://doi.org/10.1080/10630732.2017.1285123

Odendaal, N. (2003), "Information and communication technology and local governance: Understanding the difference between cities in developed and emerging economies," *Computers, Environment and Urban Systems* 27(6): 585–607.

Page, S. E. (2010). *Diversity and complexity*. Princeton, NJ: Princeton University Press.

Peres, E. (2016). *The translation of ecological resilience theory into urban systems* (Thesis (PhD)). University of Pretoria, Pretoria. Retrieved from http://hdl.handle.net/2263/56100

Peres, E., Landman, K., and du Plessis, C. (2016), "Unpacking a sustainable and resilient future for Tshwane." Presented at the Urban Transitions Global Summit, Shanghai, China: Procedia Engineering (under review).

Pierre, J. (2005), "Comparative urban governance: Uncovering complex causalities," *Urban Affairs Review* 40(4): 446–62.

Salat, S. (2011), *Cities and forms on sustainable urbanism*. Hermann: CSTB Urban Morphology Laboratory.

Salat, S. (2017), "A systemic approach of urban resilience: Power laws and urban growth patterns," *International Journal of Urban Sustainable Development* 9(2): 107–35.

Salat, S., and Bourdic, L. (2012), "Systemic resilience of complex urban systems," *TeMA-Trimestrale Del Laboratorio Territorio Mobilità e Ambiente-TeMALab* 5(2): 55–68.

Stoker, G. (2008), "Governance as theory: Five propositions," *International Social Science Journal* 50(155): 17–28. https://doi.org/10.1111/1468-2451.00106

Trembaczowski, Ł. (2012), "Learning regions as driving forces for urban economic resilience—Two subregional examples of post-industrial city transition," *Journal of Economics and Management/University of Economics in Katowice* 10: 137–50.

United Nations and Asian Development Bank (2012), *Green growth, resources and resilience: Environmental sustainability in Asia and the Pacific*. Bangkok: United Nations and Asian Development Bank.

Walker, B., and Salt, D. (2012), *Resilience thinking: Sustaining ecosystems and people in a changing world*. Washington, DC: Island Press.

Yigitcanlar, T., and Kamruzzaman, M. (2018), "Does smart city policy lead to sustainability of cities?," *Land Use Policy* 73: 49–58.

Zhang, X., and Li, H. (2018), "Urban resilience and urban sustainability: What we know and what do not know?," *Cities* 72: 141–8.

Educating for Transformative
Planning Practices

Chapter 6
DE-COLONISING PEDAGOGIES
Exploring the Geographies of Urban Planning Education Networks

Julia Wesely and Adriana Allen

Introduction

Realising the Sustainable Development Goal (SDG) 11—'Making cities and human settlements inclusive, safe, resilient and sustainable' (United Nations, 2015)—demands urban planners with the capabilities to address complex socio-economic, environmental and political processes. Addressing inequalities is a central task of planning, which is confronted by the "simultaneous challenges of deconstructing the diagnoses from which it departs, and identifying strategies to transform urban injustices" (Allen, Lambert, & Yap, 2018, p. 365). In working towards more just and equal cities, planners need to be equipped with the skills, capacities and values to put the world's growing urban population at the centre of their actions. This, in turn, requires an education based on critical pedagogies, which in its content considers issues of gender, intersectionality and justice, and in its methods stimulates critical thinking and reflective practice (Tasan-Kok, 2016).

This chapter aims to contribute to efforts advocating a radical re-framing, transforming and de-colonising of current urban planning education (UPE) in two closely related regards: First, by conceptualising and practising urban planning as a networked field of governance rather than a single profession or discipline. Particularly in the context of cities of the Global South, professional planners are only one part of a wide network of urban practitioners, who are collectively and individually, formally and informally, building and shaping cities. Second, by articulating this wider understanding of planning practice to stimulate UPE within and beyond the higher education sector. This aligns closely with SDG 4—'Ensuring inclusive and equitable quality education and promoting lifelong learning opportunities for all' (United Nations, 2015)—which advocates broadening up the understanding of a wide range of education forms. Therefore, this chapter understands UPE as inclusive of, but not limited to, higher education and

DOI: 10.4324/9781003178545-9

sees the building of capacities, skills and values of a range of urban practitioners as fundamental drivers of urban equality.

Despite momentum for change being created by the SDGs as well as the New Urban Agenda, research has shown that UPE paradoxically remains itself as one of the drivers producing and reproducing urban inequality (MacDonald et al., 2014). This manifests in inequalities in access to UPE itself, as well as others reproduced through its contents and pedagogical approaches (Allen et al., 2018). In other words, de-colonising planning involves addressing both inequalities within the political economy of higher education institutions in UPE, and the blind spots reinforced through outdated colonial curricula that render 'formal' planning as the main process responsible for building cities across the Global South, while ignoring the role and struggles of 'informal' city-makers.

Previous investigations on cities of the Global South have identified several shortfalls in current planning education. These include distributive inequalities and large quantitative deficits in the availability of, and access to, planning education. For example, a report by the Asian Development Bank highlights that India had only an estimated 5,000 registered planners, which suggests a severe shortage of professional capacity considering that already by 2011 there were 377 million people living in about 8,000 urban centres (Revi et al., 2012). Acknowledging current shortfalls and estimated rates of urbanisation in India, the Committee of Experts in Town Planning and Architecture for Policy on Education estimates a demand for educating 8,000 planners per year in the run to 2035 (South Asia Urban Knowledge Hub, 2015). Compounded with this challenge, come praxeological shortfalls and epistemological inequalities, which manifest in the teaching of planning as development control with a largely technical and modernistic focus that fails to consider the wider political economy and ecology of contemporary urban change (Tasan-Kok, 2016). In many parts of the world, planning curricula continue teaching colonial approaches, without recognising everyday planning practices in the way cities are built and managed (Odendaal, 2012; Kunzmann, 2015). Bhan (2019), for example, critiques that many planning and urbanism curricula transmit knowledge about simplistic tools and solutions, rather than building the capacity of urban practitioners to work with the messy modes of repair and auto-construction that are essential to Southern urban practices.

In this chapter, we seek to deepen the understanding of the relations between UPE and urban inequality, following a three-dimensional conceptualisation of urban justice and equality which has been developed by Fraser (1998, 2005) and adopted for higher education by Walker and Unterhalter (2007). The first dimension concerns distributive equality, which has been the most dominant, resourcist approach to measuring, for example, access to education, number of graduates or student-teacher ratios across different social categories. Taken alone, distributive equality often overlooks the contextual factors that shape the learning outcomes of different individuals and groups. Therefore, it is paramount to complement calls for re-distribution together with those for reciprocal recognition, thus, scrutinising the ways in which planning education either challenges or reinforces politics of difference. The third dimension, parity of political participation, is essential for opening up the political space for learners to activate their agency and utilise their capacities. This requires working towards an equality of capabilities, whereby addressing power relations is fundamental to entitle learners to translate their learning into reflective action with a justice-oriented intent (Walker, 2006).

The following sections examine higher education and distributional inequality in UPE as entry points to identify levers and barriers for re-framing planning education. Aligned with the notion of planning as a networked field of governance, which demands radical change at scale, we focus on the role of planning education networks, which are umbrella associations that link different schools in the field worldwide. The analysis is based on a literature review and online repositories of national, regional and global planning education and professional planner's associations.

Secondary data from these networks were used to develop a series of maps, which, in turn, served as an input for interrogating issues of urban inequalities in 19 semi-structured interviews. These were held between November 2018 and March 2019 with planning educators from Latin America (2), Asia (7) and Africa (4), as well as UK- and US-based ones (6), all with several decades of experience working in the Global South. In addition, several interviewees are active participants in planning education associations and work in close collaboration with governmental and civil society organisations (CSOs).

A critical reading of maps involves examining not just the geographical distribution of UPE schools but also the broader context of what and who is being recognised and made visible and in what ways (Lambert & Allen, 2017). In other words, the reasons and implications of absences and presences in planning education networks are highly contextual and are therefore best interpreted through consideration of the historical, political, socio-economic and cultural conditions that shape UPE in specific geographies.

Networks in Higher Education and Urban Planning

Previous research has found several motivations for the emergence of planning education networks, which include forging connections between and across schools, establishing a professional profile and signalling key historical junctures in the development of planning as a networked field of governance (Kunzmann, 1999). The decision for forming the Association of African Planning Schools (AAPS), for example, was strongly influenced by the idea of re-connecting planning schools across the region in a post-apartheid and post-colonial context (Watson & Odendaal, 2013). Moreover, the initiative recognised the shared institutional, legal and pedagogic challenges faced by many African cities and the urgent need to collaboratively develop more radical curricula and pedagogies to equip learners with the capacities required to address such challenges (Odendaal, 2012).

The benefits of connecting with other members and regional and global networks are manifold, with the potential to enhance resources, recognition, visibility and alliances. Resources include funding for projects and activities and publications, databases and other sources of information. In the case of the

AAPS, a project called 'Revitalizing Planning Education in Africa' was implemented in 2009 with funding from the Rockefeller Foundation. The project produced, amongst other outputs, a post-graduate curriculum framework, which was co-developed at an AAPS meeting in Dar es Salaam in 2010 (Odendaal & Watson, 2018). With support from the AAPS, this framework has been contextually appropriated and formally established as an MSc in Spatial Planning at the University of Zambia in Lusaka. Considering that only one other available planning degree exists in Zambia, this initiative is an essential step to form a new generation of urban practitioners through innovative pedagogies that bridge practice and theory (Interview 2, January 31, 2019).

Moreover, the AAPS network was essential to share the above experience regionally, which provided opportunities for learning and exchange across other cities and universities (Interview 1, January 9, 2019). Associations are critical in facilitating translocal knowledge exchange, either across schools facing similar urban planning issues or through the exposure to new and unfamiliar situations. These take the form of visiting scholarships, collaborative workshops and professional training courses. Further, regular conferences provide critical moments for networking among members and for sharing and discussing knowledge with wider audiences (Galland & Elinbaum, 2018). Regional and global conferences, such as the World Planning School Congresses, along with related publications, including the book series *Dialogues in Urban and Regional Planning* and the *Journal of Planning Education and Research*, and special issues like the *diSP Planning Review 2018*, have raised the visibility and recognition of ongoing efforts to transform UPE across networks and the wider (academic) field of planning.

In the following section, we read the presence of planning education associations and their members as a proxy indicator for the potential benefits outlined in this section, while examining the implications for de-colonising UPE and for building the capabilities of urban practitioners to address urban equality. However, the focus on potential benefits does not mean that we see networks of urban learning and practice uncritically. We assume that these networks are fundamental to achieve change at scale based on experiences from urban poor federations like Shack/Slum Dwellers International (SDI), or grassroots activist networks like the Habitat International Coalition (HIC), which have a rich history and tradition of learning the city. For example, SDI's horizontal learning exchanges represent an important methodology for members to learn about each other's programmes and processes. Moreover, sharing knowledge across the network also strengthens political advocacy and changing relations between the state and CSOs through counterhegemonic approaches to advance habitat rights (Bradlow, 2015; Allen et al., 2020). However, previous research has already identified that in some instances collaboration with dominant actors might potentially put these networks at risk of replicating, rather than transforming existing rationalities of governmentality (Roy, 2009). Complementary to those tensions and opportunities in grassroots networks, we see a need for interrogating more conventional networks of UPE to scope their potential benefits for planners to learn within these networks as well as across them.

Reading the Geography of UPE Associations

Several reports commissioned by the Commonwealth Association of Planners (CAP), UN-Habitat and different regional planning education associations have aimed at benchmarking the distribution of UPE at the regional and global scale and in relation to network memberships. A global study by UN-Habitat (2009) argues that the major challenge for UPE does not lie in absolute numbers of planning students, graduates and schools, but in the maldistribution of planning schools across and within different regions. Of the 550 identified planning schools worldwide in 2009, 320 were located in 10 countries. The report reveals that 53% of these planning schools were located in the Global North, a region hosting 20% of the world's population (UN-Habitat, 2009). In terms of networks in many countries of the Global South, low-regional network membership coupled with a substantial number of schools that do not operate under an accreditation system is seen as explaining the relative isolation of academic staff and limited opportunities to share and exchange curricula and pedagogic practices (Stiftel, 2009).

Using openly accessible membership data by the Global Planning Education Association Network (GPEAN), we have updated existing baseline information on UPE schools and their geographical distribution based on associations websites. GPEAN emerged after the first World Planning Schools Congress in 2001 in Shanghai, China. It was formed by several regional planning school associations, which recognised the need for a global umbrella organisation that brings together national as well as (cross-)regional planning schools. GPEAN comprises the following associations:

- Association of African Planning Schools (AAPS; 57 member schools, 18 countries). AAPS was founded in 1999 as a voluntary peer-to-peer network of tertiary education institutions across Africa.
- Association of Collegiate Schools of Planning (ACSP; 132 members, 5 countries). ACSP was established in 1969 with a clear mandate to shape pedagogic theory and practice for planning professionals.
- Association of European Schools of Planning (AESOP; 160 member schools, 39 countries). AESOP emerged in 1987, motivated to create a forum of exchange similar to the previously established ACSP.
- Australian and New Zealand Association of Planning Schools (ANZAPS; 25 member schools, 2 countries). ANZAPS represents planning schools and educators; its main activities are annual conferences, which have been organised since 1994.
- International Association for the Promotion of Learning and Research of Urban Planning (APERAU; 35 member schools, 6 countries). APERAU was founded in 1984 with an explicit multidisciplinary discourse on planning.
- Asian Planning Schools Association (APSA; 52 member schools, 14 countries). APSA focuses on the particularly Asian planning education challenges and organises major regional congresses since 1991.
- Association of Latin American Schools of Urbanism and Planning (ALEUP; 15 members, 4 countries). ALEUP was founded in 1999 as regional platform

which supports the legitimisation of undergraduate degrees in urbanism and planning.
- Association of Canadian University Planning Program (ACUPP; 18 members, 1 country). ACUPP started in 1977, focusing on the relations between planning education, research and practice.
- National Association of Postgraduate Studies and Research in Urban and Regional Planning (ANPUR; 78 members, 1 country). ANPUR has rapidly expanded in Brazil since its foundation in 1983 and brings together schools in regional and urban planning.
- Association of Schools of Planning in Indonesia (ASPI; 59 members, 1 country). ASPI was established in 2000 with a particularly explicit agenda to align planning education with the goal of welfare production in the Indonesian society.
- Association of Planning Schools of Turkey (TUPOB; 19 members, 1 country). As a national organisation, TUPOB was founded in 2004 by Heads of Planning Schools and the Chamber of City Planners, in response to demands for quality assurance in education as well as professional qualifications.

As of October 2018, we identified 650 higher education institutions, which are members of the GPEAN in 80 countries. With 389 of them based in the Global North (Australia, Canada, Europe, New Zealand and the US), and 261 located in Africa, Asia, the Middle East and Latin America and the Caribbean. These schools are part of different higher education institutions (including polytechnics), and include fields such as urban planning, regional planning, urbanism and development. Their distribution is mapped in Figure 6.1.

An interrogation of the global distribution of GPEAN members reveals five main trends, which host explanatory power for distributive, recognitional and participatory equality. These trends concern: geographic density and gaps; capital cities; language; post-colonial networks; and the existence of alternative networks, including other (higher) education networks and professional planner's organisations.

Geographic Density and Gaps

Figure 6.1 indicates that national and regional planning education associations have relatively and absolutely more members in the Global North and BRICS countries (excluding Russia). However, there are some countries in the Global South, which seem exceptionally well-represented. This applies to Indonesia (59 members), as well as Nigeria (9 members of the AAPS) and small states covered by the Commonwealth (St. Lucia, Trinidad and Tobago, Belize and Brunei). On the other hand, the map also reveals large gaps in associations in the Middle East, North-West and Central Africa, as well as Eastern Europe. The latter gap has been acknowledged by the European association AESOP, with devoted efforts to recruit schools from countries such as Ukraine, Latvia and Russia. However, these efforts had only limited success, identifying costs and language as major barriers to membership acquisition and to obtaining the expected benefits (Frank

De-Colonising Planning Education   **109**

FIGURE 6.1 Location of the members of the GPEAN. Note that TUPOB, ALEUP and ASPI are not included in this map for reasons of legibility.

Source: Authors.

et al., 2014). Other requirements for becoming a member—such as having national accreditation as a planning education school—also hinder the incorporation of potential members.

There are several cautions to reading the geographic distribution of this map in isolation. These include that membership is voluntary, hence, does not reflect the entirety of schools in any region. Further, as will be explored below, alternative networks might exist which provide similar benefits to planning schools. Finally, it is important to emphasise that the distribution of members does not indicate the scale and scope of activities of the network. Even if structures are in place, networking and collaborative research activities are strongly shaped by funding resources to support, for example, travel exchanges and sustained communication. An interviewee from the Brazilian association ANPUR, for example, highlighted that following the abolition of the Ministry of Cities and reduced national funding for universities, the network re-focused its work to seek stronger alliances with social movements rather than government authorities (Interview 4, February 11, 2019).

Capital Cities

Most member organisations are located in urban centres, although many schools are also responsible for regional and rural planning. The map shows higher concentrations of associations in coastal cities, which coincide with large urban areas and ports. This is particularly obvious in Brazil, but also in cities such as Lagos (Nigeria), Dar es Salaam (Tanzania), Cape Town (South Africa), Karachi (Pakistan), Accra (Ghana) and Sydney (Australia).

Out of the 650 GPEAN members, about one-sixth (102) are located in capital cities, while 23 countries do not have any member planning schools outside of their capitals. This can either be attributed to highly centralised planning systems, or explained by the fact that many countries face an overall high quantitative deficit of planning schools with only one member school in the country (e.g. Uganda, Ethiopia). There are only few exceptions, such as Bangladesh and Malawi, where member organisations are, respectively, based in Khulna and Blantyre, rather than in their capital cities. However, as highlighted by an interviewee from Mexico, particularly in decentralised countries of Latin America, planning schools may have started from the capital city but are now more distributed across the country (Interview 8, January 28, 2019). In Mexico, this is reflected in their approach to 'territorial' (rather than urban) and human settlements planning.

Language

Examples of the importance of language as a boundary to regional and inter-regional networking manifest in Latin America through the division between ALEUP (Spanish-speaking) and ANPUR (Portuguese-speaking). Similarly, only five of the 57 member schools of the AAPS are located in countries that are not de jure anglophone. These are two universities in Mozambique, one in

Togo, one in Morocco and one in Ethiopia (albeit the latter can be considered de facto anglophone). APERAU is the only network explicitly positioning itself as francophone UPE network. It links members across Europe and North Africa and Canada, and forms part and receives funding from the wider network of francophone universities (L'Agence Universitaire de la Francophonie).

At the global level, however, English remains the dominant language in network conferences as well as academic publications, among other exchange means. In the context of Latin America, Galland and Elinbaum (2018, p. 51) note that some academics carry "a (well-founded) prejudice against the top-indexed Anglo-Saxon journals that arguably attempt to impose their problems and methods on southern countries." The authors see Spanish journals such as Colombia's *Bitácora*, *Cuadernos de Geografía*, *Cuadernos de Vivienda y Urbanismo* and Chile's *EURE* and *Revista INVI* as fundamental structures for alternative knowledge dissemination and exchange (Galland & Elinbaum, 2018). Further, many members deliver planning education in English while planning practice takes place in local languages. In India, local planning practice and academic research have to be transmitted between English and the country's 21 other official languages (Kunzmann, 2015).

Post-Colonial Networks

Evidently, questions of language cannot be detached from strong colonial influences on UPE, which take on different shapes in a post-colonial context. For example, of the 109 members in regional Asian and African Associations (AAPS and APSA), more than half (62) belong to nations of the Commonwealth; of a total 135 members of APSA, AAPS and AESOP (outside Europe and the UK), 84 are former British colonies or protectorates.

In the case of Commonwealth nations, this has several implications for linking planning education and planning professionals. The CAP, which represents about 40,000 planners in 27 countries, commissioned a report to review capacity building and planning education across the different regions of the Commonwealth (Levy, Mattingly, & Wakely, 2011). Considering distributive equality, this study found an overall quantitative deficit and severe mismatches between the locations of schools and locations experiencing rapid urban demographic growth, growing inequality and the urbanisation of poverty. Further, the report welcomes the increasing formation of regional and international networks; however, it sees scope for improvement particularly in regard to strengthening the capacities of cross-continental, global networks. This strengthening of cross-regional networks and the simultaneous critical interrogation of colonial legacies becomes particularly crucial considering the continued dominance of Western curricula.

Alternative Networks

Levy et al. (2011) also highlight the importance of considering the different ways in which 'urban planning' is conceptualised in each region. These can, for example, reflect inherited planning concepts, such as mainstream interpretations of 'territorial development' and 'urbanism' in the Latin American and French traditions. One interviewee, with vast working experience in Africa and Asia, reflected comparatively on the manifestation of colonial legacies across the Global South:

> For me, what was always interesting about the Latin American context is that it was free of the British colonial history that was the huge imprint on the planning that I worked with in Africa and Asia. And at the same time, planning was very late in the Latin American context where you had any kind of legal framing of planning as an activity…whereas in African and Asian cities this statutory basis for planning was part of a colonial heritage. So, it created a completely different dynamic and also therefore a different planning education that emerged.
> *(Interview P1, November 21, 2018)*

When looking at the distribution of planning networks, it is therefore relevant to ask what institutions are identified as planning schools, and consequently, which ones might see benefits in affiliating themselves with certain networks. In Latin America, the Brazilian network ANPUR has strong representation across the country, bringing together about 70 post-graduate programmes in disciplines such as geography and economics, urban and regional planning (Interview 4, February 11, 2019). Comparatively smaller seems the regional network ALEUP, which only represents 15 members in four countries. However, there is an alternative regional network, which is not part of GPEAN: the Network of Postgraduate Studies from the Latin American Council of Social Sciences (CLACSO). This network offers 101 Master and Doctoral degrees across 60 institutions in 17 Latin American countries (plus Spain and Portugal) in disciplines related to urbanism and territorial development (see Figure 6.2). It fulfils similar functions to the GPEAN members, such as organising regional conferences and providing space for knowledge exchange about urban planning pedagogies. While these functions do not necessarily explain CLACSO's absence in GPEAN, an analysis of alternative networks shows that gaps in the map of regional GPEAN associations can have several reasons and implications.

Similar to CLACSO, alternative networks have a prominent role in larger nations such as China. China has only eight members in APSA, which hardly represents the hundreds of UPE programmes offered by engineering, architecture and geography schools. In the Chinese context, planning education has become increasingly demanded and well-regarded particularly since the early 2000s, due to the boom of the urban economy and increased search for urban competitiveness (Hou, 2018). Rather than becoming part of global networks, Chinese planning education organisations seem to focus their networking on two other levels. On the one hand, strong bilateral relationships between Chinese and anglophone universities in the Global North are emerging, which are manifested, for example, in the joint venture of the Xi'an Jiatong–Liverpool University. On the other hand, national-level networks are particularly strong between planning education and professional practice, as evidenced in the close

FIGURE 6.2 Members of the Latin American networks ANPUR (black), ALEUP (grey) and CLACSO (white).
Source: Authors.

collaboration between academic institutions, the government's visions of urban planning and its role for the market and industry (Hou, 2018).

Finally, it is also important to consider the increasing role of digital networks, which allow for fluid interactions and collaborations across urban practitioners and pedagogues. The web-based SDG academy, for example, provides access to a wide range of Massive Open Online Courses (MOOCs), which are taught by academic faculty as well as NGOs, CSOs and government officials. Moreover, the potential of MOOCs and digital tools to target groups who are not part of localised networks is becoming increasingly popular. The large scale and wide reach of these digital networks, and their simultaneous ability to respond to specific contexts as well as wider principles open new avenues to re-dress inequalities in access to UPE.

Networking (Higher) Education Institutions

Investigating the work of GPEAN members reveals that UPE is delivered across a range of academic disciplines. While planning has institutionally established itself in some contexts in the form of departments or faculties, many members are hosted in geography, engineering, architecture, environmental studies, urban studies, law, development studies, public policy, political science, economics, sociology, anthropology and other social sciences. In Brazil, for example, urban planning is to a large extent taught in postgraduate degrees, as undergraduate students demand to study a 'recognised profession' in order to find employment, especially in the public sector. Hence, students often prefer the above-mentioned disciplines for their first degrees, and opt for urban planning as a postgraduate specialisation (Interview 4, March 11, 2019). The multitude of pathways to urban practice has challenged many planning schools in their aims to form and strengthen a distinct profession at national, regional and global scales (Kunzmann, 1999). Nevertheless, many academics welcome the interdisciplinary diversity and flexibility of planning education approaches reflecting the contextually specific challenges and institutional structures they emerge from (Davoudi & Pendlebury, 2010; Bertolini et al., 2012). Essentially, this aligns with long-standing calls for planning to identify its core in a more dynamic way, which does not wait for planning to be redefined every decade (Sandercock, 1999).

Professional Accreditation

The difficulties in grasping the professional identity of planners and planning education due to the variety of disciplines involved are frequently discussed in reference to the accreditation of planning schools and professional planners. The implications for equality are ambiguous: on the one hand, international accreditation systems have been critiqued for operating as gatekeepers that are not sufficiently contextualised and tend to replicate Western ideas of planning, which, moreover, risk duplicating or side-lining existing national accreditation processes. On the other hand, contextualised accreditation has been lauded for providing quality assurance and accountability, for facilitating access to government funding and resources and for enabling knowledge exchange and collaborations within networks of professional planners and schools (UN-Habitat, 2009). However, there is a delicate balance to achieve, as national accreditation bodies are also feared to control and limit explorations and creativity in planning education, while lack of international accreditation might leave schools unable to demonstrate their quality and transferability of degrees (Levy et al., 2011).

The Indian Institute of Town Planners is an example of nationally contextualised accreditation. It recognises formal degrees as well as work-study programmes, which reflect the reality of on-the-job education and professional training, as important modes of learning. Work-study programmes imply that people working in certified planning offices need to follow a programme of self-managed updates and undertake a certain amount of work experience in order to become professionally certified.

De-Colonising Planning Education 115

To tease out issues of accreditation and their assumed relations with the recognition, resourcing and visibility of planning schools, we contrasted the GPEAN map with those of planning education organisations identified by the International Society of City and Regional Planners (ISOCARP). The following map includes 564 planning education organisations based on the ISOCARP database, compiled by the University of Oregon (see Figure 6.3). The organisations were registered by database managers with basic information such as websites, key contact details and affiliation with professional and educational bodies, which includes GPEAN regional associations. The ISOCARP registration does require any formal accreditation process, which means that the network includes a wider range of universities as well as a small number of educational institutions outside higher education.

The comprehensiveness and validity of the ISOCARP data has to be viewed with caution; however, it is notable that 212 of the 564 educational institutions, which have been part of the database by October 2018, did not register any affiliation with one or more of the regional planning education associations of the previous GPEAN map. What this suggests is, first, that reframing planning education for urban equality at scale requires an engagement with educational institutions beyond those formally accredited or recognised by regional and global networks. Second, the ISOCARP network might indicate the motivation of institutions to affiliate themselves with cross-regional, global networks (and their potential benefits mentioned before), aspects somehow hindered by accreditation requirements. Third, compared to the GPEAN map, the ISOCARP map seems geographically wider distributed, as it fills some of the gaps in Eastern Europe, Latin America and South Asia that became apparent in Figure 6.1. However, although accreditation and gaining recognition might play a role in the ability to network, geographical gaps in

FIGURE 6.3 Distribution of 564 self-registered educational planning institutions.
Source: Authors.

parts of Asia, the Middle East and North-West Africa in Figure 6.3 indicate gaps in capturing the full body of organisations actively engaged in UPE across the world.

Bridging Professional and Educational Associations

What remains less clear in Figures 6.1 and 6.3 is the extent of articulation across higher education networks and other forms of education, as well as between higher education, professional and insurgent planning practices. For example, the two aforementioned maps do not capture ongoing engagements between universities and networks of grassroots organisations, such as collaborations between the AAPS, SDI and Women in Informal Employment —Globalizing and Organizing (WIEGO) through case- and field-study-based pedagogies (Odendaal & Watson, 2018). The specific rules and mechanisms of these engagements vary widely, with some collaborations facilitating frequent studio-based workshops over the period of a term and with others implemented over intensive international fieldwork and knowledge exchanges.

Overall, these kinds of collaboration reflect an increase in co-learning approaches of academics, students, civil society and grassroots-based organisations, which have been lauded for their potential learning outcomes to provide planning students with more grounded capacities and sensibilities to address urban inequalities (Allen, Lambert & Yap, 2018). As such, co-learning falls within a long-ongoing shift from traditional education that unidirectionally sees to 'fill' students with professional skills and competences, towards learning—as technical, analytical, inter-cultural, ecological and design literacies (Sandercock, 1999). Pedagogies for building these literacies often engage with practices of insurgent planning and claim new spaces of participation (Miraftab, 2016; Porter et al., 2017). They thereby contribute to disrupting the normalised order of planning and destabilising implicit hierarchies of knowledge between the wide range of urban practitioners and planning professionals. However, these pedagogic efforts are still to be applied at the scale required to challenge urban inequalities worldwide.

Beyond the aforementioned efforts, many civil society and grassroots networks are themselves critical actors and learning networks outside of higher education. An example of this is the experience of Habitat International Coalition—Latin America (HIC-AL), which has the explicit vocation to act as a 'School of Grassroots Urbanism' (*Escuela de Urbanismo Popular*) through multiple autonomous schools, in which network members collectively learn in action to make visible, defend and produce habitat rights (Wesely et al., 2021).

In addition to a deeper exploration of the generative pedagogies produced and enacted by civil society networks like HIC, there is a need for further investigating the links and interactions between professional and educational associations. For example, one interviewee, who is a practitioner in the US with vast experience in international planning education, remarked that throughout his career, he often found limited room to discuss what being a reflective practitioner means in mainstream planning conferences. While the interviewee acknowledged an increasing 'flow' from theory to practice, i.e., more practitioners

FIGURE 6.4 Distribution of EDUcational, FEDerations, GOVernment agencies, INStitutes, NGOs and PROfessional organisations.
Source: Authors based on ISOCARP.

receiving theory-informed higher education qualifications, he critiques that this flow remains largely unidirectional, with little practice-based theorising finding its way into education and planning curricula (Interview 5, February 14, 2019).

To start investigating the disjuncture between educational and practitioner networks, we mapped the geographical distribution of the ISOCARP database, which is covering professional and educational organisations, as it includes in total more than 1,800 planning agencies, associations, institutes, government ministries, NGOs and universities. Figure 6.4 is particularly interesting, as it shows planning organisations in many countries which are not covered by previous maps, such as Mongolia, Yemen, Senegal and many Pacific and Caribbean islands. Further, one-coloured circles highlight that in many countries only one type of planning organisation exists, implying locations where educational and practice institutions do not overlap. Further research is required to reveal the reasons and implications for urban equality in these countries, exploring, for instance, links to the increasing mobility and translocal learning flows across cities and institutions, i.e., where planners learn in contexts that are different to the ones where their practice is based.

Conclusion

This chapter aimed to contribute to decolonising and reframing UPE through an examination of the multiple geographies in which this wide field of thinking, learning and practice operates. We provided an analysis of the geographies of planning education networks through mapping and interviews, thereby raising interrelated concerns related to geographical density and gaps, language, colonial legacies, gaps between academia and planning practice, and the role of professional accreditation in either hindering or advancing planning approaches that talk to context-specific urban equality challenges.

What are the implications of the various geographies of the analysed global networks through which UPE manifests itself? What do the biases and omissions, absences and presences in the distribution of these maps tell us about UPE and its required re-invention to become an effective driver of justice? Returning to the tri-dimensional conceptualisation of urban equality advocated at the beginning of this chapter, we conclude by highlighting two key challenges that might help steering further analyses and pedagogic practice.

The first relates to the reciprocal recognition of the different actors in, and modes of, planning education. Higher education networks, for their benefits to members as well as their rapidly growing scale and reach, reveal potential to re-invent UPE at scale. However, their geographical gaps show that they can also reinforce rather than contest inequalities, especially in relation to membership barriers like accreditation standards and language differences between and within networks. These, among other factors, tend to reproduce certain centres of gravity and hegemonic relations within existing networks and constrain the recognition of the many modes and sites of learning within and beyond higher education. We identified several alternative networks as well as links between higher education and other (networked) urban practitioner organisations that are increasingly reshaping the landscape of UPE in collaborations with CSOs (as in the case of SDI and AAPS). What seems to be missing is a better recognition of the practices of alternative educational networks and their implications for urban equality. This includes exploring their articulation with formal higher education associations, and their actual and potential impact in de-colonising urban planning through a more inclusive mobilisation of ideas and practices that challenge the notion of planning as a single discipline.

Second, working towards equality of capabilities and using the notion of planning as a networked field of governance demands careful consideration of the power relations between member schools, affiliated and collaborating organisations, funders and other actors shaping UPE within the examined regional and global networks. These relations have so far been captured in research around increasing mobility and internationalisation of planning and higher education. An examination of issues like international accreditation and coloniality reveals an additional challenge in transforming UPE through UPE networks to work towards an equal recognition of capabilities. This implies avoiding the subordination of 'situated' learning processes and practices in specific localities to the often-presumed scalar authority and legitimacy of an increasingly global planning industry.

To sum up, more than ever in the past, we currently witness the emergence of UPE as a polycentric and networked field, with significant concerted efforts to transform the current shortcomings of planning to work towards SDG 11. But while distributive deficits have by far received more attention, it is worth noticing that what is required is not just an expanded geography for professional planning to be taught and accredited. More fundamentally, achieving transformations calls for variegated re-inventions of planning to flourish across the Global South and to be recognised with equal voice in forging critical epistemologies, pedagogies and practices. Planning education networks can play a key role in this endeavour but their scope for transformative change depends on whether they privilege the rescuing of discipline-producing professionals with certain competences, or to nurture the development of de-colonising knowledges and praxes to equip urban practitioners with the capabilities and sensibilities required to address urban inequality, both in its situated manifestations and in its structural drivers.

References

Allen, A., Cociña, C., and Wesely, J. (2020), "Habitat International Coalition: Networked practices, knowledges and pedagogies for translocal housing activism," *Radical Housing Journal* 2(2): 181–92.

Allen, A., Lambert, R., & Yap, C. (2018), "Co-learning the city: Towards a pedagogy of poly-learning and planning praxis," in V. Watson, G. Bhan, and S. Srinivas, eds. *Companion to planning in the global South* (pp. 355–67). London: Routledge.

Allen, A., Revi, A., Bhan, G., Sami, N., Anand, S., and Wesely, J. (2018), "Re-framing planning education for urban equality" (Unpublished Positioning Paper WP5-1, August 2018). London: Knowledge in Action for Urban Equality. Unpublished manuscript.

Bertolini, L., Frank, A., Grin, J., Bell, S., Scholl, B., Mattila, H., and Mäntysalo, R. (2012), "Introduction: Time to think," *Planning Theory and Practice* 13(3): 465–90. https://doi.org/10.1080/14649357.2012.704712

Bhan, G. (2019), "Notes on a Southern urban practice," *Environment and Urbanization* 1(2): 116–23. https://doi.org/10.1177/0956247818815792

Bradlow, B. H. (2015), "City learning from below: Urban poor federations and knowledge generation through transnational, horizontal exchange," *International Development Planning Review* 37(2): 129–42. https://doi.org/10.3828/idpr.2015.12

Davoudi, S., and Pendlebury, J. (2010), "Centenary paper: The evolution of planning as an academic discipline," *Town Planning Review* 81(6): 613–46. https://doi.org/10.3828/tpr.2010.24

Frank, A. I., Mironowicz, I., Lourenço, J., Franchini, T., Ache, P., Finka, M., and Grams, A. (2014), "Educating planners in Europe: A review of 21st century study programmes," *Progress in Planning* 91: 30–94. https://doi.org/10.1016/j.progress.2013.05.001

Fraser, N. (1998), "From redistribution to recognition? Dilemmas of justice in a 'post-socialist' age," in C. Willet, ed. *Theorising multiculturalism: A guide to the current debate* (pp. 19–49). Oxford and Malden, MA: Blackwell.

Fraser, N. (2005), "Reframing social justice in a globalizing world," *Anales de La Cátedra Francisco Suárez* 39: 89–105.

Galland, D., and Elinbaum, P. (2018), "A 'field' under construction: The state of planning in Latin America and the Southern turn in planning—Introduction to the special issue on Latin America," *DiSP–The Planning Review* 54(1): 18–24. https://doi.org/10.1080/02513625.2018.1454665

Hou, L. (2018) "Six decades of planning education in China: Those planned and unplanned," in A. I. Frank and C. Silver, eds. *Urban planning education: Beginnings, global movement and future prospects* (pp. 81–100). Cham: Springer.

Kunzmann, K. R. (1999), "Planning education in a globalized world," *European Planning Studies* 7(5): 549–55. https://doi.org/10.1080/09654319908720537

Kunzmann, K. R. (2015), "The state of the art of planning and planning education in Asia," *DisP–The Planning Review* 51(4): 42–51. https://doi.org/10.1080/02513625.2015.1134961

Lambert, R. and Allen, A. (2017), "Mapping the contradictions: An examination of the relationship between resilience and environmental justice," in A. Allen, L. Griffin, and C. Johnson, eds. *Environmental justice and urban resilience in the global South* (pp. 231–58). New York: Palgrave Macmillan.

Levy, C., Mattingly, M., and Wakely, P. (2011), *Commonwealth capacity building for planning: Review of planning education across the commonwealth*. Edinburgh: Commonwealth Secretariat.

MacDonald, K., Sanyal, B., Silver, M., Ng, M. K., Head, P., Williams, K., and Campbell, H. (2014), "Challenging theory: Changing practice—Critical perspectives on the past and potential of professional planning," *Planning Theory and Practice* 15(1): 95–122. https://doi.org/10.1080/14649357.2014.886801

Miraftab, F. (2016), "Insurgent planning: Situating radical planning in the global South," in S. Fainstein and J. DeFilippis, eds. *Readings in planning theory*, Fourth edition (pp. 480–97). Hoboken, NJ: John Wiley & Sons. https://doi.org/10.1002/9781119084679

Odendaal, N. (2012), "Reality check: Planning education in the African urban century," *Cities* 29(3), 174–82. https://doi.org/10.1016/j.cities.2011.10.001

Odendaal, N., and Watson, V. (2018), "Partnerships in planning education: The association of African planning schools (AAPS)," in A. Frank and C. Silver, eds. *Urban planning education: Beginnings, global movement and future prospects* (pp. 147–60). Cham: Springer.

Porter, L., Matunga, H., Viswanathan, L., Patrick, L., Walker, R., Sandercock, L., and Jojola, T. (2017), "Indigenous planning: From principles to practice," *Planning Theory and Practice* 18(4): 639–66. https://doi.org/10.1080/14649357.2017.1380961

Revi, A., Idicheria, C., Jain, G., Anand, G., Sudhira, H. S., Seddon, J., and Srinivasan, S. (2012), *Urban India 2011: Evidence*. Bangalore: Autumn Worldwide.

Roy, A. (2009), "Civic governmentality: The politics of inclusion in Beirut and Mumbai," *Antipode* 41(1): 159–79. https://doi.org/10.1111/j.1467-8330.2008.00660.x

Sandercock, L. (1999), "Expanding the 'language' of planning: A meditation on planning education for the twenty-first century," *European Planning Studies* 7(5): 533–44.

South Asia Urban Knowledge Hub. (2015), *Review paper of urban planning curricula of leading national planning schools*. New Delhi: South Asia Urban Knowledge Hub.

Stiftel, B. (2009), "Planning the paths of planning schools," *Australian Planner* 46(1): 38–47. https://doi.org/10.1080/07293682.2009.9995289

Tasan-Kok, T. (2016), "'Float like a butterfly, sting like a bee': Giving voice to planning practitioners," *Planning Theory and Practice* 17(4): 621–51. https://doi.org/10.1080/14649357.2016.1225711

United Nations. (2015), *Transforming our world: The 2030 agenda for sustainable development*. New York: UN-General Assembly.

UN-Habitat. (2009), *Global report on human settlements 2009: Planning sustainable cities*. London: UN-Habitat.

Walker, M. (2006), *Higher education pedagogies*. Maidenhead: Open University Press and The Society for Research into Higher Education.

Walker, M., and Unterhalter, E., eds. (2007), *Amartya Sen's capability approach and social justice in education*. New York: Palgrave Macmillan.

Watson, V., and Odendaal, N. (2013), "Changing planning education in Africa: The role of the association of African planning schools," *Journal of Planning Education and Research* 33(1): 96–107. https://doi.org/10.1177/0739456X12452308

Wesely, J., Allen, A., Zárate, L., and Emmanuelli, M. S. (2021). "Generative pedagogies from and for the social production of habitat: Learning from HIC-AL School of grassroots urbanism," *plaNext - next generation planning*. Online first (31 May 2021). https://doi.org/10.24306/plnxt/72

Chapter 7

TRANSFORMING PLANNING EDUCATION

Practicing Collaborative Governance and Experiential Learning in a Graduate Level Planning Studio[1]

Imge Akcakaya Waite, Elif Alkay and Sinem Becerik Altindis

Introduction

Several studies have emphasized the importance of building on an international perspective when dealing with local agendas in planning education (Zinn, Lyons, and Hinojosa, 1993; Teitz, 1996; Nijkamp & Kourtit, 2013; Wu, 2016). Central to debates in contemporary international planning are the questions of sustainability and sustainable development goals: the New Urban Agenda adopted at the United Nations Conference on Housing and Sustainable Urban Development (Habitat III) in 2016 represents a shared vision for a better and more sustainable future, declaring that urbanization, if well-planned and well-managed, can be a powerful tool for sustainable development in both developing and developed countries (The United Nations Conference Report, 2017). Here, the planning model—or paradigm—adopted is a key influence on the role of the planner, helping to define the form, content and function of plans and plan-making activities.

A critical comparison of international planning studio literature and planning studio education in Turkey reveals two main differences. For one, the dominant form of planning education in Turkey is chiefly associated with the rational comprehensive model of the Chicago school, whose traditional planning thought, and thus studio education, has evolved into more contemporary models and paradigms since the 1970s in western counterparts. This gap is critical for young Turkish planners faced with the challenge of keeping up with the most recent developments of contemporary planning models and integrating them into their practice, which they learn primarily through studio experience. Second, while studio teaching methods have been evolving internationally, thanks to progressive planning studios that incorporate new pedagogical approaches to real-life planning problems, Turkish planning studios have been more reticent to try new teaching methods, perhaps as a continuation of their stance on traditional theory.

DOI: 10.4324/9781003178545-10

More recent and practice-oriented approaches seem to be better aligned with today's millennial students, who demand to be in the thick of planning issues and planning sites in order to fully understand and dedicate themselves to the task at hand. The planning studio is no longer a task to be carried out mostly inside the studio and through desk or jury criticisms alone; it requires students to be on site continuously, interacting with the stakeholders affected by the planning decisions that the student has a significant role in making. This study argues that the resulting need to close these two gaps calls for a fundamental change in the Turkish planning studio curriculum that addresses concurrently the planning paradigm and learning methods. It examines this recommendation through a review of a recent attempt to address the gaps: a two-semester graduate-level planning studio experience from Istanbul Technical University (ITU).

A Critical Look at the Planning Studio in Turkey

The first urban and regional planning department in Turkey was established at Middle East Technical University in 1962. As more planning departments were founded at different universities in late 1970s and early 1980s, the planning education they have provided grew to have a pervasive impact on the Turkish planning discipline and urban planning practice. To this day, planning departments are located in schools of architecture, engineering and design, with education modules focused on creating livable cities (TUPOB, 2007).

Because urban planning developed under the discipline of architecture, planning education has focused on physical design rather than spatial solutions that might alleviate socio-economic problems (Keleş, 1987; Ersoy, 2007; Köroğlu, 2011), which conflicts with the interdisciplinary aspects of planning studies. The educational process has called for the inclusion of basic conceptual issues such as urbanization and urban models and practical issues like visual studies, zoning and urban design into planning studios, which have been at the forefront of planning education in terms of the synthesis of practical experience and theoretical information (Ersoy, 2007; Günay, 2007; Erdoğan, 2018). However, as Köroğlu (2011) discusses, the structure of the resulting planning studios brings, among others, four obvious problems: they (1) do not create a strong bridge between studio education and theoretical courses, which can lead to an understanding of theory and space as isolated; (2) do not provide theoretical and methodological basis for decision-making processes in planning; (3) focus on hierarchical and linear causality and scales rather than thematic spatial solutions and (4) expect the students to develop city-wide physical plans through desk or jury criticisms alone, rather than on-site observations and user perspectives. The last point in particular results in concerns about the promotion of individualistic and exclusive planning approaches, the elimination of environmental concerns and local values, social and economic aspects, and an ignorance towards responsive, participatory and inclusive planning practices. Along these lines, a critical comparison of the international planning studio literature and planning studio education at ITU reveals significant differences in the planning approach taken and the conventional teaching methods followed in-studio education.

Early planning education at ITU adopted the survey-analysis-plan process of the Chicago school's rational comprehensive model while emphasizing the city and the preparation of a plan intended to control the future of the city. Because this approach considered the physical dimension of the city overrated, neither the policy perspective nor an inclusive planning process was internalized as an integral part of planning studio education. In the following decades, this understanding resulted in a deficiency in theoretical underpinning and creativity in urban studies and planning, while also failing to impart an international perspective to education and prepare students to practice effectively in a variety of contexts around the world. Discussions of the spatial aspects of sustainability and new urban forms, as well as topics such as community development, citizen participation, responsive local design, conservation of space, more attractive living environments and conflict resolution, have hardly made their way into planning studio education. These deficiencies are critical for young Turkish planners faced with the challenge of keeping up with the most recent developments of contemporary planning models and integrating them into their practice, skills which they should learn primarily through studio experience.

The criticisms above, as well as ongoing academic research in the department and experiences in studio education over the years, have sufficiently proven the necessity of a structural transformation in planning studio education. The tendency so far has been to follow the current global planning and urban agenda and structural reforms in Turkish planning law and transform the approach to studio education from positivist to constructivist. This tendency, although a step in the right direction, has yet to become a consistent structural transformation.

Since reforming studio education is a challenging job, master's degree classes might provide a fertile ground for imparting momentum to this transformation because of their smaller class sizes and the independence of studio instructors in setting out more contemporary planning problems and applying new approaches and methods in the process. Although this contribution might seem small, the potential of these classes for opening a discussion ground for students who have sufficient academic knowledge of planning studies raising the bar in both master's study and planning practices, and creating a framework for undergraduate-level planning studio education is considerable. This study therefore focuses on a two-semester graduate-level studio experience from ITU, undertaken in the Urban Planning Master's Program during the 2018–19 academic year. We hope these efforts and experiences may foster and accelerate the movement of planning studios towards contemporary approaches in undergraduate education at local level and beyond it.

Departing from Conventional Studio Education

Planning education in ITU has been limited to defining and solving problems exclusively within the Turkish context; however, local planning problems have obvious global implications, and discussions about and solutions for such problems must take into account this larger scale. Accordingly, if planning education aims to train competent professionals who will be able to practice effectively as planners, it must include larger contemporary challenges. Such challenges include but are not limited to natural resource depletion, climate crisis, intensive urbanization, incentive structure under global competitiveness, government interventions in plans, societal transformation, the changing nature of space brought on by new information technology and pandemics and replacing an exclusive understanding of planning with an inclusive one and establishing the importance of public participation in the planning process.

In order to trigger a departure from conventional approaches and increase planning-related skills, planners must be able to use a variety of tools that are fostered by teaching methods and adapted to real-world settings and challenges. Students may gain experience in the application of these methods and the ability to make sense of new, uncertain or unique situations (Zinn et al., 1993). Thus, unlike the case that used to be at ITU and other planning schools in Turkey (for example see Erdoğan, 2011; Köroğlu, 2018), today's planning studio should foster students to be on site continuously, interacting with the stakeholders affected by planning decisions. Corburn (2003) emphasized that local knowledge gathered through the participation of the local community and other relevant stakeholders improves planning in at least four ways: it (1) adds to the knowledge base of environmental policy; (2) includes new and previously silenced voices; (3) provides low-cost policy solutions and (4) highlights inequitable distributions of environmental burdens. Accordingly, urban planning students need to learn new ways of incorporating the local knowledge embedded in the communities they work in. This, obviously, cannot happen in studio through desk studies. Contemporary planning methods—deliberative planning approaches rather than positivist ones—and their counterpart teaching methods—experiential learning (EL) rather than in studio teaching dominated by the instructor—seem to be a strong and supportive way to foster the professional abilities of planning students.

Collaborative Planning and Governance as an Alternative Paradigm

Healey's *Collaborative Planning* (1997) argued that the challenges of urban development in the neoliberal era could no longer be handled effectively by government alone but required the participation of all sectors of society in a form of planning that involved dialogue and negotiation among stakeholders seeking an actionable consensus (also see Friedmann, 2008). Consensus building among parties with conflicting interests, however, often requires the intervention of mediators, and so mediation became an important new branch not only for planning but for legal studies as well (LeBaron, 2002). Larry Susskind and John Forester have made key contributions to this new specialization, the first in a series of publications culminating in the book by Susskind, McKearnen, and Thomas-Lamar (1999), *The Consensus Building Handbook: A Comprehensive Guide* to *Reaching Agreement*, the second in Forester's *The Deliberative Practitioner: Encouraging Participatory Planning Processes* (1999). Other contributions to collaborative methods and consensus building as a mode of planning and policy-making in the last two decades include the works of Innes and Booher (1999), Sager (2002), and Ansell and Gash (2007). These scholars found that such processes could be creative and effective, offering planners substantial roles. Communicative, or collaborative, planning thus became a focus in planning theory.

Parallel to collaborative planning, most planning literature uses the term collaborative governance to describe a participatory relationship between public institutions and non-state stakeholders. For example, Reilly (2001) describes collaborative efforts as a type of problem-solving that involves the 'shared pursuit of government agencies and concerned citizens.' Smith (1998) argues that collaboration involves 'representation by key interest groups.' Connick and Innes (2003) define collaborative governance as including 'representatives of all relevant interests.' Such definitions set standards for the participation of non-state stakeholders, which makes collaborative governance never a merely consultative process. It is thus no surprise that in their collaborative governance model, developed through the analysis of 137 cases, Ansell and Gash (2007) define the features of their cyclical collaborative governance process as face-to-face dialogue, trust building, commitment to the process, shared understanding and intermediate outcomes.

EL in Planning Education

Much as collaborative planning and governance call for a strong pluralism and inclusion in undertaking planning affairs, planning education can be improved through the increased involvement of its main target group—students. EL serves this very purpose, corresponding well with collaborative planning by including not only students but also the stakeholders of the planning issue studied.

As the process of learning from experience, EL has been labeled and defined in various ways throughout its evolution. For instance, John Dewey (Dewey and Dewey, 1915) discussed "learning by doing," while Wolfe and Byrne (1975) used the term "experience-based learning." David Kolb (1994), who is extensively cited in the EL literature, defined the term as "the process whereby knowledge is created through the transformation of experience. Knowledge results from the combination of grasping and transforming experience" (p. 41). Here, Kolb reinforces the idea that reflecting on an experience can potentially result in a transformation.

Perhaps the most recent definition is offered by Beard and Wilson (2018), who stress the inner and outer world of the learner and the experience of learning. In their words, "learning through the outer world" (p. 3), more specifically real-life experiences, is now synonymous with terms such as fieldwork, applied learning, learning by doing, hands-on learning, problem-based learning and EL. The growing emphasis on this kind of learning in higher education is made clear by a simple keyword search through scholarly literature. Such definitions support Kolb's (1984) much-cited model, which challenges relevant past theories and reveals the complex nature of EL (Figure 7.1).

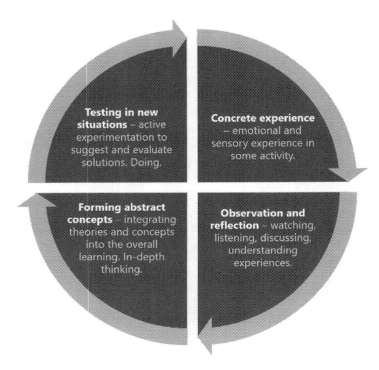

FIGURE 7.1 Kolb's experiential learning cycle.
Source: Adapted from Baldwin and Rosier (2017) and Kolb (1984).

Since the 1980s, inspired by Kolb's model, EL has attracted more attention in and entered into numerous education fields, including planning. Planning literature has demonstrated considerable interest in EL; for example, the *Journal of Planning Education and Research* released a special issue in 1998 dedicated to community outreach partnerships (Volume 17, Issue 4), which treats first-hand learning outside the four-walled classroom setting as central to the teaching of planning (Kotval, 2003).

In general, planning studios provide a quasi-real world situation not offered by classroom courses. They focus on planning-related tasks or issues that involve creative thinking and critical analysis to produce a practical solution or outcome (Higgins, Aitken-Rose, and Dixon, 2009). They offer students the opportunity to acquire skills managing other people, themselves and their time in addition to more abstract project details. They promote learning outcomes that focus on process, involving both individuals and groups, alongside the application of skills (Grant and Manuel, 1995). However, the complexity and uncertainty encountered in real-life situations cannot be duplicated in a traditional studio education (Roakes and Norris-Tirrell, 2000). When coupled with EL, planning studios can better delve into the legal, financial and collaborative challenges of actual planning cases—a point that was investigated through the case study outlined in this chapter.

Case Study Methodology

The case study explores the application of a select planning paradigm; collaborative planning and governance; and a teaching method, EL, in the conduct of a master-level planning studio. The empirical research that assessed the studio experience attempted (1) to reveal the extent to which the master-level students have or have not benefitted from select contemporary planning and teaching approaches, and (2) to derive lessons for improving the instruction and experience of this and other planning studios at ITU and beyond.

In order to reach these aims, the study utilized mixed methods in data collection and analysis. The studio process was analyzed through a review of the secondary data produced within the case studio experience, namely the two-semester syllabi and the maps, diagrams and reports produced by the students over the course of the studio (also see Waite, Alkay, and Becerik, 2019). Primary data was collected via a student course assessment survey and instruction notes. The anonymous survey was designed to reveal their perceptions of the planning approach and teaching method in question. More specifically, the survey guide included brief descriptive information about the students, followed by their assessments of the course plan design, studio activities, student performance and the impacts of the studio on their academic and professional competence.

Following the final submissions of the second semester, the survey was conducted with a total of 20 students, 18 of whom responded, which yielded a significant sample size with a 5% margin of error and at an 80% confidence interval. The quantitative data were analyzed through a number of statistical correlations and group mean comparisons through multiple choice questions and grids, while a content analysis was applied to the answers to open-ended survey questions. The qualitative analysis was reinforced by the structured observation notes compiled during the studio instructors' two-semester experience. The findings were then used to further assess and improve the impacts of the proposed approaches and methods through case-based recommendations derived for future planning studio practices in Turkey and the world, rather than the mere generalization of the study findings. As a final note, one possible research validity concern may arise from the different institutional backgrounds of the students who participated in the studio and the survey. In order to alleviate the risk of biased findings, substantial differences between undergraduate and graduate studios were reported, and where applicable, ITU graduates' responses were sequestered from those coming from other institutions.

Description of the Studio

The case studio undertook the decades old redevelopment problems of a multi-generational informal housing area in the dense Pınar neighborhood of the Sarıyer district, which primarily houses the modern CBD and is adjacent to the northern forests of Istanbul. Selected by the students, Pınar offered an interesting study area, with tangible and intangible site characteristics, intervention areas and pluralistic approaches. The studio aimed to make the best of these potentials, focusing on the planning of the neighborhood with a thorough organization of relevant stakeholders and their fair involvement in planning decisions so as to achieve successful and sustainable planning outcomes towards the betterment of the local public's well-being. The studio curriculum was planned as a two-semester process which included the two compulsory studio courses ITU's Urban Planning Master's students are required to take in the 2018–19 academic year: Project 1 and Project 2 (Table 7.1).

Collaborative approaches were embedded into the planning context through theoretical readings and a comprehensive review of relevant international cases, followed by a thematic analysis of the study area, including an advanced stakeholder analysis, and the production of models for physical, financial, participatory and collaborative plans and processes. Collaborative planning models were then advanced into collaborative governance models borrowed from the literature. These models were tested and further tailored through the criteria of community perception, risk—mainly conflict—management, good governance and legal compliance. The EL methods used to conduct the studio process involved, in addition to the more conventional desk criticisms and jury assessments, multiple structured site visits that included frequent communication with the municipality, surveys and semi-structured interviews with community members, focus groups with local stakeholders, jury assessments with municipality officials and a final feedback colloquium on site to communicate the refined planning models to the stakeholders and fine-tune planning decisions. Thanks to the more prominent attention given to theoretical background and planning models in Project 1, the use of EL methods was denser in Project 2.

In both semesters, students were expected to read, review and reflect on related literature while determining and solving the planning problems of the study area. They were provided with lists of relevant literature readings to steer their theoretical research. They worked in groups of four or five during and outside studio meetings to produce a planning study in an inherently collaborative process; they presented their work using written, oral and graphic expression techniques throughout the semesters. Studio meetings served to frame and review weekly topics, further off-studio production and allow for an inclusive discussion, thus enabling learning from different teams' work. This process was reinforced with a total of three jury meetings in which studio instructors and local municipality officials served as members of the jury. A more detailed description of the project process and outcomes with examples of student submissions can be found in a former study of the authors (Waite, Alkay, and Becerik, 2019).

TABLE 7.1 Weekly program and topics

Project 1		Project 2	
Weeks	Topics and deliverables	Weeks	Topics and deliverables
1	Introduction to the studio & logistics	1	Introduction to the studio & logistics
2–3	Site visit for analyses	2–3	Site visit for further analysis • Refining synthesis & assessments • Refining physical & financial plans
4–5	Stakeholder analysis & world cases with collaborative/participatory approaches	4–5	• Collective overview of world cases • Refining collaborative plans with input from literature
6–7	Assessments: Synthesis & problem areas	6–7	Collaborative governance model
8	Fall break	8	Spring break
9	1st JURY: Analyses & preliminary assessments	9	Focus group preparation workshop in studio
10–12	• Planning interventions & collaborative scenarios • Possible conflicts & their mediation • Policies for public interest and well-being	10–12	Focus group study with local stakeholders • Analyzing focus group study • Revisiting collaborative governance models • Possible model pitfalls and responses
13–14	Refining and concretizing proposed project model & policies	13–14	• "Good governance" in action • Implications for good governance in current Turkish governance legislation
15	2nd JURY: Revised analyses and assessments, planning interventions, collaborative approaches, consensus building scenarios, resulting project model and policies	15	FINAL JURY: Revised models with adaptive strategies and good governance inputs; refined policies for governance practices in Sarıyer and Istanbul, Turkey

Students' Perceptions

The survey sections designed to reveal the students' perceptions inquired about syllabus design and implementation, EL methods and their application, project activities, the students' individual and/or group performance inside and outside the studio and how and to what extent the studio impacted their academic and professional competence. The students' perceptions were derived over a 5-point Likert scale, through which they were asked to compare conventional undergraduate planning studios and the graduate case studios, and Project 1 and Project 2, as relevant to the section topics. The Likert scale ranged from −2 to 2, where −2 referred to highly favoring undergraduate or Project 1 experience, 2 referred to highly favoring graduate or Project 2 experience and 0 referred to a balanced view between the two experiences. The multiple choice grids, with Likert ranges of 'useful vs. not useful' and 'agree vs. disagree,' were analyzed similarly. Finally, all survey sections were complemented by open-ended questions to help students elaborate on their assessments and derive recommendations to improve future studio experiences.

Comparisons Based on Conventional vs. Case Studios, and Project 1 vs. Project 2

An analysis of the student survey reveals interesting findings when comparing the group means of the abovementioned survey sections. In all groups, the students favored graduate studios over undergraduate studios, and Project 2 over Project 1. The former finding explicitly demonstrates the students' preference for the alternative planning approach over what they had experienced in undergraduate studios, regardless of their undergraduate institution and the education they received, whether in different institutions and/or from different instructors. The latter finding can be explained by the fact that compared to Project 1, Project 2 concentrated more on critical planning through collaboration and governance rather than more global problem-solving approaches and involved a wider and more intense use of EL methods (e.g. on-site interviews, focus group study and the participatory colloquium).

A closer examination of the course plan design and implementation reveals that students found graduate studios' course plans more original, timely, coherent, instructive and consistent compared to those of the undergraduate studios they had taken (Table 7.2). In particular, they appreciated how the collaborative planning and governance literature provided by the instructors steered their studio work, and how the literature and the studio instruction encouraged them to research the relevant theory and practice. The students also found that the design and conduct of the studio enabled them to better receive and reflect on project feedback and reach initial studio objectives compared to their undergraduate experience. When assessing these and other relevant criteria to compare the two semesters, they had a more balanced view, only slightly favoring Project 2 over Project 1. One reason for this level of preference might have been due to a certain extent to the accumulation of knowledge and skills over Project 1, which enabled a more confident and deliberate studio experience in the second semester.

The cohort believed that the EL methods they practiced in Project 1 and Project 2 were highly useful, with all responses being placed in the first and second quartiles, while they favored Project 2 activities slightly more than Project 1 (Table 7.3). They viewed themselves as having particularly benefitted from the formal brief they received at the local municipality at the beginning of Project 1 and the jury assessments whose panels included informed municipality officials. Although they found structured surveys useful, the students thought semi-structured interviews proved to be more so, especially during Project 2, because they were better equipped with collaborative methods and able to interact with the local community more thoroughly. Among all the EL methods they

TABLE 7.2 Course plan assessment: Alternative (collaborative) planning approach

Category	Undergraduate vs. graduate	Project 1 vs. project 2
Course plan design	1.11	0.44
Originality/authenticity of studio topic	1.25	0.20
Actuality of studio topic and methods	1.5	0.10
Clarity of studio process	0.75	0.40
Clarity of methods used	0.56	0.00
Consistency of studio process flow	0.81	0.30
Introduction and guidance of relevant literature	1.63	0.70
Encouragement for theory and practice research	1.63	0.70
Enabling feedback and its reflections	1.19	0.60
Didactic quality	1.06	0.60
Contribution to professional knowledge and skills	0.69	0.80
Course plan undertaking	1.08	0.28
Announcement of a thorough and deductive course plan prior to semester (i.e. studio scope, process, conditions and evaluation criteria)	1.06	0.20
Conduct of studio according to the course plan	1.00	0.10
Coherence of weekly assignments to studio scope	1.06	0.10
Timely announcement of assignment/jury assessments	0.81	0.00
Attaining initially announced studio objectives	1.25	0.50
Coherence of studio activities to the studio scope	1.19	0.30
Conduct of project assessments in a positive atmosphere and with constructive methods	1.19	0.80

TABLE 7.3 Learning experience assessment: EL methods

Category	Project 1	Project 2
	(Useful vs. not useful)	
Stakeholder interaction methods	1.20	1.34
Structured site visit	1.10	1.00
Optional follow-up site visits	1.00	1.00
Municipality brief on site	1.45	N/A
Household/business/institution surveys	1.18	N/A
Semi-structured community interviews	1.18	1.72
Focus group with local stakeholders	N/A	1.83
Jury assessment with local municipality	1.09	1.50
Final feedback colloquium with local stakeholders	N/A	1.00

experienced, the students' favorite was the focus group study with local stakeholders. They had learned about the focus group method through an in-studio workshop and conducted it to discuss plans they had designed with the local community, businessmen and NGOs on site.

When asked to comparatively assess the EL activities of the project studios they had taken part in (e.g. site visits, local interactions, formal collaboration/ participation methods) based on the aims and insights defined in the extensive work of Baldwin and her colleagues (Baldwin et al., 2013), the students highly preferred graduate studio experiences over undergraduate, and Project 2 over Project 1, regarding the project activities as enabling community-university partnership (Table 7.4). This preference was followed by positive assessments of theory-practice dialectic and guided practice in the case studios, and better application of real-world context in Project 2.

Finally, the students were asked to evaluate the degree to which they felt competent professionally and academically based on their overall graduate studio experience. This group of questions yielded the highest mean (1.47) among the sections of the survey, with all responses belonging to the first two quartiles (Table 7.5). With reference to the Project 1 and Project 2 experiences, the students felt particularly stronger in two areas: grasping the theory on a given specific planning paradigm and constructing a case study on the relevant approaches, thus providing a two-way information between theory and practice; and interacting with and interpreting the views of the relevant stakeholders of the planning topic. They also felt confident in applying formal qualitative data collection and analysis methods to their planning research. All in all, the students strongly believed that they had gained adequate knowledge and skills in collaborative planning and collaborative governance topics, as well as EL methods and their application.

Some Correlations and Differences Regarding Comparative Perceptions and Subject Profiles

While the analysis of individual responses to the groups of questions yielded the findings referred to above, a comparison of the assessment/question groups over group mean correlations also points to a few notable findings (Figure 7.2). First,

TABLE 7.4 Learning experience/outcomes assessment: EL aims (based on Baldwin et al., 2013)

Category	Undergraduate vs. graduate	Project 1 vs. Project 2
Project activities	1.06	0.81
Purposefulness	0.88	0.20
Student-centeredness	1.00	0.60
Evaluation	0.88	0.40
Real-world context	1.00	1.40
Guided practice	1.27	0.40
Reflection	0.69	0.80
Theory-practice dialectic	1.31	1.10
Community-university partnership	1.63	1.60

Based on Baldwin et al. (2013).

TABLE 7.5 Overall course assessment: Post-studio competency

Category	Project 1 and / or Project 2
	(Agree vs. Disagree)
Professional and academic competency (*I have adequate knowledge and skills in…*)	1.47
…transferring theoretical knowledge into practice.	1.56
…transferring practice-related knowledge into theory.	1.13
…collaborative planning and governance.	1.56
…understanding different stakeholder experiences and conveying them into the planning process.	1.61
…designing and conducting a new case study.	1.56
…analyzing and modeling a new case study.	1.61
…using in-depth observation, interview and focus group methods in academic studies.	1.39
…defining, working with and collectively deciding with relevant actors in a given planning problem/topic.	1.61

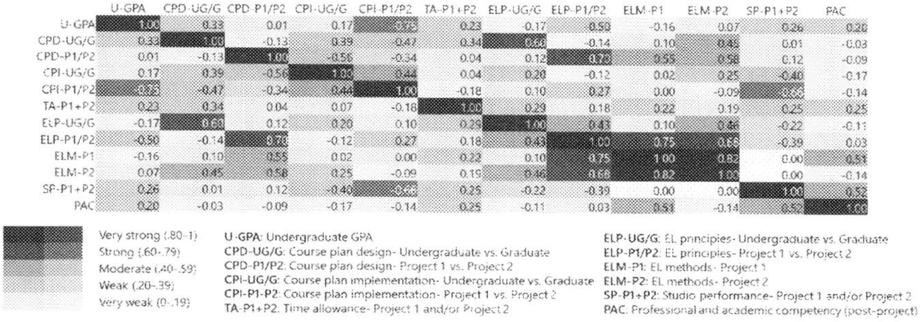

FIGURE 7.2 Group mean correlations.

a high positive correlation is observed between EL methods and EL principles, suggesting that these two features of EL supported each other throughout the studio process. The second highest set of positive correlations occurred between the graduate studios' course plan designs and meeting the EL goals and principles of the case studios, especially for Project 2. These direct positive relations are followed by the success of the EL methods and the perceived positive individual and group student performances in relation to the high post-studio competency the students felt. On the other hand, a strong negative correlation is observed between the undergraduate GPA of the students and their views on the implementation of the course plan, suggesting that those who had graduated from their undergraduate institutions with a low GPA found the application of the contemporary studio, in particular that of Project 2, more satisfactory. A similar correlation is evident between the studio performances and undertaking of the course plan; low individual and group student performance in the studio did not directly correlate to a lack of appreciation of the studio implementation, or vice versa. These and other correlations observed in the relevant table support the general argument of the study, which calls for the concurrent application of contemporary planning approaches and learning methods in planning studio education.

When searching for differences in perceptions based on student profiles or backgrounds derived from descriptive questions of the survey, the survey responses contained some interesting observations on group mean relations. Regarding the originality and clarity of the course plan design, both students who had a bachelor's degree from ITU and those who obtained one elsewhere were highly appreciative of the case studios, ITU students being on the even more positive side. Both groups favored the overall design and undertaking of the course plans at the graduate level, although ITU students were more decisive about their views.

On another note, the students who had had professional experience in planning-related fields in the public sector (e.g. ministries, municipalities, the planning department of the central government), private sector (e.g. planning, urban design and real estate firms), civil initiatives (i.e. relevant NGOs and groups at local or national level) and academia (i.e. universities and research institutes) showed considerable differences in course perceptions compared to those who had had non-planning-related or no professional experience. Although both groups favored case studios over undergraduate studios, the group with planning-related work experience found the case studios slightly less beneficial than undergraduate courses compared to those who did not have planning-related experience. Both groups found the collaboration and EL methods beneficial, while the group with prior planning experience appreciated learning and practicing these methods more than their counterpart.

Informed Recommendations to Improve the Studio Experience

Finally, the students' recommendations for improving the graduate studio experience, and thus future graduate studio designs, were centered around three tangible points. First, when there is an 'unconventional' planning paradigm at hand, theoretical discussions should carry more weight in the studio discussions in order to allow them to internalize the context, while at the same time preserving the main studio focus on practice. Second, local interactions should be expanded to a larger pool of stakeholders, both in type and in number, and to ensure gender and age balance. Third, from the course plan development to the participation methods chosen, studios should be designed to be as idiosyncratic to the case area as possible. These constructive points suggest that planning studios should be carefully designed prior to the semester to reflect the theoretical and practical structure of the course with first-hand experiences when approaching real-life planning problems. Overall, the students unanimously agreed that this innovative dual approach should be established as a new studio tradition and expanded into the undergraduate planning education as well.

Discussion: Some Implications Going ahead

The findings of the empirical research suggest that a collaboration- and governance-focused planning approach allowed the students to better keep up with and reflect on recent literature and debates. In fact, whichever planning paradigm is selected, it should reflect on the more recent debates in the planning literature rather than the conventional contexts. In this study, although the topic and problems of urban regeneration tackled in the Pınar neighborhood are rather traditional and not peculiar to Sarıyer but evident across Istanbul, Turkey, and even the world, the planning approach and its application are novel to Turkey. In this respect, this study provides an innovative alternative to the conventional planning mindset criticized, with positive outcomes reported by the students throughout the studio process, and by the local stakeholders during the post-studio colloquium in particular.

The studio experience should not rely merely on the implementation of the selected paradigm. Rather, there should be a balanced examination of both theory and practice, reinforced by literature-driven research. The lack of such an approach is a problem usually observed at the undergraduate and graduate levels. The collective studio teaching experience of the instructors demonstrates that students are by default inclined to overlook the theoretical readings assigned to them in order to merely focus on drawing plans; however, the case study suggests that when faced with an unconventional way of approaching a planning problem, the students find it more appealing to research and read the literature and start discussing alternative ways of reflecting theory into practice. In this respect, this study presents an important case for changing more archaic studio instruction.

More specifically, project site selection should be left to the students, if possible after the initial literature review on the paradigm fundamentals, so that the students have the liberty and motivation to work on sites they relate to the planning topic. Gathering and analysis of project data should be suited to the project topic and the planning issue at hand, focusing not merely on the physical aspects of the site, but also on its legal, financial, social and governance aspects. Contrary to the conventional studio approach, physical planning can be minimized depending on the planning issue. Finally, expecting model-based deliverables from students rather than maps has proven to be more successful in triggering more research and attention from the students as well as retrieving the expected outcomes of the studio.

In the case studios, the students were able to exercise the planning approach both inside and outside the studio: they experienced collaboration not only on site with different public, private and civil stakeholder groups, but also through close interactions between and among student groups. This approach also allowed for the in-depth investigation of the everyday issues faced by the local community in relation to power imbalances, legal dilemmas and political uncertainties. The students expressed strong positive learning outcomes from dealing closely with collaborative planning and governance topics in both theory and practice, highlighting the importance of such inclusive and interactive processes in building trust between planning practitioners and local actors. They learned first-hand that face-to-face dialogue goes beyond the developments of a site-based model and that the model itself is an inevitable necessity in connecting with real life. The EL methods employed, on the other hand, helped the planning studio live up to the corresponding principles reviewed in the EL literature. This compliance points at the relative success of the case studio when compared to more conventional studios in Turkey, which focus primarily on reflection and evaluation in the studio (Table 7.6).

Based on this final comparison and other implications discussed above, some tangible insights can be offered regarding the application of EL in planning studios as well. The following points build on Kotval's (2003) work to take on the insights she offers for teaching courses through EL in planning and allied disciplines:

- The importance and objectives of the planning studio at hand should be thoroughly understood and articulated not only by the faculty but by the students as well (in particular at the graduate level).

TABLE 7.6 Comparison of the conventional Turkish planning studios and the case studios in terms of EL principles and methods adopted (• indicating strong relevance; ○ indicating weak relevance; blank indicating no relevance)

	Conventional studios	Case studios
EL principles		
Purposeful	○	•
Student-centered	○	•
Theory-practice dialectic		•
Real-world context	○	•
Guided practice	○	•
Reflection	•	•
Evaluation	•	•
Community-university partnership		•
EL methods		
Structured site visit	•	
Follow-up site visits	○	•
Municipality brief on site	•	•
Household/business/institution surveys	○	
Semi-structured community interviews	○	•
Focus group w/ local stakeholders		•
Jury assessment with municipality	○	•
Final feedback colloquium		•

- The studio—and its relationship to the entire curriculum—should be structured in such a way that it reflects the unique characteristics of the alternative teaching approach; e.g. it should include a careful selection of the planning problem and site and a clear syllabus relaying both the theory and practice foci of the studio.
- The studio process should be designed to foster particularly good municipality—or other relevant planning institution—relationships to ensure good community projects and effective working partnerships.
- The instructors should regularly—but not necessarily overtly—check on the students regarding their studio experience to improve the pedagogical relationship and encourage healthy group dynamics.
- The instructors should evaluate students not only based on the maps and reports they deliver, but on all aspects of the course experience, keeping in mind that focusing on the means is at least as important as the ends of the studio experience.
- Finally, the studio outcomes and their critical analysis should be disseminated among the departmental faculty in order to encourage greater faculty involvement in new approaches.

Concluding Remarks

This study argues that in order to address contemporary planning practices and increasingly complex planning problems such as those in Istanbul, today's planning studios must explicitly focus on the means of the planning issue at hand and invite students to take on the role of actual practitioners and empathize with local stakeholders. Through studio products, instructor observations and the student survey, the findings have revealed that an interactive and inclusive studio design which actively involves both students and local actors has greater benefits for graduate students' motivation, comprehension and solution generation to real-life planning issues. Much as Kolb implies, reflecting on a hands-on experience can potentially result in a transformation of both the education and professional practice of planning in any context that is applied. As for the future of planning practice itself, this approach can yield more sustainable development outcomes through increased interest and involvement of a locality. In this way, studios may better contribute to more sustainable, inclusive and equitable planning practices.

Acknowledgments

The authors would like to thank the cohort of the two studios of the ITU Urban Planning Master's Program in the 2018–2019 academic year. They would also extend their thanks to the Sarıyer Municipality administration and its Urban Design Department. This study would not have been as effective without the eager cooperation of students, local municipality associates, and local residents.

Note

1 An earlier version of this study focusing mainly on the contents and deliverables of the said studio experience was presented at the 2019 Congress of the Association of European Schools of Planning (AESOP) in Venice. For the full paper, please see the info below or visit: https://www.aesop2019.eu/wp-content/uploads/2019/12/AESOP-Book-of-Papers_compressed.pdf Waite, I. A., Alkay, E., and Becerik, S. (2019), "Inclusive experiential learning at graduate level planning studio: A collaborative governance case," *AESOP 2019 Annual Congress: Planning in Transition*, Book of Papers, pp. 739–61. ISBN: 978-88-99243-93-7.

References

Ansell, C. and Gash, A. (2007), "Collaborative governance in theory and practice," *Journal of Public Administration Research and Theory* 18: 543–71.

Baldwin, C. and Rosier, J. (2017), "Growing future planners: A framework for integrating experiential learning into tertiary planning programs," *Journal of Planning Education and Research* 37(1): 43–55.

Baldwin, C., Rosier, J., Slade, C., Budge, T., Coiacetto, E., Harwood, A., Perkins, T. and La Vache, A. (2013), "Expanding experiential learning in Australian planning schools," Paper presented at the *49th ISOCARP Congress*, October 1–4, Brisbane, Australia. Retrieved from http://www.isocarp.net/Data/case_studies/2385.pdf (last visited on December 4, 2019).

Beard, C. and Wilson, J. P. (2018). *Experiential Learning: A Practical Guide for Training, Coaching and Education*. London, New York: Kogan Page.

Connick, S. and Innes, J. (2003), "Outcomes of collaborative water policy making: Applying complexity thinking to evaluation," *Journal of Environmental Planning and Management* 46: 177–97.

Corburn, J. (2003), "Bringing local knowledge into environmental decision making improving urban planning for communities at risk," *Journal of Planning Education and Research* 22: 420–33.

Dewey, J. and Dewey, E. (1915). *Schools of to-morrow*. London: J. M. Dent & Sons.

Erdoğan, G. (2018), "Planlama Eğitiminde Stüdyo Deneyimleri: Muğla (Menteşe) Stüdyosu," *Megaron* 13(4): 651–64.

Ersoy, M. (2007), "Planlama Eğitimi, Planlama Çevresi ve Sağlıklı Kentler." 7–8 Haziran 2007 tarihinde Bursa'da yapılacak Sağlıklı Kentler sempozyumunda sunulmak üzere hazırlanmıştır.

Forester, J. (1999), *The deliberative practitioner: Encouraging participatory planning processes*. Cambridge, MA: MIT Press.

Friedmann, J. (2008), "The uses of planning theory: A bibliographic essay," *Journal of Planning Education and Research* 28: 247–57.

Grant, J. and Manuel, P. (1995), "Using a peer resource learning model in planning education," *Journal of Planning Education and Research* 15(1): 51–57.

Günay, B. (2007), "Gestalt theory and city planning education," *METU JFA* 24(1): 93–113.

Healey, P. (1997), *Collaborative planning: Shaping places in fragmented societies*. London: Macmillan.

Higgins, M., Aitken-Rose, E. and Dixon, J. (2009), "The pedagogy of the planning studio: A view from down under," *Journal of Education in the Built Environment* 4(1): 8–30.

Innes, J. E. and Booher, D. E. (1999), "Consensus building as role playing and bricolage: Toward a theory of collaborative planning," *Journal of the American Planning Association* 65(1): 9–26.

Keleş, R. (1987). *Türkiye'de Kentbilim Eğitim*. Ankara: AÜ SBF Yayınları.
Kolb, D. (1984). *Experiential learning: Experience as the source of learning and development*. Englewood Cliffs, NJ: Prentice Hall.
Kolb, D. (1994). *Experiential learning: Experiences as a source of learning and development*. London: Prentice Hall.
Köroğlu, N. T. (2011). *Şehir ve Bölge Planlama Eğitimine Eleştirel Bir Bakış: Karar Odaklı Eğitim*. Türkiye Ekonomi Politikaları Araştırma Vakfı Yayınları.
Kotval, Z. (2003), "Teaching experiential learning in the urban planning curriculum," *Journal of Geography in Higher Education* 27(3): 297–308.
LeBaron, M. (2002). *Bridging troubled waters: Conflict resolution from the heart*. San Francisco, CA: Jossey-Bass.
Nijkamp, P. and Kourtit, K. (2013), "The "new urban Europe": Global challenges and local responses in the urban century," *European Planning Studies* 21(3): 291–315.
Reilly, T. (2001), "Collaboration in action: An uncertain process," *Administration in Social Work* 25(1): 53–73.
Roakes, S. L. and Norris-Tirrell, D. (2000), "Community service learning in planning education: A framework for course development," *Journal of Planning Education and Research* 20: 100–10.
Sager, T. (2002), "Deliberative planning and decision making: An impossibility result," *Journal of Planning Education and Research* 21: 367–78.
Smith, S. (1998), "Collaborative approaches to Pacific Northwest fisheries management: The salmon experience," *Willamette Journal of International Law and Dispute Resolution* 6: 29.
Susskind, L., McKearnen, S. and Thomas-Lamar, J. (1999). *The consensus building handbook: A comprehensive guide to reaching agreement*. Thousand Oaks, CA: Sage.
Teitz, M. B. (1996), "American planning in the 1990s: Evolution, debate and challenge," *Urban Studies* 33 (4–5): 649.
The United Nations Conference Report, (2017), *The United Nations Conference on Housing and Sustainable Development (Habitat III)*. http://habitat3.org/documents-and-archive/final-reports/ (Last visited on November 6, 2019).
Türkiye Planlama Okulları Birliği (2007), *Türkiye Planlama Okulları Birliği III. Koordinasyon Toplantısı, İstanbul Teknik Üniversitesi Buluşması Notları*, Türkiye'de Şehir ve Bölge Planlama Eğitiminde Kalite Geliştirme ve Akreditasyon ve Mesleki Yetkinlik ve Yeterlilik, http://www.spo.org.tr/resimler/ekler/be3bc32e6564055_ek.pdf?-tipi=76&turu=H&sube=0.
Waite, I. A., Alkay, E. and Becerik, S. (2019), "Inclusive experiential learning at graduate level planning studio: A collaborative governance case," *AESOP 2019 Annual Congress: Planning in Transition*, Book of Papers, pp. 739–61. ISBN: 978-88-99243-93-7.
Wolfe, D. E. and Byrne, E. T. (1975, March), "Research on experiential learning: Enhancing the process," in *Developments in Business Simulation and Experiential Learning: Proceedings of the Annual ABSEL conference* (Vol. 2), pp. 325–36. https://absel-ojs-ttu.tdl.org/absel/index.php/absel/article/view/2838 (accessed on 10 December, 2019).
Wu, F. (2016), "Emerging Chinese cities: Implications for global urban studies," *The Professional Geographer* 68(2): 338–48.
Zinn, F. D., Lyons, T. S. and Hinojosa, R. C. (1993), "Bringing a global approach to education: The case of urban planning," *Environment and Planning B: Planning and Design* 20: 557–65.

Chapter 8

PLANNERS MOVING TOWARDS THE NEW URBAN AGENDA

Research Contributions and Training

Juan José Gutiérrez-Chaparro

Approach and Guidelines for Discussion

The study of cities is a vast and complex topic which for decades has been the subject of various approaches and just as many perspectives and trends. This is even more true today seeing as though the new urban realities of the 21st century have changed the scale of interpretation and action, multiplying the dimensions of their complex condition which bring us to reflect upon the challenges for action in this new context.

The dynamic for this multidimensional process has intensified in the recent past because of the intense expansion of urbanization. City living is becoming the preferred lifestyle all over the world. Latin America and the Caribbean is not the exception, and its urbanization process expresses new ways of organizing space. This is a product of a suburban style of development which provokes new problems and challenges related to the spatial disparity, concentration of population and inequality.

Mexico is not exempt to this Latin American urbanization. Among the most important findings of the City Prosperity Initiative[1] in 2016, Mexico Report warns that our cities

> ...have followed a pattern of expansive, unsustainable and uncontrolled growth...substantially increasing the cost of quality public services and creating spatial inequality...with low quality or unequal public services which are far from places of work...worsening mobility problems and reducing environmental quality.
>
> *(ONU-Hábitat, 2016a:14)*

This argument reveals that the problem is worsening, which is supported by mounting evidence. The problem will also be explained from different

DOI: 10.4324/9781003178545-11

perspectives, offering enough elements to suggest an Urban Planning (UP) approach for this chapter. We will discuss how the challenges for this area of knowledge are greater than ever before, confronting the worsening of the urbanization process characterizing cities of the second decade of the 21st century.

Acknowledging the current limitations of territorial action, this chapter will focus on the need to update current intervention guidelines with the assumption that the knowledge available in this area is not enough to explain and/or deal with the urban problems observed in contemporary cities. We recognize that UP professional practice has not been able to tackle the challenges of contemporary urbanization, which is directly related to the training of city professionals. The World Cities Report 2016 emphasized the need to strengthen planning capabilities where teaching becomes fundamental to successful UP.

From an international perspective the need for the training of Planners is described in point 102 of the New Urban Agenda (NUA) establishing that "We will make an effort to improve the capacity for planning and …for educating urban planners" (UN-Hábitat, 2016:14). Additionally, and as a result of the discussion from the Habitat III conference and the NUA, the World Cities Report 2016 clearly shows that education in Planning is considered one of the backbones of the actions needed to reinvent UP.

From this perspective, we have no doubt that the guidelines for the transformation of UP, promoted by the UN's Habitat Program, are of the most influential in our area of knowledge, internationally. The research outlines the characteristics of a new model, answering the needs to reform the traditional model. Nevertheless, it is clear that our contributions are fitting to teaching because this new knowledge is fundamental for the training of future Planners.

With the responsibility of moving towards a formative model which responds to the needs of new urban spaces, the Faculty of Urban and Regional Planning at the Autonomous University of the State of Mexico (Toluca) has recently restructured the curriculum of the Bachelor's degree in Territorial Planning.[2] We have included several innovations, derived from the research experiences described in the new UP model, which have come out of the need for reform.

Because it is our objective to share this experience of curricular innovation, this chapter will outline the research contributions made to the obligatory courses in the Bachelor's degree. We will also evaluate the theoretical and methodological gaps in the teaching of UP in our faculty, and to confirm this, we conducted a critical evaluation of the Bachelor's degree in Territorial Planning. We compared the fundamental disciplinary elements of UP with the knowledge acquired during the degree.

Our methodological strategy is divided into two parts. First, we present the guidelines for UP transformation promoted by the Habitat Program, particularly those related to Planning Theory,[3] to use for comparison. Second, we completed an exercise of congruency between the fundamental elements of UP and the knowledge acquired in the Bachelor's degree in Territorial Planning from the analysis of the courses selected. Finally, we will present the results of the work done by the Curriculum Committee for the Bachelor's degree in Territorial

Planning which was completed at the end of 2015, and after which a restructuring of the study plan was approved.

Our experience with updating the curricula is emphatic in approaching Planning Theory as its own field of knowledge due to the recent initiatives of the Habitat Program. The reason also comes from the explicative nature of the transformation process as well as the gradual adoption of alternative models in response to the complexity of today's world.

UP under the Scope of the Habitat Program

Recognizing the complexity of urban systems from the planning state implies changing our way of thinking and acting away from simplistic solutions based on the Cartesian analytical disjunction in order to correct problems and instead transcend towards an articulated thinking including all parts, order and disorder, the object and the environment, the continuous and the discontinuous, the abstract and the concrete. All of these issues must be organized and regulated in a way that predicts the behavior of the whole system, even with the complexity involved.

With this chapter it is important to point out the contributions of the United Nations Habitat Program. The guidelines dealing with human settlements are of the most influential internationally. Since the introduction of the guidelines at the conference in Vancouver in 1976, as part of the Habitat Program, there has been a constant effort to improve and reform UP around the world.

This is especially true with the contributions of the Global Report on Human Settlements 2009 which revealed the necessity of an evaluation and review of the assumptions and fundamental elements of UP in the 21st century. The objective is to recover its role as a driving force in urban development and, more than ever, accompany that with sustainability and social justice. Notwithstanding, this document recognizes that UP has changed very little and that in many developing countries, like Mexico a traditional perspective remains. This has caused an urgency to begin a process of reflection concerning the reach of the current model.

From this perspective, the Report mentions that the new style of planning must incorporate the following elements, which emerge from at least five of the main phenomena observed in contemporary cities:

1. Environmental challenges due to climate change
2. Demographic challenges from an accelerated urbanization which expresses, among other phenomena, the rapid growth of small and medium centers and the constant growth of the number of youths in developing countries, while in developed countries the problem is the shrinking of cities and the aging population
3. The economic challenges of uncertain future growth
4. The growing socio-spatial challenges, territorial inequality, uncontrolled urban growth and unplanned peri-urbanization
5. The challenges and opportunities of democratization of the decision-making process

To add to this, since 2006 the Global Planners Network proposes a group of principles to reach new ways of reacting to territorial phenomena. Some of the more important ones are as follows: the promotion of sustainable development, collaboration among representatives, associated planned actions with variable types of funding (public and private funds) in order to make the actions more feasible, inclusive actions which recognize the diversity and promote equality based on flexible planning which adapts to the institutional guidelines as well as the needs of the new urban space.

Based on these considerations, the need for UP reform is obvious. It is important to point out that the reflection done with Habitat has strengthened. Among the lessons learned in the last few years, we would highlight International Guidelines of Urban and Territorial Planning published by the Habitat Program in 2015. This chapter became a framework for planning and a fundamental element for the definition of NUA. It includes sustainable urban development since it was adopted during the Habitat III conference in Quito in October 2016.

As we will see in the following section, because of the recent Habitat III conference, the guidelines are destined to become a framework for the strengthening of the policies and instruments on the road to achieving more compact, socially inclusive, integrated and connected cities and territories which promote sustainable development.

UP with Habitat III. Discussion and Recent Guidance

We have had an open line of discussion when it comes to UP, at least since 2009 and in October 2016 in the Habitat III conference, these ideas were summarized highlighting the importance of urban development in improving the welfare of the population and achieving better conditions of habitability in cities.

This global objective was born out of the NUA and today is considered one of the most influential instruments on this subject. And as expected, the guidelines are today considered one of the fundamental criteria for the definition of this instrument at a global level when it comes to planning and management of urban development. This is expressed in article 93 of the New Agenda, recognizing that the strategies contained in the guidelines will be considered guiding principles in this area for the next several decades (UN-Habitat, 2016:13).

As we know, the guidelines are organized into four main areas, within which 12 principles have been developed to guide decision-makers in the design and development of policies and instruments for urban action. They are designed to meet the needs of various territorial scales, from the multinational level to the neighborhood level. Many different approaches and instruments have been used, but the successful implementation of the plans depends upon strong political support for the norms and transparent outlines which include the participation of members of society.

Several tasks and responsibilities are outlined for different areas of public management in the city and transversally. UP is considered a fundamental instrument in reaching global goals and a way of making the policy a reality. It mentions the strict observance and application of plans at all levels, being precise about the compliance needed by leadership and political willingness. This includes an adequate judicial and institutional framework, efficient management, increasingly better coordination and the participation of the private sector.

Together with the guidelines, the road to the construction of NUA was paved by the 22 Issue Papers which provided the main elements for the definition of the New Urban Agenda. The documents tackle a variety of topics associated with many of the urbanization worries in the world and in relation to the advice in the guidelines; it is important to note Issue Paper No. 8 about UP and Design. This document insists on the need to rewrite the current UP model and expressly indicates that through the publication and application of the guidelines, it will be possible to have a global example to improve UP and design from different areas of action.

In order to achieve this global proposal, five principles of action are defined:

1 City systems are dynamic networks whose influence extends beyond its own administrative limits.
2 UP is more efficient when it is promoted as a participative, flexible and continuous process instead of rigid rules associated with a blueprint.
3 The process of UP should be inclusive and providing benefits for all.
4 In order for UP to be effective, a variety of dimensions must be integrated, including spatial, institutional and financial.
5 Good urban design contributes to habitability, sustainability and aids in the economic potential of the city.

This unavoidable reform was ratified with the World Cities Report 2016 published after the conference and insists on the need to reform the UP model considering the demands of the new context and the ambitions of the NUA. Actually, the Report expressly indicates that "Planning is essential for this reinvention, as inclusive process, continuous, instead of a unique design with a master vision…" (ONU-Habitat, 2016b:123), and in consequence, we need to move towards planning systems which are renewed, democratic, participative, inclusive, transparent, continuous and flexible instead of a unilateral, rigid and prohibitive as with the traditional perspective.

According to these approaches, it is possible to confirm that since Habitat began to identify its first responses to the situation and the Word Cities Report 2016 we have seen the notion of the *The Planned City* as a way of understanding the rational load of a modern UP Project, and, in contrast to that notion, *A City that Plans* is one that expresses the aspirations of the new model. This model is based on the principles of communicative rationality[4] and both flexibility and participation, which legitimize the process and the action of planning.

Communicative rationality has substituted the technical rationality of Modernism. The communicative planning model is considered the emerging paradigm in our area of knowledge and comes out of the recent discussion in the area of Planning Theory. This model is characterized by its wish for dialogue and negotiation as a channel to achieve a consensus, and, as in the past, the topics of debate revolve around implementation and action. The discussion is now focused on the advantages of communication and negotiation.

This also means a paradigm change in the understanding of UP and the city because of Habitat. Many different considerations show us the intention for change, but it is important to note that *The Planned City* is still often reduced to territorial codes and simple cartographic expression of social interactions. With the new plan, and with the notion of *A City that Plans*, we hope that UP will have the ability to stimulate, guide and coordinate actions between different players, as well as have the ability to grow and strengthen the relationships between the private sector and the government, among social groups and institutions.

Following these guidelines, it is clear that we must begin a process of reflection and reform of the fundamental elements of UP. The objective is to adapt them to the demands of the international community, from a disciplinary perspective as well as a public action perspective. It is not a small feat. On the contrary, it is a difficult challenge for the training of future professionals in the city, above all. A decade after Habitat warned us that traditional UP is obsolete,[5] countries like Mexico are still not breaking from the modernist model.

Evidence from the international agenda strengthens the argument we have been putting forward about the traditional model being obsolete. This preliminary research in Mexican cities indicates that the current model still, is influenced by modernist ideas and is connected to the new empirical and scientific information.

Planning Theory and Training Challenges

From different points of view, city professionals have warned that the current UP style has caused crises all over the world. Cities and the powers that form them frequently have rigid and prohibitive zoning rules. Mexico is not the exception. This has been an inefficient style of planning for our cities.

In response, including in classrooms, it is possible to observe the historical tendency of an unfinished, unreflective transformation which often lacks theory or urban models produced in other places. It is also obvious that there is a tendency to adopt fashionable thinking. In any case, we have not been able to consolidate clear action and our own thinking about our reality. And above all, we need to be faithful to the fundamental elements of our field of knowledge.

The study of Planning cannot be limited to numbering of repetitive concepts and classifications. When it comes to higher education, there is a need to highlight the theoretical component of Planning in order to identify its evolution and its recent tendencies. These new tendencies have modified the notions of rationality, effectiveness, efficiency and transcendence, which are part of our discipline.

This obligates us to recognize that Planning is a field of knowledge which has a high level of difficulty, not only in relation to the complexity inherent in the life of man in society, but also because of the diversity of the complementary fields involved. Nonetheless, identifying points of discussion that allow us to advance and define the area has been a focus of many academics. These discussions have identified this field as complex and at the same time as flexible. Through intromission and meditation in multiple situations, the field adapts and rebuilds itself as a body of knowledge which never loses its main purpose: a vehicle for conduct, anticipation and action.

Once this was established, we heard the call, as researchers and as teachers to contribute to this discussion. There is no doubt that we need to focus our efforts on the study of our field of knowledge. Actually, from this perspective, Planning Theory, including the complexity inherent to the concept, the content and guidance, is an essential topic for the discussion. From a classic perspective, this is known as *the problem* of Planning Theory. Using its framework, we will need to identify elements which help student overall comprehension.

The *problem* of Planning Theory has been approached from different perspectives, in particular by authors like Faludi (1976). His work identified, as a point of inflection from Planning Theory, the coexistence of two types of complementary theories which are necessary for its definition, development and practice: Theory *about* Planning or Procedural Theory and Theory *in* Planning or Substantial Theory.

Faludi argues this distinction and identifies two fields of action and knowledge. The first is part of Planning (Theory about Planning), and the second refers to knowledge that is from another field (Theory of Planning) but is incorporated into Planning in particular situations, where needed.

Once this was established, the underlying *problem* of Planning Theory defined by this author is the imbalance between both components, Planning teaching and practice, that are excessively oriented towards a body of knowledge that is not part of Planning. The *problem* in Planning Theory is not ignorance of the function, utility and complementarity of the substantive areas of knowledge in Planning; on the contrary, the problem is the need to promote the maximum integration of these areas. Procedural Theory complemented with Substantial Theory is needed for this case.

The Challenges for Teaching at the Faculty of Urban and Regional Planning

Even though the *problem* of Planning Theory was brought to light many decades ago, evidence shows that in Mexico the problem remains, and at the Faculty of Urban and Regional Planning, we have not been able to contribute to resolving the problem. Neither our discussions in the area, nor our teaching in the classroom have been focused on these fundamental areas. Adding to the problem, in Mexico we have not adopted this new knowledge and our cities are growing with multiple problems. We somehow recognize that UP has evolved in response to the changes observed in the object of the study, but we have not consolidated and transcended initiatives that show evidence of change.

Higher education is not the exception. Since its creation in 1986, and at least until the end of 2015 when the new curriculum was approved, the faculty has not registered any actions to this effect. No action has been taken to strengthen the curriculum for training Planners with theory or methodology. The objective should be for students to familiarize themselves with and understand the origin of UP, evaluate its reach from a critical perspective and redirect it in the context of recent developments in their own disciplinary area. All three undergraduate programs were offered for at least 30 years[6] with topics associated with the object of study but taken from complementary disciplines such as architecture or geography.

From the perspective of evaluation, which will be presented further on, we can anticipate that, in the case of UP, this bias translates into a clear tendency to deal with topics like cities, regions, land use, housing, transportation, among others in an isolated fashion. Except for studies about the effects of urbanization or those of a sectorial nature, Mexico does not have previous studies that consider the process of evolution of our discipline.

This affirmation is backed up by a wide body of work in which an exercise was carried out contrasting the fundamental disciplinary elements of UP and the knowledge acquired during the undergraduate degree. The contents of the three degrees offered by the faculty were analyzed. Methodologically, it is important to point out that the analysis of the first degree program from 1986 is only a reference. The document was not available for review. We were able to review the "Project: Faculty of Urban and Regional Planning. Autonomous University of the State of Mexico. September 1983" as well as a couple of pamphlets from the School of Urban and Regional Planning.

In relation to the contents to evaluate, it was clear to us that in order to advance with the definition of the function, means and spaces of UP intervention, the study should consider aspects that begin with the roots of its history and up until contemporary cities. When it comes to the means of intervention, using the urbanization process as a base phenomenon, it was necessary to divide the topics into two main groups:

1   The study of the characteristics and function of UP from its origin, linking it directly with the story of urbanism and the day-to-day work of Architecture, as well as the complex Latin American urban experience, is influenced by a style of rational, developmental planning, ending with the case of Mexico. In Mexico, the UP styles most used are not a result of our own intellectual development, but a complex mix of styles and models from other countries adapted to our context.
2   As a complement to knowledge about its origins and evolutions, and as a tool for behavior and processes of occupation and transformation of cities, it is important to include the study of Planning Theory. Planning Theory contributes to the interpretation of the rational character of the current UP model in our country. It is a fundamental aspect in order to know the evolution of Planning, offering the student a larger panorama of the different models which have been developed in the field.

According to this, the first stage of analysis of course content was to identify the courses that had the word Planning in the title, assuming that the objectives and specific content would include the study of the discipline from some perspective. After this first selection, it was necessary to review the objective of each course and eliminate courses that do not have the correct objective.

From this exercise, we identified a second group of courses that had at least one objective associated with our study, and this number was quite small. The third stage of analysis consisted of a review of the contents per unit and the topics, in order to corroborate whether they were explicitly dealing with UP.

As a result, we observed that from each of the degree programs only 2, in the case of the 1993 plan and also 2 from the present course plan would be part of the content analysis by unit and by topic in order to confirm that the objective and the contents are linked to the teaching of our discipline from some perspective.

Specifically we were able to prove that the contents of the "Fundamentals of Planning and Public Administration" and "Planning Processes and Methods" of the 1993 plan as well as the "Fundamentals of Administration and Levels of Planning in Mexico" of the current plan were judicial and institutional in nature. The development of technical abilities which complement this education is not enough to strengthen the disciplinary component.

Consequently, the subject "Theory and Process of Territorial Planning" from the 2003 plan was the only one which showed a clear link to our field. Nevertheless, this one course cannot be considered because a review of the bibliography revealed that none of the texts offered the student or the teacher the minimum elements to understand the concept or the evolution of UP, a main objective of their training.

We would also like to add that none of the courses contained elements of the two main groups of fundamental concepts described above. There was especially no mention of the history of UP, which is part of the objective of this study. The intention is to then complement that history with topics from the discipline, but we found no evidence of these topics during our analysis.

Final Result:

- Between 1986 and 2003 no courses were offered which contributed training elements related to the field of UP (Theory and History).
- Between 2003 and 2015 only one course contained elements of what a future Planner could superficially link to the field of UP (Theory and History)

Training Update from the Field of Planning Theory

The Faculty of Urban and Regional Planning has been repeating a pattern for at least three decades which lacks the foundation a Planner needs to learn about and explore the fundamental elements of the degree and their own field. Fortunately, this situation is changing due to work done by the Curriculum Committee of the Bachelor's degree in Territorial Planning. Near the end of 2015, the approval was awarded for a restructuring of the current degree program. The fundamental elements of our field are a priority for the contents of the program. This way we will achieve more of a balance between the procedural and the fundamental components. These concepts, contents and vehicles for action will be permanent.

The restructuring of the curriculum for the Bachelor's degree in Territorial Planning means an important change as a whole and for the contents of the courses. The diagnostic study of the current plan (2003) showed that 60% of the total credits of the Bachelor's degree were part of courses which are predominantly technical. The weight of the credits in practical objectives is even more evident when compared with the credits in theory. Course content with disciplinary theoretical content directly associated with Territorial Planning was only 3.5% of the total curriculum[7] while close to 40% of the credits are distributed among interdisciplinary courses like Territorial and Environmental Economic Politics and Society, Natural Resources and the Environment, among others.

The current diagnostic plan is emphatic in pointing out that in these conditions the students usually receive a predominantly technical education, while the theory is missing. It is surprising that the courses involved in this degree tend to come from other disciplines and not from Territorial Planning, created from a concept we will call multi-meaning.

Fortunately, this technical tendency was modified in favor of a theoretical tendency in the 2015 plan, which recognizes that

> the study of Territorial Planning requires a interdisciplinary approach which in a teaching setting requires a dynamic and systematic integration of theories, methods and instruments from distinct disciplines with the purpose of finding solutions to territorial phenomena which have been conceived from an comprehensive perspective
>
> *(FaPUR, 2015:198)*

at a time when Planning and Urbanism are central in Territorial Planning.

The objective of the program is to:

> Train professionals able to design adaptable instruments that allow them to deal with territorial problems in relation to: urban structures, infrastructure, equipment, urban image, urban mobility, housing, basic services and a legal framework, territorially and environmentally, through the acquisition of theoretical, methodological and axiological knowledge, for the planning, order, regulation, and control of the use of land, derived by rural, urban, political, economic, social and environmental processes, among others...
>
> *(FaPUR, 2015:213)*

And where it says "...through the acquisition of theoretical, methodological and axiological knowledge, for the planning ..." is where we find a niche of opportunity to integrate the two courses related to Planning Theory, which are part of the Territorial Planning section.[8]

Planning Theory 1 and 2 are part of the basic nucleus in the study plan with eight credits each, which translates to four hours of theory to study these topics during two school semesters. Theory 1 is taken during third semester and Theory 2 during fourth semester. According to the content, these courses offer a disciplinary base for Territorial Planning that, together with the practical and technical base, improves professional performance. As mentioned from different perspectives, the important thing is to strengthen education in the field, something that is absent and has been recovered with the restructuring of the plan.

The following describes in detail the objectives and content of each course:

Theory of Planning 1

Analyze the evolution of the rationality in the decision-making process from the main schools of thinking in the Theory of Planning (see Table 8.1).

TABLE 8.1 Contents per unit, course 1

Unit 1. Basic planning concepts

Objective: Discuss and explain concepts and basic ideas about planning from previous personal and group knowledge to establish a base of common knowledge which allows for a glimpse of the work of planning from an ample perspective

Contents
1.1. Planning as an act of human rationality
1.2. Planning and everyday experiences
1.3. Territorial Planning from common sense

Unit 2. The Scientific Method and Scientific Theories

Objective: Discuss the principles of the scientific method as a rational resource and an explanatory foundation of the scientific theories

Contents
2.1. The scientific method
2.2. Scientific theories
2.3. The scientific method in the social sciences
2.4. Social theories

Unit 3. Rationality as a principal for planning

Objective: Explain the significance of rationality and its implications in the decision-making process

Contents
3.1. Illustrated thinking and rationality
3.2. Instrumental rationality
3.3. Public decisions and rational choice

Unit 4. Planning Theory

Objective: Discuss the main contributions to schools of classical thought and the fundamental elements of Planning Theory

Contents
4.1. What is Planning Theory?
4.2. Traditions and schools of thought
4.3. The problem with Planning Theory
4.4. The classic model: Comprehensive rational planning

Planning Theory 2

Analyze the tendencies and recent developments in Planning Theory based on the contributions to the study of territory and the decision-making process that allows us to distinguish emerging models of intervention (see Table 8.2).

TABLE 8.2 Contents per unit, course 2

Unit 1. The critique of rationality

Objective: Analyze the critical positions of Planning Theory
Contents
1.1. Limited rationality (Simon)
1.2. Incremental focus (Lindblom)
1.3. Mixed exploration (Etzioni)
1.4. Advocacy planning (Davidof)

Unit 2. Recent tendencies

Objective: Discuss the recent tendencies in Planning Theory
Contents
2.1. Postmodern thinking
2.2. Official history and invisible minorities
2.3. Emerging alternatives

Unit 3. Communicative planning

Objective: Highlight the contributions to communicative rationality and analyze the foundations of communicative planning
Contents
3.1. Instrumental rationality
3.2. Communicative rationality
3.3. Communicative planning

Unit 4. The new paradigm in planning: case studies

Objective: Discuss the possibilities of adopting the new communicative model in the public sector and territorial studies
Content
4.1. Case studies

These two courses were first offered in August 2016. We believe the experience has been positive for the students who have received this theory training thus far;

nevertheless, we have had to confront two specific circumstances for which we have not found a practical solution for. The first is the level of complexity inherent to theoretical and epistemological topics. This is even more difficult because it requires the knowledge of a second language. The bibliography for the course is in English, and the students do not have a high enough level of the language to understand the texts. For this reason, we must design parallel teaching strategies.

Conclusion

A substantial part of this research is based upon sharing our experiences with the scientific community, and with theory and as they relate to changes in curricula. Though the ideas are generalized, they create a group of contributions to the field of UP, like those in Planning Theory, an important foundation in order to evaluate the relevance and the belonging of our object of study.

Both areas of analysis are justified, not only because of the implicit importance of generating knowledge, but also because of the lack of formal education in these topics at the university level, in Bachelor's and Master's degrees in Mexico. These topics are not included in the programs registered in the National Association of Educational Institutes for Territorial Planning, Urbanism and Urban Design (ANPUD, México).

There may be different paths to achieving this, but according to the objectives of this chapter, there is a need to include the necessary knowledge in the curriculum of future professionals in UP. It is also necessary that they evaluate the reach of this knowledge from a critical perspective and redirect this perspective in the context of recent developments in their own field.

Under this premise, it is essential that the different educational organisms responsible for the training of future Planners establish points of convergence in the topics which allow us to construct knowledge about the reality of urban Latin America. This should be done with a long-term perspective and offering interpretive frameworks of the phenomena that underline the current urban reality.

As with so many other emerging topics in the context of UP, there is no doubt of its usefulness within the study plans; however, in order to be able to contribute to improving the training of future professionals, with new and constant knowledge about the field, there needs to be a closer relationship between research and teaching. Research gives teachers the ability to offer new knowledge to the student, and as researchers, we can contribute to the construction of a theoretical and methodological body of knowledge specific to the needs of new urban spaces and knowledge that can adapt to the complex demands of the environment, society and territory.

Notes

1 A focus promoted by the UN-Habitat since 2012 to measure the current and future progress of cities.

2 The Bachelor's degree in Territorial Planning is one of the precursors in the field from the National Association of Educational Institutes for Territorial Planning, Urbanism and Urban Design. ANPUD—Mexico.
3 Main line of research for our project became the foundation for our training proposal.
4 As a basis for the strategy to reinvent UP, exploring the possibilities of *A City that Plans* brings us to the study of Planning Theory, an area of knowledge which is the foundation for our training proposal.
5 Global Report on Human Settlements 2009.
6 The first (1986–93) with the Bachelor's degree in Urban and Regional Planning, the second (1993–2003) with the Bachelor's degree in Territorial Planning and the third (2003–15) also from the Bachelor's degree in Territorial Planning.
7 The results of our evaluation confirm the absence of a theoretical base in Planner training.
8 The objective is to

> Analyze the process, evolution and strengthening of the city, as well as emergence of Territorial Planning from a theoretical and methodological perspective for the design and implementation of proposals and alternatives that contribute to the decision making which will answer territorial issues.
>
> (FaPUR, 2015:216)

References

Faludi, A. (1976). *Planning Theory*. Pergamon Press.
FaPUR, Facultad de Planeación Urbana y Regional (2015). *Plan de Estudios de la Licenciatura en Planeación Territorial*. Universidad Autónoma del Estado de México. Toluca México.
ONU-Hábitat, Programa de la Naciones Unidas para los Asentamientos Humanos (2016a). *Índice de Prosperidad Urbana en la República Mexicana*. Programa de la Naciones Unidas para los Asentamientos Humanos. México.
ONU-Hábitat, Programa de la Naciones Unidas para los Asentamientos Humanos (2016b). *Urbanización y Desarrollo: Futuros emergentes. Reporte Ciudades del Mundo 2016*. Programa de la Naciones Unidas para los Asentamientos Humanos. Nairobi, Kenia.
UN-Habitat. United Nations Human Settlements Programme (2016). *Habitat III. New Urban Agenda*. United Nations Human Settlements Programme. Nairobi, Kenia.

Chapter 9

URBAN PLANNING IN GUADALAJARA, MEXICO

The New Urban Agenda and Experience of Its Application Locally

José Luis Águila Flores and Raúl Agraz Joya

Introduction

This work provides a general description of an unprecedented case for the municipality of Guadalajara and the Metropolitan Area it forms a part of, and has to do with the elaboration of planning instruments 2017–18 by the government of Guadalajara. The planning project was directed by professionals working for the city council, but with strong support from the University of Guadalajara, through a group of young graduates. The whole process involved bringing the municipality's planning instruments up to date and in line with the legal frameworks of Mexico and the State of Jalisco.

With the overlapping of interests, and changes made to national policies of urban development since the previous urban planning instruments of Guadalajara had been introduced 14 years before, new development plans were designed, which may be regarded as an example worth knowing about and sharing nationally, especially since Mexico's recent adoption of the New Urban Agenda (NUA) published by Habitat III, which establishes guidelines to be followed in matters of urban development and planning in favor of a re-densification suited to local reality, thus countering the consequences of outdated planning suffered in a number of cities in Mexico and Latin America. The present work explains, in three sections, how the planning instruments for Guadalajara were elaborated: the first section shows how the NUA was applied in the context of Mexico; the second section provides a brief summary of the historical antecedents of planning instruments in Guadalajara, and also describes the problems that forced the government of Guadalajara to update its urban legislation; and the third presents the characteristics of the team who formulated the new planning instruments, the methodology they applied, the tools they used and the changes they have

DOI: 10.4324/9781003178545-12

proposed to the new urban development strategies for the municipality of Guadalajara, showing how they fit in with the policies of urban development of higher levels of government.

According to Guay (1989), with the institutionalization of professionals and of the university people brought in to work on territorial management, attempts were made to create theories that applied specifically to planning. This can be seen in the strategies followed and actions applied in particular population centers to determine the most appropriate development under the prevailing conditions. Taking the elaboration of planning instruments for Guadalajara as an example, to meet current urban development challenges and for the necessary professional work to be done, teachers had to bring to their classrooms the right kind of instruction, based on international theories and paying attention to urban legislation. Similarly, students and graduates require the skills and the knowledge they will need to apply in their daily professional and public service work in order to benefit citizens in general, as, after all, the city is everyone's home.

The New Urban Agenda and Its Application in Mexico

In response to the current challenges of urban development, the United Nations Organization (UNO), Habitat and its member states adopted commitments and guidelines to direct the growth of cities and to move towards a sustainable model of urban development. Examples of these agreements are the creation of Agenda 2030 for Sustainable Development, and the NUA. Agenda 2030, passed in September 2015, is a document containing 17 objectives for Sustainable Development; some of its aims are to end poverty, to fight against inequality and to deal with climate change, leaving no one behind. The point of view adopted in the agenda stretches to 2030. The NUA, in turn, approved at the United Nations Conference on Housing and Sustainable Urban Development (Habitat III), held in Quito, Ecuador, in 2016, is a document setting out the commitments made by countries of the United Nations to encourage the Sustainable Development of cities for the long term, and it concentrates on the promotion of cities that are compact, secure, resilient, participatory, sustainable and inclusive. Both agendas were ratified by Mexico and integrated into national public policies for urban development (UN-Habitat, 2016).

In Mexico, the management of development, and of planning for urban areas, is a subject of national importance, and over the last five years this has been seen in laws, programs and plans at all three levels of government: federal, state and municipal. Its importance can be seen in the fact, published in the Inter-census Survey of 2015, that the urban population in Mexico had reached 75.1 million people, representing 62.8% of the national population; and also because the number of metropolitan zones had increased, from 59 in 2010 to 74 in 2015 (SEDATU and INEGI, 2015).

Following Chaparro (2017), the report *The Evolution of National Urban Policies: A Global Overview* (UN-Habitat, 2014) explains that in Mexico planning and urban development face the following challenges:

I   Obsolete legislation
II Inflexible and inappropriate institutions (for example, subsidies to encourage suburban housing)
III No vision of urban development
IV Uncertainty for private investment
V   Weak, short-term, local governments

The report quoted points out that the National Development Plan 2013–18 promotes a sustainable and intelligent urban development model, to obtain decent housing and compact cities with greater population density and development opportunities for the inhabitants. In 2014, in line with this plan, there followed the National Urban Development Programme, and even though it was designed before the NUA was published, the Programme coincided with several of the objectives of the Agenda, as the objectives and strategies of the NUA were really conclusions arrived at after various studies had been made and events had been held in preceding years. Subsequently, in 2015 Mexico officially adopted Agenda 2030 for Sustainable Development, and in 2016, the NUA, after which, in the same year, the new General Law of Human Settlements, Territorial Management and Urban Development (*Ley General de Asentamientos Humanos, Ordenamiento Territorial y Desarrollo Urbano,* LGAHOTDU) was passed, requiring new urban planning policies in Mexico to follow a development model that would encourage protection of the environment, prevent the expansion of urban areas, encourage sustainable mobility, diminish the vulnerability of citizens to natural and man-made disasters, while also promoting the regularization of land tenure and a reduction in urban inequality.

The fifth transitory article of LGAHOTDU (2016) establishes a two-year deadline for the urban development plans and programs of states and population centers of over 100,000 inhabitants, to adjust to the new guidelines for urban development in the Law. The World Resources Institute (WRI), the Mexican Institute for Competition (*Instituto Mexicano para la Competitividad,* IMCO) and the Mario Molina Centre (*Centro Mario Molina,* CMM, 2016) determined that two years is not long enough, and noted that not having committed financial resources for the training and hiring of staff and external advisors to produce the necessary adjustments to the urban laws of the states was going to make it difficult for the adjustments to be made. This observation can be considered correct, as by the time the present work was in progress, no physical results of applying the NUA had been recorded beyond reports, plans and urban development programs. Further, as highlighted by the report *The Evolution of National Urban Policies: a Global Overview* and IMCO (2016), with the municipal governments changing every three years, there is little time to implement urban development strategies showing continuity, which makes their monitoring and evaluating them difficult;

though with the electoral reform of 2014 that allowed municipal presidents to be re-elected, from 2018 onwards, these effects of the short administrative periods would be lessened.

Some examples given as reference for local governments to follow in their application of the NUA are the "Guide for the implementation of Transit-Oriented Development policies and projects" published by Institute for Transportation and Development Policy (ITDP) in collaboration with the Secretariat of Agrarian, Territorial and Urban Development (SEDATU); and the "New Methodology for the Elaboration and Updating of Municipal Urban Development Programs." According to SEDATU, only 6 out of the 32 states that constitute Mexico had adapted their state legislation in the area of urban development to align with the LGAHOTDU by the end of the period running from October 2017 to January 2018. Of these 6 states, 2 created a law for urban development, while the remaining 4 only reformed existing legislation[1] (including Jalisco).

These reforms were applied to the Urban Code for the State of Jalisco (CUEJ), and include subjects such as reducing environmental impacts, and improving resilience, sustainable urban mobility and universal accessibility. Another action executed by the State was to upgrade the 2013 State Development Program in 2016, to make it agree with the objectives of the Agenda 2030 for Sustainable Development. Within the upgraded objectives of the 2013–33 Jalisco State Development Plan (2016), the topics that stand out are increasing the sustainability of the environment; a development model with transport as its priority; reducing vulnerabilities from natural or anthropogenic disasters and the improvement of urban mobility. Deriving from this plan, the Sectoral Urban and Territorial Development Program came in, whose main objectives are to reverse the urban sprawl, prevent the depopulation of city centers of the state and to diminish the demands on territory and ecosystems. This program focuses most strongly on the case of the Guadalajara Metropolitan Area (GMA) (Gobierno de Jalisco, 2014).

In summary, since 2013 public policies and legislation regarding planning and urban development in Mexico have been directed towards fostering the development of more compact cities with the aims of decreasing the consumption of natural resources and reducing inequality (Águila, 2019). By adopting the NUA objectives in 2016, this vision for Mexican cities was strengthened. However, as it has only recently come into play, the states and municipalities are still in the process of aligning with public policies and they do not all have the same conditions for the execution of the objectives. Authors such as Chaparro (2017) indicate that the chances of actually applying the NUA policies in the states and municipalities are rather limited, due to the complexity and obsolescence of the legislation for urban development in most of the states.

Alignment of the Planning Instruments of Guadalajara

Guadalajara, founded in 1542, is the capital of the State of Jalisco and the central municipality of the GMA, which hosts 4,865,122 inhabitants (Gobierno de Guadalajara, 2017a). It is the second most populous metropolitan area in the country.

Guadalajara has an interesting dynamic, influencing the west of the country as a result of the infrastructure and urban facilities with the regional range that it has. It is one of the UNESCO World Heritage Sites and has a unique cultural identity within Mexico (where it is thought of as the land of mariachi and tequila). The city has developed industrial activities and services, such as the tequila industry and, lately, activities related to high-tech and information technologies, to the extent of being called the Mexican Silicon Valley.[2] Guadalajara has hosted international spectacles such as various FIFA World Cup games (1970 and 1986), the XVI Pan American Games (in 2011) and the yearly International Book Fair (FIL)—the largest book fair in the Spanish-speaking world. Guadalajara's urban development deserves particular attention, as that of an attractive city with great potential internationally.

For purposes of land management and planning in Guadalajara, the Constitution of the United Mexican States of 1917 recognizes three levels of government: federal, state and municipal, which have judicially determined attributes, degrees of autonomy and restraints (Arias, 2011). Based on Article 115 of the Constitution, municipalities have the faculty to manage their territory through the formulation, approval and management of zoning and urban development plans, as well as the control of land use (within their jurisdictions), the granting of licenses and building permits and the power to regularize land ownership and to determine the regulations for land management. Starting from this order, in 1933 the earliest example of planning instruments in Guadalajara, the Law of Cooperation, Planning and Public Works was passed, with the purpose of regulating urban centers, especially Guadalajara. This law restructured the city's physical space and its adjuncts, such as urban facilities, roads and water and sewage infrastructure (Arias, 2011).

During the second half of the 20th century Guadalajara experienced an accelerated demographic growth and urban sprawl, seen in its conurbation with the neighboring municipalities of Zapopan, San Pedro Tlaquepaque and Tonalá from 1970 to 2000, and later, others. Jiménez and Cruz (2015) define these three municipalities as the first periphery. Due to the new conditions of a conurbation, in 1982 the Management Plan of the Conurbation of Guadalajara was published, with the aim of integrally regulating and coordinating metropolitan growth. In 1983, Article 115 of the Constitution was reformed, now defining urban planning as a fundamentally municipal activity, which resulted in a restructuring of state urban planning. One of the consequences of this reform was the declaration in 1993 of the Law of Urban Development of the State of Jalisco. This law was prior to the Urban Code for the State of Jalisco, which came into force in 2009. The new law established the joint participation of state and municipal governments in management of the territory, as well as the creation of a system of planning instruments, from which the Urban Development Partial Plan proceeds (Arias, 2011).

From 2005, the municipalities of El Salto and Tlajomulco were incorporated into the conurbation as the population of the core municipality was reduced and those living on the outside of the city increased in number, forming a second peripheral ring. This phenomenon emerged during the 1990s, and it was

Urban Planning in Guadalajara, Mexico   **159**

not unique to the city of Guadalajara, as the same pattern can be seen in other Latin American cities (Jiménez and Cruz, 2015). Nowadays, the GMA (see Figure 9.1) has extended into the municipalities of Ixtlahuacán, Juanacatlán and Zapotlanejo (IMEPLAN, 2016); even though these last municipalities are not totally conurbated, they possess connectivity and interactions with the central municipality. Consequently, the Territorial Management Plan of the Guadalajara Metropolitan Area (POTMet) was created in 2016, to answer the new conditions of urban growth, that had not been addressed since 1982; and to coordinate the urban planning of the nine conurbated municipalities with that of the state government; in other words, to require the joint participation of the various levels of governance.

The municipality of Guadalajara which is at the core of the Metropolitan Area had a negative population growth rate from 1990 to 2015, while the peripheral municipalities showed positive rates of growth. Table 9.1 contains the area of built space in the GMA from 1990 to 2015, where the variation in Guadalajara is minimal compared to that in the other municipalities. In Figure 9.2 we see the absolute variation in the number of inhabitants in Guadalajara between 2000 and

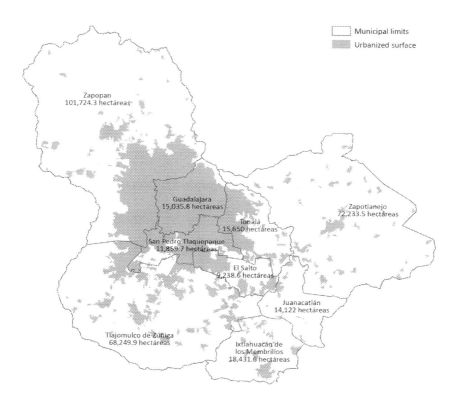

FIGURE 9.1   Guadalajara Metropolitan Area (GMA) 2016.
Source: Gobierno de Guadalajara, 2017, p. 84.

TABLE 9.1 Built Space Area in the GMA (In Ha, from 1990 to 2015)

Municipality	1990	2000	2010	2015	Annual growth rate (1990–2015) (%)	Increase between 1990–2015 (Ha)
Guadalajara	12,499	13,098	13,170	13,604	0.34	1,105
Zapopan	8,974	12,482	16,965	20,906	3.44	11,932
Tlaquepaque	3,827	5,320	7,019	8,186	3.09	4,359
Tonalá	2,413	3,698	5,700	7,012	4.36	4,599
Tlajomulco	1,952	3,391	7,654	11,094	7.20	9,141
El Salto	910	1,854	3,008	4,027	6.13	3,117
Ixtlahuacán	370	650	1,084	1,525	5.82	1,155
Juanacatlán	125	186	260	410	4.88	285
Zapotlanejo	608	932	1,436	2,475	5.77	1,867
Total	**31,630**	**41,610**	**56,296**	**69,240**	**3.18**	**37,561**

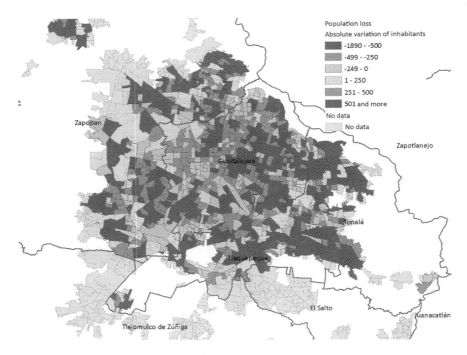

FIGURE 9.2 Absolute variation of inhabitants.
Source: Gobierno de Guadalajara, 2017, p. 90.

2010, where the municipality of Guadalajara shows a variation of as much as 1809 inhabitants within its limits; while in parts of the neighboring municipalities there is an increase of more than 500 inhabitants.

In 2017–18 Guadalajara issued the Municipal Program of Urban Development, its Population Center Plan of Urban Development and 53 Partial Plans

Urban Planning in Guadalajara, Mexico **161**

of Urban Development (PPUD), all based on the State System of Urban Development Planning (CUEJ 2008, Art. 78). The partial plans determine secondary zoning, that is, the land use destinations, and establish the rules for estate and property use. The process of formulating the PPUD, securing approval for them and getting them applied is governed by the CUEJ and binds the municipal authority to have the plans reviewed every three years to consider their upgrading or ratification. For this reason, the 2015–18 administration of the Municipality of Guadalajara decided to update its instruments, as the previous PPUD were from 2004, 2008 to 2011 (see Figure 9.3).

In Figure 9.3, there were different upgrades and criteria for each district dependent on the year of their elaboration, but the zones that presented a 14-year lag were in the center and west, where there was even more pressure on real estate as a result of the municipality's physical and economic conditions (see Figures 9.4–9.6). To understand this situation, the history of Guadalajara should be taken into account, where an East-West socio-spatial segregation has always benefited development in the West of the city, from the foundation of the city by the Spanish in 1542, on the western side of the San Juan de Dios river, till the end of the

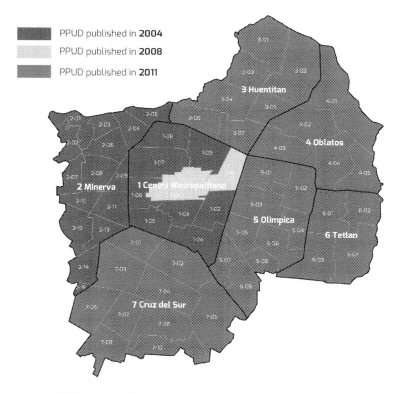

FIGURE 9.3 Valid PPUD at the time of analysis.
Source: Gobierno de Guadalajara.

19th century with the settlement of the Americana and Lafayette neighborhoods, and in the 20th century the development of neighborhoods like Chapalita and Providencia (Verduzco and Valenzuela, 2018). This segregation is the origin of one of the challenges currently faced by the municipality: the inequality of urban development between the East and the West of the territory, which the planning instruments prior to 2018 were not able to resolve efficiently.

As well as failing to address development inequality, the PPUD from before 2018 were also obsolete regarding the state of urban mobility in Guadalajara. In 2014, taking its cue from the federal policies of Sustainable Development and compact cities, the government of Jalisco, in collaboration with the federal dependencies, started the construction of a new line for the light rail system (line 3) and the extension of one of the existing lines (line 1), for the purpose of increasing the mass public transport network of the GMA, which at the time of writing in 2018 had 2 light rail lines and a BRT (Macrobús) service, as shown in Figure 9.7.

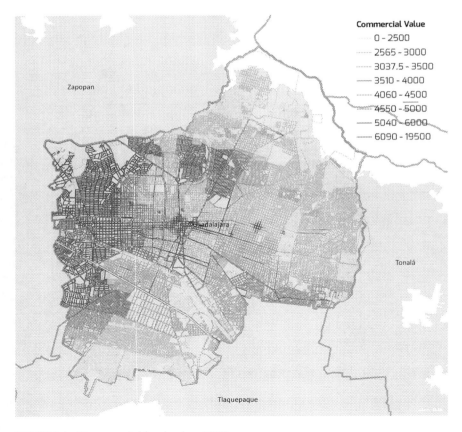

FIGURE 9.4 Commercial land value, 2016.
Source: Gobierno de Guadalajara, 2017, p. 157.

Urban Planning in Guadalajara, Mexico **163**

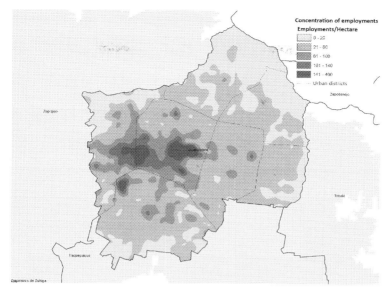

FIGURE 9.5 Concentration of employment.
Source: Gobierno de Guadalajara, 2017, p. 114.

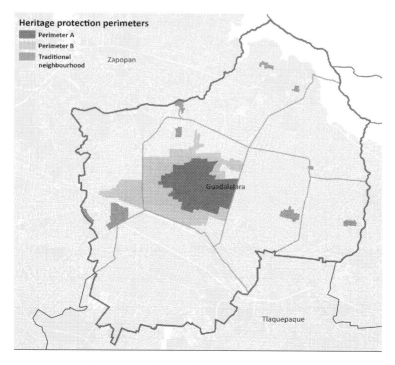

FIGURE 9.6 Built heritage protection perimeters.
Source: Gobierno de Guadalajara, 2017, pp. 232–33.

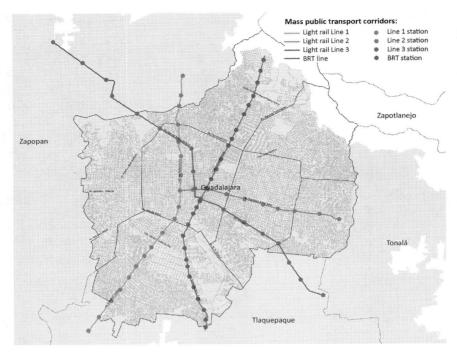

FIGURE 9.7 Mass public transit corridors.
Source: Gobierno de Guadalajara, 2017, p. 172.

This infrastructure, complemented by cycling infrastructure promoted by the state and municipal governments, represents an opportunity for public mass Transit-Oriented Development (TOD) to encourage new residential and commercial zones inside the municipality of Guadalajara and achieve a more balanced and more sustainable urban development of the territory; and in addition to countering the depopulation[3] of the municipality of Guadalajara, especially in its historic center.

University and Professional Participation in the Elaboration of the PPUD 2018

Seeking alignment with federal and state legislation and to meet the other challenges mentioned previously, on June 30, 2016, the Government of Guadalajara 2015–18 authorized the revision, elaboration and approval of a new Municipal Program of Urban Development and the planning instruments deriving from it: the Population Center Plan of Urban Development and the PPUD. Their elaboration was conducted by the municipal government itself. It is relevant to mention this fact, because since the establishment of the PPUD, these had been elaborated by private consultancy offices, and as a result, in some cases where more than one consultancy office took part, the final projects contained criteria that differed from one project to another, giving rise to various inconsistencies and incompatibilities. On this occasion, the consultancy offices were only asked to give advice on how to strengthen the legal and technical points of the plans, and this translated into savings for the government.

The Government of Guadalajara looked for people with the right profiles to manage this project, and chose mainly academics and alumni from the University of Guadalajara (UDG); among them are architects, urbanists, geographers, civil engineers and lawyers. The participation of the university in the PPUD project was spontaneous, and even though team members did not have to be from the same university, it was in fact useful for them all to have come from the University of Guadalajara, for reasons of coordination and project implementation. Most of the team members had graduated from the University Center for Art, Architecture and Design (CUAAD), specifically with degrees in Urbanism and the Environment, or in Architecture, so they had a common background in studies of urban centers. Also taking part were graduates from other campuses, such as geographers and lawyers from the University Centre of Social Sciences and Humanities (CUCSH) and civil engineers from the University Centre of Exact Sciences and Engineering (CUCEI). The diversity of profiles of the people who made up this team made it possible for the subjects covered by the PPUD to be approached from different angles, since each of the team members focused on a specific subject according to his or her aptitudes and interests, ranging from the diagnosis of demographic factors, and of the natural environment, to mobility studies, built heritage, public spaces, infrastructures and legal alignment; and including socialization, and the design and layout of the final documents. It was necessary to check, of course, that the technical work of this team was revised by other areas of the municipal government, and took into account their advice. These were the departments of Environment, Transport and Mobility, Public Works and Public Spaces, all of them under the General Office of City Management, and the office of the Municipal Ombudsman that was legally responsible for the municipal government.

The concentration of human capital and the size of the city interact to increase knowledge and raise the level of productivity (Glaeser and Resseger, 2009); people learn faster, and the flow of ideas is more efficient. The characteristics of this team of professionals facilitated to prove such a hypothesis. The team members benefited from the knowledge and abilities of each other; some effects were the following: to master specialized software for geographic information systems (GISs) or image editing and design; to implement writing, research, data analysis and project management techniques; to get to know how municipal and state legal processes work; and to deal with the public to socialize the project or just to learn more about diverse subjects related to urbanism. Thanks to the abilities acquired during the work, the PPUD project was completed in the appointed time and correct form.

The legal methodology for projecting the 2018 planning instruments was adopted on the basis of stipulations in the Urban Code (Articles 78 and 122) and the LGAHOTDU (Articles 45 and 46). However, several ambiguities concerning mobility, environment, urban facilities, infrastructure and risks were identified in the law. This situation leaves some of the PPUD content open to interpretation. Since each of the PPUD addresses one urban subdistrict of the municipality, a particular scenario was defined for everyone, with reference to the territorial policies laid out in the planning instruments of a higher rank, and with reference to the affected population; this therefore conditioned the contents of each PPUD. As the urban subdistricts are not isolated territorial units, for the analysis it was decided to apply categories of the same magnitude; in other words, the diagnosis and strategies take as a reference the whole district they belong to. For this reason also, the attributes and obligations of those involved in the application of the PPUD were defined.

One of the innovations in the creation of the 2018 PPUD was the use of a corporate geodatabase stored on a municipal server; it should be noted that Guadalajara was the first municipality in the country to implement this tool. The geodatabase facilitated analysis of the municipality's geographical phenomena and exploited the full potential of census, cadastral and geographical data. Another advantage of the geodatabase was that it allowed the operation of multi-user and integrated control of any changes; the project was therefore able to work simultaneously for the dependencies that generate geographical information, such as the departments of the Environment, Mobility and Land Management, or the Municipal Institute of Housing (IMUVI); in addition, it reduced the incidence of mistakes (Gobierno de Guadalajara, 2018). One of the benefits of implementing this mode of work was seen in the information produced, which will serve for digital platforms, such as *"Visor Urbano."* This platform was one of the winning projects in the 2016 Mayors Challenge, awarded by Bloomberg Philanthropies. *Visor Urbano* allows geo-referenced information and urban laws to be consulted, and building or operating licenses to be obtained; it was included with the aim of tackling corruption in the awarding of urban development permits, to speed up the processes, to channel investment in specific areas of the city and to allow all citizens access to information (Gobierno de Guadalajara, 2017b).

The 2018 PPUDs respect the NUA by aligning themselves with national and state urban policies, which are promoting a compact, connected city with development opportunities for all its inhabitants. Their main strategy is the repopulation of the municipality through the application of a TOD model in the corridors that host mass public transport routes in the city, intending thereby to direct densification strategies and distribute the building potential suitable for each zone. The TOD model is focused mainly on the areas shown in Figure 9.8.

These corridors capture the projections of heights, land use mixes, redensification and the redistribution of the building potential of the municipality, which coincides with the polygons of areas that are a priority for densification, as seen in Figure 9.9. It should be mentioned that the population density in these corridors is low compared to the job density, which justifies the TOD strategy and is consistent with the area where it is to be applied.

Urban Planning in Guadalajara, Mexico **167**

FIGURE 9.8 Influence area of mass public transit.
Source: Gobierno de Guadalajara, 2018, p. 93.

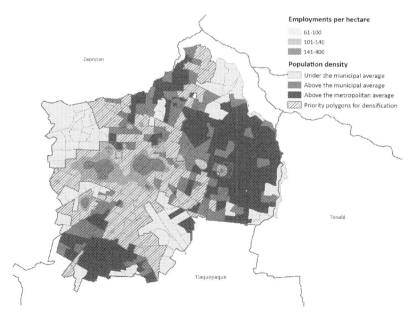

FIGURE 9.9 Priority polygons for densification.
Source: Gobierno de Guadalajara, 2018, p. 95.

168 José Luis Águila Flores and Raúl Agraz Joya

Based on the analysis above, the building potential of the municipality is redistributed, and this will direct the actions of the new PPUD. The redistribution is seen in Figure 9.10 which shows how the building potential was distributed in the PPUD in force at the time of the analysis of the situation of the municipality (see Figure 9.11), in comparison with the result of the new PPUD following the TOD model. Thanks to this strategy, the renovation of the city will be promoted through verticalization at different scales and degrees of compactness, which

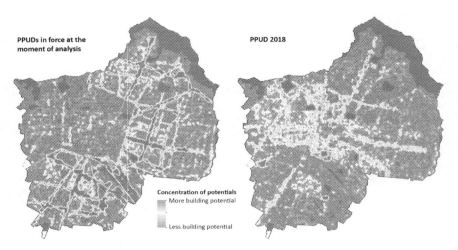

FIGURE 9.10 Redistribution of building potential.
Source: Gobierno de Guadalajara, 2018, p. 185.

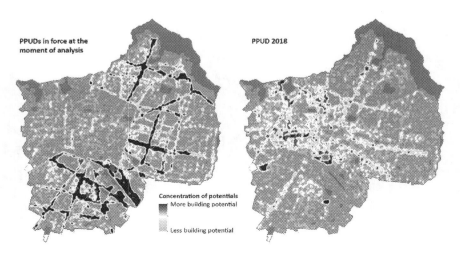

FIGURE 9.11 Redistribution of building potential.
Source: Gobierno de Guadalajara, 2018, p. 185.

will have the effect of encouraging the repopulation, economic competitiveness, mixture of land uses and the improvement of the habitability of the municipality (Gobierno de Guadalajara, 2018).

During the public consultation process of the PPUD there were coincidences in the proposals, observations and concerns of citizens, academics and private initiatives; these included regulation of the heights of buildings, the use of building potential, the compatibility of land uses and the preservation and use of the built heritage. In order to address these issues, the following general urban planning rules were formulated, which, compared with the rules of the previous PPUD, allow better use of the land, while protecting the context of the area where construction is sought.

The general urban regulations are the following:

1. Situations outside official planning or contrary to the PPUD: urbanization activities developed prior to the approval of the PPUD are now regulated.
2. Building lot conditions: to facilitate the use of intra-urban land.
3. Limits on the height of buildings: the negative impact of the height of buildings on neighboring lands is controlled, protecting sunlight provision, ventilation and the urban image of the place where they are built.
4. Increase in Occupancy and Land Use Coefficients (ICOS and ICUS): the new rules require contributions to be paid for any increase in building potential, in order to compensate for the lack of infrastructure in underutilized and low population density areas, especially those with high centrality.
5. Family housing plot division: to allow the development of a second or third dwelling on a property with permission to be used for single-family housing.
6. Road sections: liberate the strict division of roads, allowing greater preference for pedestrian and mass public transport lanes.
7. Conditions of building restrictions: to clarify the restrictions to which buildings are subject, mainly in high-rise buildings and with respect to subsequently built adjacent buildings.
8. Housing: to promote the construction of housing of social and economic interest, in order to privilege densification and verticality and to use the land more efficiently.
9. Transfer of Development Rights: the plan sets out the generalities of the system for the transfer of urban development rights, in order to improve the conditions of the estates with buildings of heritage or environmental value.
10. Design criteria for roads and parking management: basic geometries for design are set out.
11. On the conservation of the built cultural heritage: the plan establishes the applicable technical criteria for conservation and restoration to homologate the characteristics of all the movable and immovable components that make up the urban landscape.
12. Recession of façades: the plan guarantees the preservation of the urban image and prevents the destruction or degradation of the built cultural heritage.

13 Noise control: contains the first standard of this nature, which attempts to zonify noise by minimizing negative elements in mixed land use areas.

The outcome of the participation of young graduates from the same university as the academics directing them was satisfactory and unprecedented. The implementation of the project was efficient, under the guidance of leaders with adequate experience and skills added to the team's intellectual capital, its rapid learning capacity and its adaptation to available resources; and effective, in producing the PPUD in the required times and with content consistent with the urban reality of Guadalajara and national and state urban development policies.

Although on this occasion the participation of the University of Guadalajara was spontaneous and indirect, the project of the 2018 PPUD may provide a precedent for formalizing an association of the University with the municipal government in order to improve the quality of life in the city. Graduates have the abilities and the knowledge to apply them in practice, as observed with the members of the 2018 PPUD team; however, questions arose about how to project the planning instruments and their scope and how the particular disciplines involved can contribute to the design of the strategies; therefore, it is important, starting in the classroom, to go deeper into understanding the formulation of planning instruments, the different reaches of urban legislation and how these urban policies materialize in the city.

Regarding the city-university relationship, the Hixon Center for Urban Ecology of Yale University (2017) argues that there is mutual benefit, as the generation of information and the possession of intellectual capital and trained human resources, all complement each other. First of all, the university generates information based on city data and then uses the new data to guide the city's policies and actions, which will result in feedback for the university. Second, the university generates intellectual capital or trains human resources, and the city provides an opportunity for practice. The university also offers to help with three aspects of forging this partnership: leadership, which is the commitment, communication and dedication of both parties; building a culture of association, by formalizing the association and identifying who will intervene and how; finally, funding: explaining what is to be provided and alternative methods of financing. Webber (2012) agrees with these criteria, but adds that this type of association can begin when the university takes the initiative to improve its immediate context, that is, the neighborhood or area where it is located.

In Mexico there is no parameter for university-city collaboration that goes beyond intermittent projects or agreements for professional practice or social service by university students in municipalities in contrast to the Hixon Center for Urban Ecology and Webber (2012), where there are cases of collaboration between the two institutions that transcends research, planning and project management, such as those of UBC-Vancouver City, University of Chicago-City of Chicago, and the University of Wisconsin-Madison-City of Madison, to name a few. For the University of Guadalajara, an association of this kind would be feasible, since there are university centers and schools of higher secondary education that are points of reference in the areas where they are located and, due to their influence, to generate housing zones, commercial activities, infrastructure and complementary urban facilities around them; the same happens with the campuses of the other universities located in the GMA. For these reasons, it would be valuable for the collaboration of the University and local government to be formalized, as there is potential to generate mutually beneficial projects and information.

Conclusions

The correct application of the NUA in Mexico will depend on the states and municipalities. Due to the fact that it is recent, most of the state and municipal legislations are not aligned with the national urban development policy. Additionally, each state and municipality presents conditions in its particular natural, demographic, urban and economic context, which implies applying the NUA using different strategies; moreover, the human resources and the intellectual capital that each entity counts on have an influence at the moment of elaboration of their respective planning instruments. Now with the new electoral reform, there is a chance of continuity in the programs and plans of urban development, as the length of time of the municipal administrations is doubled, including the time to monitor their actions. In contrast, cases like those of the State of Jalisco and the Municipality of Guadalajara count with the legal and urban conditions and the human resources that allow them to apply the national urban development policies. Of course, citizen participation within the formulation process is always a priority.

The analysis of Guadalajara is important, since it is one of the few municipalities that have upgraded their legislation and urban instruments, adhering to the new urban demands and general guidelines. The inclusion of young professionals and academics from the University of Guadalajara in the elaboration of the 2018 PPUDs was a lucky coincidence that provided the opportunity for a city-university association to be formalized, which implies maintaining a source of intellectual capital and human resources that can contribute to the city while, at the same time, the city enriches the knowledge of the new professionals. Guadalajara also hosts several other universities, so the idea of a university network with the municipal government should be considered.[4]

Notes

1 https://www.gob.mx/sedatu/acciones-y-programas/fortalecimiento-para-la-reforma-del-desarrollo-urbano-y-el-ordenamiento-territorial-147027
2 https://elpais.com/tecnologia/2017/03/12/actualidad/1489275848_767120.html
3 Around 200,000 inhabitants from 1990 to 2015.
4 The original version of the article was published in the document titled "Libro de Actas del XIV Congreso de la Asociación Latinoamericana de Escuelas de Urbanismo y Planificación" (ISNN 2452–4573).

References

Águila, J. L. (2019). (Re)densificación y condominio; la perspectiva urbana de Guadalajara. Universidad de Guadalajara y Unión Iberoamericana de Municipalistas. México y España.

Arias, C. F. (2011). "Evolución de la legislación urbanística e instrumentos de planificación en Jalisco y Guadalajara, de 1933 a 1995 y hasta la actualidad." in *Derecho urbanístico* (pp. 449–61). Universidad Nacional Autónoma de México, Coordinación de Humanidades, Programa Universitario de Estudios sobre la Ciudad.

Chaparro, J. J. (2017). "México y la Nueva Agenda Urbana. Hoja de ruta con trazos invisibles. [in] capacidades institucionales en el Estado de México," *Bitácora Urbano Territorial* 27(2): 35–43. doi:10.15446/bitacora.v27n2.63133

Código Urbano para el Estado de Jalisco CUEJ (2018). Congreso el Estado de Jalisco.

Glaeser, E. and Resseger, M. (2009). "The Complementarity between Cities and Skills." doi: 10.3386/w15103

Gobierno de Guadalajara. (2017a). Mayors Challenge: https://guadalajara.gob.mx/GIC-GDL/.

Gobierno de Guadalajara (2017b). Programa Municipal de Desarrollo Urbano 2017–2042.

Gobierno de Guadalajara (2018). Planes Parciales de Desarrollo Urbano.

Gobierno de Jalisco (2014). Programa Sectorial de Desarrollo Territorial y Urbano.

Gobierno de Jalisco (2016). Plan Estatal de Desarrollo Jalisco 2013–2033; Actualización 2016.

Guay, L. (1989), "Connaissance et action en planification / John Friedmann. Planning in the Public Domain: From Knowledge to Action, Princeton, Princeton University Press, 1987." *International Review of Community Development* 22: 198–200. doi:10.7202/1034029ar

Hixon Center for Urban Ecology (2017). *Forging University-Municipality Partnerships toward Urban Sustainability.* https://hixon.yale.edu/events/conference/forging-university-municipality-partnerships-toward-urban-sustainability

IMCO (2016). Índice de Competitividad Urbana 2016: Reelección municipal y rendición de cuentas: ¿Cómo lograr el círculo virtuoso? http://imco.org.mx/indices/reeleccion-municipal-y-rendicion-de-cuentas/introduccion

IMCO, WRI, and CMM (2016). Observaciones y recomendaciones a la Ley General de Asentamientos Humanos, Ordenamiento Territorial y Desarrollo Urbano: https://imco.org.mx/desarrollo_urbano/observaciones-y-recomendaciones-a-la-ley-general-de-asentamientos-humanos-ordenamiento-territorial-y-desarrollo-urbano/

IMEPLAN (2016). POTmet del AMG.

Jiménez, E. R. and Cruz, H. (2015). "Opportunities and Challenges for Consolidated Informal Urbanization in the Metropolitan Area of Guadalajara," In Ward, P.M., Jiménez Huerta, E.R., & Di Virgilio, M.M. (Eds.), *Housing Policy in Latin American Cities: A New Generation of Strategies and Approaches for 2016 UN-Habitat III* (1st edn, pp. 47–72). Routledge. https://doi.org/10.4324/9781315773001.

Ley General de Asentamientos Humanos, Ordenamiento Territorial y Desarrollo Urbano LGAHOTDU (2016), Gobierno de México. DOT 28-11-2016.

SEDATU (2017). Nueva Metodología para la elaboración y actualización de Programas Municipales de Desarrollo Urbano.

SEDATU, INEGI y CONAPO (2018). Delimitación de las Zonas Metropolitanas de México 2015.

UN-Habitat (2014). The Evolution of National Urban Policies: A Global Overview." Nairobi, Kenya: UN-Habitat: https://unhabitat.org/books/the-evolution-of-national-urban-policies/

UN-Habitat (2016). Agenda 2030 y Objetivos de Desarrollo Sostenible; Una oportunidad para América Latina y el Caribe.
Verduzco, B. and Valenzuela, B. (2018). Los distritos urbanos gastronómico-turísticos: conflictos y problemas de gestión pública. Guadalajara, México. *Revista EURE—Revista De Estudios Urbano Regionales* 44(132): 237–62.
Webber, H. (2012). *Building Effective City-University Partnerships: Lessons from the Heartland* (Summary of policies) Rappaport Institute for Greater Boston, Radcliffe Institute for Advanced Study: https://www.hks.harvard.edu/centers/rappaport/research-and-publications/policy-briefs/building-effective-city-university-partnerships

Research and Evaluations of Transformative Policy Initiatives

Chapter 10

TOWARDS CIRCULAR ECONOMY IMPLEMENTATION IN URBAN PROJECTS

Practices and Assessment Tools[1]

Federica Appendino, Charlotte Roux, Myriam Saadé, and Bruno Peuportier

Introduction

Over the last ten years, the concept of circular economy (CE) has gained momentum in politics, business and academia (Kampelmann 2016; Reike, Vermeulen, and Witjes 2017) to overcome the contradictions between economic and environmental prosperity (Geissdoerfer et al. 2017). The current economic model, characterised as 'linear' and based on a 'take-make-consume-throw away' approach of resources, is reaching its limits. Alternatively, CE forms an "economic system of trade and production which, at all stages of the product lifecycle, aims to increase the efficiency of resource use and reduce the impact on the environment, while developing the well-being of individuals" (ADEME 2014). For these reasons, CE represents already the core theme of major European plans and regulations (Petit-Boix and Leipold 2018), such as the 'Circular Economy Package' adopted in 2015.

Today several disciplines ranging from economics to urban planning are studying CE, in close relation with sustainable development issues (Kirchherr, Reike, and Hekkert 2017). However, no univocal and shared definition of CE has yet been developed, despite a wide dissemination of the concept (Prieto-Sandoval, Jaca, and Ormazabal 2017). Thus, CE constitutes an evolving notion (Merli, Preziosi, and Acampora 2018), rather ambiguous and vague (Korhonen et al. 2017) whose potential "still needs to be unlocked" (OECD 2020).

The built environment, given its important contribution to several environmental issues, is supposedly one of the main targets of CE strategies. However, scientific literature on the subject remains limited (Adams et al. 2017; Bocken et al. 2017), and concrete application of the principle is so far slowly implemented (Adams et al. 2017; Pomponi and Moncaster 2017; Tingley, Giesekam, and Cooper-Searle 2018). CE is mainly understood as waste recycling and

DOI: 10.4324/9781003178545-14

management (Ghisellini et al. 2018), and the potential effects of its implementation at urban scale are poorly investigated (Haupt, Vadenbo, and Hellweg 2017). Then, little consensus exists on how to best approach and deal with this concept in the building sector, and the knowledge and tools required to enact it remain to be developed (Leising, Quist, and Bocken 2018).

Subsequently, the international scientific community calls for a better understanding of the role played by the built environment in translating the CE concept into action. Furthermore, there is still a need to demonstrate and assess the environmental impacts of such translation. Implementing CE initiatives generates not only potential benefits, but also a number of environmental risks. 'Closing the loop' does not always positively affect the environment, and therefore, 'circularity' should be assessed with relevant indicators (Kampelmann 2016; Petit-Boix and Leipold 2018). The CE is supposed to be "not an end per se, but a means to an end: it provides an opportunity to do more with less" (OECD 2020), and it is necessary to ensure the implementation of the most environmentally relevant initiatives. For this reason, the application of systemic methods and tools corroborating the environmental relevance of the CE applied to the built environment is now required (Haupt et al. 2017; Haupt and Zschokke 2017).

This chapter explores how CE is (or is planned to be) implemented at neighbourhood scale and which assessment tools are used. In the following sections, the contribution provides an analysis of four 'circular neighbourhood' projects located in Europe. The next section briefly summarises the literature debate on CE in the built environment. The third section describes the methodology, and the fourth section presents the analysis of the case studies. The fifth section compares and discusses the main findings. Highlighting a diverse representation of the CE paradigm in urban projects, our analysis stresses the usefulness of assessment tools, particularly to avoid the implementation of environmentally harmful actions promoted as circular.

CE in the Built Environment: From the 'Circular City' to the 'Circular Neighbourhood'

The CE approach is gaining momentum in the field of urban sustainability. Several studies, as well as some international meetings, have investigated the role that CE can play to ensure a more sustainable development of cities. References on the subject are growing (Cities Foundation 2017; Ellen MacArthur Foundation 2017; Prendeville, Cherim, and Bocken 2018).

From the scientific literature, Pomponi and Moncaster (2017) identify three scales of CE deployment: the 'macro scale' of the city, the 'meso scale' of the buildings and the 'micro scale' of the construction elements. Academic research has so far consistently apprehended the macro scale, through the assessment of urban metabolism and eco-parks, as well as the micro scale, particularly materials and building components. The meso scale remains however poorly investigated.

Considering their pressures on the environment, urban research on CE has focused on 'circular cities.' Several cities, such as Berlin, Rotterdam, Paris, London, Milan and Amsterdam, have recently adopted strategic plans and are launching specific actions and projects to make their economy more circular. For instance, the City of Amsterdam adopted in 2014 'The Circular Metropolis Amsterdam 2014–2018,'[2] a strategic document aimed at transforming the city into a competitive and sustainable European metropolis. This document, which comprises part of the Amsterdam Smart City initiative, relies on the 'City Circle Scan' approach identifying areas where major CE progress can be made. Based on this tool, Amsterdam decided to focus on the construction sector as well as the organic production and biomass sector. In addition, Amsterdam became in 2016 a Fab-City, part of an international initiative bringing approximately 20 cities together with the goal of becoming self-sufficient.[3]

Similarly, the City of Rotterdam linked CE to the Smart City Initiative, adopting the 'Roadmap Circular Economy Rotterdam'[4] in 2016. The actions proposed to ensure the city's sustainable and circular development by 2030 are based on the results of the 'Rotterdam Metabolism' study, which provided a comprehensive picture of urban flows. Rotterdam's CE strategy focuses primarily on the city's port area for implementing biosourced projects (Prendeville et al. 2018).

More recently, London and Paris presented guidance documents in 2017. Following the 2015 General Assembly of the Circular Economy, Paris adopted its first 'Circular Economy Plan 2017–2020'[5] and its operational roadmap. London similarly published a 'Circular Economy Route Map,'[6] containing actions involving the construction, food, textile, plastic and electrical industries. A complementary economic analysis estimated at £2.8 billion the benefits of the Map in terms of wealth creation, activities and employment.

Initiatives and actions are multiplying in parallel with the creation of global networks bringing together several cities. The Circular Europe Network (CEN),[7] for example, gathers dozens of European cities to exchange best practices. At the international level, the Open Source Circular Economy (OSCE)[8] collects innovative solutions linking CE and open data. But research on CE has hitherto dedicated little attention to the meso scale, even though authors have stressed the importance of orienting CE research towards the built environment and the building scale (Glass, Greenfield, and Longhurst 2017; Pomponi and Moncaster 2017; Leising et al. 2018). In Europe, the built base represents almost half of the total energy consumption, and more than 50% of all extracted materials (BPIE 2011). In France, it is responsible for nearly 40% of energy consumption, 60% of electricity consumption and approximately a quarter of national greenhouse gases emissions (ADEME 2012). In addition, the construction sector generates nearly three-quarters of the national waste[9] volume and consumes approximately 600 km^2 of natural areas per year.[10]

In this context, the built environment could represent an essential cornerstone for the implementation of effective CE strategies in the city. Several authors have pointed out that the 'neighbourhood scale,' linking the city and the building, is the most relevant for addressing different environmental problems (Lotteau 2017). In Europe, the attention paid to the neighbourhood scale has even become central to the sustainable city discourse (Souami 2009). However, research on CE application in neighbourhoods remains limited, and there is a lack of comprehensive studies reviewing recent advances. A number of pathfinder projects are however emerging, and the number of 'circular urban projects' is increasing in practice, raising questions about their effects on urban project dynamics and their environmental performances. To answer this, assessment tools have been developed (Popovici and Peuportier 2004; Herfray and Peuportier 2010; Roux Peuportier and Herfray 2013) and applied to the design of urban projects at neighbourhood scale (Peuportier 2005, 2015; Peuportier, Vorger and Herfray 2012).

However, only little attention has been paid to study, characterise (Appendino, Roux and Peuportier 2018) and evaluate the environmental impacts of such projects (Girard and Nocca 2019). A recent literature review pointed out that current academic discourses focus only marginally on CE indicators and assessment tools (Appendino et al. 2018). To date, assessment frameworks do not provide adequate tools to measure effectively the progress made in the field (OECD 2019). On these bases, the present chapter aims to address the two following questions:

Q1) How can CE be implemented in a neighbourhood?
Q2) What assessment tools are used?

Methodology

This study analyses and compares four case studies of a 'circular neighbourhood.' The case study method was selected because it enables integrating theory and practice, aptly suiting the exploratory nature of this research (Leising et al. 2018). First, we conducted a literature review to identify relevant 'circular neighbourhood' cases. In addition to scientific papers, reports and urban planning documents completed the corpus. Scientific literature was indeed mostly limited to theoretical discussion with little attention to the neighbourhood scale. The research involved English, French and Italian references. Four case studies were found and selected: the first concerns the neighbourhood of Buiksloterham (Amsterdam), which will develop into a sustainable district, based on circular principles; the second neighbourhood is Kera (Espoo), an industrial area destined to become a 'liveable circular economy neighbourhood.' The last two cases are located in Paris, namely, the Groues and Saint-Vincent-de-Paul eco-neighbourhoods, both considered 'EC living labs.' The selection of all cases responded to two fundamental criteria: the willingness to implement CE principles at the neighbourhood scale and the existence of a comprehensive CE strategy at the city level, within which the project fits in.

Following the case selection, CE initiatives and actions were identified and classified using document analysis and integrating data collected through semi-structured interviews with local stakeholders involved in the projects. Finally, we defined a conceptual framework analysis based on three criteria: CE practices, strategic city scale integration and tools employed. We applied this analytical framework to the four case studies for comparison.

Case Studies Analysis

The selection of the four case studies relies on their innovative character and central relevance of the CE. In all four urban projects, CE appears as a key pillar.

As illustrated in Table 10.1, despite the differences in size and location, the analysed neighbourhoods present some common features. For instance, all four cases constitute urban regeneration projects, and at the same time, they are experimental, functioning as showcases to test the CE principles. It is also important to underline that all projects are recent and at different stages of implementation. None of them is yet completed. For this reason, the analysis focuses on the design phase.

Buiksloterham, Amsterdam

Amsterdam represents one of Europe's pioneering cities in terms of CE. CE constitutes one of the main pillars of the Sustainable Amsterdam Agenda (2015). The Agenda sets targets for 2020 by reducing energy consumption by 20% and increasing renewable production by 20% compared to 2013 (van der Hoek, Struker, and de Danschutter 2017). In this strategic document, the Buiksloterham neighbourhood is considered "an engine for the broader transition of Amsterdam" (Metabolic 2015) towards a circular city. Part of a larger redevelopment plan of the northern banks of the river, Buiksloterham is characterised by abandoned

TABLE 10.1 Case studies

Case	Buiksloterham	Kera	Les Groues	Saint-Vincent-de-Paul
City and Country	Amsterdam, Netherlands	Espoo, Finland	Nanterre, France	Paris, France
Size	1000 hectares	22 hectares	65 hectares	4 hectares
Site	Requalification industrial areas	Requalification industrial areas	Requalification industrial areas	Requalification hospital complex
Main Objective	"key innovation zone for circular development"	"a showcase district for circular economy"	"circular economy living-lab"	"a privileged space to develop and test circular economy"
Starting date	Around 2015	Around 2018	Around 2018	Around 2018

factories, wastelands and docks. Once the site of Amsterdam's most polluting industries, the neighbourhood could become according to the city's vision "a key innovation zone for circular urban development" (Metabolic 2016). The municipality proposed a bottom-up approach for the area's redevelopment in order to build a more comprehensive sustainability strategy. To this end, approximately 20 stakeholders, including local actors, organisations, associations and companies, signed in 2015 the 'Circular Buiksloterham Manifesto.' This innovative manifesto included the shared guiding principles for redeveloping Buikloterham, such as the zero-waste objective, the implementation of clean technologies or the use of biosourced materials.

Reckoning the urgency for a clear operational strategy, all involved stakeholders commissioned an Urban Metabolism Scan in order to understand the neighbourhood's complete workings from a systemic perspective. The analysis, carried out by the Metabolic and published in 2015, involved three stages: context analysis, stakeholder analysis and metabolism analysis. The 'Urban Metabolism Scan' focused on material and energy flows, biodiversity, environmental conditions, socio-economic factors, local actors, urban planning documents and plans, health and living environment.

A study on the neighbourhood's CE potential followed this analysis. On these bases, the priority objectives for redeveloping Buikloterham as a 'living lab for CE' by 2034 were translated into eight priority issues (Table 10.2).

With regard to the built environment, it is interesting to note that a 'Circular Building Standard' applies for all renovations or new constructions. This innovative assessment tool, which is still in the development phase, would allow tax

TABLE 10.2 Buiksloterham's objectives

Objectives	
Energy	Buiksloterham is energy self-sufficient with a fully renewable energy supply
Materials and products	Buiksloterham is a zero-waste neighbourhood with a near 100% circular material flow
Water	Buiksloterham is rainproof and has near 100% resource recovery from wastewater
Ecosystems and biodiversity	Buiksloterham's ecosystems are regenerated, and its base of natural capital is self-renewing
Infrastructure and mobility	Buiksloterham's Infrastructure is maximally used and local mobility has zero emissions
Socio-cultural	Buiksloterham has a diverse and inclusive culture, and a high-quality, liveable environment
Economy	Buiksloterham has a strong local economy that stimulates entrepreneurship and encourages the creation and exchange of multiple kinds of values (social, environmental, cultural)
Health and well-being	Buiksloterham is a healthy, safe and attractive environment with recreational activity space for all residents

credits once the standard has been reached. Among the key recommendations, all building roofs are equipped for clean energy production and rainwater collection, and all materials are registered in a digital passport to facilitate their identification. In addition, prefabricated building elements are preferred, facilitating deconstruction and reuse.

To ensure these objectives, a first action plan was developed. The proposed actions consisted of two types: systemic, aimed at ensuring the district's long-term transition, and technical, concerning specific issues. For the definition of the actions, prioritisation work was carried out. In particular, the actions considered most urgent related to new constructions and infrastructures. Consequently, the priority actions concerned the energy efficiency of the built stock, the flexibility of new infrastructures, the development of fresh mobility, water recovery and management (Metabolic 2016).

Kera, Espoo

The City of Espoo, Finland, is one of the pioneering cities in terms of sustainable development, as demonstrated in a comparative assessment study of 15 European cities carried out in 2017 by the University of Tilburg.[11] Initiatives led by the municipality within the framework of the Helsinki Metropolitan Plan, as well as the Helsinki Metropolitan Area Smart and Clean Cooperation project, are multiplying, with the objective of becoming carbon neutral by 2050.[12] In most cases, CE constitutes a central issue.

In this context, the Kera neighbourhood, located in the eastern part of Espoo and close to the train station, represents a unique opportunity for the municipality to experiment with innovative CE solutions. Previously an industrial area, headquarter of Finland's largest distribution group, Kera will be transformed into a mixed-use and dense neighbourhood of 14,000 residents. In addition to commercial services and offices, the project includes day-care centres, schools, sports and recreation services.[13]

The municipality's objective is to transform by 2035 this industrial park into a liveable neighbourhood with a strong CE focus (Table 10.3). The goal of the project is to make Kera "a showcase district for circular economy,"[14] as well as "an international example of circular economy."[15] It is with this perspective that the case of Kera was presented as an example of a 'circular neighbourhood' at the World Circular Economy Forum of 2017.[16]

The ongoing project was the winner of the Kera Challenge,[17] launched in 2015 with the aim of identifying a vision and project for Kera's future, based on the principles of sustainable urban planning and EC. In the winning project, Co-op City, CE is supposed to be achieved through a "large range of different measures, from boosting resources efficiency and creating closed loop systems to involving the local residents."[18]

The main solutions to support CE put forward in the project relate to the recycling of the industrial architecture, the development of sharing economy and

TABLE 10.3 Kera's objectives

Objectives				
The first Nordic neighbourhood built according to the CE principles	A 20-minute walkable neighbourhood, where everyday destinations are within walking distance	A sustainable planning and construction process, by using ecological and innovative building technologies and materials	A network of green infrastructure and multifunctional public places	A versatile, dense, mixed use, human scale urban fabric

digital services, the creation of mobile platforms for smart mobility services and the conception of a resilient green infrastructure of public spaces.

In particular, with respect to the built environment, the 'Kera Design Manual' describes the considered EC practices. In the manual, all constructions are required to be biodegradable or fully recyclable to phase out gradually construction waste. The flexibility of the constructed buildings represents one of the documented principles. This flexibility provides the basis for the possibility of a future 'circular regeneration' of the built stock. In this perspective, Life Cycle Assessment (LCA) will be mandatory. In addition, for new constructions, all materials used are required to be fully biodegradable or recyclable in order to reduce construction waste.

Concerning reuse and recycling, attention is paid both to existing materials, such as asphalt, which must be recovered, and to the construction elements of existing buildings, such as beams, slabs and columns. In addition, the temporary use of some existing buildings is highlighted as an EC practice. It is interesting to note that 100% of the primary energy demand will be produced from renewable sources, some of which produced on site. Solar, geothermal and wind energies are planned and will feed into an intelligent energy grid. For new constructions, passive solutions are preferred.

Les Groues, Nanterre

The urban redevelopment project of Les Groues in Nanterre, led by the Etablissement Public d'Aménagement de la Défense Seine-Arche (EPADESA), aims to create a mixed district, offering housing, office space, shops, services and equipment, accommodating nearly 12,000 inhabitants and as many jobs.[19] Close to the business district of La Défense and served by a future line of the Grand Paris metro, the Les Groues neighbourhood covers approximately 65 hectares. It is characterised by numerous wastelands and distressed buildings. The goal of the Les Groues development project is to become a "laboratory for a dynamic, green

TABLE 10.4 Les Groues' objectives

Objectives				
Energy transition and the fight against climate change	Biodiversity and respect for natural resources	Protection against nuisances and creation of healthy and comfortable environments	Creation of an economic innovation ecosystem integrating a diversity of actors and co-design approaches	Laboratory of circular and solidarity economy

and inclusive neighbourhood,"[20] and more generally, to become "an experimental laboratory for the sustainable city of tomorrow."[21] In particular, the project aims to be exemplary in environmental matters and to obtain the EcoQuartier Label, becoming a positive energy territory.[22]

Five strategic axes constitute the foundation of the project (Table 10.4).

As such, CE represents one of the main pillars of the project's sustainable development strategy. Winner of the Call for Expression of Interest 'Circular Economy and Urban Planning' launched by the ADEME in 2015, the Les Groues project offers a place to experiment CE at neighbourhood and territorial scale. The actions planned for CE are multiple, and the built environment receives particular attention through the local management of construction site waste (choice of materials, grey energy, local management of backfill/burial) (ADEME 2017).

In addition, the ZAC project plans to place the built environment at the centre of CE's approach, as well as the project's overall energy efficiency ambition. To this end, 'life cycle thinking' is encouraged:

> the building must be understood in all its spatial and temporal integrity by real estate operators, who must understand the life cycle of their building: its manufacturing processes and materials, its duration over time and its capacity to adapt and evolve up to its deconstruction.[23]

The concepts of 'grey energy' and 'transformation capacity' are also central. Other CE practices are highlighted as well, such as rainwater harvesting, building flexibility and modularity, neighbourhood waste harvesting and reuse of existing buildings.

In addition, EPADESA launched in 2016 two calls for projects, aimed at inspiring innovative reflections and experiments on the CE theme. The first one concerns temporary urban planning approaches, allowing to extend the lifespan of existing buildings. The ephemeral initiatives presented were highly diverse, ranging from soil remediation to the reuse of building materials, or even innovative start-up incubators. The second one directly concerns new constructions and aims at developing innovative CE solutions in the construction sector. LCA has been applied to the design of five office buildings, and the environmental benefit of recycling has been studied.

The project is underway, and after this first phase of experimentation, the challenge is to bring overall coherence to these CE actions at the neighbourhood level. In particular, there is a willingness to establish fruitful local alliances mainly around the reuse of materials.

Saint-Vincent-de-Paul, Paris

Located in the 14th arrondissement of Paris, the Saint-Vincent-de-Paul former hospital remained under decommissioning for approximately ten years. In 2014, it was acquired by the Municipality of Paris to transform it into an innovative eco-neighbourhood (City of Paris 2017). Covering an area of 4 hectares, the redevelopment project of the Saint-Vincent-de-Paul Hospital represented a rare opportunity for urban transformation in the heart of Paris' particularly dense urban fabric.

In particular, the objectives pursued by Paris are as follows (Table 10.5).

In December 2016, the ZAC was created and granted to the developer Paris Batignolles Aménagement. The construction work began in 2018, planning for approximately 60,000 m^2 of total floor area, broken down into housing (including 50% social housing), facilities, equipment (including a school and a gymnasium), shops and a public garden.[24] With regard to the built environment, the future district aims to become an exemplary showcase for the entire city thanks to an ambitious environmental approach. Specifically, the Resilience Strategy adopted in 2017 described the project as the city's first resilient and carbon-neutral neighbourhood. In compliance with the city's framework documents, and as a "pilot district for sustainable development" (City of Paris 2017) involving its inhabitants, the project aims at reducing impacts on the environment and promoting innovative technologies. In this perspective, the new project provides for reversible buildings, pooling resources, conserving and converting 60% of

TABLE 10.5 Saint-Vincent-de-Paul's objectives

Objectives			
Create a predominantly residential area, promoting social diversity	Lead an exemplary environmental approach, making Saint-Vincent-de-Paul an innovative and emblematic eco-neighbourhood for the city	Think of public and open spaces as green spaces, whether on roofs, floors or facades	Enhance the heritage and history of the site

existing buildings, developing renewable energies, certifying new constructions, optimising energy systems and recovering waste.

ZAC Saint-Vincent-de-Paul aims to be "a privileged space to develop the principle of CE."[25] Several actions are put forward in the field of CE, respecting the orientations of the Parisian CE plan. With regard to the built environment, attention is being paid to reusing certain buildings, which would make it possible to limit demolitions, short circuits and temporary occupation of existing buildings, as well as to ensure continuity with the ephemeral urban planning experimentation of the Grands Voisins, including smart grids, urban agriculture and bio-waste.

The project has specific objectives related to waste generated during the construction phase, such as: material recovery by reuse in place or elsewhere (in particular, building elements such as doors and windows, which can easily find a new use, or concrete waste and bricks, which can be used as aggregates) and energy recovery from waste; to this end, a process of recovering dismountable elements likely to be reused is planned for all site operations, thanks to an inventory distributed to various local, potentially interested structures. For both new construction and rehabilitation, architects have to demonstrate the proportion of reused materials as early as the design phase of their project. CE indicators are being developed and will be introduced into the project's Building Information Modelling (BIM) to produce global indicators at the neighbourhood level. As part of the PULSE-PARIS research project, funded by ADEME,[26] LCA will also be used to evaluate Saint-Vincent-de-Paul CE actions related to deconstruction, renovation and new construction.

Cross-Case Comparison and Discussion

The results of the analysis are summarised in Table 10.6 and compared by applying the analytical grid based on the following criteria: CE practices, strategic city scale integration and tools employed. Following this three-step analysis, some significant similarities have been revealed.

First of all, the four projects are integrated into strategic documents addressing sustainable development and CE of each city, such as the Smart City Agenda, Climate Change Plan and so on. Furthermore, these documents always present the projects as 'experimental demonstrators' of CE in urban projects. Therefore, there is always a strong link between the strategic planning scale and the operational scale of the urban project. However, it is important to note that, in all reviewed cases, CE is often seen as one of the pillars of sustainable development, and sometimes, no distinction is made among the proposed actions between those related to the CE and to sustainable development.

Second, the analogies are also evident with respect to CE practices identified in the projects. With regard to the case studies analysis, it is possible to classify four categories of recurrent practices: energy, water, waste and 'other.' In particular, all cases insist on flexibility and temporary occupancy of buildings, the reuse

TABLE 10.6 Cross-case comparison

	Buiksloterham	Kera	Les Groues	Saint-Vincent-de-Paul
Strategic city scale integration	Sustainable Agenda Smart City Initiative Circular Amsterdam	Sustainable Agenda Smart City Initiative	EcoQuartier Label	Resilience Plan Territorial Climate Plan Circular Economy Plan
Tools employed	Circular Building Standard Materials digital Passport MFA	Kera design manual LCA Buildings	(LCA Perspective)	LCA Building Carbon Footprint Municipality's assessment tool
CE practices — Energy	100% Renewable energy PassivHaus Label Local energy production 100% energy recovery from wastewater	100% Renewable energy PassivHaus Label Local energy production (Géothermal, Eolic) Smart Grid	70% Renewable energy Energy recovery from wastewater	40% Electricity by photovoltaic panels PassivHaus Label Smart Grid
Waste and materials	Reuse materials 100% « circular material flow » Deconstruction Zero-waste objective	Reuse materials and construction elements Biodegradable or recyclable materials	Reuse of materials and existing buildings Local management of construction and demolition waste Waste recovery and valourisation	Reuse of materials and existing buildings Local management of construction and demolition waste Waste recovery and valourisation
Water	Rainwater collection	« Green and Blue Tools »	Rainwater collection	Rainwater collection
Other	Temporary occupancy of buildings Buildings flexibility Prefabricated constructions and structures Auto-construction Urban agriculture and local food production	Temporary occupancy of buildings Buildings flexibility	Temporary occupancy of buildings Buildings flexibility Urban agriculture	Temporary occupancy of buildings Urban agriculture Short circuits CE stakeholders point of reference

of building materials, elements and existing buildings, and eco-construction. On this subject, an important focus is placed on the energy aspects of new buildings, with precise standards to be achieved.

All case studies also insist on favouring reuse over recycling. The focus is primarily on the reuse of existing structures, which is considered to be the most preferred option in the projects. Indeed, reusing means using an item once again for the same or a different purpose, while recycling is often an energy-intensive process, wherein a used item is turned into bulk secondary material through operations such as grinding and/or melting. For this reason, the flexibility of new buildings is also emphasised, to ensure the easy reuse of structures in the future according to the renewed demands. Second, all elements such as doors, windows or even interior furnishings should be recovered and reused whenever possible, as well as building materials. For this reason, all cases refer to selective deconstruction and disassembly as best practice. In this regard, it is interesting to note that there is a need for temporary storage of materials and elements, preferably close to the site location. This is particularly difficult in dense urban areas such as Paris, where space is lacking, while it is much more feasible in the case of Kera and Buiksloterham, where terrains have been vacant for years. Furthermore, the marketplace of second-hand building elements and materials is still immature, despite the development of digital platforms connecting the different actors, the supply and the demand.[27] Very precise rules (technical, legal and economic) govern the use of construction materials, limiting the possibility of reuse (ADEME 2016).

Interventions related to the temporary use of buildings seem to require a relatively low investment and are easily removed. Other practices highlighted by at least two cases relate to waste management, particularly construction site waste, as well as water management and urban agriculture. More generally, the comparative table indicates a wide variety of CE practices, focusing primarily on environmental issues. The other two pillars of sustainable development, economic and social, would not appear to be central. Despite the great number of CE practices within these cases, their implications in environmental, economic and social terms do not appear to have been studied in depth. Some practices remain vague. Quantified and measurable targets relate almost exclusively to energy issues.

There is no consensus regarding the tools employed. For instance, the Dutch and Finnish cases rely on ad hoc assessment methodologies. These tools, mostly intended for the design and construction phases, would set precise standards to be achieved in the field of circular construction. However, they are still under development and only little information is presently available. In particular, the digital passport proposed in the Buiksloterham case appears to be very innovative for the easy identification and valuation of materials available at the end of the buildings' useful life. Only the case of Buiksloterham mobilised a metabolism analysis. Based on the material flow analysis (MFA) methodology, this analysis looks not only at the type and quantity of physical flows (energy, water, materials), but also at local socio-economic flows. Results founded the proposed goals and actions for moving to a circular neighbourhood. This well-identified assessment tool is often coupled with CE, but according to Elia, Gnoni, and Tornese (2017), it is not sufficient to validate the relevance of CE practices, because it does not explicitly account for the environmental impacts. MFA is an important territorial knowledge tool, but it does not allow to prioritise and make decisions among the different CE actions.

Other tools, such as LCA, could conversely support such decisions. LCA appeared in the early 1990s and even if the expression CE was not employed at that time, most ideas corresponding to CE were already integrated. For instance, recycling was one issue particularly studied to reduce environmental impacts. Some of the elaborated methods accounted for environmental benefits of recycling in the building sector, at the fabrication stage but also after deconstruction (Polster et al. 1996).

In this regard, it is interesting to note that the 'life cycle perspective' is central in all cases, but not necessarily associated with LCA tools. Some scholars consider LCA to be the most comprehensive method for the assessment of environmental impacts and CE requirements (Elia et al. 2017). Nevertheless, in the Kera case, LCA is planned only at the building scale and for new constructions. The assessment of CE practices is not directly mentioned, except in Saint-Vincent-de-Paul. The scale of the neighbourhood is never mentioned for the evaluation of CE practices using LCA.

This can lead to contradictions, because as demonstrated during the 63rd discussion forum on LCA,[28] 'circularity' does not always positively affect the environment and contradictions can arise. Purely by way of example, while material recovery practices can reduce the consumption of natural resources, they are not necessarily relevant from a climate or ecosystem point of view. In the case of a recycling site far from the worksite, the transport of heavy materials may reduce or even cancel out the environmental benefits of recycling. Similarly, the flexibility and modularity of spaces must be studied in conjunction with summer comfort: the systematic use of lightweight and low inertia partitions can lead to overconsumption of air conditioning compared to a design with heavy partitions. Moreover, while it is true that rehabilitation of a building generates less waste, it can also generate other environmental impacts.

Despite overlaps, MFA and LCA have different purposes: MFA aims to reduce the different flows, by identifying and quantifying them; on the other hand, LCA aims to characterise these different flows, in order to quantify and reduce the possible impacts on the environment. Both tools could therefore be complementary for CE assessment, but they are not coupled in the case studies.

Finally, it is important to note that all these projects are currently underway or started recently, contributing to a lack of precision regarding the performance that will actually be achieved upon delivery. For this reason, the focus is mainly on the design and construction phase, raising the question of how the CE can be perpetuated in urban projects in the following phases.

Conclusions

Our literature review shows that CE provides a useful perspective for rethinking sustainable urban development. Consequently, CE is becoming part of the urban agenda. Nevertheless, CE remains a new topic for urban planning, and research is lacking with respect to the application of CE principles to the built environment. This raises the questions of how the CE is concretely implemented in urban projects and how to measure their environmental benefit. To address this gap, this chapter also provides a comparative analysis of four 'circular neighbourhoods' to identify and discuss the CE practices implemented and the assessment tools utilised.

The results of this analysis indicate a large panel of CE practices, focusing primarily on environmental dimensions, and an important issue of experimentation and consolidation of CE models applied to urban projects. The case studies also underscore additional requirements for the implementation of the CE, such as the need to store materials to be reused.

More generally, examining the different CE practices identified in the case studies shows a significant similarity between eco-neighbourhood projects. In the sustainable eco-neighbourhoods' literature, local and renewable energy production, rainwater collection or urban agriculture are practices typically put forward. The main difference is a new emphasis on aspects related to deconstruction, management of construction and demolition waste, as well as building and materials reuse.

Furthermore, both the referenced literature and the case studies reveal a limited use of indicators and assessment tools to establish the relevance and prioritisation of these practices. This raises the questions of how to ensure that the CE generates real environmental benefits, and how to measure them. These assessment tools, when existing, are useful to avoid risks of greenwashing, guaranteeing the adoption of more sustainable and environmentally friendly practices.

Notes

1. Disclaimer: An earlier and longer version of this paper is published in Transactions of AESOP Journal, Volume 5, Issue 1, ISSN 2566-2147
2. https://amsterdamsmartcity.com/circularamsterdam
3. http://fab.city/
4. https://www.pianoo.nl/sites/default/files/documents/documents/rebusfactsheet37-gemeenterotterdam-engels-juni2017-1.pdf
5. https://www.paris.fr/economiecirculaire
6. https://www.lwarb.gov.uk/what-we-do/circular-london/circular-economy-route-map/
7. http://www.circular-europe-network.eu/
8. https://oscedays.org/
9. http://www.statistiques.developpement-durable.gouv.fr/lessentiel/ar/326/1097/dechets-secteur-construction.html
10. http://www.developpement-durable.gouv.fr/Etalement-urbain-et.html
11. https://www.espooinnovationgarden.fi/en/espoo-innovation-garden/media/news/espoo-remains-the-most-sustainable-city-in-europe/

12 https://www.espoo.fi/en-US/Housing_and_environment/Sustainable_development
13 https://www.espoo.fi/enUS/Housing_and_environment/City_planning/Master_Plan/Pending_Master_Plans/Component_Master_Plan_of_Kera/Kera_set_for_sustainable_growth(105154)
14 https://www.helsinkismart.fi/portfolio-items/an-industrial-area-turns-into-a-liveable-circular-economy-neighbourhood/
15 https://www.espoo.fi/enUS/Jobs_and_enterprise/A_dynamic_city/Locate_in_Espoo/Urban_Development/Rail_Zone/Kera
16 http://www.nordicinnovation.org/Documents/Nordic%20Built%20Cities-dokumenter/NBCC-Kera-COOP-CITY-booklet_small.pdf
17 http://uusikera.fi/wp/wp-content/uploads/2016/06/COOP-CITY-Illustrations.pdf
18 http://uusikera.fi/wp/wp-content/uploads/2016/06/COOP-CITY-Illustrations.pdf
19 https://fr.calameo.com/read/00398144113f3e65fce93
20 EPADESA. 2016. Les Groues. Plan Guide.
21 https://fr.calameo.com/read/00398144113f3e65fce93
22 http://fr.calameo.com/read/0039814413c1330021bdd
23 EPADESA. 2016. Les Groues. Plan Guide.
24 https://www.paris.fr/services-et-infos-pratiques/urbanisme-et-architecture/projets-urbains-et-architecturaux/saint-vincent-de-paul-14e-2373
25 http://www.paris-batignollesamenagement.fr/pba/sites/default/files/publications/dp_svp_1506_deflite_bd.pdf
26 The PULSE-PARIS research project led by EIVP and MinesParisTech aims to improve the relevance and operationality of eco-design approaches for urban projects in line with the CE strategic plans of the City of Paris.
27 See for example https://www.cycle-up.fr/
28 www.lcaforum.ch

References

Adams, K. T., Osmani, M., Thorpe, T. and Thornback, J. (2017). "Circular Economy in Construction: Current Awareness, Challenges and Enablers," *Proceedings of the Institution of Civil Engineers: Waste and Resource Management* 170 (1). https://doi.org/10.1680/jwarm.16.00011.

ADEME. (2012). 'Énergie et climat: Chiffres-clés.'

———. (2014). '*Économie Circulaire: Notions.*'

———. (2016). *Identification des freins et des leviers au réemploi de produits et matériaux de construction.*

———. (2017). '*Economie Circulaire—Un Atout Pour Relever Le Défi de l'aménagement Durable Des Territoires.*'

Appendino, F., Roux, C. and Peuportier, B. (2018). *PULSE-PARIS Livrable 1.* Ademe.

Bocken, N., Olivetti, E., Cullen, J.M., Potting, J. and Lifset, R. (2017), "Taking the Circularity to the Next Level: A Special Issue on the Circular Economy," *Journal of Industrial Ecology* 21 (3). https://doi.org/10.1111/jiec.12606.

BPIE-Buildings Performance Institute Europe (2011). *Europe's Buildings under the Microscope: a Country-by-Country Review of the Energy Performance of Buildings.* Brussels: Buildings Performance Institute Europe.

Cities Foundation. (2017). *The Wasted City: Approaches to Circular City Making.* Haarlem: Trancity.

City of Paris. (2017). 'Stratégie de Résilience de Paris.'

Elia, V., Gnoni, M. G. and Tornese, F. (2017). "Measuring Circular Economy Strategies through Index Methods: A Critical Analysis," *Journal of Cleaner Production* 142 (January): 2741–51. https://doi.org/10.1016/j.jclepro.2016.10.196.

Ellen MacArthur Foundation. (2017). *Cities in the Circular Economy: An Initial Exploration*. Available at: https://www.ellenmacarthurfoundation.org/publications/cities-in-the-circular-economy-an-initial-exploration

Fregonara, E., Giordano, R., Ferrando, D. G. and Pattono, S. (2017). "Economic-Environmental Indicators to Support Investment Decisions: A Focus on the Buildings' End-of-Life Stage," *Buildings* 7 (4): 65. https://doi.org/10.3390/buildings7030065.

Geissdoerfer, M., Savaget, P., Bocken, N. M. P. and Hultink, E. J. (2017). "The Circular Economy—A New Sustainability Paradigm?," *Journal of Cleaner Production*. https://doi.org/10.1016/j.jclepro.2016.12.048.

Ghisellini, P., Ripa, M. and Ulgiati, S. (2018). "Exploring Environmental and Economic Costs and Benefits of a Circular Economy Approach to the Construction and Demolition Sector. A Literature Review," *Journal of Cleaner Production*. https://doi.org/10.1016/j.jclepro.2017.11.207.

Giorgi, S., Lavagna, M. and Campioli, A. (2017). "Circular Economy, Waste Management and Life Cycle Thinking," *Ingegneria Dell'ambiente* 4 (3). http://dx.doi.org/10.14672/ida.v4i3.1141.

Girard, L. F. and Nocca, F. (2019). "Moving towards the Circular Economy/City Model: Which Tools for Operationalizing This Model?," *Sustainability*, MDPI, 11 (22): 6253.

Glass, J., Greenfield, D. and Longhurst, P. (2017). "Editorial: Circular Economy in the Built Environment," *Proceedings of the Institution of Civil Engineers—Waste and Resource Management* 170 (1). https://doi.org/10.1680/jwarm.2017.170.1.1.

Haupt, M., Vadenbo, C. and Hellweg, S. (2017). "Do We Have the Right Performance Indicators for the Circular Economy?: Insight into the Swiss Waste Management System," *Journal of Industrial Ecology* 21 (3): 615–27. https://doi.org/10.1111/jiec.12506.

Haupt, M. and Zschokke, M. (2017). "How Can LCA Support the Circular Economy?—63rd Discussion Forum on Life Cycle Assessment, Zurich, Switzerland, November 30, 2016," *The International Journal of Life Cycle Assessment* 22 (5): 832–7. https://doi.org/10.1007/s11367-017-1267-1.

Herfray, G. and Peuportier, B. (2010). "Life Cycle Assessment Applied to Urban Settlements," *Sustainable Building Conference 2010*, Madrid, avril.

Kampelmann, S. (2016). "Mesurer l'économie Circulaire à l'échelle Territoriale," *Revue de l'OFCE* 1 (145). https://doi.org/10.3917/reof.145.0161.

Kirchherr, J., Reike, D. and Hekkert, M. (2017). "Conceptualizing the Circular Economy: An Analysis of 114 Definitions," *Resources, Conservation & Recycling* 127. http://dx.doi.org/10.1016/j.resconrec.2017.09.005.

Korhonen, J., Nuur, C., Feldmann, A. and Birkie, S. E. (2017). "Circular Economy as an Essentially Contested Concept," *Journal of Cleaner Production* 175. https://doi.org/10.1016/j.jclepro.2017.12.111.

Leising, E., Quist, J. and Bocken, N. (2018). "Circular Economy in the Building Sector: Three Cases and a Collaboration Tool," *Journal of Cleaner Production* 176: 976–89. https://doi.org/10.1016/j.jclepro.2017.12.010.

Lotteau, M. (2017). *Integration of Morphological Analysis in Early-Stage LCA of the Built Environment at the Neighborhood Scale*. Theses, Université de Bordeaux. https://tel.archives-ouvertes.fr/tel-01677273.

Merli, R., Preziosi, M. and Acampora, A. (2018). "How Do Scholars Approach the Circular Economy? A Systematic Literature Review," *Journal of Cleaner Production* (in press). https://doi.org/10.1016/j.jclepro.2017.12.112.

Metabolic. (2015). *Circular Buiksloterham. Transitioning Amsterdam to a Circular City. Vision and Ambition*. Available at: https://www.metabolic.nl/publications/

———. (2016). *Circular Cities. Designing Post-Industrial Amsterdam the Case of Buiksloterham*. Available at: https://www.metabolic.nl/publications/

OECD. (2019). *1st Roundtable on the Circular Economy in Cities and Regions*. 4 July 2019. Available at: https://www.oecd.org/cfe/regionaldevelopment/roundtable-circular-economy.htm

———. (2020). *The Circular Economy in Groningen, Netherlands*. https://doi.org/10.1787/e53348d4-en.

Petit-Boix, A., and Leipold, S. (2018). "Circular Economy in Cities: Reviewing How Environmental Research Aligns with Local Practices," *Journal of Cleaner Production* 195: 1270–81. https://doi.org/10.1016/j.jclepro.2018.05.281.

Peuportier, B. (2005). "Towards Sustainable Neighbourhoods, the Eco-Housing Project, *IV International Conference "Climate change—energy awareness—energy efficiency*," Visegrad.

———. (2015). *Energétique des bâtiments et simulation thermique. Modèles—Mise en oeuvre—Etudes de cas*. Eyrolles, Paris.

Peuportier, B., Vorger E. and Herfray G. (2012). LCA application in urban design, *International Symposium Life Cycle Assessment and Construction*, Nantes, juillet 2012.

Polster, B., Peuportier, B., Sommereux, I. B., Pedregal, P. D., Gobin, C. and Durand, E. (1996). "Evaluation of the Environmental Quality of Buildings towards a More Environmentally Conscious Design," *Solar Energy* 57 (3): 219–30. https://doi.org/10.1016/S0038-092X(96)00071-0.

Pomponi, F. and Moncaster, A. (2017). "Circular Economy for the Built Environment: A Research Framework," *Journal of Cleaner Production* 143: 710–18. https://doi.org/10.1016/j.jclepro.2016.12.055.

Popovici, E. and Peuportier, B. (2004). "Using life cycle assessment as decision support in the design of settlements," PLEA Conference, Eindhoven, 2004.

Prendeville, S., Cherim, E. and Bocken, N. (2018). "Circular Cities: Mapping Six Cities in Transition," *Environmental Innovation and Societal Transitions*. https://doi.org/10.1016/j.eist.2017.03.002.

Prieto-Sandoval, V., Jaca, C. and Ormazabal, M. (2017). "Towards a Consensus on the Circular Economy," *Journal of Cleaner Production* (in press). https://doi.org/10.1016/j.jclepro.2017.12.224.

Reike, D., Vermeulen, W. and Witjes, S. (2017). "The Circular Economy: New or Refurbished as CE 3.0?—Exploring Controversies in the Conceptualization of the Circular Economy through a Focus on History and Resource Value Retention Options," *Resources, Conservation & Recycling* in press. https://doi.org/10.1016/j.resconrec.2017.08.027.

Roux, C., Peuportier B. and Herfray G. (2013), "Dynamic LCA Applied to Buildings and Urban Districts," *Sustainable Building 2013 Conference*, Munich, april.

Souami, T. (2009). *Écoquartiers, Secrets de Fabrication. Analyse Critique d'exemples Européens*. Éditions les Carnets de l'info. Paris.

Tingley, D. D., Giesekam, J. and Cooper-Searle, S. (2018). "Applying Circular Economy Principles to Reduce Embodied Carbon," in *Embodied Carbon in Buildings. Measurement, Management and Mitigation*. Cham: Springer International Publishing, pp. 443–62

van der Hoek, J. P., Struker, A. and Danschutter, J. E. M. de (2017). "Amsterdam as a Sustainable European Metropolis: Integration of Water, Energy and Material Flows," *Urban Water Journal* 14. https://doi.org/10.1080/1573062X.2015.1076858.

Zanni, S., Simion, I. M., Gavrilescu, M. and Bonoli, A. (2018). "Life Cycle Assessment Applied to Circular Designed Construction Materials," *Procedia CIRP* 69: 154–9. https://doi.org/10.1016/j.procir.2017.11.040

Chapter 11
LIVING WITH WATER IN THE ERA OF CLIMATE CHANGE
Lessons from the Lafitte Greenway in Post-Katrina New Orleans

Billy Fields, Jeffrey J. Thomas, and Jacob A. Wagner

Introduction

The growing awareness that climate change is increasing local flood risk and that structural approaches alone will not protect communities is ushering in a new framework of planning. This emerging approach seeks to augment structural flood control systems through the use of green and blue infrastructure to build resilience to storm events (Everett and Lamond 2014). The potential increase in sea levels due to climate change in low-lying areas like the Netherlands and the catastrophic flooding of New Orleans during Hurricane Katrina have been catalysts for moving toward a new *living with water* framework that focuses on green and blue infrastructure acting in concert with structural engineering systems.

This approach seeks to enhance quality of life in cities during the majority of times when an area is not threatened and to use natural systems to buffer the built environment during brief, but intense, storm events (Zevenbergen et al. 2013). This conceptual shift, as Meyer notes (2009, 432), is a change from "'fighting against the water,' (to) a new one of 'working with nature'."

While the Netherlands has begun to implement the living with water approach to flood management, this new paradigm runs counter to the entrenched engineering and disaster funding practices in the United States. Disaster recovery funding constitutes the largest source of monies available to communities in the United States seeking to invest in green and blue infrastructure. While this funding process has evolved over the last ten years and significant institutional learning has occurred as a result of the Hurricane Katrina and Superstorm Sandy experiences, existing funding structures still present numerous limitations for harnessing federal funds for green and blue infrastructure. Despite significant policy shifts toward a more resiliency-based focus over the last several years, federal policy and existing practices still often make it easier for local communities

DOI: 10.4324/9781003178545-15

to rebuild following a disaster in a status quo manner while limiting opportunities to innovate with more resilient development.

To understand how this evolving policy landscape impacts planning, we analyze post-Hurricane Katrina rebuilding in New Orleans through a case study of the Lafitte Greenway—a green infrastructure project that transformed a three-mile corridor of underutilized public land into a linear park running through flood-prone neighborhoods. Through the experience of creating the Lafitte Greenway, planners in New Orleans learned valuable lessons about US disaster rebuilding policies and how to implement green infrastructure in urban neighborhoods. This chapter analyzes the opportunities and challenges presented to New Orleans and other cities rebuilding from disasters to harness federal funds and other resources to invest in green and blue infrastructure.

This chapter is organized into three sections. First, we examine the shift from flood-resistant to flood resilience planning in the United States and the Netherlands. We examine how green infrastructure projects are being utilized as the heart of this new flood management approach. This is followed by a case study of the Lafitte Greenway in New Orleans. Finally, planning and policy implications are examined.

Methodology and Theoretical Orientation

From a theoretical perspective, we focus on the ways in which individuals and institutions reinvent policies and plans to reshape places in response to disasters and their aftermath. Our work is consistent with Healey's (1999) focus on the "place-conscious evolution" in public policy. We utilize this theory through an embedded case study (Yin 2013) to analyze the policy context and changing patterns of institutional relationships associated with green infrastructure planning. The New Orleans experience is viewed from the local perspective within the postdisaster planning process. Then, the New Orleans case is placed in the context of larger policy processes that have shifted as a result of the *living with water* approach in the Netherlands and US policy changes following Superstorm Sandy.

Our sources are diverse within the case study research design. Sources including participant observations, interviews, plans and primary documents are used to highlight the New Orleans case situated within an evolving policy landscape. We interviewed a variety of local participants and national experts involved in processes of water management, planning and public administration and activists engaged in pushing the boundaries of water management and resilience planning in US cities.[1]

Blue–Green Infrastructure: The Resilient City and the Disaster Funding Divide

Planning for climate-resilient cities is a growing challenge. Two of the largest natural disasters in the history of the United States, Hurricane Katrina and

Superstorm Sandy took place within seven years and resulted in 2,033 deaths and an estimated economic loss of approximately $219 billion (Newman 2012). The overall US population susceptible to coastal flooding or hurricane wind events is significant and growing. Of the entire US population, almost 8% are currently at risk from ocean flooding events and 28% live in areas that could experience category-one hurricane force winds (Crowell et al. 2010). As sea levels rise and hurricanes become more frequent and intense due to climate change, the population susceptible to flooding events is projected to increase 40%–45% by 2100 (AECOM 2013).

Despite these risks, most communities in the United States, especially those without hazard zoning or state and local mandates for coastal planning (Burby, Nelson, and Sanchez 2006), have limited land use regulations guiding development in high-risk areas and few, if any, dedicated local resources to invest in community-scale flood protections. Where large-scale flood infrastructure does exist, it tends to be structural in nature, using pipes, pumps and other hard systems to barricade or evacuate storm water as expeditiously as possible. This *flood resistance* model is based on resisting the entrance of water into the city and creating systems to eliminate it as quickly as possible.

Amid a paucity of preemptive resources, investment in large-scale *flood resilience* in the United States is largely relegated to those communities rebuilding after disasters that have access to federally funded recovery processes. For these communities, postdisaster settings present a critical opportunity to implement a *flood resilience* framework (see Table 11.1), particularly as officials and citizens seek to understand the disaster and how to rebuild to prevent future devastation (Campanella 2006). Such postdisaster awakening to resilience provides a chance

TABLE 11.1 Flood resistance vs. flood resilience

	Urban scale	*Management paradigm*
Flood-resistant design	Levees, floodwalls, pipes, canals and structural means to resist the entrance of water into the city and to remove it as quickly as possible.	"Flood Defense"—Policies that support, promote or require flood-resistant infrastructure, buildings and communities, such as floodwalls with the goal of keeping water out.
Flood-resilient design	Modified structural systems, integration of green and blue infrastructural solutions with the assumption that flooding will happen.	"Living with Water"—The adaptation of policies, laws and plans to allow for investment in new systems based in resilience. Treats the reduction of flood risk as an opportunity to create new amenities, active living and ecological urbanism. Adapts city infrastructure to let water into the city through urban and landscape design.

to reevaluate existing community patterns (Wagner and Frisch 2009; Olshansky, Hopkins, and Johnson 2012). In terms of urban planning, these periods can be a "design moment" that can stimulate the redesign of basic systems in a city—including infrastructure and urban environmental systems (Wagner and Frisch 2009). Rather than the more common incremental growth of a city, the magnitude and urgency of rebuilding after a disaster can spur dramatic reimagining of large-scale infrastructure and the social, economic and environmental relationships associated with these systems.

The drawback of relying on postdisaster planning and investment, however, is that it happens in a constrained timeline where an incredible number of decisions must be made quickly and amid conflicting needs and mandates. Olshansky, Hopkins, and Johnson (2012) refer to this "time compression" after a disaster as the feature that distinguishes postdisaster recovery from typical urban planning. Moreover, the "fast forward" of postdisaster planning can be further constrained by regulations that dictate both the flow of federal funds and the purposes for which they can be utilized. The result of these factors is often an uneven recovery process of "crisis driven redevelopment" (Gotham and Greenberg 2014) and the challenge of implementing an equitable redevelopment process (Blackwell 2005; Vazquez 2005).

While federal agencies are increasingly interested in using disaster funds to finance resilience from climate change, the regulations governing the use of funds are still catching up to promising policy pronouncements. Still, in an era of chronic budget shortfalls, the tens of billions of dollars in federal disaster recovery funds awarded annually nationwide are the most significant source of funding that local communities can use to enhance their flood resilience.

Living with Water: Conceptualizing the Potential of Blue–Green Infrastructure

From a safety perspective, resilience planning in coastal areas involves minimizing risk to human populations and structures by managing the location and building types exposed to flooding and/or wind risk. While there are a variety of mitigation tools that can be used to increase safety, one of the key tools that planners can utilize to enhance resiliency is the creation of open space systems with ecological, storm buffering and community benefits.

Over the last 15 years, open space planning has been transformed by the green infrastructure and ecosystem services paradigm. Green infrastructure, according to Benedict and McMahon (2002, 12), is "an interconnected network of green space that conserves natural ecosystem values and functions and provides associated benefits to human populations." These authors argue that green infrastructure is different from conservation-oriented open space planning because the green infrastructure approach "looks at conservation values in concert with land development, growth management and built infrastructure planning" (2002, 12). Rather than an open space system separate from human populations, green infrastructure seeks to help shape urban and regional development to provide multiple benefits simultaneously (Erickson 2006). Greenways, in particular, can be a catalyst for this combination of ecosystem restoration, flood management and trail-oriented development with active transportation along a linear corridor (Fields 2009).

Green infrastructure can be used as a part of integrated flood management systems while promoting urban development that is less carbon-intensive. Large green infrastructure components can be designed to provide recreation and active transportation linkages (walking and bicycling) while simultaneously providing for the capture of floodwater during storm events. Within an urbanized area, different components of a comprehensive system for managing storm water and providing community benefits can be developed at multiple scales, including bioswales, green streets and larger landscape elements to reduce storm surges.

Recently, the green infrastructure elements have been coupled with the "wet" systems of *blue infrastructure* to create a framework for managing water. Lawson et al. (2014, 115) argue that a blue–green city can be conceptualized, which "aims to recreate a naturally oriented water cycle while contributing to the amenity of the city by bringing water management and green infrastructure together." Table 11.2 provides examples of the components of this system.

Greenways emerged in the late 19th century as an urban design strategy intended to link landscapes together in a regional pattern of protected open space. The underlying concept of linked landscapes designed to steer growth has remained constant, but with significant variations depending on issues in particular eras or places (Ahern 2004; Fabos 2004). Originating with Olmsted's Emerald Necklace concept of linked parks in Boston, and George Kessler's parks and boulevards system in Kansas City, greenway planning in the United States has traditionally focused on providing access to recreation and the conservation of sensitive environmental areas (Little 1990). Olmsted's work on integrating the Muddy River into the Emerald Necklace system to improve drainage and extend park opportunities provides "early environmental restoration and green infrastructure precedents" (Eisenman 2013, 294). The greenway movement of connected open space corridors can complement a system of "wet" spaces or blueways. Beatley

TABLE 11.2 Blue and green infrastructure components

Blue infrastructure components	*Green infrastructure components*
Bayous as part of a linear drainage system	Greenways as part of a linear open space system
Wetlands as nodes within the drainage system	Parks
Ponds	Green streets
Wet water storage area	Bioswales

Source: Modified from Lawson et al. (2014).

(2014, 90) argues that coastal cities have "the chance to create a network of blue-belts that parallel the land-based greenbelts" that can be a "powerful way to reframe and reinterpret the marine spaces and places often quite near to cities but largely ignored." The concept of expanded linkages between the blue and green infrastructure systems is a useful construct for reimagining delta cities.

Blue-Green Infrastructure: A Changing Management Model

While envisioning the system is an important first step, building functional partnerships across the multiple agencies to manage these ecological and urban systems is a core challenge (Benedict and McMahon 2002). At present in the United States, the management of the blue and green systems is fractured, with agencies across multiple levels of government working towards more narrow goals than the blue–green paradigm suggests is optimal.

One promising example of redefining these relationships is developing in the Netherlands. The Netherlands is particularly vulnerable to ocean flooding and sea-level rise, with 60% of the land in the country below sea level and 70% of the country's gross national product earned in these areas (Kabat et al. 2005). After devastating flooding in the 1950s, the Dutch created an intricate engineering-based system designed to prevent future flood events called the Delta Works project. This system involves closing multiple estuary systems with dikes to prevent sea flooding. Meyer (2009) argues that the massive cost of this flood project (4.5 billion euros) was made politically acceptable because of the co-benefits of the extension of agricultural land and improved roadway connectivity that the project also accomplished. The extensive system provides a high level of safety for Netherlands residents, with the system designed to protect against a 1 in 10,000-year flood event (Meyer 2009). By contrast, US flood protection systems are mostly designed to withstand a 1 in 100-year flood event.

Despite the higher level of engineering safety built into the Dutch system, the devastating impact of Hurricane Katrina and the prospect of climate change–induced sea-level rise have prompted planners in the Netherlands to reexamine the limits of the structural system (Meyer 2009; Zevenbergen et al. 2013). The so-called Delta 2 program was passed by the Netherlands government in 2009 providing 1 billion euros per year to focus on what Zevenbergen et al. (2013, 1221) call "resilience: striving towards an appropriate balance between protection, prevention and preparedness, both now and into the future." The key to this approach is building "in (more) flexibility and/or robustness into the primary flood protection infrastructure in the Netherlands, using both natural processes, and more sustainable land use planning to create room for water to expand during high flows" (Zevenbergen et al. 2013, 1221).

A key management component of this "living with water" system is a network of agencies designed to build community resilience. Traditional bureaucracies tend to focus on a single task in isolation. This approach to planning is ill suited to coordinate the more comprehensive living with water approach (Meyer 2009).

In order for communities to organize around resilience, public agencies need to focus on active learning, flexibility and commitment to institutional change with an interdisciplinary focus on multiple benefits across sectors. Such an approach requires new funding structures to encourage agencies to build working relationships (Zevenbergen et al. 2013, 1218).

While the flood defense paradigm in the Netherlands has begun to change, Meyer (2009, 448) argues that "a new consensus" on how multiple organizations can work together "is lacking." In large measure, he argues, the modern notion that "it is possible and desirable to control nature and to subject a territory to national and rational goals concerning economic development, urbanization and society building" (Meyer 2009, 449) is still embedded within agency culture and practice. A fundamental shift in how we plan for complex urban delta and coastal regions is necessary to move to a flood resilience framework. Meyer (2009, 448) sums this up by arguing that

> a consensus can be reached only when new strategies include urban planning as well as nature, environment, new economic developments and, last but not least, effective and sustainable strategies concerning flooding. Such a comprehensive approach is only possible in a cross disciplinary approach.

This cross-disciplinary approach challenges existing patterns of bureaucratic organization and funding. While the conceptual shift to living with water has begun, as Meyer (2009) notes, a full consensus has not yet emerged. This is particularly evident in how cities prioritize the use of land that is otherwise suitable for blue–green infrastructure and in the stubborn bureaucratic hurdles to using public funding for such projects. The development of Lafitte Greenway in New Orleans following Hurricane Katrina illustrates this evolving consensus and lingering challenges.

The New Orleans Resiliency Challenge: A Delta City in Rising Sea

Recovery planning in New Orleans after Hurricane Katrina has taken place in a complicated and shifting network of federal regulations, funding sources and policy opportunities. The difficult environmental context of New Orleans as a delta city, however, exists above and apart from these rules. These relentless environmental conditions make planning innovation for climate change resilience absolutely vital for the city's survival.

Delta cities, those cities perched on the often-unstable and subsiding land between the ocean and river deltas, present immense economic opportunities for trade and challenging natural settings for urban habitation. The multifaceted setting of delta cities forces planners to simultaneously address "the complexity of the delta, as the meeting of rivers and sea... with the complexity of urban patterns, as a condition and result of economic, cultural and social life" (Meyer 2009, 432).

This multifaceted imperative of balancing nature, commerce and culture presents unique challenges to delta city planners as these locations become increasingly important to the global economy and, simultaneously, more vulnerable to rising sea levels. Managing the delta city in the era of climate change becomes the latest and one of the most difficult "wicked problems" in urban planning (Rittel and Weber 1973; Weber and Khademian 2008).

As a delta city (Shields 2008; Campanella 2010), New Orleans has long been prone to flooding and the planning history of the city is inseparable from this environmental context and condition. Early development of the city clung to higher ground along the Mississippi River and various bayou ridges utilizing natural wetland systems to buffer storm surge and flooding. In the early 20th century, this tight, higher-ground development pattern based on natural systems and limited backswamp levees was broken with the use of the massive Wood Screw Pump that allowed for draining vast areas of low-lying swampland in the early 20th century. These areas were quickly turned into new suburban neighborhoods known as Gentilly, Lakeview and New Orleans East (Lewis 2003).

These newly developed areas were, however, more susceptible to flooding. Sections of New Orleans have flooded six times because of hurricanes (1915, 1940, 1947, 1965, 1969 and 2005) in the last century (Seed et al. 2006). In response to massive flooding in 1965 by Hurricane Betsy, a network of engineering systems was developed focusing on levee and flood control structures coupled with massive pumping stations linked to a network of outfall canals for storm protection from the tidal Lake Pontchartrain, the main source of potential flood waters for the core area of the city.

This structural approach to flood control was inadequately designed and poorly maintained, which resulted in "a system in name only" (Bea 2006). When the storm surge of Hurricane Katrina began to fill the outfall canals in the heart of the city, the structures crumbled at levels below the design tolerance of the system, which flooded 80% of the city and resulted in 767 fatalities in the City of New Orleans in 2005 (Markwell and Ratard 2012). The result of the engineering failures at key locations in the system was "the single most costly catastrophic failure of an engineered system in history" (Seed et al. 2006, xix).

Hurricane Katrina flooding exposed a complicated set of interlocking water management problems, including a poorly designed structural flood control system coupled with the dual problems of increasing vulnerability of human populations due to development in sensitive areas and massive wetland loss in adjacent coastal areas (Bea 2006; Lopez 2006; Van Heerden 2007; Fields 2009). When these difficult planning challenges are combined with land subsidence and potential sea-level rise due to climate change, the immensity of the challenges of the "Katrina wicked problem" (Fields 2013) comes into focus.

Post-Katrina Recovery Planning: Attempting to Mobilize Resilience

In this chaotic context, projects were planned and executed during the immediate recovery phase from Hurricane Katrina. Planning for disaster recovery involved a series of plans, each of which sought state and federal approval for funding. The multiple processes that resulted in a detailed project list were highly politicized and resulted in a contentious process of defining a vision for the city's recovery (Nelson, Ehrenfeucht, and Laska 2007; Olshansky et al. 2008; Fields, Wagner, and Frisch 2015).

Open space planning was particularly contentious as conceptual renderings of park space in the form of "green dots" were superimposed on existing, low-lying neighborhoods during a November 2005 presentation by the Bring New Orleans Back Commission. These "green dots," presented at a time when most citizens were not ready or able to participate in postdisaster planning, were perceived by many as signposts for wholesale abandonment of neighborhoods and conversion to parks. This fear profoundly chilled any serious discussion about integrating protective greenspace into neighborhood recovery efforts in early recovery planning (Fields 2009). Further, the changing rules governing the use of Department of Housing and Urban Development (HUD) Disaster Recovery Community Development Block Grants (CDBG-DR), Federal Emergency Management Agency Public Assistance (FEMA-PA) Grants and FEMA Hazard Mitigation Grant Program (HMGP) complicated the situation.

Federal Disaster Funding Background

Federal funding constitutes one of the largest sources of public money available to state and local governments for infrastructure investments (Stafford Act 2006; Lindsay 2014; FEMA 2015). The three largest sources of federal disaster funds—FEMA PA grants, FEMA HMGP and US Department of HUD CDBG-DR—are allocated according to the Housing and Community Development Act of 1974. The magnitude of these federal allocations can shape cities and infrastructure systems for generations.

Over the last decade, federal guidance has been altered to enhance the potential for these funding mechanisms to be used for green infrastructure. Of the three federal sources, CDBG-DR and HMGP are best tailored to finance green and blue infrastructure investment because CDBG-DR can be used to fund new infrastructure projects without connection to existing storm-damaged assets, and HMGP is awarded specifically to mitigate the risk from identified local hazards. Conversely, FEMA-PA funding is used to repair, restore or replace existing public assets that were damaged by a disaster (FEMA 2007).

Only recently have HUD and FEMA promoted the use of CDBG-DR and HMGP, respectively, as a means to invest in climate resilience. It wasn't until after Superstorm Sandy and the creation of the Hurricane Sandy Rebuilding Task Force that the federal government made specific recommendations for leveraging CDBG-DR, HMGP and other resources to "facilitate a region-wide approach to rebuilding, and promote resilient rebuilding so that the region will be better able to withstand the impacts of existing risks and future climate change" (HUD 2013).

This policy context has had significant impact on planning in New Orleans after Hurricane Katrina. During the immediate years of rebuilding, before the wave of policy innovations that followed Superstorm Sandy, neither HUD nor FEMA provided explicit guidance regarding investing in green and blue infrastructure or climate resilience generally. While the federal government's recent climate policy goals are promising, proposed green infrastructure projects using federal disaster recovery funds in both New Orleans and communities impacted by Superstorm Sandy are still making their way from design to implementation and will test the ability of FEMA and HUD bureaucracies to follow stated policy intentions.

The result in New Orleans of this federal policy context was that the recovery projects that emerged from the planning processes were not a holistic collection designed to work together to enhance resiliency. Rather, the successful projects were those that garnered enough political support to survive the competitive, political process of project selection and, simultaneously, meet the statutory regulations of the complex funding sources.

Lafitte Greenway Project: Green and Blue Infrastructure in Recovery Planning

These limitations can be explained through a case study of the planning for the conversion of the Lafitte Corridor into a greenway in post-Katrina New Orleans. The Lafitte Corridor, a three-mile corridor of underutilized industrial properties, divided several neighborhoods from the back of the French Quarter to the Lakeview neighborhood (see Figure 11.1). This stretch of open space originally served as the location for the Carondelet Canal linking the river and lake beginning in the late 1700s until it was covered over in the 1930s. The adjacent railway along the corridor existed until the early 2000s.

Prior to Hurricane Katrina, the City Planning Commission's update of the Parks, Recreation and Open Space component of its Comprehensive Land Use Plan (City of New Orleans 2002) identified the conversion of these defunct rail corridors to greenways as a community priority. In the aftermath of Hurricane Katrina, planners and citizens developed multiple plans to enhance the green infrastructure potential of the corridor. These efforts have begun to be realized with a new greenway and trail that opened in November 2015. The blue infrastructure components, on the other hand, require more significant funding allocations and a larger shift in agency culture and practices in order to reconfigure urban and regional water management. As a result, the blue infrastructure vision for New Orleans awaits far greater funding than is currently available. The following sections highlight the green infrastructure planning process and illustrate how blue infrastructure planning and implementation will require more significant state and federal policy changes.

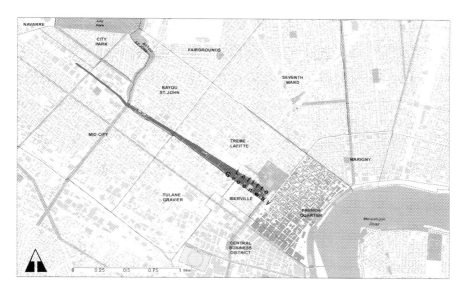

FIGURE 11.1 Map of New Orleans, Louisiana, and the Lafitte Greenway with adjacent neighborhoods.
Source: Map prepared by Jacob A. Wagner using City of New Orleans GIS data.

The Lafitte Greenway: Green Infrastructure in Recovery Planning

In early 2006, a group of local stakeholders aided by the national Rails-to-Trails Conservancy, the University of Missouri Kansas City and the Tulane School of Public Health convened a series of meetings that led to the formation of the Friends of Lafitte Corridor (FOLC). FOLC worked through the recovery planning processes in 2006 and 2007 to develop a strategy to build a three-mile greenway for active transportation (walking and bicycling) and park space. The goals of the plans for the greenway focused on four central themes: (1) expanding open space, (2) building active transportation, (3) enhancing cultural heritage and (4) neighborhood revitalization (FOLC and Brown & Danos Landdesign, Inc 2007; Schwartz, Executive Director of the Broad Community Connections Main Street, personal communication, April 20, 2015). At the outset, these goals did not include a significant blue infrastructure vision. These goals did attract a broad coalition of neighbors, active transportation activists and local businesses from multiple neighborhoods along the corridor. This group found an important, positive vision for a new, more resilient New Orleans through FOLC and the greenway project.

As advocate for the creation of a greenway and trail, FOLC was able to successfully advocate for the green infrastructure component within the recovery planning processes. The coalition-building created momentum for the project and a broader concept of disaster recovery that included open space, economic revitalization, recreation and active transportation. The greenway coalition successfully influenced city staff and elected officials to prioritize the project in the context of a competitive recovery process.

FOLC's advocacy efforts were complemented by efforts within local government to prioritize the project. Staff within public works, the planning department, the Mayor's Office of Recovery Development and Administration (ORDA) and the New Orleans Regional Planning Commission (RPC) worked with FOLC to prioritize the project in the early phases of recovery planning, which ensured that it remained on key project-funding lists.

By focusing on this "inside-outside" advocacy strategy, the Lafitte Greenway survived several rounds of planning and moved from idea toward funding. The team of advocates worked with government staff to apply for grants to plan for and implement the project. Success at receiving external funding from a diversity of sources including the Transportation Enhancement (TE) Program, Bikes Belong, Greater New Orleans Foundation and the Recreational Trails Program kept the project moving. The TE funding and Recreational Trail funding were part of larger federal transportation funds administered by the state. For greenway planning, these sources provided an opportunity to achieve multiple community goals that centered on active transportation, a key component of the larger strategy to recreate the New Orleans transportation systems in a less carbon-intensive manner. These programs, combined at the federal level as Transportation Alternatives since 2013, while outside of the traditional federal postdisaster funding, can be an important platform for green infrastructure implementation.

The state-allocated federal funds provided a foundation to begin the planning process, but were not sufficient to complete the larger vision. For this, a portion of the City's $410 million in CDBG-DR funding was sought. Since March 2009, the City has invested approximately $12.6 million in CDBG-DR to acquire land and construct the Lafitte Greenway.

The Lafitte Greenway opened in November 2015 and now forms a vital connection in the city's expanding active transportation system. Since Hurricane Katrina, New Orleans has added 87 miles of new bicycle facilities, including a mix of on-road and protected trails (Fields 2015). With the addition of the Lafitte Greenway, New Orleans has now created the backbone of a protected greenway trail system that links the French Quarter to Lake Pontchartrain. The significant expansion of this system has placed New Orleans as the top-ranked city in the south for bicycle commute mode share and fifth nationally (McCloud 2015). Further, recreational, cultural and community wellness programs are being implemented through $200,000 in grants and donations managed by the Friends of Lafitte Greenway, the offspring of FOLC.

While the realization of the two early goals of enhanced open space and active transportation expansion in the Lafitte Corridor has been achieved, the more difficult processes of neighborhood revitalization and equitable redevelopment is unresolved. With the opening of the new greenway, developers have been drawn to the enhanced amenity value of the proximate greenspace (Crompton 2001), with multiple new developments in the pipeline. These developments raise questions about who will ultimately benefit from the new greenway. A recent headline, for example, in *The Louisiana Weekly* pointedly asked "Living along the Lafitte Greenway: Is It Attainable or Unaffordable?" (Buchanan 2015). Godschalk (2004) identifies this type of conflict between livability and equity values as the gentrification conflict, where enhanced livability of an area can displace existing residents.

From the beginning of the greenway planning process, however, this issue was addressed through a parallel neighborhood revitalization process led by Providence Housing through the New City Partnership. This larger neighborhood revitalization effort has been critical to stabilize the neighborhood and maintain affordable housing while the greenway was being planned and built. A recent estimate indicates that over more than 1.2 billion dollars have been invested in housing around the greenway corridor (New City NOLA 2014).

While green infrastructure plans have been realized in the corridor, implementation of an integrated green and blue infrastructure component in the Lafitte Corridor—a new goal that was missing from the initial conceptualizations of the greenway—is now growing in importance.

Moving from Green to Blue: The Lafitte Greenway and Social Learning

The limited degree to which the greenway addresses the challenges of the City's storm water management reveals the complexities of planning for and implementing green and blue infrastructure systems. The green infrastructure orientation of the Lafitte Greenway reflects the early thinking of the advocates and government champions of the project. The green infrastructure vision embedded in the original FOLC plan began to evolve as the project was being designed. A series of exchanges between the Netherlands and United States were a catalyst for a new way of thinking about planning for water in the city. In 2010, the Dutch Dialogues 3, an international design exchange involving Dutch and US planners, focused on the opportunities of the Lafitte Corridor to implement a new vision of water management in New Orleans. Representatives of FOLC were invited to participate in this planning process.

The Dutch Dialogues team focused on the integration of the Lafitte Corridor into a citywide blue infrastructure system. The international and US-based participants began a process of reenvisioning the corridor as a key water management project along the lines of its historical roles as the Carondelet Canal. This vision included the active transportation trail system and a new "blueway" feature that would redesign the City's channelized drainage system with Bayou St. John, City Park and Lake Pontchartrain. This new design began to lay the foundation for the *living with water* concept in New Orleans. Stromberg (2010, 36) describes how the Dutch Dialogues process expanded the vision of the Lafitte Corridor "to create a 'bluegreen corridor' that would bring the underground water to the surface at selected places, establish a series of open spaces, reconnect the Lafitte Corridor with Bayou St. John, and beautify both areas."

The work of the Dutch Dialogues was expanded through the Greater New Orleans Urban Water Plan (Waggonner and Ball Architects 2013). This plan, a joint project of Waggoner and Ball Architects and the City of New Orleans, includes a vision of living with water at multiple scales, from street-level interventions to larger coastal systems. The underlying philosophy of the plan is based on an understanding of the complexity of inhabiting a delta region, and the need for a comprehensive approach to flood management with multiple lines of defense, including efforts to restore Louisiana's shrinking coast and increase local green and blue infrastructure systems inside of the city's levee system. To create an effective framework for living with water, these systems need to work together from the neighborhood scale to the region.

Beyond providing a new vision for a more flood-resilient New Orleans, the processes of developing the Greater New Orleans Water Plan and the Dutch Dialogues contributed to significant social learning among greenway advocates and local government. One participant described how the Dutch Dialogues transformed the goals of the greenway project by increasing the importance of the "blueway" component, which quickly became an important goal for the group and a major component of a new vision for New Orleans (Schwartz, Executive Director of the Broad Community Connections Main Street, personal communication, April 20, 2015). While the Dutch Dialogues and Greater New Orleans Water Plan helped to expand the blue infrastructure vision of the project, moving this plan to implementation within the preexisting disaster project funding sequences and shifting rules proved to be a difficult challenge. Two sequences help to show the difficulties of integrating the blue infrastructure component into the evolving Lafitte Greenway project.

The City's CDBG-DR funding application for design and construction of the greenway trail project was approved by state and federal authorities before the consensus around the blue infrastructure component was achieved. By the time that local advocates and city officials were beginning to understand the critical importance of the Lafitte Greenway to a flood-resilient city, the City's consultant had already begun to prepare a plan for design and construction. Because of this timing, it was difficult to integrate the new awareness into a preapproved project, and only a small number of token flood management components were included in the design of the Lafitte Greenway.

After preparation of the plan, the New Orleans City Council and advocates of the new flood resilience vision for the greenway requested that city staff assess the potential for incorporating more substantial blue infrastructure components into the project. After analysis, staff concluded that integrating the blue infrastructure components would delay the current greenway construction, require more extensive analysis and risk having to return federal funding that had been approved based on the initial design. The City argued that

> although the concept of the Blueway offers much promise conceptually toward storm water management, there is significant refinement still required

to advance it to the point of an implementable design and to know how its hydrological performance will achieve intended outcomes through its integration with other storm management systems (City of New Orleans 2013c, 9).

While the City received an additional $247 million in HMGP, in part, to invest in storm water management, the City concluded that a green–blue infrastructure project with Lafitte Greenway could not satisfy FEMA's existing benefit–cost rules for using HMGP without considerable expense and time delay that would jeopardize the availability of the project's federal CDBG-DR funding (City of New Orleans 2013c, 9).

While there have been shifts in how federal agencies value green and blue infrastructure over the past ten years, the rejection of the proposal to use HMGP to fund green and blue infrastructure in the Lafitte Greenway is a cautionary tale regarding FEMA's cost–benefit rules. The reasons are technical, but instructive of the challenges. The area surrounding Lafitte Greenway, for example, is a 1,375-acre basin composed of more than 13,500 residents across several neighborhoods (City of New Orleans 2013a, 2013b). Neighborhoods within these basins experience significant flooding during intense rain events that can exceed a foot of standing water in some locales and have resulted in dozens of non-tropical storm–related flood insurance claims since Hurricane Katrina (Bosch Slabbers, Landscape & Urban Design, Waggonner & Ball Architects 2013, 10).

Based on its current benefit–cost project calculations, FEMA determined that HMGP funding could not be used to incorporate storm water management into the Greenway because there was not enough documentable, historical evidence to demonstrate a sufficient reduction in either future federal flood insurance claims and/or property damage from a 100-year storm event—a much rarer event than those that typically cause flooding in the Greenway area (J. Trucks, interview with Jeff Thomas, telephone interview, New Orleans, LA, March 10, 2013). Absent this and the fact that FEMA does not score benefits attributed to abating subsidence or other environmental services from green and blue infrastructure, the City could not satisfy current FEMA rules and was prevented from using HMGP funds to implement the project (Thomas and DeWeese 2015). Looking ahead, HMGP will continue to be a limited option for funding green infrastructure projects until the full benefits of such investments are captured. These technical hurdles present significant challenges to communities for planning and implementing blue infrastructure projects, especially in the constrained timelines following disasters.

Planning and Policy Implications

Climate change is challenging how we plan, fund and administer key infrastructure systems in our cities. In many low-lying communities such as New Orleans, the specter of flooding from worsening storms is exacerbated by subsidence, which is often caused by inadequate ground water levels. Whether bulwarking from storm surge or seeking stability amid sinking lands, green and blue infrastructures are essential investments that communities can make to mitigate and adapt to climate change. New Orleans' development toward investing in green and blue infrastructure and the process of exploring its utility within Lafitte Greenway, in particular, highlights how the planning for local infrastructure innovation is hamstrung when paired with federal disaster monies as the main source of funding.

While post-Superstorm Sandy federal policy changes have been promising regarding climate adaption investments, many statutory and regulatory particulars of HUD and FEMA disaster funding render it difficult to fund the construction of green-blue infrastructure solutions. Pursuing these investments in a postdisaster framework, as the Lafitte Greenway case makes clear, is further complicated by the need to address complex and competing recovery demands with the same funds while political pressure builds to show progress after a disaster.

Blue infrastructure projects, in particular, are difficult to plan and implement in the tight timelines that disaster recovery periods often allow. If green and blue infrastructure plans are not in place prior to a disaster, it is difficult to incorporate them into postdisaster-spending agendas.

Finally, neither HUD nor FEMA presently has comparable funding available that can be widely used *before* a major disaster strikes. As a result, the largest sources of federal funding for green and blue infrastructure investments require a community to first suffer a major disaster to be eligible for funding. The Lafitte Greenway is an example of these limitations. The amount of time, study and cost needed to fully examine, design and construct large-scale green and blue infrastructure systems into that 3.1-mile public space would take years and millions of dollars—all the while competing with other uses of available postdisaster HUD and FEMA funding. If the Lafitte Greenway was constructed from scratch in 2015, the use of CDBG-DR would find general favor but still have to be couched in the context of national objectives and related regulations still relatively untested when financing green–blue infrastructure. The City's inquiry into the use of available HMGP revealed telling shortcomings that are relevant nationwide.

In all, the hurdles of time and regulation seen clearly in the example of Lafitte Greenway signal the need for additional pathways by which communities can plan for and invest in flood resilience. To address these issues, water system management needs to be addressed across scales through a multidisciplinary approach (Meyer 2009) focused on integrating urban planning, urban design, engineering, economic development and disaster management. In areas like New Orleans, which are also challenged by concentrated poverty and racial inequality, it is vital that these concerns be addressed as part of the larger infrastructure planning process (Blackwell 2005; Gotham 2015). Creating the institutional and professional consensus around *living with water* and then integrating these principles into planning practice and statutory guidance are a clear challenge.

TABLE 11.3 Scale, government actors and blue–green infrastructure

Blue–green government actors in New Orleans responsibility	Infrastructure	Scale
Department of Public Works	Green Streets Projects, Greenways	Local
Sewerage and Water Board	Local Drainage System	Local
Levee Boards	Levee System	Regional
Coastal Restoration Authority	Major Coastal Planning and Restoration Projects	Regional
Army Corps of Engineers	Structural Flood Control Systems	Federal
FEMA	Emergency Response	Federal
HUD	Emergency Response	Federal

Note: FEMA = Federal Emergency Management Agency; HUD = US Department of Housing and Urban Development.

In large part, achieving this interdisciplinary approach requires aligning and leveraging federal, state and local government funding sources, regulatory processes and community development mandates, along with community-based public–private partnerships and other emerging market-based tools to finance local green–blue flood protections (EPA 2015). Table 11.3 shows current actions taking place across Southeast Louisiana at multiples scales. Projects can be implemented from the block level (bioswales, green streets) to the regional level (greenway systems, wetlands restoration). Each scale requires partnerships with varying levels of government and other key actors. While the partnerships will vary depending on place, the general pattern of local advocates focused on climate-sensitive infrastructures (green and blue) combined with public space planning (greenways, open spaces, streets and drainage) working with regional, state and federal agencies, and the private sector will be required to make more resilient communities a reality.

Conclusion

The purposeful integration of local projects with community benefits, like the Lafitte Greenway, into the development of regional climate change plans is an important strategy to build consensus for the greater challenge of planning for equitable and resilient regions. A key area of future research should examine how the adaption and mitigation components of blue and green infrastructure can be better conceptualized and planned for simultaneously. Building working relationships between land use, environmental and transportation planners with networks of associated professionals in urban design, landscape architecture, architecture and engineering can help to increase resilience and at the same time create co-benefits to urban populations like trail-oriented development opportunities (Fields 2009; Meyer 2009). Building these working relationships and the political coalitions necessary to push equitable plans forward is as important a challenge as building the green and blue infrastructure itself.

Note

1 The authors were participant observers in the planning process, acting in administrative, academic, and advocacy roles.

References

AECOM. (2013). The Impact of Climate Change and Population Growth on the National Flood Insurance Program through 2100. https://www.adaptationclearinghouse.org/resources/the-impact-of-climate-change-and-population-growth-on-the-national-flood-insurance-program-through-2100.html (accessed August 9, 2021).

Ahern, J. (2004). "Greenways in the USA: Theory, Trends and Prospects." In R. Jongman and G. Pungetti, eds. *Ecological Networks and Greenways, Concept, Design, Implementation*, pp. 34–55. Cambridge: Cambridge University Press.

Bea, R. (2006). *Reflections on the Draft Final U.S. Army Corps of Engineers Interagency Performance Evaluation Task Force (IPET) Report Titled Performance Evaluation of the New Orleans and Southeast Louisiana Hurricane Protection System*. Berkeley: Center for Catastrophic Risk Management University of California, Berkeley.

Beatley, T. (2014). *Blue Urbanism: Exploring Connections between Cities and Oceans*. Washington, DC: Island Press.

Benedict, M. A. and McMahon, E.T. (2002). "Green Infrastructure: Smart Conservation for the 21st Century," *Renewable Resources Journal* 2002: 12–19.

Blackwell, A. G. (2005). *Equitable Gulf Coast Renewal: Creating Housing Opportunity through Inclusionary Zoning*. New Orleans, LA: Policy Link, New Orleans Policy Brief, October 2005.

Bosch Slabbers, Landscape & Urban Design, Waggonner & Ball Architects (2013). *Greater New Orleans Urban Water Plan: Lafitte Blueway—Transforming the Lafitte Corridor*. http://livingwithwater.com/urban_water_plan/reports/ (accessed May 1, 2015).

Buchanan, S. (2015). "Living along the Lafitte Greenway: Is It Attainable or Unaffordable?" *Louisiana Weekly*, September 29. http://www.louisianaweekly.com/living-along-the-lafitte- greenway-is-it-attainable-or-unaffordable (accessed April 15, 2016).

Burby, R. J., Nelson, A. C. and Sanchez, T. W. (2006). "The Problems of Containment and the Promise of Planning." In E. L. Birch and S. M. Wachter, eds. *Rebuilding Urban Places after Disaster*, pp. 47–65. Philadelphia: University of Pennsylvania Press.

Campanella, R. (2010). *Delta Urbanism: New Orleans*. Chicago, IL: American Planning Association.

Campanella, T. J. (2006). "Urban Resilience and the Recovery of New Orleans," *Journal of the American Planning Association* 72(2): 141–6.

City of New Orleans. (2002). *New Century New Orleans Parks, Recreation, and Open Space Plan*. City of New Orleans: Planning Commission.

City of New Orleans. (2013a). *Lafitte Greenway Master Plan. Part 1*. City of New Orleans. https://www.lafittegreenway.org/lafitte-greenway-plans (accessed August 9, 2021).

City of New Orleans. (2013b). *Lafitte Corridor Revitalization Plan*. http://www.lafittegreenway.org/lafitte-greenway-plans (accessed April 15, 2016).

City of New Orleans. (2013c). "Incorporation of 'Blueway' Design into Lafitte Corridor Altering Greenway Scope between Bayou St John and Broad Street." Unpublished memo.

Crompton, J. L. (2001). "Perceptions of How the Presence of Greenway Trails Affects the Value of Proximate Properties," *Journal of Park and Recreation Administration* 19(3): 114–32.

Crowell, M., Coulton, K., Johnson, C., Westcott, J., Bellomo, D., Edelman, S. and Hirsch, E. (2010). "Estimate of the US Population Living in 100-Year Coastal Flood Hazard Areas," *Journal of Coastal Research* 26(20): 201–11.

Eisenman, T. S. (2013). "Frederick Law Olmsted, Green Infrastructure, and the Evolving City," *Journal of Planning History* 12(4): 287–311.

EPA (US Environmental Protection Agency) (2015). *Community Based Public-Private Partnerships (CBP3) and Alternative Market-Based Tools for Integrated Green Stormwater Infrastructure: A Guide for Local Governments.* April. http://www.epa.gov/reg3wapd/greeninfrastructure/GI_CB_P3_Guide_%20EPA_R3_FINAL_042115_508.pdf (accessed May 1, 2015).

Erickson, D. L. (2006). *MetroGreen: Connection Open Space in North American Cities.* Washington, DC: Island Press.

Everett, G. and Lamond, J. (2014). "A Conceptual Framework for Understanding Behaviours and Attitudes around 'Blue–Green' Approaches to Flood-Risk Management." In D. Proverbs and C. A. Brebbia, eds. *Flood Recovery, Innovation and Response IV*, pp. 101–12. Southampton: WIT Press.

Fabos, G. J. (2004). "Greenway Planning in the United States: Its Origins and Recent Case Studies," *Landscape and Urban Planning* 68: 321–42.

FEMA. (2007). *Public Assistance Policy and Guidance (June).* http://www.fema.gov/public-assistance-policy-and-guidance/public-assistance-guide (accessed May 1, 2015).

FEMA. (2015). *Disaster Declarations by Year.* https://www.fema.gov/disaster/declarations (accessed May 1, 2015).

Fields, B. (2009). "From Green Dots to Greenways: Planning in the Age of Climate Change in Post-Katrina New Orleans," *Journal of Urban Design* 14(3): 325–44.

Fields, B. (2013). "Confronting the Wicked Problem: Disaster Planning in Post-Katrina New Orleans," *Good Governance Worldwide* July 2(6): pp. 1–8.

Fields, B. (2015). *Accessing the Mega-Region: Evaluating the Role of Livable Community Patterns in Gulf Coast Mega-Region Planning* (No. SWUTC/15/600451-00109-1).

Fields, B., Wagner, J. and Frisch, M. (2015). "Placemaking and Disaster Recovery: Targeting Place for Recovery in Post- Katrina New Orleans," *Journal of Urbanism* 8(1): 38–56.

FOLC (Friends of Lafitte Corridor) and Brown & Danos Landdesign, Inc. (2007). *Lafitte Greenway Master Plan.* New Orleans, LA: FOLC.

Godschalk, D. R. (2004). "Land Use Planning Challenges: Coping with Conflicts in Visions of Sustainable Development and Livable Communities," *Journal of the American Planning Association* 70(1): 5–13.

Gotham, K. F. (2015). "Limitations, Legacies, and Lessons Post- Katrina Rebuilding in Retrospect and Prospect," *American Behavioral Scientist* 59(10): 1314–26.

Gotham, K. F. and Greenberg, M. (2014). *Crisis Cities: Disaster and Redevelopment in New York and New Orleans.* New York: Oxford University Press.

Healey, P. (1999). "Institutionalist Analysis, Communicative Planning, and Shaping Places," *Journal of Planning Education and Research* 19: 111–21.

HUD (US Department of Housing and Urban Development). Hurricane Sandy Rebuilding Task Force. (2013). "Hurricane Sandy Rebuilding Strategy: Stronger Communities, A Resilient Region." August. http://portal.hud.gov/hudportal/documents/huddoc?id=hsrebuildingstrategy.pdf (accessed May 1, 2015).

Kabat, P., Vierssen, W., van, Veraart, J. and Vellinga Aerts, P. J. (2005). "Climate Proofing the Netherlands," *Nature* 438: 283–4.

Lawson, E., Thorne, C., Ahilan, S., Allen, D., Arthur, S., Everett, G. and Wright, N. (2014). "Delivering and Evaluating the Multiple Flood Risk Benefits in Blue–Green

Cities: An Interdisciplinary Approach," *Flood Recovery, Innovation and Response IV* 184: 113–24.
Lewis, P. (2003). *New Orleans: The Making of an Urban Landscape*. Charlottesville: University of Virginia Press.
Lindsay, B. R. (2014). "FEMA's Disaster Relief Fund: Overview and Selected Issues," *Congressional Research Service*, May 7, p. 6.
Little, C. E. (1990). *Greenways for America*. Baltimore, MD: Johns Hopkins University Press.
Lopez, J. A. (2006). "The Multiple Lines of Defense Strategy to Sustain Coastal Louisiana (Metairie, LA: Lake Pontchartrain Basin Foundation)." http://www.SaveOurLake.org/ (accessed May 1, 2015).
Markwell, P. and Ratard, R. (2012). "Deaths Directly Caused by Hurricane Katrina." http://www.dhh.state.la.us/assets/oph/Center-PHCH/Center-CH/stepi/specialstudies/KatrinaDeath1.pdf (accessed June 23, 2016).
McCloud, K. (2015). "Updated: Bike Commute Data Released." League of American Bicyclists. http://bikeleague.org/content/updated-bike-commute-data-released (accessed December 4, 2015).
Meyer, H. (2009). "Reinventing the Dutch Delta: Complexity and Conflicts," *Built Environment* 28(4): 432–51.
Nelson, M., Ehrenfeucht, R. and Laska, S. (2007). "Planning, Plans, and People: Professional Expertise, Local Knowledge, and Governmental Action in Post-Hurricane Katrina New Orleans," *Cityscape* 9(3): 23–54.
New City NOLA. (2014). http://newcitynola.org/projects/ (accessed June 27, 2016).
Newman, Andy. (2012). Hurricane Sandy vs. Hurricane Katrina. *New York Times City Room*. https://cityroom.blogs.nytimes.com/2012/11/27/hurricane-sandy-vs-hurricane-katrina/ (accessed August 8, 2021).
Olshansky, R., Hopkins, L. and Johnson, L. (2012). "Disaster and Recovery: Processes Compressed in Time," *Natural Hazards Review* 13(3): 173–8.
Olshansky, R. B., Johnson, L.A., Horne, J. and Nee, B. (2008). "Longer View: Planning for the Rebuilding of New Orleans," *Journal of the American Planning Association* 74(3): 273–87.
Rittel, H. and Webber, M. (1973). "Dilemmas in a General Theory of Planning," *Policy Sciences*, 4: 155–69. Amsterdam: Elsevier Scientific.
Seed, R., Bea, R., Abdelmalak, R., Athanasopoulos, A., Boutwell Jr., G. Bray, J., Briaud, J-L., Cheung, C., Cobos-Roa, D., Cohen- Waeber, J., et al. (2006). "Investigation of the Performance of the New Orleans Flood Protection Systems in Hurricane Katrina on August 29, 2005. Vol 1." http://www.ce.berkeley.edu/projects/neworleans/report/VOL_1.pdf (accessed May 1, 2015).
Shields, R. (2008). "Delta City." In P. E., Steinberg, and R. Shields, eds. *What Is a City? Rethinking the Urban after Hurricane Katrina*, pp. 78–93. Athens: University of Georgia Press.
Stafford Act (The Robert T. Stafford Disaster Relief and Emergency Assistance Act of 1988), Pub. L. No. 100-707, 42 U.S.C. §§ 5121–5207 (2006). Originally published November 23, 1988.
Stromberg, M. (2010). "Putting the Water to Work," *Planning* 76(6): 34–36.
Thomas, J. J. and DeWeese, J. (2015). *Reimaging New Orleans Post-Katrina: A Case Study in Using Disaster Recovery Funds to Rebuild More Resiliently*. Washington, DC: Georgetown Climate Center.
Van Heerden, I. L. (2007). "The Failure of the New Orleans Levee System following Hurricane Katrina and the Pathway Forward," *Public Administration Review* 67(1): 24–35.

Vazquez, L. (2005). "A Plan for Democratic and Equitable Planning in New Orleans," *PLanetizen*, November 7, 2005. http://www.planetizen.com/node/17769 (accessed April 30, 2016).

Waggonner & Ball Architects. (2013). *Greater New Orleans Urban Water Plan*. http://livingwithwater.com/urban_water_plan/reports/ (accessed May 1, 2015).

Wagner, J. A. and Frisch, M. (2009). "Introduction: New Orleans and the Design Moment," *Journal of Urban Design* 14(3): 237–55.

Weber, E. P. and Khademian, A.M. (2008). "Wicked Problems, Knowledge Challenges, and Collaborative Capacity Builders in Network Settings," *Public Administration Review* 68: 334–49.

Yin, R. K. (2013). *Case Study Research: Design and Methods* (Applied Social Research Methods). Thousand Oaks, CA: Sage.

Zevenbergen, C., Van Herk, S., Rijke, J., Kabat, P., Bloemen, P., Ashley, R., Speers, A., Gersonius, B. and Veerbeek, W. (2013). "Taming Global Flood Disasters. Lessons Learned from Dutch Experience," *Natural Hazards* 65(3): 1217–25.

Chapter 12

THE ROLE OF LOCAL LEADERS REGARDING ENVIRONMENTAL CONCERNS IN MASTER PLANS

An Empirical Study of China's 80 Large Municipalities

Lei Zhang, Rachel M. Tochen, Michael Hibbard, and Zhenghong Tang

Introduction

Master plans, also called general plans or comprehensive plans, are important documents for the future vision of local jurisdictions (Levy 2003). Environmental concerns typically refer to the awareness of environmental problems and prioritizing policies and actions to tackle these problems. Generally, master plans that address more environmental concerns may improve local collective action in regard to ecosystem protection, climate change and smart growth (Berke et al. 2013; Norton 2008). The extent of environmental concerns in master plans varies from place to place depending on the degree to which the state mandates attention to environmental issues, as well as the role played by local education, political will, officials and planners in the development of the master plans (Brody, Highfield and Carrasco 2004; Norton 2008).

Though these factors influencing master plans in North America and Australia are well discussed in the planning literature (Berke and Godschalk 2009; Stevens 2013; Tang and Brody 2009; Tang et al. 2011), little research has been conducted in China, where the master planning process is different in terms of nationwide statutory requirements, powerful local leaders, party-state regime and a planning culture dominated by modernization and physical planning (Abramson 2006; Leaf 2005; Tian and Shen 2011; Zhang 2002). In particular, the effects of local leaders' attributes on environmental concerns in master plans are not well explored, although some studies have found that local leaders have a prominent role in China's local public affairs (Li and Zhou 2005; Zhang 2002).

In this chapter, first, we report the findings of a study that evaluates environmental concerns in 80 municipal master plans (MMPs) from China and explores the impacts of local leaders. The research can contribute to a body of knowledge on plan evaluation with the master plans from China, a region not well covered

DOI: 10.4324/9781003178545-16

by the existing plan evaluation research. Second, the word count method we utilize is especially appropriate in a context in which a hierarchical administration and planning system dominates the planning process. Third, we explain factors influencing environmental concerns in Chinese master plans, in particular, the factors from local leaders, which can give a distinctive explanation as to why some MMPs show more environmental concerns than the others. In doing so, we address two research questions: (1) To what extent are environmental concerns expressed in China's MMPs? (2) What kinds of influence do local leaders impose on the level of environmental concerns expressed in the MMPs?

We begin by drawing on the literature to establish a theoretical framework to explain the presence of environmental concerns in master plans and the influence of local leaders' personal characteristics on those concerns. Then we describe the methods used to collect and analyze the plan quality and their influential variables. Next, we present our findings and discuss the implications of the findings for promoting environmental concerns.

Literature Review

Environmental Concerns in MMPs from China

Environmental concerns generally refer to "the degree to which people are aware of problems regarding the environment and support efforts to solve them and/or indicate a willingness to contribute personally to their solution" (Dunlap and Jones 2002). Master plans are important documents for thinking about a city in an integrated way (Levy 2003). Therefore, it can reflect the environmental concerns of cities, meaning to what extent these cities express an awareness of environmental problems and priority on policies and actions to tackle these problems. They are especially important, in that the scope of master plans has expanded from land use to addressing social issues, economic needs and environmental crises (Kaiser and Godschalk 1995). As Berke et al. (2013) recommended, it is time to incorporate environmental thinking into comprehensive plans, but the approach must consider different planning regimes.

Most existing frameworks of plan evaluation, covering broad issues like environmental protection, affordable housing, climate change actions, hazard mitigation, community plans, ecosystem protection and smart growth, are derived from plans in the United States, Australia, New Zealand and Canada (Baker, Sipe and Gleeson 2006; Berke, Song, and Stevens 2009, 2013; Berke and Godschalk 2009; Brody et al. 2004; Lyles and Stevens 2014; Tang et al. 2011). Plans from these countries, based on the principle of representative democracy, are engaged with elected officials and the general public. Therefore, comprehensive plans in these local contexts can express openly and freely the future viewpoint and trade-off between economic development and environmental protection (Loh and Norton 2015; Norton 2005). Master plans in China, however, are still dominated by a hierarchical system and party-state regime, despite the growing effects from the market and the local public. Under the institutional context, the central government sets down general goals of economic development, social equality and environmental protection, and local governments cannot openly express disagreement on these goals in their master plans, but can make implicit choices by emphasizing some goals and neglecting others.

The standard procedures of municipal master planning in China include four steps. First, the municipal government will offer the master planning work to a certified planning institute. Second, the commissioned planning institute will survey, collect data and interview cadres from different departments and other stakeholders from the public. During the process, the municipal mayor and the municipal Chinese Communist Party (CCP) secretary will express their opinions for the future image of the city to the planners. The institute will finish several preliminary drafts of the master plan based on "scientific" data analysis, discussions with local cadres and opinions of municipal leaders, while also incorporating national laws, ordinances and statutory technical guidance. Then planners can display the positive and negative responses to preliminary drafts to local leaders, planning staffs and cadres from other departments. Based on the feedback they receive, planners will then form one single draft of the master plan. In the process of communication and plan adjustment, local leaders play a dominant role in directing the strategy of the final draft. Some planners even complain that during master planning "it is the local leader doing the planning and planners doing some drawing" (Zhang 2002).

The third step is public involvement, hearings and consultation. The final draft must be open to experts and the general public for their suggestions and opinions. The planners can then adjust the master plan according to the suggestions of the experts and the public. However, the effects of public involvement vary widely across cities because local governments can choose both the form that public involvement takes and the extent to which the opinions of the public and experts are accepted or rejected.

Later the revised version of the MMP of a large municipality (with an urban population of more than 1 million) is submitted to the State Council for approval. A committee led by the Ministry of Housing and Urban-Rural Development (MHURD), the national department in charge of urban planning, and joined by 14 other related ministries checks whether the MMP complies with the state's mandated planning goals according to laws, ordinances, policies and statutory guidance and standards. The approved MMP will then become a statutory plan. It is in fact a negotiated result between the state and local government, and reflects preferences of local governments balancing multiple objectives of economic development, environmental protection and social stability.

Evaluating Environmental Concerns by Word Counting

MMPs in China reflect local preference in a different way than western plans, it is necessary to rethink a plan evaluation method suitable to the distinctive context. Until now, the most common approach to plan evaluation content analysis is by item coding with an established framework of good plans (Berke et al. 2013; Berke and Godschalk 2009; Brody 2003; Brody et al. 2004; Godschalk et al. 1999; Stevens 2013; Tang and Brody 2009). The plan evaluation process of item coding generally includes developing a conceptual framework, constructing a protocol of items, coding items by a single or multiple trained coders and checking the reliability and validity of results (Berke and Godschalk 2009; Lyles and Stevens 2014; Stevens 2013). Though the item coding approach holds a potential in evaluating plans beyond the North America and Europe, Counting Word Frequency (CWF) can be a reliable approach with three advantages to measure environmental concerns of MMPs in China.

First, CWF method, based on a naïve Bayes assumption in content analysis that "a text is represented as vector of word counts or occurrence" (Slapin and Proksch 2008), has been commonly used in content analysis in political science, public management and, to a lesser extent, urban planning (Klüver, 2009; 2013; Laver, Benoit, and Garry 2003; Quinn et al. 2010). Though having poor performance in flexibility and complexity, the CWF approach, with the help of computer aided program, can reduce the likelihood of human error and personal bias associated with code noting (Grimmer and Stewer 2013). Moreover, in case of using CWF for English text, it is necessary to simplify the vocabulary with *stemming*, which reduces the complexity by mapping words that refer to the same basic concept to a single root. In Chinese, however, there are no separate singular and plural forms for nouns, and no verb conjugation to denote sense or match with the corresponding subject. For example, family, families, familial all use the same word of *jiating* (family) in Chinese. Therefore, the stemming work for Chinese texts can be much easier than that for English texts.

Second, MMPs in China reflect local preference in an implicit approach. As previously mentioned, the central government sets down general goals of economic development, social equality and environmental protection, and local governments cannot openly express their disagreement on these goals but can make a choice among them, emphasizing some goals and neglecting others. As for the words and expression on environmental concerns, few plans that use these environment-related words with negative expression, such as a municipality should neglect the environment, environmental protection, climate change, etc. For instance, a municipality prioritizing economic growth even at the expense of the environmental degrading will not express its idea in plans with a sentence of "strengthen the economic growth, and disregard environmental protection" but replace it with "strengthen the economic growth," which mentions no ideas on environmental protection. Thus, the frequency of words in a certain domain can reveal the extent to which a municipality prioritizes the issue. The approach of measuring the level of policy priority through the number or relative proportion of documents or terms on different issues is commonly used in studies of environmental issues in an authoritarian political setting (Huang et al. 2010). The reluctance to use negative expression on environment-related words partly relieve the problem of the different meaning that a same word may have within various text in MMPs.

Third, China's MMPs are very standardized in their structure of drafts and similar in language style. MHURD issues a series of guidelines and requirements for drafting urban and rural plans. These guidelines regulate the structures and styles that the text of master plans in China should obey. Moreover, planners making MMPs in China are required to pass the Chinese Registered Planner (CRR) certification exam, the only nationwide, official verification of planners' qualifications in China. Once passed, they also need to complete several training courses required each year for CRR certification maintenance. The China Association of City Planning led by the MHURD is in charge of both the CRR exam and the subsequent training programs, assuring that all registered planners are familiar with the guidelines and requirements for drafting master plans.

Both the standardized form and the reluctance to use negative expression can make CWF a suitable method to measure the environmental concerns in China's MMPs. But it should also be mentioned that all languages are complex. There is no exception for Chinese language. CWF method will not eliminate the need for careful thought by researchers, nor remove the necessity of reading texts. Therefore, it is also necessary to supplement the CWF method with careful human reading and confirm results with the common approach of item coding.

Local Leaders' Effects on Environmental Concerns in China

Early plan evaluation research discussed methods to evaluate the differences in the quality of plans, but more recent studies focus on factors that explain these differences. They broadly include planning contexts (e.g. population, wealth, education) (Berke 1996; Brody, Carrasco, and Highfield 2006; Brody, Godschalk, and Burby 2003; Stevens 2013; Tang et al. 2010); local jurisdictions (e.g. local political supports, the values and preferences of decision-makers, statutory obligations and interplay with higher levels of governance) (Berke 1996; Betsill 2001; Burby and Dalton 1994; Burby and May 1998; Tang et al. 2010; Urwin and Jordan 2008); planning agencies and planners (Burby and May 1998; Loh and Norton 2015; Tang and Brody 2009); and public participation (Brody et al. 2003).

Among these four explanations, planning scholars have consistently stressed the dominant role of decision-makers on the policy focus of local plans (Betsill 2001; Burby and May 1998; Tang et al. 2010). The difference in their awareness of, commitment to deal with and capacity to solve issues may lead to differences in the policy focus of local plans (Burby and May 1998; Norton 2005; Tang et al. 2010). However, many of these debates on the role of decision-makers (e.g. mayors) on local plans are based in a North American or European context, where local regimes are based on representative democracy. Although the policy focus may not entirely reflect the preference of the general public, the policy preference in a local representative government should align with the public preference as closely as possible (Loh and Norton 2015).

Local governments in China differ from those of North America and Europe in their accountability and commitment. Effects of local leaders in China are also distinctive from their counterparts in North America or Europe. The state exerts more influence on public affairs, and local officers are more accountable to the central government than to the local public (Abramson 2006; Zhang 2002).

Leaders in China's municipalities answer to both the CCP secretary and the mayor, which reflects the dual presence of the communist party and administrative government (Li and Zhou 2005; Zheng et al. 2014). CCP city secretaries have somewhat more authority than the mayor according to laws that regulate the government under the leadership of the CCP. In practice, CCP secretaries are mainly in charge of personnel and political affairs, and mayors are responsible for the administration of economic development, environmental protection, education and so on. Neither municipal CCP secretaries nor mayors are directly elected by residents of the jurisdiction. Rather, they are selected by those serving in higher tiers of government.

China's municipal leaders are powerful and strongly influence local public affairs (Eaton and Kostka 2014). Since the economic reform in 1978 and the tax-sharing reform in 1994, the central government has decentralized most decision-making and given partial budgetary control to local governments (Li and Zhou 2005; Tsui and Wang 2004). Moreover, local governments may also acquire extra-budgetary revenues through their monopolistic power over the land market (Tao et al. 2010). Municipal leaders wield significant authority and influence over almost all major decisions in a municipality, especially those involving the appointment of sub-level officials and economic problems (Eaton and Kostka 2014).

However, these powerful municipal leaders do not operate without constraints. As agents of the state, municipal leaders are evaluated by metrics and held directly accountable to higher levels of government (Li and Zhou 2005). Since economic reform in 1978, the central government has adjusted these metrics from political ideology and loyalty to the ability to promote economic growth (Bo 1996). The effects of these changes have been shown in the literature, confirming the positive connection between economic growth and official promotion in provincial, municipal and township levels (Edin 2003; Li and Zhou 2005; Martis et al. 2000). Most recently, facing severe problems of environmental degradation along with economic growth, the central government has increasingly focused on environmental issues in evaluating local leaders (Ran 2013; Wu 2009). The transition, sometimes defined as "*authoritarian environmentalism*," is top-down and rooted in the statutory power of the central state (Gilley 2012) and differs from *democratic environmentalism* in western countries, which relies more on public concerns, elections and mobilization (List and Sturm 2006).

However, the environment-oriented transition of the central government has not generally aligned with practical outcomes in localities (Gilley 2012; Yu,

Pagani, and Huang 2012). Ran (2013) attributes the failure to the central government, which provides little political, financial and moral incentive to encourage local leaders to focus on the long-term (e.g. environmental protection) instead of tangible and short-term outcomes (e.g. economic growth). Economy (2004) and Lo and Tang (2006) blamed local governments as the key obstacle in including environmental concerns, because of their popular pro-growth values and weak control from the central government.

Further research shows that local leaders' performance levels vary with key attributes, including their duration, education, age and working experience (Eaton and Kostka 2014; Lorentzen, Landry, and Yasuda 2010). Among them, Eaton and Kostka (2014) found that short duration generates significant negative effects on environmental policy implementation. Lorentzen et al. (2010) showed that local leaders' education, such as training abroad and training in law, can promote more expedited implementation of environmental amenities and higher levels of environmental transparency. However, little research has explored the effects of local leaders' attributes on environmental concerns in master plans.

Methods and Data

The first step in carrying out our study was accessing the MMPs. Given the fact that full versions of MMPs in most of China's large municipalities are inaccessible to the public, we collected MMPs adopted from 2000 to 2012 by direct requests to planning authorities or planning institutes participating in master planning, by emails and phone calls. Some of them refused to provide their plans, resulting in us collecting 80 MMPs, which accounted for 76.2% of the total 105 MMPs for China's large municipalities during this period. They covered all 31 provincial level administrations in Mainland China.

Then we measured the environmental concerns by CWF method, comparing the probability of environmentally related words within each master plan draft. We counted the occurrence of environmental-related words in master plans in three steps. First, we briefly read all texts of master plans. Then we listed the frequency of all Chinese words in texts using Rost CM 6.0 (a software for Chinese content analysis), and excluded all conjunctions, adverbs and adjectives (Chinese does not have articles). The most common word used in the 80 master plans is development (*fazhan*), with the frequency of 8.28 per thousand, and the frequency of the 100th common word is 0.26 per thousand. The average frequency of the most common 100 words is 1.57 per thousand, in contrast to 0.03 per thousand of the succeeding 100 most common words. So we just chose the words related to environment from the 100 most common words, and came up with seven words, including environment (*huanjing*), environmental protection (*huanbao*), sustainable (*kechixu*), ecological (*shengtai*), carbon emission (*tanpaifang*) and climate change (*qihoubianhua*). The frequency of these seven common environmental-related words was calculated for each plan as the variable reflecting the environmental concerns.

To confirm the reliability of the CWF method, we also employed a correlation analysis between the result of environmental concerns from word counting and that of the common approach of item noting in plan quality research. The protocol for item noting draws in part upon the common seven dimensions of plan quality developed by Godschalk et al. (1999), as well as the framework of direction and action recently developed by Berke et al. (2013). Since this study focuses on the environmental concerns as a whole, rather than individual dimensions of plan quality, we regard the *fact base* as awareness for environmental issues and combine dimensions of *goal, policies, implementation and monitoring and coordination* as one reflecting the willingness, and support to improve environment. Each item of the protocol was established by the authors and two research assistants with consensus on score assignments after coding five master plans other than those under study. Each item was scored on a 0 or 1. 1 means that the indicator was included, and 0 means not. The protocol originally contained 60 items. After coding all 80 master plans under study, 6 items were excluded because their intercoder reliability was less than 80%, a standard that most existing plan quality studies meet (Berke and Godschalk 2009).

Because master plans differ in both their length and number of environmentally related words, we employed a logistic model for grouped data to analyze the possible effects on environmental concerns using STATA 12.0. Each draft of the master plan is regarded as a group, within which each word is defined as environmentally related (coded as 1) or not (coded as 0). Then the effects on the probability of environmentally related words occurring could be explored by the logit model, which produces maximum-likelihood logit estimates on grouped data (Hamilton 2013; Hosmer, Lemeshow, and Sturdivant 2013; Rabe-Hesketh and Everitt 2004).

We analyzed these variables on environmental concerns in two stages. First, variables of local leaders' attributes, planning consultants and public participation were separately examined with logit regression. Then in the second stage, we combined all three groups of variables into one model and confirmed variables being statistically significant.

Attributes of Local Leaders

As we discussed above, both the mayor and CCP secretary have predominant effects in the process of master planning. Their effects on environmental concerns in finalized master plans possibly differ according to their age, education and working experience, as has been identified in studies of environmental policy implementation and environmental transparency (Eaton and Kostka 2014; Lorentzen et al. 2010). Therefore, we chose age, education level, major and working experience of both CCP city secretary and mayor as variables possibly affecting environmental concerns in a master plan (as Table 12.1 shows).

We first divided local leaders into three age groups of young (40s), middle (50s) and aged (60s) based on their age when plans are made, because the 50 and 60 are important age points for higher level governments to promote local leaders. Second, *education level* of local leaders was classified into three levels: high level refers to these officers with a full-time master's degree or a bachelor's degree from China's top 39 universities sponsored with the "program 985" (top university funding) by the Ministry of Education of China. Middle level refers to those with a full-time bachelor's degree from a university other than the top 39 universities. Low are those without a full-time bachelor's degree. We posit that education level of local leaders may have a positive effect on environmental concerns. Another variable reflecting education of local leaders is whether or not their *major* is related to the environment. Training in environmentally related fields provides local leaders more professional skills and knowledge, which could possibly promote environmental concerns in master plans. The last variable on the personal characteristics of local leaders is whether or not their *working experience* is related to the environment. It is possible that an officer with environmentally related working experience would be more concerned about environmental issues. The personal information of city leaders was collected from the website of *Baidu Baike*, which provides both the curriculum vitae of local leaders under research, and their links with the official website of city governments.

City Context

The variables of city context control for the possible impacts of the general socio-economic background on local environmental concerns in master plans. In this study, city context variables are *wealth, education, scales, industrial structure* and the *time* being adopted. All city context data, except for the *time*, are collected from the officially government-issued China City Statistical Yearbooks from 2001 to 2013.

The *wealth* of a city possibly contributes to the environmental concerns in plans because with increased income, the general public concerns itself more with environmental issues (Scott and Willits 1994; Selden and Song 1995). In addition, wealthier cities have more financial, human and technical resources, which could also contribute to high-quality plans reflecting more environmental concerns (Tang et al. 2010). Finally, wealthy cities in China face less pressure on economic growth in the race for GDP, and, as a result, can possibly lead to a relatively high environmental priority in their master plans. Therefore, we measure the wealth of the 80 municipalities according to their per-capita GDP value in the year when their plans were finished. The per-capita GDP values in different years are all converted to that of 2000.

In addition to the *wealth*, municipalities with *industrial structure* highly dependent on secondary industry can also lead to more attention on environmental concerns in their master plans. The reason is that these municipalities confront more pollution due to the heavy weight of the secondary industry (Shen 2006), and the national transfer to environmental priority promoted by the central government forces cities with serious environmental degradation to be more responsible for environmental degradation, no matter if they prefer or not (Gilley 2012; Ran 2013). We measure the *industrial structure* by the GDP share of the secondary industry.

Education is the third city context variable that can influence environmental concerns in master plans. A highly educated population may influence the planning process and encourage an increased interest in environmental concerns (Brody et al. 2004; Howell and Laska 1992; Tang et al. 2011). We measure the education level by ranking incidence of highly educated people of the total population of the city in the year the plan was made.

China's large municipalities also differ in population size (ranging from 1 million to more than 10 million) and administrative level (the highest is provincial-level city, and the lowest is prefecture-level city) (Abramson 2006). Large-scale cities or communities can potentially raise more concern about environmental issues in plans (Tang and Brody 2009). High administrative level means the municipal leaders should comply more with the central government's environmental concerns. In China, these two variables are closely intertwined, with a larger urban population in most cases acquiring higher administrative level. So we combine both size of urban population and political position into a variable of *scale*, and code provincial-level city, sub provincial-level and provincial capital municipalities as 1, and all others as 0.

Environmental concerns in MMPs may also differ because of the time of adoption. National efforts to tackle environmental problems have been increasing over the last two decades, particularly after 2007, when a cabinet-level environmental ministry was established and environmental targets were adopted in the National 12th Five Year Plan. We divided the MMPs into those being issued after 2007 (code 1) or not (code 0) to check the possible effects of increased environmental concerns from the state mandates.

Planning Consultants and Public Participation

We also have control variables for planning institutes and public participation. There are three types of planning institutes in China (Abramson 2006): local planning institutes subordinated to provincial and municipal governments, the national planning institute subordinated to MHURD and planning institutes at departments of universities. Because none of our sample MMPs were done by a university planning department, we divided the planning institutes as either national (coded as 1) or local (coded as 0). In general, the national planning institute has a more highly esteemed professional reputation and better-developed social networks with the central government, while local planning institutes take advantage of local knowledge and social networks with local governments.

The role of public participation has been thoroughly discussed in European and North American planning circles (Berke et al. 2013; Brody et al. 2003; Tang et al. 2010), but it is a new topic for China's urban planning. Most municipalities began to incorporate public participation during the planning process by posting a MMP draft either onsite or online for public suggestions or recommendations.

However, great differences still exist in practice. Some city governments exhibit draft master plans for a long time at sites that are popularly known and easily accessed by the general public, while others do not. Similarly, some planning staffs in municipalities actively reply to popular opinions online, whereas those in other municipalities do not. Therefore, we take two variables to measure public participation in master planning. One is whether or not the city has an accessible and fixed place to exhibit the draft plans (coded as 1) or not (coded as 0). Another is whether planning staff reply to general suggestions (coded as 1) or not (coded as 0) about master plans on their official website. The information for these two variables was collected online via the official websites of municipal urban planning bureaus, planning exhibition halls, etc.

Results and Discussion

The results confirm that there are great differences in the degree of environmental concern in master plans, in the degree to which large municipalities in China express their awareness on environmental problems and in priority on policies and actions to curb environmental problems. Table 12.1 shows the mean frequencies of environmental words in master plans is 245.3 words with a standard deviation of 105.31. In addition, the mean length of master plans is 48,811.06 words with a standard deviation of 15,187.85.

TABLE 12.1 Variable definition and summary statistics

Variable	Definition and data source	Mean	Standard deviation
Dependent variable environmental concerns			
Words for environment	The amount of words related on environment[a]	245.83	105.31
Words in plans	Total amount of words in each master plan[a]	48811.06	15187.85
City context			
Regions located	Region located[b]		
Eastern	Cities in eastern region (1 = yes, 0 = no)	0.46	0.502
Central	Cities in central region (1 = yes, 0 = no)	0.20	0.403
Western	Cities in western region (1 = yes, 0 = no)	0.20	0.403
Northeastern	Cities in northeastern region (1 = yes, 0 = no)	0.14	0.347
Political status	Administration level (1 = provincial, vice-provincial cities and provincial capital, 0 = prefectural level)[b]	0.425	0.497
Wealth	GDP per capita (unit: CNY)[b]	26,462	15,644
Education	Rank of the percentage of high education (from 1 to 80)	40.50	23.24

Role of Local Leaders in Masterplanning

Industrial structure	The share of secondary industry[b]	47.77	10.780
Time	Plans issued after 2007 (yes = 1, no = 0)[a]	0.72	0.454
Planning consultant	National planning institute = 1 local institute = 0[a]	0.44	0.499
Public participation			
Plan exhibition	With a plans exhibition hall (yes = 1, no = 0)[c]	0.42	0.497
Reply public on line	Reply to public suggestions and communication on master plans online (yes = 1, no = 0)[c]	0.62	0.488
Leader's attributes			
Age_M	Age group mayors belong to[d]		
60s	Mayors aged 60s (yes = 1, no = 0)	0.13	0.336
50s	Mayors aged 50s (yes = 1, no = 0)	0.54	0.502
40s	Mayors aged 40s (yes = 1, no = 0)	0.33	0.474
Age_S	Age group CCP secretary belong to[d]		
60s	CCP secretary aged 60s (yes = 1, no = 0)	0.13	0.336
50s	CCP secretary aged 50s (yes = 1, no = 0)	0.68	0.470
40s	CCP secretary aged 40s (yes = 1, no = 0)	0.18	0.386
Education_M	The education level of the mayor[d]		
High	With master's degree or bachelor's degree from the top 39 universities (yes = 1, no = 0)	0.39	0.493
Middle	With bachelor's degree from non-top universities (yes = 1, no = 0)	0.40	0.493
Low	Without bachelor's degree (yes = 1, no = 0)	0.20	0.406
Education_S	The education level of the CCP secretary[d]		
High	With master's degree or bachelor's degree from top universities (yes = 1, no = 0)	0.45	0.500
Middle	With bachelor's degree from non-top universities (yes = 1, no = 0)	0.45	0.500
Low	Without bachelor's degree (yes = 1, no = 0)	0.11	0.309
Major_M	Mayor with degree related to environment (1 = yes, 0 = no)[d]	0.385	0.490
Major_S	CCP secretaries with degree related to environment (1 = yes, 0 = no)[d]	0.45	0.500
Work Experience_M	Mayor with environmental working experience (1 = yes, 0 = no)[d]	0.167	0.375
Work Experience_S	CCP secretaries with environmental working experience (1 = yes, 0 = no)[d]	0.05	0.222

Notes: GDP=gross domestic product; CNY=Chinese yuan; CCP=Chinese Communist Party.
[a] Data based on the content analysis of master plans by research team;
[b] Data from the China City Statistical Yearbook from 2001 to 2013;
[c] Data collected from websites of planning authorities of 80 large municipalities under the study in 2014;
[d] Data collected from the website of *Baidu Baike* http://baike.baidu.com and websites of city governments of 80 large municipalities under the study in 2014.

In a different way, item noting based on established protocol also confirms the difference of the 80 master plans under study in environmental concerns. As Table 12.2 shows, the mean score from the protocol of environmental concerns was 34.85, with a standard deviation of 4.44.

Table 12.3 shows the Pearson correlation coefficient between the score when environmental concerns are evaluated by item noting and the frequency from environmental word counting. The correlation is positive and strong with a value of 0.883, as well as being statistically significant. Moreover, we also separately analyze the correlations between frequency of environmentally related words and score of *awareness,* and that of *willingness and supports* by item coding. Both the *awareness* and *willingness and supports* are important aspects of environmental concern. *Awareness,* referring to the extent to which a municipality is aware of environmental problems, is measured by score of fact base by item coding within MMPs. The *willingness and supports* to improve environment is measured by the score of goal, policies, implementation and monitoring and coordination in MMPs. Both of the two correlations are positive with the value of 0.633 and 0.718. All results from the correlation analysis confirm the credibility of the method that using word frequency counting evaluates environmental concerns in China's MMPs.

Using the probability of environmentally related words, Table 12.4 reports the maximum likelihood estimates resulting from four logit models. Model 1, Model 2 and Model 3 separately explore effects from variables of local leaders' attributes, city context, planning consultants and public participation. Model 4 then combines all three groups of variables.

TABLE 12.2 Summary statistics for the environmental concerns score from code noting

Variable	Number of items	Mean	Minimum	Maximum	Standard deviation
Environmental concerns	54	34.85	26	44	4.44
Awareness	16	5.14	0	13	3.06
Willingness and supports	38	29.73	24	35	2.79

TABLE 12.3 The correlation analysis between the score from code noting and frequency of word counting

Variable	Frequency of environmentally related words
Scores of environmental concerns	0.883***
Scores of awareness	0.633***
Scores of willingness and supports	0.718***

★ $p < 0.1$, ★★ $p < 0.05$, ★★★ $p < 0.01$.

TABLE 12.4 Logistic regression on environmental issues

Variable	Model 1 Coeff.	Z	Model 2 Coeff.	Z	Model 3 Coeff.	Z	Model 4 Coeff.	Z
Local leader's attributes								
Age_Mayor (Reference = 60s)								
50s	−0.115***	−0.025					−0.030	−1.00
40s	−0.059**	−0.026					−0.039**	−2.03
Age_Secretary (Reference = 60s)								
50s	−0.083***	−0.024					−0.110***	−1.86
40s	−0.120***	−0.028					−0.242***	−8.57
Education_M (Reference = Low)								
Middle	−0.038**	−0.018					0.053***	2.24
High	0.100***	−0.020					0.075***	3.78
Education_S (Reference=Low)								
Middle	−0.014	−0.016					−0.009	−0.46
High	0.039	−0.029					0.137***	4.18
Major_M	0.148***	−0.018					0.151***	7.92
Major_S	0.075***	−0.017					0.056***	3.17
Work Experience_M	−0.036*	−0.021					−0.017	−0.72
Work Experience_S	0.089***	−0.032					0.062	1.41

(*Continued*)

Variable	Model 1 Coeff.	Z	Model 2 Coeff.	Z	Model 3 Coeff.	z	Model 4 Coeff.	z
City context								
Scale			0.188***	7.27			0.183***	6.21
Region (Reference=Cities in Eastern Region)								
Middle			−0.117***	−5.26			−0.029	−1.04
Western			0.052**	2.09			−0.022	−0.74
Northeastern			0.056**	2.04			0.085***	2.64
Industrial structure			0.003***	3.52			0.002**	2.17
GDP rank			2.21e^{-06}**	2.03			5.58e^{-06}***	4.48
Education level			−0.002***	−2.83			−0.004**	−3.94
Time			−0.020	−1.12			0.017	0.89
Planning institute and public participation								
Planning institute					−0.056***	−0.373	−0.035**	−2.12
Planning exhibition					0.058***	3.94	0.053***	2.91
Reply public on line					0.057***	3.74	0.049***	2.44
_cons	−5.224***	−0.029	−5.653***	−66.31	−5.308***	−0.020	−5.937***	−53.50
Prob > chi2	0.0000		0.0000		0.0000		0.0000	

Note: Coeff. = coefficient; GDP = gross domestic product.
* $p < 0.10$, ** $p < 0.05$, *** $p < 0.01$.

Local Leaders' Attributes

The results of models 1 and 4 indicate that the attributes of local leaders are closely associated with environmental concerns in MMPs. Among them age, personal education level and major are statistically significant, while work experience related to the environment is not.

First, the results indicate that the age of local leaders, both mayors and CCP secretaries, connects positively to environmental concerns in MMPs. MMPs of large municipalities with local leaders aged 60 years or over have, in general, more environmental words than those with local leaders aged less than 60 years, and hence MMPs with local leaders aged 50–59 years more than those with local leaders aged less than 50 years. The results correlate with the argument (e.g. Li and Zhou 2005; Zheng et al. 2014) that that since China's cadre personnel system prefers to promote young leaders, the aged CCP secretaries and mayors who have lost their chance for promotion can afford to be more concerned about long-term municipal environmental issues rather than short-term economic growth.

The education of local leaders also positively correlates with environmental concerns. Both the mayors and CCP secretaries with environmentally related majors correlate positively with the degree of environmental concerns. Moreover, the education level of mayors shows more significant positive effects than that of CCP secretaries. Models 1 and 4 indicate at a statistically significant level ($p < 0.01$) that highly educated mayors show a greater concern about environmental issues than mayors with a middle or low level of education. However, the effects of CCP secretaries' education level are not so confirmed, giving the result that the dummy variables of both highly educated and middle educated are not statistically significant in separated model 1, and only variables of the highly educated are statistically significant in combined model 4 ($p < 0.01$). Even so, we can say that China's large municipalities with local leaders having higher and more environmentally related education can positively affect environmental concerns in their MMPs.

Finally, the working experience of local leaders related to the environment contributes little to environmental concerns, as in the popular Chinese saying, *"the position of officers directs their thinking."* Some local leaders may have working experience of the environment, but that does not strengthen their value toward the environment. When they are promoted to be a mayor or CCP secretary, no difference exists between them and those without environmentally related working experience.

City Context

Our study also identified several contextual factors influencing environmental concerns in master plans. First, the wealth of a city contributes to more environmental concerns in its master plan. The result comes from the fact that the wealth rank of a city has a negative effect on the degree of environmental concerns of master plans in both separate model 2 and combined model 4. Another parallel result is that education makes a difference in terms of environmental concerns in master plans. In China, high education level of urban residents also promotes more concern about environmental issues, which is reflected in the master plans as well.

In addition, cities with higher shares of secondary industry also have positive effects on environmental concerns. It is understandable that cities with high shares of secondary industry face more challenges in reducing environmental problems, as well as increasing pressure from the central government, which has begun to prioritize national environmental goals. Even if implementation is difficult, the fact that the MMPs have an environmental focus reflects their awareness of, and willingness to consider potential action to address the problem.

Planning Consultants and Public Participation

The results also found that planning institutes have effects on environmental concerns. Models 2 and 3 show a statistically negative effect from the national planning institute ($p < 0.01$). It is quite strange that the national planning institute, with its high professional planning reputation, induces less environmental concerns than local planning institutes. One possible explanation is that the national planning institute is much more familiar with professional guides, procedures and requirements for approving MMPs, and has a strong social network with the MHURD as well. These two advantages may make it easier to receive approval from the central government on a MMP with less environmental concerns. Another possible reason is that local planning institutes, familiar with local knowledge, have more awareness about local environmental challenges and express them more in MMPs.

Public participation also has some positive effects on the environmental policy focus in MMPs. First, the cities with stable plan exhibition places accessible to the general public promote more environmental concerns in MMPs. The result is statistically significant in both separate Model 3 ($p < 0.01$) and combined Model 4 ($p < 0.01$). In addition, the positive effects of the variable on *reply public on line* are also statistically significant in both Model 3 ($p < 0.01$) and Model 4 ($p < 0.05$). The two results confirm that a municipality in which planning staff actively reply to the public online or display more information onsite can increase the extent to which environmental concerns are expressed in master plans.

Conclusion

This study answers the question of the extent to which environmental concerns are expressed in China's MMPs, in the case of 80 large municipalities, and the question of what kinds of influence local leaders impose on the level of environmental concerns. The two questions are significant in understanding the planning process and accountability of local governments in systems that are different than those based on representative democracy in Europe and North America. Moreover, we focused on environmental concerns because the environment has become an issue of note for both China's central government and the general public. To what extent the environmental concerns were combined in master plans could extensively reflect the roles of the local leaders, central government, general public and planners in the planning process and planning outcomes under certain city contexts.

We evaluated environmental concerns in MMPs with CWF method. The result shows that environmental concerns are differently addressed in MMPs of China's large municipalities. We also confirmed the result by correlation analysis with that of item coding, the common approach to plan evaluation. The positive and statistically significant correlations confirm the potential of the CWF method, being used in plan evaluation within the institutional context of the hierarchy planning system, party-state regime and the standardized form of master plans.

We also found that personal characteristics of local leaders, the CCP city secretary and the mayor do affect the level of environmental concerns expressed in master plans based on a logit regression for 80 master plans. Among these personal attributes, their education and age generally play a positive role on environmental concerns. In addition, there are no obvious effects from their working experience. The reason for the positive effect of age may be partially explained by the existing cadre evaluation system, where aged local leaders, with less chances for promotion, could pursue more long-term environmental concerns instead of the short-term objective like economic growth. While higher education and environmentally related majors improve local leaders' environmental values, which become infused into the planning process.

Moreover, we identified positive effects of contextual variables like wealth, general education level and public participation. These results are similar to that of cities in Europe and North America. While it is quite interesting that in some countries based on representative democracy, state mandates on the environment have an obvious effect on environmental concerns (Berke and French 1994; Tang et al. 2011); in China, a country with strict hierarchal administrative structure, the increasing central mandates on environment are not reflected in MMPs of large municipalities. The explanations for this deviation are difficult, but show that the existing planning system in China is far from the ideal hierarchal structure, and local governments in reality hold more autonomy in local plans. To improve the environmental focus in MMPs, a more collaborative approach should replace these top-down and coercive mandates.

Our study also suggests that improving environmental concerns in plans may reflect various strategies under different local regimes. For China's large municipalities, more environmentally related training could cause considerable effects on promoting environmental concerns in MMPs. Also the existing cadre evaluation system, which prefers young officers, should be readjusted to reduce local leaders' incentive to implement short-term metrics.

However, our research does not explore the processes by which these local leaders exert their personal influence on MMPs through planning institutes and planners. Also our study is limited, in that we did not consider the role of public servants and managers in the planning bureaus, the important agents who connect local leaders, the general public and local knowledge with planning institutes and planners, because the personal information of the managers and planning staffs of planning bureaus in most large municipalities, unlike these local leaders, is inaccessible to the public. Therefore, further studies on the master plan-making process by case study could deepen our understanding of how these mayors and CCP secretaries influence master plans through communication with planning staffs, planning institutes and planners, or vice versa.

Acknowledgment

We would like to thank Jian Zhang, Yiming Jiang, Xingxing Chen, Haiquan Song and Ruiying Wang for assistance with data collection. Thanks also goes to Saul Wilson, the anonymous reviewers and *JPER* editors who offered constructive suggestions and valuable comments on an earlier manuscript.

Declaration of Conflicting Interests

The authors declared no potential conflicts of interest with respect to the research, authorship and/or publication of this chapter.

Funding

The work for this chapter was supported by Renmin University of China.

References

Abramson, D. B. (2006), "Urban Planning in China: Continuity and Change: What the Future Holds May Surprise You," *Journal of the American Planning Association* 72 (2): 197–215.

Baker, D. C., Sipe, N. G. and Gleeson, B. J. (2006), "Performance-Based Planning: Perspectives from the United States, Australia, and New Zealand," *Journal of Planning Education and Research* 25 (4): 396–409.

Berke, P. and Godschalk, D. (2009), "Searching for the Good Plan: A Meta-Analysis of Plan Quality Studies," *Journal of Planning Literature* 23 (3): 227–40.

Berke, P., Song, Y. and Stevens, M. (2009), "Integrating Hazard Mitigation into New Urban and Conventional Developments," *Journal of Planning Education and Research* 28 (4): 441–55.

Berke, P., Spurlock, D., Hess, G. and Band, L. (2013), "Local Comprehensive Plan Quality and Regional Ecosystem Protection: The Case of the Jordan Lake Watershed, North Carolina, U.S.A," *Land Use Policy* 31: 450–59.

Berke, P. R. (1996), "Enhancing Plan Quality: Evaluating the Role of State Planning Mandates for Natural Hazard Mitigation," *Journal of Environmental Planning and Management* 39 (1): 79–96.

Berke, P. R. and French, S. P. (1994), "The Influence of State Planning Mandates on Local Plan Quality," *Journal of Planning Education and Research* 13 (4): 237–50.

Betsill, M. M. (2001), "Mitigating Climate Change in US Cities: Opportunities and Obstacles," *Local Environment* 6 (4): 393–406.

Bo, Z. (1996), "Economic Performance and Political Mobility: Chinese Provincial Leaders," *Journal of Contemporary China* 5 (12): 135–54.

Brody, S. D. (2003), "Measuring the Effects of Stakeholder Participation on the Quality of Local Plans Based on the Principles of Collaborative Ecosystem Management," *Journal of Planning Education and Research* 22(4):407–19.

Brody, S. D., Carrasco, V. and Highfield, W.E. (2006), "Measuring the Adoption of Local Sprawl: Reduction Planning Policies in Florida," *Journal of Planning Education and Research* 25 (3): 294–310.

Brody, S. D., Godschalk, D. R. and Burby, R. J. (2003), "Mandating Citizen Participation in Plan Making Six Strategic Choices," *Journal of American Planning Association* 69 (3): 245–64.

Brody, S. D., Highfield, W. and Carrasco, V. (2004), "Measuring the Collective Planning Capabilities of Local Jurisdictions to Manage Ecological Systems in Southern Florida," *Landscape and Urban Planning* 69 (1): 33–50.

Burby, R. J. and Dalton, L. C. (1994), "Plans Can Matter! The Role of Landing Use Plans and Sate Planning Mandates in Limiting the Development of Hazardous Areas Development," *Public Administration Review* 54 (3): 229–38.

Burby, R. J. and May, P. J. (1998), "Intergovernmental Environmental Planning: Addressing the Commitment Conundrum," *Journal of Environmental Planning and Management* 41 (1): 95–110.

Dunlap, R. E. and Jones, R. E. (2002), "Environmental Concern: Conceptual and Measurement Issues," in: R. Dunlap and W. Michelson, eds. *Handbook of Environmental Sociology*. Westport, CT: Greenwood Press, pp. 482–524.

Eaton, S. and Kostka, G. (2014), "Authoritarian Environmentalism Undermined? Local Leaders' Time Horizons and Environmental Policy Implementation in China," *The China Quarterly* 218: 359–80.

Economy, E. C. (2004), *The River Runs Black: The Environmental Challenge to China's Future*. Ithaca, NY: Cornell University Press.

Edin, M. (2003), "State Capacity and Local Agent Control in China: CCP Cadre Management from a Township Perspective," *The China Quarterly* 173: 35–52.

Gilley, B. (2012), "Authoritarian Environmentalism and China's Response to Climate Change," *Environmental Politics* 21 (2): 287–307.

Godschalk, D. R., Beatley, T., Berke, P. R., Brower, D. and Kaiser, E. (1999), *Natural Hazard Mitigation: Recasting Disaster Policy and Planning*. Washington, DC: Island Press.

Grimmer, J. and Stewart, B. M. (2013), "Text as Data: The Promise and Pitfalls of Automatic Content Analysis Methods for Political Texts," *Political Analysis* 21 (3): 267–97.

Hamilton, L. C. (2013), *Statistics with STATA Updated for Version 12*. Boston, MA: Brooks/Cole.

Hosmer, D. W., Lemeshow, S. and Sturdivant, R. X. (2013), *Applied Logistic Regression*. 3rd edition. Hoboken, NJ: Wiley.

Howell, S. E. and Laska, S. B. (1992), "The Changing Face of the Environmental Coalition: A Research Note," *Environment and Behavior* 24 (1): 134–44.

Huang, X., Zhao, D., Brown, C. G., Wu, Y. and Waldron, S. A. (2010), "Environmental Issues and Policy Priorities in China: A Content Analysis of Government Documents," *China: An International Journal* 8 (2): 220–46.

Kaiser, E. and Godschalk, D. R. (1995), "Twentieth Century Land Use Planning: A Stalwart Family Tree," *Journal of the American Planning Association* 61 (3): 365–85.

Klüver, H. (2009), "Measuring Interest Group Influence Using Quantitative Text Analysis," *European Union Politics* 10 (4): 535–49.

Klüver, H. (2013), "Lobbying as a Collective Enterprise: Winners and Losers of Policy Formulation in the European Union," *Journal of European Public Policy* 20 (1): 59–76.

Laver, M., Benoit, K. and Garry, J. (2003), "Extracting Policy Positions from Political Texts Using Words as Data," *American Political Science Review* 97 (02): 311–31.

Leaf, M. (2005), "Modernity Confronts Tradition: The Professional Planner and Local Corporatism in the Building of China's Cities," in: B. Sanyal, ed. *Comparative Planning Cultures*. New York and London: Taylor & Francis Group, pp. 91–111.

Levy, J. M. (2003), *Contemporary urban planning*, 6th edition. Upper Saddle River, NJ: Prentice Hall

Li, H. and Zhou, L. A. (2005), "Political Turnover and Economic Performance: The Incentive Role of Personnel Control in China," *Journal of Public Economics* 89 (9–10): 1743–62.

List, J. A. and Sturm, D. M. (2006), "How Elections Matter: Theory and Evidence from Environmental Policy," *Quarterly Journal of Economics* 121 (4): 1249–81.

Lo, C.W.-H. and Tang, S-Y. (2006), "Institutional Reform, Economic Changes, and Local Environmental Management in China: The Case of Guangdong Province," *Environmental Politics* 15 (2): 190–210.

Loh, C. G. and Norton, R. K. (2015), "Planning Consultants' Influence on Local Comprehensive Plans," *Journal of Planning Education and Research*. doi:10.1177/0739456X14566868

Lorentzen, P., Landry, P. and Yasuda, J. (2010), "Transparent Authoritarianism? An Analysis of Political and Economic; Barriers to Greater Government Transparency in China," UC Berkeley Working Paper. http://cega.berkeley.edu/assets/cega_events/25/

Lyles, W. and Stevens, M. (2014), "Plan Quality Evaluation 1994–2012: Growth and Contributions, Limitations, and New Directions," *Journal of Planning Education and Research* 34 (4): 433–50.

Norton, R. K. (2005), "Local Commitment to State-Mandated Planning in Coastal North Carolina," *Journal of the American Planning Association* 25 (2): 149–71.

Norton, R. K. (2008), "Using Content Analysis to Evaluate Local Master Plans and Zoning Codes," *Land Use Policy* 25 (3): 432–54.

Quinn, K. M., Monroe, B. L., Colaresi, M., Crespin, M. H. and Radev D. R. (2010), "How to Analyze Political Attention with Minimal Assumptions and Costs," *American Journal of Political Science* 54 (1): 209–28.

Rabe-Hesketh, S. and Everitt, B. (2004). *A Handbook of Statistical Analyses Using Stata Third Edition*. Boca Raton, FL: CRC Press.

Ran, R. (2013), "Perverse Incentive Structure and Policy Implementation Gap in China'S Local Environmental Politics," *Journal of Environmental Policy & Planning* 15 (1): 17–39.

Selden, T. M. and Song, D. (1995), "Neoclassical Growth, the J Curve for Abatement and the Inverted U Curve for Pollution," *Journal of Environmental Economics and Management* 29 (2): 162–8.

Scott, D. and Willits, F. (1994), "Environmental Attitudes and Behavior," *Environmental Behavior* 26 (2): 239–61.

Shen, J. (2006), "A Simultaneous Estimation of Environmental Kuznets Curve: Evidence from China," *China Economic Review* 17 (4): 383–94.

Slapin, J. B. and Proksch, S-O. (2008), "A Scaling Model for Estimating Time-Series Party Positions from Texts," *American Journal of Political Science* 52 (3): 705–22.

Stevens, M. R. (2013), "Evaluating the Quality of Official Community Plans in Southern British Columbia," *Journal of Planning Education and Research* 33 (4): 471–90.

Tang, Z. and Brody, S. D. (2009), "Linking Planning Theories with Factors Influencing Local Environmental-Plan Quality," *Environment and Planning B: Planning and Design* 36 (3): 522–37.

Tang, Z., Brody, S. D., Li, R., Quinn, C. and Zhao, N. (2011), "Examining Locally Driven Climate Change Policy Efforts in Three Pacific States," *Ocean and Coastal Management* 54 (5): 415–26.

Tang, Z., Brody, S. D., Quinn, C., Chang, L. and Wei, T. (2010), "Moving from Agenda to Action: Evaluating Local Climate Change Action Plans," *Journal of Environmental Planning and Management* 53 (1): 41–62.

Tao, R., Su, F., Liu, M. and Cao, G. (2010), "Land Leasing and Local Public Finance in China's Regional Development: Evidence from Prefecture-Level Cities," *Urban Studies* 47 (10): 2217–36.

Tian, L. and Shen, T. (2011), "Evaluation of Plan Implementation in the Transitional China: A Case of Guangzhou City Master Plan," *Cities* 28 (1): 11–27.

Tsui, K-Y. and Wang, Y. (2004), "Between Separate Stoves and a Single Menu: Fiscal Decentralization in China," *The China Quarterly* 177: 71–90.

Urwin, K. and Jordan, A. (2008), "Does Public Policy Support or Undermine Climate Change Adaptation? Exploring Policy Interplay across Different Scales of Governance," *Global Environmental Change* 18 (1): 180–91.

Wu, F. (2009), "Environmental Politics in China: An Issue Area in Review," *Journal of Chinese Political Science* 14 (4): 383–406.

Yu, W., Pagani, R. and Huang, L. (2012), "CO_2 Emission Inventories for Chinese Cities in Highly Urbanized Areas Compared with European Cities," *Energy Policy* 47: 298–308.

Zhang, T. (2002), "Planners in Transitional China," *Journal of Planning Education and Research* 22 (1): 64–76.

Zheng, S., Kahn, M. E., Sun, W. and Luo, D. (2014), "Incentives for China's Urban Mayors to Mitigate Pollution Externalities: The Role of the Central Government and Public Environmentalism," *Regional Science and Urban Economics* 47: 61–71.

Chapter 13

FURTHER OPPORTUNITIES TO REDUCE THE ENERGY USE AND GREENHOUSE GAS EMISSIONS OF BUILDINGS

David Hsu, Ting Meng, Albert T. Han, and Daniel Suh

Introduction

This chapter argues that further opportunities exist for planners to reduce the energy use and the associated greenhouse gas (GHG) emissions of buildings using the existing powers and jurisdiction of local governments. This is an argument with two parts or threads that will run throughout this chapter. First, to motivate the subsequent analysis and findings, we begin by observing that buildings and energy systems are shaped by many different disciplines working together within many different kinds of departments and agencies with a wide range of powers and jurisdictions spread throughout local governments. Second, in New York City in 2014, buildings were responsible for 73% of all GHG emissions (City of New York 2016a). By analyzing a large, comprehensive dataset of almost 4,000 buildings, we identify new opportunities for planners to reduce energy use and GHG emissions by focusing on different mechanisms and/or collaborations.

Motivation for this chapter comes from a number of trends and facts that help to frame our approach. First, this chapter focuses on buildings specifically because they are a major pathway for energy use. Worldwide, approximately 40% of primary energy consumption and 30% of GHG emissions occur in buildings, and these high levels are similar for most developed countries and are forecasted to grow further in many regions (Perez-Lombard, Ortiz, and Pout 2008; Urge-Vorsatz and Novikova 2008). Recent policy analyses indicate that mitigating climate change to any meaningful extent still requires a significant reduction of the GHG emissions associated with the energy use of buildings (International Energy Agency and International Partnership for Energy Efficiency Cooperation 2015; Höhne et al. 2017).

Another common-sense assumption of this chapter is that since buildings are large, durable and expensive objects, and comprise much of the built

DOI: 10.4324/9781003178545-17

environment, they are almost never built by any single individual or discipline working in isolation, or with a singular purpose in mind. Rather, buildings are shaped by many overlapping disciplines, including but not limited to planning, architecture, engineering or real estate. Buildings also can be seen as the synthesis of competing interests, including but not limited to aesthetics, affordability, location and integration with the overall city. Finally, the shaping of buildings is certainly not done by planners within planning departments alone, but is influenced by many things, including local infrastructure, the construction industry and customs, development interests, financial incentives and regulation by many agencies for a number of different social purposes ranging from technical fire codes to standards for affordability.

This chapter also focuses on New York City and its municipal government (henceforth, NYC) because it is both a unique and generalizable example. NYC is unique because of its implicit leadership as the largest, densest city in the United States; it is a policy leader in reducing energy consumption in buildings, and it is a global city amidst continuing urbanization and megacity growth worldwide. But this chapter also focuses on NYC specifically because of the diversity of the departments engaged in policy efforts around building energy use, and because this policy experience should be of general interest to many other cities.

Furthermore, though this is a book largely written by and for planners, this chapter also seeks to emphasize that the energy use of buildings is often best addressed by planners working together with other disciplines within different agencies and institutions with a wide range of missions, authorities and jurisdictions. Even if these agencies and institutions are also charged with other tasks such as development, housing, sustainability, utilities or infrastructure, planners should consider the full range of the tools available for them to affect energy use in buildings through a wide range of agencies. Cities that mix planning with other functions include the following: Boston, which has a joint planning and development agency; Kansas City, which has a joint planning and development department; Seattle, which has separate departments for planning and community development, construction and inspections, and neighborhoods, in addition to municipally owned water and energy utilities; and Philadelphia has the usual departments of housing and community development, a housing authority and a city planning commission, in addition to a water department, a land bank and offices dedicated to sustainability, property assessment and public property. Not only do planners already work with and within all of these departments, this chapter will show that the diverse features related to energy use in buildings mean that planners need to seek further opportunities and collaborations with other professionals within these departments and to take advantage of their existing powers and jurisdictions.

The structure of this chapter is as follows. We begin with the theoretical argument that planners operate within diverse institutional landscapes, and show this in the context of both NYC and the academic literature. The subsequent sections of this chapter describe how we created the dataset of energy consumption for

4,000 large buildings in NYC, and then analyzed it using relative importance metrics, a method similar to analysis-of-variance (ANOVA) approaches that assess the relative contribution of categories of data in explaining a particular response. Since we are interested in identifying opportunities to reduce the energy consumption of buildings, we group our data according to conceptual categories that align with how buildings are shaped by particular policy instruments, and then obtain metrics for these categories. This chapter concludes with a discussion of some tools and policies that planners should consider further, especially those that can be implemented at the local level.

Diverse Institutional Landscapes in NYC and Other Cities

Reducing energy consumption in buildings is a necessary step towards climate action in NYC, since the energy used in buildings is far greater than the energy used in any other sector including transportation (City of New York 2014b). The history of how these policies were implemented in NYC also shows that much of the effort to reduce energy use in buildings was done outside of planning agencies. The Mayor's Office of Long-Term Planning and Sustainability (OLTPS) under the Bloomberg administration (now part of the Office of Recovery and Resiliency in the De Blasio administration) created the original PlaNYC 2030 plan in 2007, and the Greener, Greater Buildings Plan in 2009. These policies to reduce energy consumption in buildings were conceived of and implemented by a diverse group of departments. Significant roles were played by the Departments of Design and Construction; Citywide Administrative Services; Housing Preservation and Development; and the NYC Housing Authority, in addition to City Planning (ICLEI 2011; NYC 2014). Furthermore, the Department of Finance collects property taxes and offers abatements and incentives for various programs, and the Department of Buildings is responsible for maintaining and enforcing NYC's building codes, including the city's energy conservation code, and administering programs for solar, green and cool roofs (Anuta 2014). More recently, NYC has released two reports developing a roadmap to reducing energy use and associated GHG emissions in buildings by 80% by 2050 (City of New York 2014a, 2016b) that cite the contributions and responsibilities of eight different departments. This chapter focuses on NYC as a case study but the examples of Boston, Kansas City, Seattle and Philadelphia indicate that this institutional diversity exists in other U.S. cities as well.

The more general theme—that local governments have significant powers to shape the built environment towards environmental goals—also emerges from a variety of literatures. Local governments have always been recognized to have substantial regulatory and enforcement powers over building practices and construction. For example, the United Nations' Agenda 21 broadly recognized that

> local authorities construct, operate and maintain economic, social and environmental infrastructure, oversee planning processes, establish local

environmental policies and regulations, and assist in implementing national and subnational environmental policies. As the level of governance closest to the people, they play a vital role in educating, mobilizing and responding to the public to promote sustainable development....

(UN 1992)

Second, consider for a moment the range of jurisdictions and powers that local governments exert over the built environment just in the United States. Not only do local governments zone and plan land use, they also collect more than 70% of all local tax revenues and more than 30% of all state and local tax revenues through property taxes (Tax Policy Center 2016a, 2016b); represent more than 75% of total spending on transportation and water infrastructure (Congressional Budget Office 2015); and own 30% of all electrical utilities, with growing interest in public ownership (Cardwell 2013). Third, planning functions exist in agencies and institutions that often mix planning with other governmental functions, such as buildings, housing, economic development and/or sustainability (Albrechts, Alden, and Pires 2001).

Surprisingly, there is relatively little work in the academic planning literature studying the regulatory authority of planners over buildings. Raymond Burby and others have argued that planners have significant latitude to create and enforce effective regulations with significant impacts on real estate markets for both better and worse (Burby, May, and Paterson 1998; Burby et al. 2000; Burby, Salvesen, and Creed 2006). Some researchers have critically examined the effectiveness of planning in terms of evaluation, implementation and conformance (Talen 1997; Laurian et al. 2004; Lyles, Berke, and Smith 2015). Finally, lack of explicit jurisdiction or previous disciplinary boundaries have not stopped planning and other disciplines from arguing that better planning of the built environment is necessary to address diverse issues such as sustainability (Portney 2003; Saha 2009), food systems (Pothukuchi and Kaufman 1999), climate change (Wilson 2006; Wheeler 2008; Bassett and Shandas 2010) and public health (Frank and Engelke 2001; Perdue, Stone, and Gostin 2003).

Related Work on the Energy Consumption of Buildings

Works related to the topic of energy consumption in buildings vary considerably by discipline in their focus on explanatory variables and approaches to research. Architecture and engineering are the dominant disciplines in the study of energy consumption in buildings by sheer number of publications, but this research often focuses on the building energy performance of small groups or individual buildings. Critiques of this prevalent approach can be seen in a number of recent papers that argue the need for broader and more data-driven approaches to understanding large numbers or the "stock" of buildings (Ravetz 2008; Kohler, Steadman, and Hassler 2009; Hamilton et al. 2013). In contrast, the planning literature has focused on aggregate characteristics of the built environment like land use, urban form and density. One way to summarize the two approaches might be the "micro" approach of architects and engineers versus the "macro" approach of planners. This seems to be the result of professional practice rather than the result of any inherent research differences, since the architectural and engineering professions are focused on the production of individual buildings while the planning profession has focused on producing comprehensive plans. Nonetheless, this divergence can be clearly seen in the literature and will be discussed further below.

Because of the diversity of agencies and institutions in which planners operate, we therefore take a very broad view in thinking about how planners can work to reduce the energy use of buildings. Since buildings are expensive, long-lived and durable objects, we categorize our data in terms of both the authority of planners to intervene and phases throughout the life of buildings. However, all of our reviewers helpfully pointed out that we use conceptual categories that are similar but not identical to phases in lifecycle analysis (LCA). LCA considers buildings in terms of the phases of manufacturing or construction; operations and management; and demolition, waste or recycling. Instead, we develop conceptual categories for the different features of buildings and how the existing literature addresses them:

- Building characteristics: it is relatively difficult to change some of the fundamental characteristics of buildings through subsequent renovation or retrofitting, such as the basic construction, materials, structure and layout of buildings. In addition, fundamentally changing energy or fuel systems is relatively expensive but not impossible (Gregory 2014). Therefore, these issues should be addressed at the planning, design or construction phase. Policy instruments focused on these categories such as building codes and mandated certification like Leadership in Energy and Environmental Design (LEED) are often implemented in agencies that oversee planning and construction (Cidell 2009; Halverson, Shui, and Evans 2009).
- Occupancy and use patterns: this has traditionally been a difficult area for planners to engage in, although this is a growing area of interest for energy analysts. Rapidly spreading policies in this category include mandated benchmarking, disclosure or retro-commissioning for existing buildings (Mills 2011; Hsu 2014).
- Surroundings: this refers to metrics for land use, urban form and density as typically addressed by the planning literature and will be discussed further below.

While there are a number of papers focusing on each of these three categories, few papers address all three, or their effects relative to one another. The following sections therefore describe the existing literature in these conceptual categories, and present key findings regarding the effects of building characteristics, occupancy and use patterns; surroundings on energy consumption; and how they relate to one another.

Building Characteristics

The disciplines of green building design and mechanical engineering assume that construction plays a crucial role in determining the performance of building energy use. This has also been consistently confirmed in recent empirical studies that take into account construction along with other characteristics at a variety of scales. In the United States, Min, Hausfather and Lin (2010), Kaza (2010), Pitt (2013) and Estiri (2014) all use data from the Residential Energy Consumption Survey (RECS) to find that house area and construction style are significant determinants of energy use for houses across the United States in terms of their heating, cooling and other energy uses. Using smaller datasets, Guerra Santin, Itard and Visscher (2009) demonstrated that building construction characteristics explain 42% of total energy use in a dataset of residential buildings in the Netherlands; Ratti, Baker and Steemers (2005) and Steadman, Hamilton and Evans (2014) find strong correlations between building shape and energy consumption; and Kolter and Ferreira (2011) find that characteristics of building construction are important factors in predicting the monthly energy consumption of both residential and commercial buildings in Cambridge, Massachusetts. Using similar data sources as this chapter, both Hsu (2015) and Kontokosta (2014) examine data for commercial and multifamily buildings in NYC and find that construction characteristics remain significant and should be included in regression models predicting energy consumption, even when other social, economic and demographic data is included.

Occupancy and Use

Harvey (2009) argues using a broader literature review that significant energy reductions are only possible with enlightened occupant behavior. However, until recently, there were relatively few empirical studies in this area due to the variability of building types and uses. Obtaining disaggregated data that can be matched to observed energy use remains a significant challenge to studying the effects of occupancy with other factors. Unusual recent examples include Ingle et al. (2014), who find that modest changes in occupant behavior can yield equivalent savings to retrofits; Yu et al. (2011), who apply cluster analysis to data from 80 residential buildings in Japan to find proximate characteristics for occupant behavior; and Estiri (2014), who finds that households have almost as large an effect as buildings on energy consumption. However, Guerra Santin, Itard and Visscher (2009) find in their study that only 4.2% of building energy use can be attributed to occupant characteristics and behavior, while ten times that (42%) is related to construction characteristics.

More recently, the International Energy Agency has convened an Annex 66 working group specifically on occupant behavior and energy use with an extensive bibliography effort (see https://www.annex66.org/?q=biblio). There has been a recent flourishing of papers on interactions between occupant behavior and building construction or systems (Azar and Menassa 2014; Langevin, Gurian, and Wen 2015; Hong et al. 2016; Schweiker and Wagner 2016), but rarely do they consider the intersection of occupancy and construction *with* surroundings which is most relevant to understanding further opportunities for planners.

Surroundings

A number of recent papers, especially in the planning literature, seek to understand the effect of building surroundings on observed energy consumption. None of these are direct causal studies because of the usual challenges of experimental design with cities, but instead these studies seek to associate either observed energy consumption with microclimatic effects, or allocated densities and space with subsequent energy consumption.

The most familiar hypothesis for land use planners is the idea that higher densities will lead to smaller homes and more multifamily buildings, both of which use less energy than single-family homes at low density. A number of papers specifically address energy use with respect to the spatial distribution of buildings, using relatively large energy consumption surveys and statistical approaches; however, the results remain inconclusive since both negative and positive relationships with urban density have been found (Hui 2001; Steemers 2003; Norman, MacLean and Kennedy 2006; Ewing and Rong 2008; Kaza 2010; Heinonen, Kyrö and Junnila 2011; Ko 2013).

Most studies do not use building-level microdata, since it is often difficult to obtain comprehensive data about construction, occupancy, use and urban form at this scale. Kaza (2010), Kontokosta (2014) and Scofield (2014) all note that a key characteristic missing from their and other studies is solar insolation, i.e., the amount of solar exposure for buildings. Notable exceptions either use surveys or multilevel models to get at neighborhood characteristics, and find surrounding areas have a significant influence on the energy consumption of buildings in addition to the physical and operational characteristics of buildings themselves (Wilson 2013; Choudhary and Tian 2014; Tso and Guan 2014).

Conceptual Framework and Methodology

The response variables of interest for buildings are on-site energy consumption and GHG emissions. A logarithmic transformation is used in order to correct for a left-hand skewed distribution of observed building energy data. As discussed above, predictor variables associated with each building are divided into the three categories described above: building characteristics including the construction of the shell, structure and energy systems; occupancy and use patterns, including measurements of activities inside of each building; and the building's surroundings as indicated by land cover information and solar insolation. The process of data analysis is shown in Figure 13.1 and discussed in the following sections.

: Assess relative importance

Step 1: standardize and categorize variables

Step 2: within-category regression

Step 3: overall regression using representative variables

Step 4: calculate metrics of relative importance for each category

Step 5: calculate confidence intervals using bootstrapping

: Identify determinants

Step 1: standardize data except dummies

Step 2: over all GLS regression

Step 3: backward variable selection.

FIGURE 13.1 Data analysis process.

Assessing Relative Importance

In general, there are three main definitions of relative importance (Achen 1982): dispersion importance, which explains the variance of response variable in terms of the contribution of specific predictor variables; level importance, which explains the mean of the response variable; and theoretical importance, which links changes in the predictor variables to changes in the response variable. This study uses the definition of dispersion importance first through a multivariate linear regression, and then by applying the ANOVA-like metrics. These decisions and steps are explained further below.

First, predictor variables are grouped into categories (in our case, building characteristics, occupancy and use, and surroundings), and within each category, a linear regression model is applied to model the response variable as a function of representative predictor variables within each category. We use combinations of variables because this does not remove any information from the analysis. These representative variables are then used as predictor variables to model the logarithm of energy consumption and GHG emissions.

The metric of relative importance, or called averaging over orderings of predictor variables as suggested by Lindeman, Merenda and Gold (1980) referred to as LMG henceforth, is recommended when focusing on causal importance and decomposing the proportion of explained variance, or R-squared (Grömping 2006). The LMG metrics of relative importance are similar to an ANOVA-type analysis, in that ANOVA calculates sequential sums of squares in order to calculate contributions to the overall explained variance. However, since the order of regressors has a strong impact on the relative importance of regressors in ANOVA, the LMG method averages over all possible permutations of the orderings of the regressors in order to decompose the proportion of explained variance, or R-squared, into non-negative contributions from each regressor or set of regressors. Grömping (2006) describes this as "the average over average contributions in models of different sizes." Since these calculations are computer-intensive for a large number of predictor variables, Grömping (2006) also presents "relaimpo," a related statistical package to implement this within the R statistical computing environment. Finally, in order to assess the uncertainty in these metrics, the 95% confidence intervals for LMG metrics are computed using bootstrap simulations.

Examining the Significant Determinants

After assessing the relative importance of each category on building energy use, we then identify significant predictor variables that affect total energy consumption and carbon emissions, respectively, and quantify the magnitude of their marginal effects. A multiple regression model is applied in the current study using all of the characteristics associated with each building as predictor variables (Equation 1):

$$Y = \beta + X_C \beta_C + X_O \beta_o + X_S \beta_S + \varepsilon \quad (1)$$

where for N observations, Y, a N by 1 vector, denotes the response variable (i.e., the logarithm of total energy consumption or GHG emissions); X_C (N by p_1), X_o (N by p_2) and X_S (N by p_3) denote predictor variables for the categories of building characteristics, occupancy and use, and surroundings, respectively; the ps are the number of variables in each category; βs are the corresponding coefficients to be estimated; and ε (N by 1) represents the stochastic error term vector. All continuous variables are standard-normalized before estimation, so the estimated coefficients can be interpreted in units of Y in terms of standard deviations as X changes away from their means. Generalized least squares (GLS) regression is used to address heteroscedasticity. Backward stepwise selection is used to reduce the larger number of predictor variables only to those that are found to be statistically significant below the 10% level, and results in only significant variables being reported.

Data

The dataset used in this study was created by joining NYC's 2013 energy benchmarking data, generated by Local Law 84, with four other data sources—the

U.S. Environmental Protection Agency's (EPA) Energy Star Portfolio Manager (PM), the City of New York's Primary Land Use Tax Lot Output (PLUTO), CoStar data and NYC Open Data. The composite dataset assembled using these data sources provided a comprehensive record of most buildings over 50,000 square feet, which is the threshold for the mandated energy benchmarking law. For instance, the PM data contains energy use information such as total energy use and GHG emissions; the PLUTO data includes land use information including building and lot sizes, zoning and built year; the CoStar commercial building data includes building characteristics such as materials and amenities; and the multiple datasets retrieved from NYC Open Data include building perimeter and land cover types, which were used to produce variables representing the surrounding urban form for each building. Some of the variables such as solar insolation and building orientation were processed using collected building information and spatial data.

Because our data came from various sources, it was necessary to conduct extensive data cleaning and joining processes. The PM energy dataset obtained from the NYC OLTPS initially contained 14,144 records. First, we eliminated duplicate records and observations missing key variables. In addition, we removed records that had more than one building per block to ensure one-to-one matching between Block Identification Numbers (BBL10) and Building Identification Numbers (BIN). CoStar data was geocoded using the latitude and longitude coordinates so that it could be spatially joined to the PM data. Once the initial data joining process was completed, we conducted additional cleaning processes to improve the overall data quality, such as eliminating building outliers with exceptionally high or low energy use based on engineering judgment. Among various building uses, we focused our research on buildings that were predominantly composed of either office or multifamily uses, which constituted more than 90% of the entire dataset. After all of the sequential data joining and processing steps, the final dataset contained 3,863 records representing 755 office buildings and 3,108 multifamily buildings.

Most commercial office buildings are located in midtown and lower Manhattan, while multifamily buildings are distributed throughout all five boroughs of NYC (Figure 13.2). The variables in this study are displayed in Figure 13.3, and summary of their descriptive statistics is displayed in Tables 13.1 and 13.2. The sections below highlight particular aspects of the data that require additional explanation or discussion that is common to the entire building population, as well as issues specific to office and multifamily buildings.

Common Variables

There are many variables serving as predictors for building energy performance. As discussed in the previous section, these building characteristics were grouped into the three categories of building characteristics, occupancy and use, and surroundings. Office and multifamily buildings share many of the same predictor variable types for building characteristics and surroundings, though of course

248 David Hsu et al.

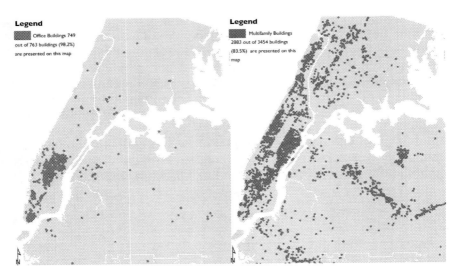

FIGURE 13.2 Map of office and multifamily buildings. Most office properties are located on the island of Manhattan (running diagonally from bottom left to top right).

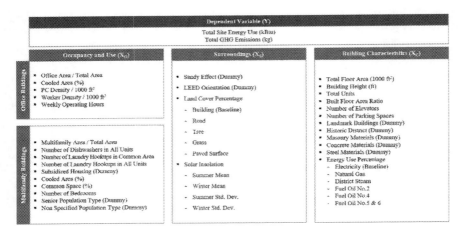

FIGURE 13.3 Organization of variable into conceptual categories.

with different values. Predictor variables describing building surroundings included location, orientation, land cover and solar insolation. In addition, the dataset in this study covers the one-year period in which the events of Hurricane Sandy left Lower Manhattan and other parts of NYC without power for a number of days, so in order to capture the potential disruption of energy service and use in particular areas, a binary variable was created to indicate buildings in Manhattan located below 34th Street. Variables for surrounding urban form and areas included land cover information in terms of shares of different land cover

TABLE 13.1 Summary of descriptive statistics for office buildings ($N = 755$)

Variable name (unit)		Mean	Std.	Min.	Max.
Dependent variable (original number)					
Total site energy use (1000's kBtu)		28,897	48,846	160	586,445
Total GHG emissions (kg)		2,524	4,238	12	51,335
Dependent variable (log transformation):					
Total site energy use (1000's kBtu)		10.27	10.79	5.08	13.28
Total GHG emissions (kg)		7.83	8.35	2.48	10.84
Independent variable					
Occupancy and use	Office area/total area	0.95	0.06	0.75	1.00
	Cooled area (%)	97.26	12.03	0.00	100.00
	PC density (/1000 SF)	2.83	2.19	0.00	45.93
	Weekly operating hours	60.61	22.94	5.00	168.00
	Worker density (/1000 SF)	2.78	1.93	0.00	36.75
Surroundings	Sandy effect dummy	0.42		0.00	1.00
	LEED orientation dummy	0.05		0.00	1.00
	Land cover percentage (0–1)				
	Building (Baseline)	0.54	0.11	0.11	0.74
	Paved surface	0.22	0.06	0.09	0.60
	Road	0.23	0.07	0.07	0.53
	Tree	0.04	0.06	0.00	0.93
	Grass	0.01	0.02	0.00	0.19
	Solar insolation				
	Summer mean (Wh/m^2)	128,980	31,822	7,439	168,185
	Winter mean (Wh/m^2)	19,253	8,287	1,108	32,725
	Summer std. (Wh/m^2)	25,892	13,958	43	60,069
	Winter std. (Wh/m^2)	4,304	2,611	26	13,153
Building characteristics	Total floor area (1000s ft^2)	312	393	14	3,637
	Building height (ft)	274.45	156.03	43.41	951.97
	Total units	34.02	91.96	0.00	2,000
	Built FAR	13.98	6.53	0.37	43.23
	No. of elevators	6.58	7.80	0.00	67.00
	No. of parking spaces	11.73	61.31	0.00	780.00
	Landmark dummy	0.06		0.00	1.00
	Historical district dummy	0.12		0.00	1.00
	Masonry materials dummy	0.53		0.00	1.00
	Concrete materials dummy	0.08		0.00	1.00
	Steel materials dummy	0.26		0.00	1.00
	Energy use percentage				
	Electricity use (Baseline)	0.63	0.21	0.00	1.00
	Nature gas use	0.09	0.17	0.00	0.97
	District steam use	0.11	0.18	0.00	1.00
	Fuel oil no.2 use	0.03	0.12	0.00	1.00
	Fuel oil no.4 use	0.05	0.14	0.00	1.00
	Fuel oil no.5.6 use	0.10	0.20	0.00	1.00

Note: SD = standard deviation; GHG = greenhouse gas; PC = personal computer; LEED = Leadership in Energy and Environmental Design; FAR = flood area ratio.

TABLE 13.2 Summary of descriptive statistics for multifamily buildings ($N = 3108$)

Variable name		Mean	Std.	Min.	Max.
Dependent variable					
Total site energy use (1000's kBtu)		8,207	4,668	2,275	27,218
Total GHG emissions (kg)		606	390	97	7,854
Dependent variable (log transformation)					
Total site energy use (1000's kBtu)		9.01	8.45	7.73	10.21
Total GHG emissions (kg)		6.41	5.97	4.57	8.99
Independent variable					
Occupancy and use	Multifamily area/total area	0.98	0.04	0.76	1.00
	No. of dishwashers in all units	31.36	59.69	0.00	780.00
	No. of laundries in common area	5.53	8.24	0.00	130.00
	No. of laundries in all units	11.02	33.28	0.00	484.00
	Subsidized housing dummy	0.05		0.00	1.00
	Cooled area (%)	46.14	45.03	0.00	100.00
	Common space (%)	10.51	9.37	0.00	107.00
	No. of bedrooms	124.90	105.27	0.00	1,560
	Senior population-type dummy	0.69		0	1
	Other population-type dummy	0.01		0	1
Surroundings	Sandy effect dummy	0.11		0.00	1.00
	LEED orientation dummy	0.13		0.00	1.00
	Land cover percentage				
	Building (baseline)	0.45	0.10	0.07	0.76
	Paved surface	0.28	0.07	0.10	0.69
	Road	0.23	0.08	0.00	0.56
	Grass	0.04	0.05	0.00	0.47
	Tree	0.18	0.13	0.00	0.97
	Solar insolation				
	Summer mean (Wh/m^2)	155,053	18,343	13,485	167,501
	Winter mean (Wh/m^2)	25,433	5,350	833	34,016
	Summer std. (Wh/m^2)	10,120	12,499	2	58,001
	Winter std. (Wh/m^2)	2,429	2,327	0	16,720
Building characteristics	Total floor area (1000s ft^2)	108,360	67,023	9,024	826,290
	Building height (ft)	138.64	74.88	43.41	800.36
	Total units	94.15	61.06	0.00	707.00
	Built FAR	7.32	37.57	0.19	2,088
	No. of elevators	0.20	0.89	0.00	30.00
	No. of parking spaces	6.19	28.35	0.00	400.00
	Landmark dummy	0.01		0.00	1.00
	Historical district dummy	0.13		0.00	1.00
	Masonry materials dummy	0.75		0.00	1.00
	Concrete materials dummy	0.01		0.00	1.00
	Steel materials dummy	0.02		0.00	1.00
	Energy use percentage				

Electricity use (Baseline)	0.26	0.18	0.00	1.00
Nature gas use	0.36	0.37	0.00	1.00
District steam use	0.03	0.12	0.00	0.93
Fuel oil no.2 use	0.05	0.18	0.00	1.00
Fuel oil no.4 use	0.08	0.22	0.00	1.00
Fuel oil no.5.6 use	0.23	0.34	0.00	1.00

Note: SD = standard deviation; GHG = greenhouse gas; PC = personal computer; LEED = Leadership in Energy and Environmental Design; FAR = flood area ratio.

TABLE 13.3 Building materials

Material	Office	Multifamily
	Percentage	
Steel	25.8	1.6
Reinforced concrete	7.5	1.1
Masonry	52.7	74.5
Other	13.9	22.8

types (e.g., road, paved surface, tree and grass), calculated by the Zonal Statistics tool of ArcGIS. In addition, many building energy studies claim that orientation affects the passive solar insolation on buildings, and therefore, energy is used for lighting, heating and cooling (Kontoleon and Eumorfopoulou 2010; Krüger, Pearlmutter, and Rasia 2010). Therefore, a binary variable indicating good building orientation was created based on building geographic angle according to U.S. Green Building Council standards for green buildings (USGBC 2015), i.e., whether the principal east-west axis of the building is within 15 degrees of due east-west. Another characteristic calculated was the direct solar insolation on vertical surfaces, which was computed by spatially joining building footprints to a digital elevation model (DEM), extruding the footprints to the building heights, then using the solar analysis feature of ArcGIS to calculate shading and exposure of buildings to the sun.

Fundamental and hard-to-change building characteristics were expected to influence total energy use and carbon emissions, such as total floor area, height, the number of total units, energy use percentage by type, the number of facilities (i.e., elevators and parking spaces) as well as built materials. The majority of buildings are made of masonry, accounting for 52.7% of office buildings and 74.5% of multifamily buildings (Table 13.3). Dummy variables for landmarked and historically designated buildings also serve to indicate the unique construction characteristics associated with those types of buildings. The building height was calculated using the number of floors from the PM database and height per floor coefficients based on guidance from the Council on Tall Buildings and Urban Habitat (2015). A variety of fuel types are used in NYC buildings, including electricity, natural gas, district steam and fuel oils. Electricity is the main fuel type in office buildings, while the major energy type of multifamily buildings is natural gas.

Variables Specific to Commercial and Multifamily Buildings

In contrast to the common variables for surroundings and building characteristics discussed above, occupancy and use variables are quite different between office and multifamily buildings. We included a number of control variables to allow for subgroups of buildings to be different than others and to remove bias for the other estimated coefficients, although this should not affect the overall effects from the categorical groupings of features. For example, a large number of computers in a particular office building might differentiate it from others. For office buildings, major characteristics describing the occupancy and use behaviors in the office are the density of personal computers (PC), hours of operation, worker density and the share of total building area for office use. For multifamily buildings, operational variables include the number of household appliances (e.g., dishwashers and laundry machines)—whether it is subsidized housing or not—the number of bedrooms, percentages of cooling area and resident type. In terms of appliance use, the distinction between individual units and common areas captures varying energy use patterns in multifamily buildings.

Results and Discussion

Relative Importance of Building Characteristics, Occupancy and Use, and Surroundings

Results for relative impacts of our categories of variables (i.e., building characteristics, occupancy and use, and surroundings) on energy consumption and GHG emissions in office and multifamily buildings are displayed in Table 13.4. Overall, within the same building use type, metrics of relative importance are nearly the same in terms of building energy consumption and the associated GHG emissions. This is not surprising because of the way EPA calculates energy consumption and GHG emissions from fuel types and corresponding conversion factors (U.S. Environmental Protection Agency 2014). However, the variance contributed by each category varies significantly across building use types. For office buildings, the major contributors of energy consumption ordered from high to low are building characteristics (83%), surroundings (10%), and then occupancy and use (7%); the order of these metrics are the same for GHG emissions. This indicates that in office buildings, building characteristics explain the majority of building energy performance, in contrast to the role of occupancy and use and surroundings, which are relatively small. The ranking of the categories for multifamily buildings is similar but not the same, with the main impacts on energy consumption from building characteristics (72%), occupancy and use (24%), and surroundings (4%); this pattern holds true for GHG

TABLE 13.4 Relative impacts for energy consumption and GHG emissions measured by LMG Metrics

		Building characteristics	Occupancy and use	Surroundings	R2
Office	Energy consumption	83.6 (79.6, 87.0)	6.6 (4.3, 9.6)	9.8 (6.7, 13.4)	78.3
	GHG emissions	83.3 (79.3, 87.0)	6.8 (4.3, 9.8)	9.9 (6.9, 13.2)	78.6
Multifamily	Energy consumption	72.0 (69.7, 74.2)	24.2 (22.1, 26.2)	3.8 (2.9, 5.0)	72.0
	GHG emissions	71.1 (69.2, 73.3)	24.0 (21.9, 25.8)	4.9 (3.9, 6.0)	73.6

Note: All figures are in percentages. Parentheses display 95% confidence intervals based on 1,000 bootstrap replicates. LMG = Lindeman, Merenda and Gold (1980); GHG = greenhouse gas.

emissions as well. Compared with metrics in office buildings, the fundamental characteristics of multifamily buildings still dominate but occupancy and use are much more important. Surroundings are also relatively unimportant in multifamily buildings.

Significant Determinants for Energy Consumption and GHG Emissions

In addition to the assessment of relative impacts discussed above, this study also investigated the significant determinants of building energy performance through a multiple regression model. Estimation results regarding office and multifamily buildings are illustrated in Tables 5 and 6, respectively. We also computed the variance inflation factor (VIF) for each explanatory variable, and the VIFs are all less than 10 and most of them are less than 5, so the results are not affected by multicollinearity. Since the relationship between energy use and GHG emissions is roughly linear in the reported data because of how EPA calculates carbon emissions, as mentioned above, only the coefficients for energy use will be discussed further below. Because the results vary between the different building types, we discuss the results for office buildings and multifamily buildings at greater length in separate sections.

Office Buildings

As shown in Table 13.5 for office buildings, significant determinants of total energy consumption and GHG emissions are PC density, road cover percentage, the solar insolation mean and standard deviation, and building construction characteristics, as well as different energy use percentages.

Confirming the findings of relative importance using the LMG metrics, fundamental construction variables such as the total floor area of the building, the built flood area ratio (FAR) and the material used for construction (steel and concrete) were among the largest magnitude effect sizes (0.520, 0.173, 0.161, 0.198, respectively), with the binary variable for buildings built in the 1960s indicating that they use significantly more energy (0.156). The energy systems used in the building itself were also associated with large effect sizes, particularly for the buildings that have larger percentages of district steam (0.143) and No. 5/6 fuel oil (0.182), though the squared term for No. 5/6 fuel oil indicates that as the proportion of this fuel becomes larger, its effect on overall energy consumption goes down significantly (−0.278).

Among the occupancy and use variables, PC density and its square term were found to have the largest effect sizes and to be significant (0.138 and −0.119, respectively). This indicates that in the office buildings, energy consumption and GHG emissions increase as the PC density grows, but at a decreasing rate, meaning that large numbers of computers may use more energy but more efficiently on a per computer basis. However, this cannot be interpreted as the efficiency achieved by data centers: one limitation of this study is that buildings that indicated that they had data centers were excluded from the office building category, but the rapid growth of data centers and server rooms means that some of the effects of these technologies cannot be observed in these results.

With regard to the surrounding environment of the building, the only land cover variable that seems to be important is road cover percentage, which is significant but relatively small in magnitude (0.046). In addition, energy use and carbon emissions were found to vary significantly with solar insolation, specifically increasing as a result of higher mean insolation in the summer (0.135), lower mean insolation in the winter (−0.098) or a larger standard deviation in winter insolation (0.046). These relationships match our intuition, which is that during summer, buildings with higher solar insolation demand larger cooling loads, while in the winter lower levels of solar insolation and larger variations are closely associated with larger heating loads. However, good building orientation, as deemed by LEED, also was not significant for office buildings: this result reflects ongoing debates about the actual energy impacts of the LEED certification process (Newsham, Mancini, and Birt 2009; Scofield 2009).

Multifamily Buildings

Estimation results for multifamily buildings are summarized in Table 13.6. Similar variables and relationships include total floor area, which was the large expected effect on energy consumption (0.421) and binary variables indicating construction in the 1960s (0.185) and 1990s (0.225), compared to the baseline category of buildings from the 1940s or earlier. Masonry and especially concrete buildings use less energy (−0.070 and −0.246, respectively). In terms of energy use, natural gas and heavy oil (No. 5 and 6 fuel oils) dominate energy use among multifamily buildings (0.701 and 0.711, respectively), with relatively

TABLE 13.5 Estimation results of determinants of energy consumption and GHG emissions in office buildings

Variable name	GHG emissions Coeff.	Std. err.	Coeff.	Std. err.
Intercept	−0.077***	0.026	−0.077***	0.026
Occupancy and use				
PC density	0.138***	0.035	0.145***	0.035
PC density square	−0.119***	0.035	−0.124***	0.035
Surroundings				
Land cover percentage				
Road	0.046**	0.020	0.051**	0.020
Solar insolation				
Summer mean	0.135***	0.036	0.134***	0.036
Winter mean	−0.098***	0.036	−0.102***	0.036
Winter standard deviation	0.046**	0.023	0.046**	0.022
Building characteristics				
Total floor area	0.520***	0.027	0.507***	0.027
Built FAR	0.173***	0.026	0.178***	0.026
Concrete materials dummy	0.161**	0.077	0.173**	0.076
Steel materials dummy	0.198***	0.056	0.200***	0.055
Built decade 1960s dummy	0.156**	0.076	0.144*	0.075
Energy use percentage				
Natural gas use	0.040*	0.023	–	–
District steam use	0.143***	0.027	0.130***	0.025
Fuel Oil no. 2 use	−0.068***	0.021	−0.082***	0.020
Fuel Oil no. 4 use	−0.074***	0.023	−0.088***	0.021
Fuel Oil no. 5.6 use	0.182***	0.056	0.176***	0.052
Fuel Oil no. 5.6 use square	−0.278***	0.050	−0.288***	0.049
Log likelihood	−614.788		−603.448	
Pseudo R-square	0.74		0.74	

* $p < 0.1$; ** $p < 0.05$; *** $p < 0.01$.

Note: All variables except dummy variables were standard-normalized. GHG = greenhouse gas; Coeff. = coefficient; SE = standard error; PC = personal computer; SD = standard deviation; FAR = floor area ratio.

smaller effects from higher percentages of steam, No. 2 and 4 fuel oils (0.282, 0.328 and 0.434, respectively).

Other variables are quite different from the office category and are interpreted quite differently. The total number of units has a strong effect on energy use

(0.291). Buildings with a landmark designation or located in a historical district are notably more associated with larger energy use (0.254 and 0.075).

A number of variables in the occupancy and use category are found to affect energy performance significantly among multifamily buildings, including large effect sizes for the number of bedrooms (0.192), but this has a negative effect for the squared term, indicating that this effect decreases as the number of bedrooms increases to higher levels (−0.154). Other significant effects, but with relatively small magnitudes, include the share of common space (−0.032) and the percentage of multifamily area to the whole area of the building (−0.075), which in New York usually indicates the presence of retail and office spaces also. An interesting and intuitive finding is that laundry machines in common areas and in individual units have totally opposite effects on building energy use (−0.031 and 0.045); while it seems logical that the usage of laundries in common areas shared among residents is related to better energy performance than ones in individual units, these effects are ultimately quite small when compared using standard-normalized coefficients.

Similar to what was found in office buildings, the only surroundings or urban form variables that had a significant effect on higher energy consumption were found in buildings with a larger road cover percentage (0.038) and higher levels of solar insolation in the summer (0.024). This confirms that microclimates affect energy use in both office and multifamily buildings but the effect sizes remain small. Similar to the office buildings above, good building orientation as defined by LEED was not a significant determinant of energy use in multifamily buildings either.

There are several limitations of these results, associated with the data sources and geographic focus on NYC. First, NYC buildings are not like other buildings in rest of the United States, since they are larger, denser and better served by public transit. Second, the City of New York focused its policies on larger buildings because they consume a relatively large proportion of energy, while smaller buildings and residential homes use roughly 25% of all energy in the United States. Third, and with regard to the density and urban form of NYC buildings, the descriptive statistics in Tables 13.1 and 13.2 show a wide range of percentages of land cover; however, this little-known variation across the entire area of the City of New York actually assists in estimating the effects of land cover, so this strengthens the internal validity but still perhaps does not aid the external validity. Fourth, this study does not capture the proportion of energy used in transportation, a strong area of existing planning research. However, since the proportion of energy used in buildings in NYC is high regardless of energy used in transportation, we believe that this justifies a separate analysis focused on buildings. Fifth, and finally, since this chapter focuses on an argument (why) and a general method (how) for planners and other professionals to identify further opportunities to reduce energy use and GHG emissions in buildings, it remains to be seen if the same approach when applied to other datasets would lead to similar conclusions in other cities.

TABLE 13.6 Estimation results of determinants of energy consumption and GHG emissions in multifamily buildings ($N = 3108$)

Variable name	Energy consumption		GHG emissions	
	Coeff.	Std. err.	Coeff.	Std. err.
Intercept	−0.004	0.023	−0.004	0.023
Occupancy and use				
Multifamily area/total area	−0.075***	0.011	−0.075***	0.011
No. of laundries in common area	−0.031***	0.012	−0.031***	0.011
No. of laundries in all units	0.045***	0.012	0.040***	0.011
Common space percentage	−0.032***	0.011	−0.030***	0.010
No. of bedrooms	0.192***	0.021	0.178***	0.021
No. of bedroom square	−0.154***	0.018	−0.144***	0.018
Surroundings				
Land cover percentage				
Road	0.038***	0.011	0.030***	0.010
Solar insolation				
Summer mean	0.024**	0.011	0.026**	0.011
Building characteristics				
Total floor area	0.431***	0.020	0.409***	0.019
Building height	0.112***	0.015	0.105***	0.015
Total units	0.291***	0.019	0.272***	0.019
No. of elevators	−0.030***	0.011	−0.026**	0.010
Landmark dummy	0.254*	0.146	0.240*	0.142
Historical district dummy	0.075**	0.032	0.060*	0.031
Masonry materials dummy	−0.070***	0.024	−0.072***	0.024
Concrete materials dummy	−0.246**	0.100	−0.235**	0.097
Built decade 1950s or not	0.066*	0.036	0.070**	0.035
Built decade 1960s or not	0.185***	0.034	0.178***	0.032
Built decade 1970s or not	0.025**	0.011	0.024**	0.011
Built decade 1980s or not	0.093**	0.046	0.117***	0.045
Built decade 1990s or not	0.225***	0.082	0.231***	0.079
Built decade 2000s or not	0.132***	0.047	0.147***	0.046
Energy use percentage				
Nature gas use	0.701***	0.025	0.276***	0.024
District steam use	0.282***	0.013	0.225***	0.013
Fuel Oil no. 2 use	0.328***	0.015	0.223***	0.014
Fuel Oil no. 4 use	0.434***	0.017	0.302***	0.016
Fuel Oil no. 5.6 use	0.711***	0.023	0.549***	0.022
Log likelihood	−2,728.371		−2,629.817	
Pseudo R-square	0.63		0.70	

* $p < 0.1$; ** $p < 0.05$; *** $p < 0.01$.

Note: All variables except dummy variables were standard-normalized. GHG = greenhouse gas; Coeff. = coefficient; SE = standard error; FAR = floor area ratio.

Conclusions and Implications

Energy consumption and GHG emissions by buildings have been recognized by policymakers and researchers in recent years as an increasingly important issue. As discussed at the beginning of this chapter, planners work in diverse departments and agencies in many cities. In the section on previous work, we summarized much of the previous research done in this area by architects and engineers as not addressing large populations of buildings. While the planning literature does examine urban form in aggregate, the planning literature has mostly focused on urban form, building density and land cover. Few studies have observed the effect of characteristics throughout the life of buildings on energy consumption, taking together fundamental building characteristics, occupancy and use, and surrounding urban form. The results of this study indicate that the relative importance of these three aspects is quite different. For office buildings, fundamental building characteristics have the greatest effect on energy consumption and GHG emissions (80%–87%), followed by surroundings (7%–13%), and occupancy and use (4%–9%). Similarly, fundamental building characteristics are important in multifamily buildings (79%–87%), but occupancy and use are relatively more important (22%–26%), and surroundings less so (3%–5%).

However, we do not interpret these results as meaning that better engineering of new construction is most important, and the planning, occupancy or use of the surrounding built environment less so. On the contrary, in the spirit of Willie Sutton, we believe that this indicates that planners and other professionals should focus their attention on where the actual energy is, or at least on where and when the key decisions are made that will affect the energy use of the actual building throughout its lifetime. This has distinct and different implications for how we approach energy use in buildings, particularly existing buildings and new construction.

Half of all buildings in 2030 will still be comprised of existing buildings more than 30 years old (Nelson 2004), so policies proven to affect operations and occupancy of existing buildings should be studied further. Along with traditional tools like zoning changes, codes, permits and enforcement, emerging policy instruments such as mandated energy efficiency retrofits, retro-commissioning and building energy disclosure policies are all ways in which we can shape the existing buildings that we have now and will have for the foreseeable future. Considering how to use policies to affect occupancy and use patterns could further accelerate technological changes in electric vehicle charging, smart grids or building controls.

For the other half of buildings in 2030 that are expected to be relatively new construction, interpreting the meaning of these results requires a more complex discussion of how planning policies can be used to achieve lower energy use and GHG emissions. While the effects of land use, land cover and microclimate on the observed energy consumption and GHG emissions of buildings are all relatively small, we believe that planners have many further opportunities to affect other fundamental building characteristics if they pursue them.

This has further implications for planning practice. First, this means that planners may need to change their regulatory frame of mind, or at least the objects of their attention and focus. Since buildings are regulated at the municipal level, and planning functions are quite often grouped with or within departments such as economic development and housing, and building regulation, in many cases planners or their close colleagues can again use their existing authority in zoning, codes, permitting, enforcement and assessing property taxes, all to shape significantly future demand for energy-efficient buildings. Planning practitioners need to embrace the powers often shared within departments and with other disciplines, and researchers need to give them a better sense of how to focus these powers on the buildings that use the most energy and have the most impact on GHG emissions. Recent work by Andrews et al. (2016) demonstrates some of the existing tensions between energy codes and other types of planning for existing buildings. Other work by Burby, May and Paterson (1998) and Burby et al. (2000) argues that building codes and enforcement remain an open opportunity to improve the regulatory environment of cities and therefore development patterns. One of the reviewers suggested that planners could become more literate about energy subcodes, in order to participate in the code development and adoption process, so they can advocate more effectively for codes that meet both planning and energy objectives. This was a particularly astute suggestion, because this reminded us that this is exactly what the City of Seattle has done for the past 20 years or so, with the municipally owned energy utility sponsoring staff within the planning department dedicated to developing cutting-edge energy codes for buildings.

A second and additional direction for planners to pursue in future research is how land use regulations can be shaped to guarantee that the outcome of these policies results in more energy-efficient buildings themselves. While planners generally believe in and advocate for higher densities and certain urban forms for many reasons, including the expectation that this leads to higher and better use of land and hopefully more energy-efficient buildings, recent literature on plan evaluation, implementation and conformance indicates that there is much more work to be done to be able to guarantee these outcomes (Oliveira and Pinho 2010; Lyles, Berke, and Smith 2015). This chapter is merely an initial step to attempt to understand better which key opportunities exist in the life of buildings affect energy consumption, but it is intended to point the way towards design, planning and policy processes that deliver buildings that use less energy and generate less GHG emissions when built and in use.

References

Achen, C. H. (1982), *Interpreting and Using Regression*. Vol. 29. SAGE.
Albrechts, L., Alden, J. and Pires, A. da R., (2001), *The Changing Institutional Landscape of Planning*. Ashgate Pub Ltd.
Andrews, C.J., Hattis, D., Listokin, D., Senick, J.A., Sherman, G.B. and Souder, J. (2016), "Energy-Efficient Reuse of Existing Commercial Buildings," *Journal of the American Planning Association* 0 (0): 1–21. doi:10.1080/01944363.2015.1134275.

Anuta, J. (2014), "9 of 10 Building Plans Fail Basic Test," *Crain's New York Business*. August 18. http://www.crainsnewyork.com/article/20140818/REAL_ESTATE/308179994/9-of-10-building-plans-fail-basic-test.

Azar, E. and Menassa, C.C. (2014), "A Comprehensive Framework to Quantify Energy Savings Potential from Improved Operations of Commercial Building Stocks," *Energy Policy* 67 (April): 459–72. doi:10.1016/j.enpol.2013.12.031.

Bassett, E. and Shandas, V. (2010), "Innovation and Climate Action Planning—Perspectives from Municipal Plans," *Journal of the American Planning Association* 76 (4): 435. doi:10.1080/01944363.2010.509703.

Burby, R.J., May, P.J., Malizia, E.E. and Levine, J. (2000), "Building Code Enforcement Burdens and Central City Decline," *Journal of the American Planning Association* 66 (2): 143–61. doi:10.1080/01944360008976095.

Burby, R.J., May, P.J. and Paterson, R.C. (1998), "Improving Compliance with Regulations: Choices and Outcomes for Local Government," *Journal of the American Planning Association* 64 (3): 324–34. doi:10.1080/01944369808975989.

Burby, R.J., Salvesen, D. and Creed, M. (2006), "Encouraging Residential Rehabilitation with Building Codes: New Jersey's Experience," *Journal of the American Planning Association* 72 (2): 183–96. doi:10.1080/01944360608976738.

Cardwell, D. (2013), "Cities Weigh Taking over from Private Utilities," *The New York Times*, March 13. http://www.nytimes.com/2013/03/14/business/energy-environment/cities-weigh-taking-electricity-business-from-private-utilities.html.

Choudhary, R. and Tian, W. (2014), "Influence of District Features on Energy Consumption in Non-Domestic Buildings," *Building Research & Information* 42 (1): 32–46. doi:10.1080/09613218.2014.832559.

Cidell, J. (2009), "Building Green: The Emerging Geography of LEED-Certified Buildings and Professionals," *The Professional Geographer* 61 (2): 200–215. doi:10.1080/00330120902735932.

City of New York (2014a), "One City Built to Last: Technical Working Group Report: Transforming New York City Buildings for a Low-Carbon Future," http://www1.nyc.gov/assets/sustainability/downloads/pdf/publications/TWGreport_04212016.pdf.

——— (2014b), "New York City Local Law 84 Benchmarking Report," The City of New York, Office of Long Term Planning and Sustainability.

——— (2016a), "Inventory of New York City Greenhouse Gas Emissions in 2014," http://www1.nyc.gov/assets/sustainability/downloads/pdf/publications/NYC_GHG_Inventory_2014.pdf.

——— (2016b), "New York City's Roadmap to 80 X 50," City of New York. http://www1.nyc.gov/assets/sustainability/downloads/pdf/publications/New%20York%20City's%20Roadmap%20to%2080%20x%2050_Final.pdf.

Congressional Budget Office (2015), "Public Spending on Transportation and Water Infrastructure, 1956 to 2014," *Congressional Budget Office*. March 2. https://www.cbo.gov/publication/49910.

Council on Tall Buildings and Urban Habitat (2015), "CTBUH Tall Building Height Calculator," Accessed January 7. http://www.ctbuh.org/TallBuildings/HeightStatistics/HeightCalculator/OnLineCalculator/tabid/1068/language/en-GB/Default.aspx.

Estiri, H. (2014), "Building and Household X-Factors and Energy Consumption at the Residential Sector: A Structural Equation Analysis of the Effects of Household and Building Characteristics on the Annual Energy Consumption of US Residential Buildings," *Energy Economics* 43 (May): 178–84. doi:10.1016/j.eneco.2014.02.013.

Ewing, R. and Rong, F. (2008), "The Impact of Urban Form on U.S. Residential Energy Use," *Housing Policy Debate* 19 (1): 1–30. doi:10.1080/10511482.2008.9521624.

Frank, L.D. and Engelke, P.O. (2001), "The Built Environment and Human Activity Patterns: Exploring the Impacts of Urban Form on Public Health," *Journal of Planning Literature* 16 (2): 202–18. doi:10.1177/08854120122093339.

Gregory, K. (2014), "Cost Among Hurdles Slowing New York City's Plan to Phase Out Dirty Heating Oil," *The New York Times*, April 6. http://www.nytimes.com/2014/04/07/nyregion/cost-among-hurdles-slowing-new-yorks-plan-to-phase-out-dirty-heating-oil.html.

Grömping, U. (2006), "Relative Importance for Linear Regression in R: The Package Relaimpo," *Journal of Statistical Software* 17 (1): 1–27.

Guerra Santin, O., Itard, L. and Visscher, H. (2009), "The Effect of Occupancy and Building Characteristics on Energy Use for Space and Water Heating in Dutch Residential Stock," *Energy and Buildings* 41 (11): 1223–32. doi:10.1016/j.enbuild.2009.07.002.

Halverson, M.A., Shui, B. and Evans, M. (2009). *Country Report on Building Energy Codes in the United States*. http://www.osti.gov/energycitations/servlets/purl/978981-CXfXMI/.

Hamilton, I.G., Summerfield, A.J., Lowe, R., Ruyssevelt, P., Elwell, C.A. and Oreszczyn, T. (2013), "Energy Epidemiology: A New Approach to End-Use Energy Demand Research," *Building Research & Information* 41 (4): 482–97. doi:10.1080/09613218.2013.798142.

Harvey, L.D.D. (2009), "Reducing Energy Use in the Buildings Sector: Measures, Costs, and Examples," *Energy Efficiency* 2 (2): 139–63. doi:10.1007/s12053-009-9041-2.

Heinonen, J., Kyrö, R. and Junnila, S. (2011), "Dense Downtown Living More Carbon Intense due to Higher Consumption: A Case Study of Helsinki," *Environmental Research Letters* 6 (3): 34034. doi:10.1088/1748-9326/6/3/034034.

Höhne, N., Kuramochi, T., Warnecke, C., Röser, F., Fekete, H., Hagemann, M., Day, T. et al. (2017), "The Paris Agreement: Resolving the Inconsistency between Global Goals and National Contributions," *Climate Policy* 17 (1): 16–32. doi:10.1080/14693062.2016.1218320.

Hong, T., Taylor-Lange, S.C., D'Oca, S., Yan, D. and Corgnati, S.P. (2016), "Advances in Research and Applications of Energy-Related Occupant Behavior in Buildings," *Energy and Buildings* 116 (March): 694–702. doi:10.1016/j.enbuild.2015.11.052.

Hsu, D. (2014), "How Much Information Disclosure of Building Energy Performance Is Necessary?," *Energy Policy* 64: 263–72. doi:10.1016/j.enpol.2013.08.094.

——— (2015), "Identifying Key Variables and Interactions in Statistical Models of Building Energy Consumption Using Regularization," *Energy* 83 (April): 144–55. doi:10.1016/j.energy.2015.02.008.

Hui, S. (2001), "Low Energy Building Design in High Density Urban Cities," *Renewable Energy* 24 (3): 627–40.

ICLEI (2011), "Case Study: New York City's Greener, Greater Buildings Plan," http://www.nyc.gov/html/gbee/html/plan/related_ggbp.shtml.

Ingle, A., Moezzi, M., Lutzenhiser, L. and Diamond, R. (2014), "Better Home Energy Audit Modelling: Incorporating Inhabitant Behaviours," *Building Research & Information* 42 (4): 409–21. doi:10.1080/09613218.2014.890776.

International Energy Agency, and International Partnership for Energy Efficiency Cooperation (2015), "Building Energy Performance Metrics," http://www.iea.org/publications/freepublications/publication/building-energy-performance-metrics.html.

Kaza, N. (2010), "Understanding the Spectrum of Residential Energy Consumption: A Quantile Regression Approach," *Energy Policy*, Energy Efficiency Policies and Strategies with regular papers., 38 (11): 6574–85. doi:10.1016/j.enpol.2010.06.028.

Ko, Y. (2013), "Urban Form and Residential Energy Use: A Review of Design Principles and Research Findings," *Journal of Planning Literature* 28 (4): 327–51. doi:10.1177/0885412213491499.

Kohler, N., Steadman, P. and Hassler, U. (2009), "Research on the Building Stock and Its Applications," *Building Research & Information* 37 (5–6): 449–54. doi:10.1080/09613210903189384.

Kolter, J.Z. and Ferreira, J. (2011), "A Large-Scale Study on Predicting and Contextualizing Building Energy Usage," in *Proceedings of the Twenty-Fifth AAAI Conference on Artificial Intelligence*. http://www.aaai.org/ocs/index.php/AAAI/AAAI11/paper/download/3759/4088.

Kontokosta, C.E. (2014), "A Market-Specific Methodology for a Commercial Building Energy Performance Index," *The Journal of Real Estate Finance and Economics*, August, 1–29. doi:10.1007/s11146-014-9481-0.

Kontoleon, K.J. and Eumorfopoulou, E.A. (2010), "The Effect of the Orientation and Proportion of a Plant-Covered Wall Layer on the Thermal Performance of a Building Zone," *Building and Environment* 45 (5): 1287–303. doi:10.1016/j.buildenv.2009.11.013.

Krüger, E., Pearlmutter, D. and Rasia, F. (2010), "Evaluating the Impact of Canyon Geometry and Orientation on Cooling Loads in a High-Mass Building in a Hot Dry Environment," *Applied Energy* 87 (6): 2068–78. doi:10.1016/j.apenergy.2009.11.034.

Langevin, J., Gurian, P.L. and Wen, J. (2015), "Tracking the Human-Building Interaction: A Longitudinal Field Study of Occupant Behavior in Air-Conditioned Offices," *Journal of Environmental Psychology* 42 (June): 94–115. doi:10.1016/j.jenvp.2015.01.007.

Laurian, L., Day, M., Berke, P., Ericksen, N., Backhurst, M., Crawford, J. and Dixon, J. (2004), "Evaluating Plan Implementation: A Conformance-Based Methodology," *Journal of the American Planning Association* 70 (4): 471–80. doi:10.1080/01944360408976395.

Lindeman, R.H., Merenda, P.F. and Gold, R.Z. (1980). *Introduction to Bivariate and Multivariate Analysis*. Scott, Foresman Glenview, IL. http://www.sidalc.net/cgi-bin/wxis.exe/?IsisScript=COLPOS.xis&method=post&formato=2&cantidad=1&expresion=mfn=005517.

Lyles, W., Berke, P. and Smith, G. (2015), "Local Plan Implementation: Assessing Conformance and Influence of Local Plans in the United States," *Environment and Planning B: Planning and Design*, September, 265813515604071. doi:10.1177/0265813515604071.

Mills, E. (2011), "Building Commissioning: A Golden Opportunity for Reducing Energy Costs and Greenhouse Gas Emissions in the United States," *Energy Efficiency* 4 (2): 145–73. doi:10.1007/s12053-011-9116-8.

Min, J., Hausfather, Z. and Lin, Q.F. (2010), "A High-Resolution Statistical Model of Residential Energy End Use Characteristics for the United States," *Journal of Industrial Ecology* 14 (5): 791–807. doi:10.1111/j.1530-9290.2010.00279.x.

Nelson, A.C. (2004). *Towards a New Metropolis: The Opportunity to Rebuild America*. Washington, DC: Brookings Institution.

Newsham, G.R., Mancini, S. and Birt, B.J. (2009), "Do LEED-Certified Buildings Save Energy? Yes, But...," *Energy and Buildings* 41 (8): 897–905. doi:10.1016/j.enbuild.2009.03.014.

New York City (2014), *PlaNYC 2030: Progress Report 2014*. http://www.nyc.gov/html/planyc2030/downloads/pdf/140422_PlaNYCP-Report_FINAL_Web.pdf.

Norman, J., MacLean, H.L. and Kennedy, C.A. (2006), "Comparing High and Low Residential Density: Life-Cycle Analysis of Energy Use and Greenhouse Gas

Emissions," *Journal of Urban Planning & Development* 132 (1): 10–21. doi:10.1061/(ASCE)0733-9488(2006)132:1(10).

Oliveira, V. and Pinho, P. (2010), "Evaluation in Urban Planning: Advances and Prospects," *Journal of Planning Literature* 24 (4): 343–61. doi:10.1177/0885412210364589.

Perdue, W.C., Stone, L.A. and Gostin, L.O. (2003), "The Built Environment and Its Relationship to the Public's Health: The Legal Framework," *American Journal of Public Health* 93 (9): 1390–94. doi:10.2105/AJPH.93.9.1390.

Perez-Lombard, L., Ortiz, J. and Pout, C. (2008), "A Review on Buildings Energy Consumption Information," *Energy and Buildings* 40 (3): 394–8. doi:10.1016/j.enbuild.2007.03.007.

Pitt, D. (2013), "Evaluating the Greenhouse Gas Reduction Benefits of Compact Housing Development," *Journal of Environmental Planning and Management* 56 (4): 588–606. doi:10.1080/09640568.2012.692894.

Portney, K.E. (2003). *Taking Sustainable Cities Seriously: Economic Development, the Environment, and Quality of Life in American Cities (American and Comparative Environmental Policy)*. The MIT Press.

Pothukuchi, K. and Kaufman, J.L. (1999), "Placing the Food System on the Urban Agenda: The Role of Municipal Institutions in Food Systems Planning," *Agriculture and Human Values* 16 (2): 213–24. doi:10.1023/A:1007558805953.

Ratti, C., Baker, N. and Steemers, K. (2005), "Energy Consumption and Urban Texture," *Energy and Buildings* 37 (7): 762–76. doi:10.1016/j.enbuild.2004.10.010.

Ravetz, J. (2008), "State of the Stock—What Do We Know about Existing Buildings and Their Future Prospects?," *Energy Policy* 36 (12): 4462–70. doi:10.1016/j.enpol.2008.09.026.

Saha, D. (2009), "Empirical Research on Local Government Sustainability Efforts in the USA: Gaps in the Current Literature," *Local Environment* 14 (1): 17–30.

Schweiker, M. and Wagner, A. (2016), "The Effect of Occupancy on Perceived Control, Neutral Temperature, and Behavioral Patterns," *Energy and Buildings* 117 (April): 246–59. doi:10.1016/j.enbuild.2015.10.051.

Scofield, J.H. (2009), "Do LEED-Certified Buildings Save Energy? Not Really....," *Energy and Buildings* 41 (12): 1386–90. doi:10.1016/j.enbuild.2009.08.006.

——— (2014), "ENERGY STAR Building Benchmarking Scores: Good Idea, Bad Science," in *Proceedings of the 2014 ACEEE Summer Study on Energy Efficiency in Buildings.* Asilomar, CA. http://www.energytaxincentives.com/files/proceedings/2014/data/papers/3-725.pdf.

Steadman, P., Hamilton, I. and Evans, S. (2014), "Energy and Urban Built Form: An Empirical and Statistical Approach," *Building Research & Information* 42 (1): 17–31. doi:10.1080/09613218.2013.808140.

Steemers, K. (2003), "Energy and the City: Density, Buildings and Transport," *Energy and Buildings* 35 (1): 3–14.

Talen, E. (1997), "Success, Failure, and Conformance: An Alternative Approach to Planning Evaluation," *Environment and Planning B: Planning and Design* 24 (4): 573–87. doi:10.1068/b240573.

Tax Policy Center. (2016a), "Local Property Taxes as a Percentage of Local Tax Revenue," *Tax Policy Center.* June 21. http://www.taxpolicycenter.org/statistics/local-property-taxes-percentage-local-tax-revenue.

——— (2016b), "Property Taxes as a Percentage of State and Local Taxes," *Tax Policy Center.* June 21. http://www.taxpolicycenter.org/statistics/property-taxes-percentage-state-and-local-taxes.

Tso, G.K.F. and Guan, J. (2014), "A Multilevel Regression Approach to Understand Effects of Environment Indicators and Household Features on Residential Energy Consumption," *Energy* 66 (March): 722–31. doi:10.1016/j.energy.2014.01.056.

United Nations (1992), *Agenda 21: The United Nations Programme of Action from Rio*. United Nations.

Urge-Vorsatz, D. and Novikova, A. (2008), "Potentials and Costs of Carbon Dioxide Mitigation in the World's Buildings," *Energy Policy* 36 (2): 642–61. doi:10.1016/j.enpol.2007.10.009.

U.S. Environmental Protection Agency. (2014), "Greenhouse Gas Emissions, Energy Star Portfolio Manager Technical Reference," https://portfoliomanager.energystar.gov/pdf/reference/Emissions.pdf.

US Green Building Council (2015), *Building Orientation for Passive Solar | U.S. Green Building Council*. http://www.usgbc.org/credits/homes/v4-draft/eac6.

Wheeler, S.M. (2008), "State and Municipal Climate Change Plans: The First Generation," *Journal of the American Planning Association* 74 (4): 481. doi:10.1080/01944360802377973.

Wilson, B. (2013), "Urban Form and Residential Electricity Consumption: Evidence from Illinois, USA," *Landscape and Urban Planning* 115 (July): 62–71. doi:10.1016/j.landurbplan.2013.03.011.

Wilson, E. (2006), "Adapting to Climate Change at the Local Level: The Spatial Planning Response," *Local Environment* 11 (6): 609–25. doi:10.1080/13549830600853635.

Yu, Z., Fung, B.C.M., Haghighat, F., Yoshino, H. and Morofsky, E. (2011), "A Systematic Procedure to Study the Influence of Occupant Behavior on Building Energy Consumption," *Energy and Buildings* 43 (6): 1409–17. doi:10.1016/j.enbuild.2011.02.002.

Chapter 14

INFLUENCES OF PLANNING POLICIES ON COMMUNITY SHAPING IN CHINA

From Past to Present

Jian Liu

Introduction

In China, as in other countries of the world, communities are shaped and influenced by many factors. Scholars have made analyses on this issue from different perspectives, such as from the perspectives of city history (Davis et al., 1995; Heng, 1999), social life (Dutton, 1998; Pow, 2009), urban space (Wang and Murie, 2000; Bray, 2005), urban governance (Huang, 2006; Wu, 2018), housing policy (Wu, 1996; Lu et al., 2001), service production (Salmenkari, 2011) and architectural and urban morphology (Hui, 2009; Rowe et al., 2016). Different from all these studies, this chapter approaches the issue of community shaping from a planning perspective and tries to answer the questions of how Chinese communities have been physically shaped throughout history and what influences the planning policies have on communities' scales, forms and functions. Hereby, the planning policies concern not only the spatial organization, but also the social management of communities. The research is elaborated chronologically, dividing the history of community development in China roughly into four periods according to socio-economic development trends, planning objectives and community characters. They are the following: hierarchical *Li-Fang* communities shaped by traditional city building principles in the pre-modernization period before the 1900s; various *Danwei* communities shaped by urban planning for industrialization in the planned economy period from the 1950s to the 1970s; commodity housing communities shaped by market-oriented urban planning in the economic transition period from the 1980s to the 2000s and comprehensive community improvement shaped by quality-oriented urban planning in the era of new urbanization after the 2010s. The narration is mainly based on literature work and case studies, with a focus on the social and spatial characters of urban communities in terms of scale, form and function.

DOI: 10.4324/9781003178545-18

Pre-Modernization Period before the 1900s: Hierarchical *Li-Fang* Communities Shaped by Traditional City Building Principles

China's community development can be dated back to about 4,000 BC when primitive human settlements appeared. They were mostly built by tribes based on lineage relations. The first recorded settlement in a written document stems from the Shang Dynasty (1600 BC–1046 BC) and has been verified by archaeological findings in today's Henan Province. In the Zhou Dynasty (1046 BC–221 BC), China's traditional principles of city building were elaborated in *Zhouli*, or *Rites of Zhou*, particularly in the *Kaogongji* chapter which includes a normative descriptions on city form, functional layout, road configuration, and building codes. Meanwhile, a hierarchical administrative system was established in both the urban and rural areas of the country to facilitate the state's regime, within which *Lü* and *Li* were the basic administrative units of urban and rural areas, respectively (Li and Ren, 2014; see Table 14.1). Since then, this *Lü-Li* system became the prototype of Chinese communities until the early 20th century, despite the separation between the urban and rural systems and the variations of terminologies along with their historical evolutions, such as *Li-Fang*, *Bao-Jia* and *Fang-Xiang*. The traditional city building principles aiming at facilitating and highlighting the regime of the state have been a decisive factor in shaping communities of Chinese cities throughout its feudal history (He, 1996).

According to the *Zhouli*, *Lü* (*Li*) was a walled and gated residential community which was composed of five *Bi* (*Lin*), a grassroots neighborhood of five households, and four *Lü* (*Li*) constituted a clan of *Zu* (*Zan*) which was configured into four wards and equivalent to 100 households (see Figure 14.1). In the shape of a square, both *Lü* (*Li*) and *Zu* (*Zan*) were a unified unit of social management and spatial organization of different levels, for purposes of organizing tax collection, reinforcing feudal governance, maintaining social order and facilitating military conscription. The *Zhouli* also regulated the equipment of service facilities in urban communities, such as a day inn for every 10 *Lü* (*Li*), a guesthouse for every 30 *Lü* (*Li*) and a market for every 50 *Lü* (*Li*). Taking into consideration that the average family size at that moment was about 4–7 people, *Lü* (*Li*) was a neighborhood of 100 to 180 people, while *Zu* (*Zan*) was a clan of 400–700 people.

TABLE 14.1 The hierarchical administrative system of the Zhou Dynasty in both urban and rural areas

Urban area	Administrative unit	Xiang	Zhou	Dang	Zu	Lü	Bi
	Composition	5 Zhou	5 Dang	5 Zu	4 Lü	5 Bi	5 households
Rural area	Administrative unit	Sui	Xian	Bi	Zan	Li	Lin
	Composition	5 Xian	5 Bi	5 Zan	4 Li	5 Lin	5 households

Source: Revised based on Li and Ren (2014).

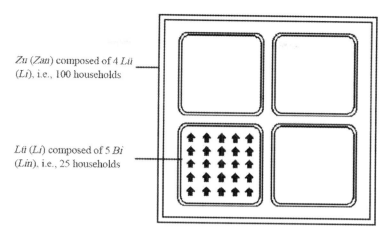

FIGURE 14.1 Li-Zu system of Zhou Dynasty.
Source: Drawn by Ong Huay Ying.

The communities were mainly self-governed in line with Confucian principles, with the practice of compassion and rituals serving as a means of communal activities to foster self-cultivation and establish communal order (Rowe et al., 2016).

The blood and kinship relation of communities started to collapse in the Eastern Zhou Dynasty (770 BC–221 BC) when pragmatic Legalism arose. Different from Confucianism, it advocated an autocratic state that was governed by impersonal norms and standards, instead of individual morality or blood relations. The practice of compassion or benevolence and rituals was extended from families to neighborhoods and then to a community, so that each individual was always related to others, helping to foster self-cultivation and to establish a communal order. The Legalistic administrative bureaucracy was established which included a system of mandatory population registration and the creation of mutual responsibility groups of five households for each. It meant that the five households might not be from the same clan, but they shall be responsible for each other. This collective compliance of communities was reinforced during the Qin Dynasty (221 BC–206 BC) when *Li*, a walled and gated neighborhood, became territorialized, leading to the differentiation between an inclusive and an exclusive community (Rowe et al., 2016).

The social relation-based communities were further developed in the period of Three Kingdoms (220–280) when frequent wars forced people to move to remote areas and build new settlements for self-defense. Due to the displacement, these new settlements were usually composed of people from various social hierarchies, including elite clans and non-family elements, such as household staff, soldiers and commoners. This resulted in the rising of communitarians who believed that the order of communities should be maintained through self-governance for mutual cohesion and consensus. Religions, such as Buddhism and

Taoism, became the bonds of collective, and community leaders were elected through recommendation based on reputation.

Although the term *Fang* was used to describe urban communities of ancient Chinese cities since the Eastern Han Dynasty (25–220), sometimes even replacing the term *Li*, *Lü-Li* remained the official terminology until it was renamed *Li-Fang* in the Sui Dynasty (581–618), which was popularized in the Tang Dynasty (618–907). Different from the *Lü-Li* system which guided the social management and spatial organization of the communities in both urban and rural areas, the *Li-Fang* system was mainly used to guide the shaping of urban communities in two aspects: Li mostly as a unit of social management, while Fang served as unit of spatial organization. Since then, the units of social management were gradually separated from the units of spatial organization in the physical environment. Meanwhile, compared with *Lü* (*Li*), both the size, quantity and density of *Li-Fang* remarkably increased due to the enlargement of cities, and the functions of *Li-Fang* also changed accordingly. For example, Chang'an City, the capital of the Tang Dynasty, was laid out according to the traditional Chinese city building principles depicted in the *Kaogongji*. It was composed of 108 *Li-Fang* delimited regularly by a chess-board grid, with a *Li* being composed of 100 households, while a *Fang* composed of 1,000–2,000 households, or even over 5,000 households. Being walled and gated communities which covered an area varying from 26.7 ha to 94.3 ha (He, 1996), both *Li* and *Fang* were under the administration of their respective leaders, with *Li* as a uniquely residential community, while *Fang* as a multi-functional community, like market *Fang* for instance (see Figure 14.2). The differentiation between *Li* and *Fang* inadvertently led to the social segregation of housing, separating the commoners from the royals, government officers, official residences, military barracks and storehouses.

As the *Li-Fang* system was a governance mechanism based on law enforcement and civil control at the grassroots level, it had prevailed through the following dynasties until the Qing Dynasty. It should be noted that the Song Dynasty (960–1279) witnessed remarkable transformations of the physical environment along with the prosperity of commercial activities. Some of the once walled and gated *Li* and *Fang* were opened to have a direct access to the arterial street. This led to the rising of commercial streets and mixed land use within the communities, as depicted by Zhang Zeduan in his famous painting, *Riverside Scene at Qingming Festival* in the city of Dongjing (now Kaifeng), the capital of the Northern Song Dynasty. Consequently, the spatial pattern of an open ward-lane community was invented for pre-modern urban neighborhoods, replacing some of the previous closed and inward *Li* and *Fang*. However, the openness of the *Li-Fang* system was not completed afterward due to the slow development of market economy, as well as due to strict requirements in city governance.

Today, the influences of traditional city building principles on the community shaping of feudalistic Chinese cities are still visible in the layout of the Old City of Beijing. As China's capital city in the Yuan (1267–1368), Ming (1368–1664) and Qing (1616–1911) dynasties, Beijing was planned and built strictly according

Influences of Planning Policy on Community **269**

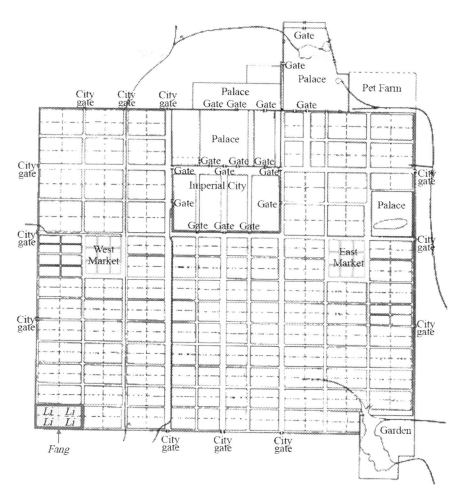

FIGURE 14.2 The layout of the Li-Fang pattern in Chang'an City of the Tang Dynasty. *Source*: Drawn by Ong Huay Ying based on He, 1996.

to traditional Chinese city building principles depicted in the *Kaogongji* chapter, even though the city was shifted and expanded southward in the Ming Dynasty. Being a walled city covering an area of 62 km^2, it was geometrically laid out along a central axis of 7.8 km long and spatially zoned in a concentric way according to social hierarchy, starting from the Forbidden City for the Emperor at the center, followed by the Imperial City for the imperial families, the Inner City for the nobles and the Outer City for civilians. Its functional layout was based on a hierarchical road grid, with the Palace at the center, the Temple of Ancestors to its left, the Altar of Grains to its right, the Court in its front and the Market to its back. Apart from the capital functions, neighborhoods and communities were developed simultaneously within the areas delimited by the hierarchical road

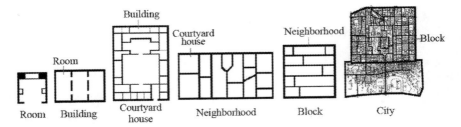

FIGURE 14.3 The composition of the Old City of Beijing based on the Fang-Xiang system.
Source: Drawn by Ong Huay Ying.

grid, along with the construction of courtyard houses by individuals according to the building codes for architectural facade, height, style, material, and color, etc., which also distinguished the differentiation of social classes. In the physical environment, the social management system was further separated from the spatial organization system. In terms of social management, communities were organized according to the *Pai-Jia* system based on population size, with 10 households for 1 *Pai,* 10 *Pai* for 1 *Jia* and 10 *Jia* for 1 *Bao.* In terms of spatial organization, neighborhoods were organized according to the *Fang-Xiang* system based on a hierarchical principle. Several courtyard houses were linked by a Hutong to form one *Xiang* (a neighborhood served by a lane), several Hutong neighborhoods linked by streets to form one *Fang* (an urban block or ward served by streets) and several wards linked by avenues to form a city (see Figure 14.3).

Planned Economy Period from the 1950s to the 1970s: Various *Danwei* Communities Shaped by the Planning for Industrialization

After China initiated its modernization in the mid-19th century, along with the process of colonization, modern urban planning was introduced to China from the West in the early 20th century (Liu, 2014). The way of community shaping in Chinese cities completely changed. After China adopted a planned economy system and implemented the industrialization strategy since the 1950s, the *Danwei* became the unit of the country's socio-economic development. It played a decisive role in industrial production and social management, as well as in spatial organization (Bjorklund, 1986; Bray, 2005; Bonino and De Pieri, 2015), in the 30 years of the planned economy. Socially, it was responsible for all the social welfare of employees including public services and housing allocation, acting as a "micro-government" at the grassroots level. Physically, it was often referred to gated compounds in blocks integrating employees' working with living on closed territories. Both led to the emergence of the *Danwei* community, a new kind of self-contained community. At the same time, for the purpose of turning consummative cities into productive cities, modern urban planning was taken as a technical tool of planned socio-economic development to support industrialization. It was quickly developed in China with the help of the former Soviet Union, being applied to guiding both the construction of industrial cities and *Danwei* communities. Moreover, a new community administration system was set up in 1954 according to the *Ordinance on the Urban Residents' Committee* promulgated by China's State Council. The Urban Residents' Committee became the autonomous organization of local residents for self-management, self-education and self-service. In line with the principle of facilitating self-governance, it was composed of 100–700 households according to the actual situation of habitation, which could be further divided into a maximum of 17 small neighborhoods, each with 15–40 households. Its establishment, annulment and adjustment were to be decided by the local district or city government, and its operation was to be under the guidance of the local governmental agency, i.e., sub-district office.

Compared with the traditional *Li-Fang* community, the *Danwei* community was a new spatial system of a residential quarter in blocks with multiple functions, though it remained gated and closed in spatial form. It was planned and built by either government agencies or state-owned enterprises with public investments, following the theory of Neighborhood Unit which was put forward in the 1920s by Clarence Perry, an American architect. Being housing construction equipped with public services, it was large in scale and mixed in functional composition. In terms of spatial organization, it was either part of a mixed compound with both working and living facilities, or a compound of living facilities neighboring working facilities (see Figure 14.4). In terms of social management, it could be under the administration of one or several residents' committees according to

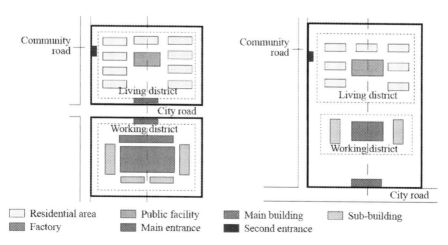

FIGURE 14.4 Different spatial patterns of *Danwei* community.
Source: Revised by Ong Huay ying based on Zhang et al., 2014.

the quantity of households it hosted, which ran under the direction of a local sub-district office and an enterprise as well (Hamama et al., 2019).

The development of *Danwei* communities in Beijing during the 1950s to the 1970s can be taken as an example to justify the influences of urban planning on community shaping in that period. Till 1949, Beijing was not an industrial city, and most of its communities were in the form of the traditional *Fang-Xiang* system. There were only very few industrial enterprises scaled to more than 100 employees and the industrial workers only accounted for a very small part of its urban population, making its industries play an insignificant role in either the socio-economic development or the spatial development of the city. After becoming the capital of the People's Republic of China in 1949 and in line with the national strategy of industrialization, Beijing was declared to be "not only a political center, but also a cultural, scientific, and artistic city, as well as an industrial city." Since then, thanks to a series of city planning schemes issued in the 1950s, industrial development became one of the key goals of Beijing's urban development and the industrial layout became one of the key contents of its urban planning (Liu, 2015). A number of industrial zones were planned and developed on the periphery of the urban center, which, by the end of 1957, occupied a land of 14.9 km^2 and hosted 67 industrial enterprises of over 1,000 employees. Meanwhile, in order to facilitate the organization of industrial production, a number of large-scale residential areas, i.e., *Danwei* communities, were built up nearby, following the principle of integrating working with living (see Figure 14.5 and Zhang et al. 2009).

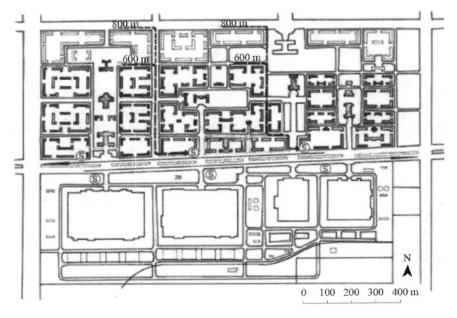

FIGURE 14.5 Typical *Danwei* communities neighboring factories in the east of Beijing.
Source: Zhang et al., 2009.

These *Danwei* communities were mostly in the form of an inward territory, regardless of being walled and gated or not, in order to facilitate the community management by the enterprises to which they belonged. Implementing the Neighborhood Unit theory, they were delimited by urban arteries and equipped with an internal grid, so as to get rid of the disturbance of by-pass traffic. They were composed of several residential blocks, with multi-leveled apartment buildings on the perimeter of each, surrounded by either a garden or a square as semi-public space, or a kindergarten or a boiler or electricity room as affiliated public utility. There were also blocks at the center of communities dedicated to public facilities, such as parks, a primary or middle school, clinic, post office, bank and market, whose type and scale were decided by the quantity of local residents. Thus, when communities were walled and gated, they would form quite large-scale multi-functional and self-contained compounds, i.e., the so-called "*Dayuan* (big-yard compound)." The prototype of *Danwei* community, including that of big-yard compound, was adopted by not only industrial enterprises but also governmental agencies, research institutes and universities. The campus of Tsinghua University is a typical example of the big-yard compound of *Danwei* community. Expanding gradually since the 1950s, it now covers an area of about 4 km^2 to accommodate about 80,000 residents, including most of its students, some of its staff and their families, a set of teaching and research facilities and almost all kinds of public facilities for daily life. Its social management is conducted by eight residents' committees under the direct guidance of one sub-district office and the university authority as well.

Economic Transition Period from the 1980s to the 2000s: Commodity Housing Communities Shaped by Market-Oriented Planning

In the following 30 years from 1980 to 2009, thanks to the reform and opening-up initiated in the late 1970s, China had undergone an accelerating process of urbanization supported by a sustained economic growth. On average, the urbanization rate increased annually by 1 percentage point, implying an annual migration of 14 million people from the countryside to cities. Together with increasing demands for a higher living standard, this resulted in huge urban constructions to provide them with houses and jobs, as well as various services, with the volume of the newly completed floor area doubling or even tripling every five years. For example, in order to tackle the issue of housing shortage due to the slow housing development in the planned economy period, Chinese cities made a huge investment in housing construction. The annual completed housing floor area increased from 172.6 million m^2 in 1982 to 886.4 million m^2 in 2009. At the same time, the national housing floor area per capita increased from 6.3 m^2 in 1988 to 23.7 m^2 in 2007.

In order to facilitate the transformation from a planned to a market economy, China had simultaneously implemented a series of critical reforms in many aspects of its socio-economic development, some of which played a significant role in the transformation of its urban communities, in terms of both social management and spatial organization. For example, the housing system reform initiated in 1980 characterized by the commercialization of housing changed the mode of housing supply from the free allocation by the government or *Danwei* as social welfare to being available for purchase as a commodity by individuals on the market after 1994 (Deng et al., 2011). In the 15 years from 1995 to 2009, the share of commodity housing as a percentage of newly completed floor area increased from 29.0% to 67.3%, with an annual increase of 2.6 percentage points. The land system reform marked by the promulgation of the *Land Administration Law of the People's Republic of China* in 1986, as well as its amendments and revisions in the following years, changed the mode of construction land utilization from free land use to land use at compensation. The enterprise system reform conducted in succession since 1978 to establish a modern enterprise system, characterized by the elaboration of property rights, the clarification of rights and responsibilities, the separation of government and enterprise and the scientific management changed the role of the *Danwei* from a "micro-government" to an independent market entity, with its responsibility of providing its employees with a full set of social welfare including housing and public services being returned to either the government or the society.

As a consequence, the hierarchical administration system composed of the city government, district government, sub-district office and residents' committee, which was originally established in the period of the planned economy based on the *Danwei*, gradually showed its inadaptability to the new situation of the market economy, though the *Law of Urban Residents' Committee Organization of the People's Republic of China* promulgated in 1989 reaffirmed the role of the urban residents' committee as the autonomous organization of local residents for self-management, self-education and self-service. Along with the withdrawal of *Danwei* from the social management of urban communities (Tian and Lu, 2009) and the proceeding of housing privatization, both sub-district offices and local residents' committees appeared incapable of providing urban communities with basic public services, which was once the responsibility of either the *Danwei* or certain local governmental agencies. Under these circumstances, the *Shequ* (i.e., community) sociological theory was introduced from the West to China in the late 1980s, in the hope of taking the place of the *Danwei* and local governmental agencies in public service supplying and complementing the incapabilities of the existing community administration system (Jiang and Hu, 2002; Tong and Zhao, 2006). In 2000, the *Opinions on Promoting Community Building Nationwide* issued by China's Ministry of Civil Affairs clarified the definition of community and its relationship with the residents' committee, as well as the connotation of community building. In 2003, the *Property Management Ordinance* promulgated by China's State Council legalized the Proprietors' Committee (also known as Owners' Committee) as a new kind of self-governance organization in commodity housing communities and regulated its rights and responsibilities in the property management of commodity housing communities, as well as its relationship with local residents' committees. This marked the beginning of community management with public participation under the new situation of housing privatization and commercialization.

Meanwhile, in terms of spatial organization, the *Code for Urban Residential Areas Planning & Design* (*Code GB 50180-93* hereinafter) was issued in 1993 and revised in 2002, based on the *Urban Planning Law of People's Republic of China* promulgated in 1989, aiming at regulating the large-scale construction of residential areas under the circumstance of housing commercialization. However, in spite of the reform and opening-up, the *Code GB 50180-93* still had a strong planning ideology. It advocated a three-level hierarchical community system composed of the *Juzhu Qu* (residential district), *Juzhu Xiaoqu* (residential quarter) and *Juzhu Zutuan* (residential cluster), which were categorized according to the quantities of both households and residents (see Table 14.2) corresponding, respectively, to the service of a middle school, a primary school and a kindergarten. A set of public facilities was also listed to be equipped in the three-level communities, for the purpose of supporting the development of complete and self-contained communities. The technical tool of a thousand-resident quota was applied to regulate the capacity of each kind of public facility.

Among the planning and design codes in the *Code GB 50180-93*, two have had a particular strong influence on the physical form of communities, i.e., the quota of sunlight spacing and residential land use per capita. The quota of sunlight spacing refers to the minimum distance between two neighboring buildings latitudinally laid out, which allows the natural sunshine of certain hours during a certain period through a full window on the ground floor of the back-row building on the day of either Winter Solstice or Great Cold. This rule is represented by the sunlight spacing coefficient which is the proportion of the height of the front-row building to the perpendicular distance between two buildings. As the required minimum natural sunshine time varies from one hour to three hours in different climate

TABLE 14.2 Category of the three-level community system in terms of household and resident: a comparison between the *Code GB 50180-93* and its revision in 2002

	Household quantity		Resident quantity	
	1993	2002	1993	2002
Residential district	10,000–15,000	10,000–16,000	30,000–50,000	30,000–50,000
Residential quarter	2,000–4,000	3,000–5,000	7,000–15,000	10,000–15,000
Residential cluster	300–700	300–1,000	1,000–3,000	1,000–3,000

Source: The *Code GB 50180-93* and its revision in 2002.

zones and according to the population size of cities, the quota of sunshine spacing also varies from one climate zone to another, according to the orientation of buildings (see Table 14.3). For example, the standard sunlight spacing coefficient of Beijing, i.e., that for south- to north-oriented housing of new constructions, is 1.7, while that of Shanghai is 1.2 and that of Harbin is 1.8. In spite of the variations, the quota of sunshine spacing results, without exception, in the decrease of east- to west-oriented buildings and the disappearance of perimeter blocks, as well as in the popularization of south- to north-oriented barracks with quite large open space between them. The quota of residential land use per capita refers to the land use area per capita for residential use, including housing, public facility, road, and green land, which also varies according to climate zones, residential community levels and the number of housing floors, whereby more housing floors lead to smaller quotas. Thus, under the circumstances of land use at compensation and housing commercialization, the quota of residential land use per capita inevitably results in the preference for high-rise buildings, rather than multi-story or low-rise buildings, so as to maximize the floor area on the same land area.

In the case of Beijing, the city went through a rapid process of suburbanization from 1980 to 2009, which was physically characterized by continuous urban expansion under the driving forces of economic restructuring and demographic growth. Statistics show an annual demographic increase of 360,000 and an annual construction land increase of 37.3 km^2 in a mono-centered pattern. In order to settle the problems caused by the continuous mono-centered urban expansion, including serious housing shortage, the city master plans of 1993 and 2004 highlighted in succession the policy of decentralization through regional development. As a result, when the Old City of Beijing was undergoing urban renovations in different ways, large-scale urban constructions took place in suburban areas, including commodity housing development projects in the form of "mega-communities" (Lin, 2006). Among them, Fangzhuang and Huilongguan built, respectively, in the mid-1980s and late 1990s, can be taken as typical examples.

TABLE 14.3 Regulations on natural sunlight time

Architectural category of climate zones	I, II, III and IV Climate zones		IV Climate zone	V and VI Climate zones
	Big city	Medium- and small-sized cities	Big city	Medium- and small-sized cities
Standard day Sunshine time	Day of Great Cold ≥ 2 h	≥ 3 h	Day of Winter Solstice ≥ 1 h	
Effective sunshine period Base point	From 8 am to 4 pm Lower windowsill		From 9 am to 3 pm	

Source: The *Code GB 50180-93* and its revision in 2002.

Located to the southeast of the Old City of Beijing, Fangzhuang residential area is the first large-scale and multi-functional community built up through planning with due attention to new requirements for modern facilities, societal life and commercial management after the reform and opening-up (Wu, 1987). The construction was initiated in 1985 after the housing commercialization reform was implemented in certain cities and was finished about ten years later before the policy of housing commercialization was implemented all over the country. At the transition period of housing privatization and commercialization, the planning of Fangzhuang abandoned the prototype of *Danwei* community and adopted the three-level community system of the *Juzhu Qu*, *Juzhu Xiaoqu* and *Juzhu Zutuan*, though the *Code GB 50180-93* was not officially issued yet. Covering a planned area of 2 km^2 delimited by four urban arteries and divided into four parts by two crisscrossing artery roads, this residential district of mega-community is composed of four residential quarters, accommodating a total of 76,000 residents. Centering on a park of 6.5 ha, each of the four residential quarters, a self-contained unit served by an inward road system to get rid of by-pass traffic, is further divided into several residential clusters which are either centered on a green land or linked by a green belt (see Figure 14.6). This spatial organization corresponded well to the new management system of the Fangzhuang Management Committee, the predecessor of the Fangzhuang Sub-District Office, which took the responsibility of social management of the community in collaboration with the local residents' committees. Its planned built floor area is 2.66 million m^2, including 1.81 million m^2 for housing and 0.85 million m^2 for public facilities, such as shops and markets; hospitals and clinics; high, middle and primary schools; kindergartens; and sports centers, as well as hotels and offices (Wu, 1987). Facing the rising housing market under the circumstance of housing commercialization, it adopted an architectural typology of high-density and high-rise buildings, so as to have more floor area. 80% of its buildings were planned to be high rises, which were interwoven with a number of multi-story and low-rise buildings in barrack style. All these made it distinguished, in physical term, from the prototype of the *Danwei* community which was physically characterized by perimeter blocks, though both were planned to be gated and self-contained. Nowadays, it is a built-up area of 3.14 km^2 composed of 15 communities (or residents' committees), hosting a population of around 100,000 (Xu, 2013).

Different from Fangzhuang, Huilongguan, officially named as Huilongguan Cultural Residential Area, is an updated mega-community under the circumstance of housing commercialization. It was the biggest of the 19 economically affordable housing projects announced by the Municipal Government of Beijing in 1998, located in Huilongguan Town of Changping District to the northwest of Beijing's urban center, not far away from Zhongguancun Science Park, a national-level High-Tech Industrial Development Zone established in 1988. Covering an area of 11.23 km^2, it was planned to be a comprehensive urban area with multiple functions including residence, employment, education and recreation, and a complete set of public and commercial facilities, accommodating a population of 230,000 on a floor area of 8 million m^2 to serve Zhongguancun

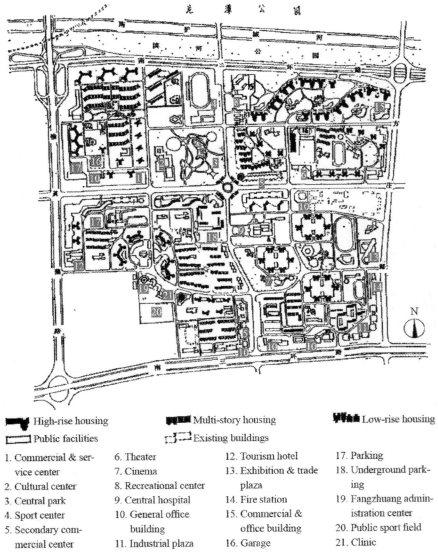

FIGURE 14.6 Site plan of Fangzhuang residential area.
Source: Revised by author based on Wu, 1987.

Science Park. The spatial organization of its residential areas was under the guidance of the *Code GB 50180-93*, with a number of gated residential quarters delimited by the road grid (see Figure 14.7). Its construction was initiated in 1999, and, by the end of 2007, a floor area of 4.88 million m^2 was completed, accounting for more than 60% of the planned quota, among which 4.42 million m^2 was for 38,000 apartments and 460,000 m^2 for public and commercial facilities

Influences of Planning Policy on Community   279

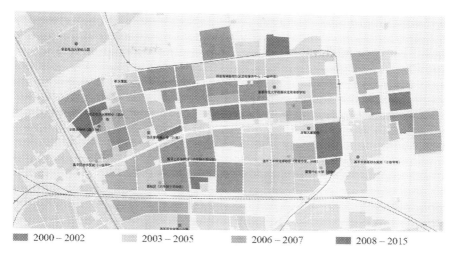

■ 2000–2002   ■ 2003–2005   ■ 2006–2007   ■ 2008–2015

FIGURE 14.7 Phasing of completion of Huilongguan cultural residential area.
Source: Revised by Ong Huay Ying based on Wang and Wang, 2018.

for education, administration, health care, civil utility, community service, etc. They were all organized into 31 residential quarters (Wang, 2008). The same as Fangzhuang, it adopted the spatial layout of gated community in barrack style. Different from Fangzhuang, it adopted the architectural typology of multi-story buildings in order to be more competitive in market. Nowadays, it accommodates more than 400,000 people under the administration of two sub-district offices and keeps the identity of the biggest economically affordable housing project of Beijing and a mega-residential community.

New Urbanization Period after the 2010s: Comprehensive Community Improvement Shaped by Quality-Oriented Planning

In 2011, after its urbanization rate surpassed 50%, China welcomed the coming of the urban society. In view of the problems occurring during the process of urbanization in a traditional mode, the Chinese government issued the policy of new urbanization in 2014, in the hope of improving the quality of urbanization. New urbanization advocates a people-oriented urbanization to ensure equity and sharing, the synchronous development of informatization, industrialization, urbanization and agricultural modernization to ensure the balance between urban and rural areas and among various regions. It also highlights a reasonable city layout to ensure intensive and efficient land use; the ecological civilization to ensure green development, recycling development and low-carbon development; and the cultural continuity to ensure local identity. The new policy implies that future trends of urbanization would shift from economy-oriented to human-oriented, from quantity-oriented to quality-oriented, from disregarding the environment to being environment-friendly and from increment-based to inventory-based. Its influences on the community building of Chinese cities were then presented in various aspects, including the improvement of the physical environment of residential areas and the rising of public participation in community life.

Considering that large-scale gated or inward communities, including both the *Danwei* communities of big-yard compound and the mega-communities of commodity housing, became a kind of thrombus worsening the traffic jam in cities and hindering the land use efficiency on the market, the National City Working Meeting held in Beijing in 2015 proposed the development of a *Jie-qu* (lane-block) system. The concept was reaffirmed in the following year by the *Opinions on Further Strengthening Urban Planning, Construction and Management Works*, which required the opening of existing big-yard compounds and prohibited the construction of new gated communities in future. Different from the spatial pattern of the traditional *Danwei* and mega-communities characterized by a sparse grid, wide roads and super blocks, the *Jie-qu* system is a new spatial pattern featuring a dense grid, narrow streets and small blocks, which is more adaptable to the traffic situation and the land market of modern cities. However, the implementation of this policy brought about wide debates in Chinese society, with concerns on the issues of property right, privacy and security, especially regarding the opening-up of the existing gated communities. The introduction to the planning practice of Barcelona from small blocks to super blocks for the purpose of making streets more pedestrian-friendly furthered the debates (Liao and Cai, 2018).

Under the new circumstances, the *Code GB 50180-93* was revised again in 2018. In order to be in line with the requirements of new urbanization for quality development and to be more adaptable to the market environment, it tries to decrease its sense of planning ideology, with its role being changed from compulsory to guiding. A new four-level hierarchical community system was set up to replace the previous one consisting of the *Juzhu Qu*, *Juzhu Xiaoqu* and *Juzhu Zutuan*, giving priority to the walking distance to local community service center, rather than only the quantities of households and residents. The new category includes 15-minute, 10-minute and 5-minute pedestrian-scale neighborhoods and neighborhood block, with correspondence to certain number of households and residents which are comparatively smaller than the previous ones (see Table 14.4). Moreover, the new *Code GB 50180-93* set higher standards for green lands and public services and concerned the renewal of old housing and the quality of the living environment. All these new guiding standards were soon accepted and implemented in the master planning of some mega-cities, such as Beijing and Shanghai, which became important references for other Chinese cities. In the same year, comments were invited for the draft version of the *Code for Residential Building*, which set up the standards for the energy performance, comfort equipment, land use, spatial layout, building code, construction structure and interior environment of residential buildings. It prescribes the maximum height of 80

TABLE 14.4 Community category proposed by the *Code GB 50180-93*: a comparison between the revisions in 2002 and 2018

Community hierarchy	Radius	Household quantity	Resident quantity
15-Minute pedestrian-scale neighborhood	800–1,000	17,000–32,000	50,000–100,000
10-Minute pedestrian-scale neighborhood	500	5,000–8,000	15,000–25,000
5-Minute pedestrian-scale neighborhood	300	1,500–4,000	5,000–12,000
Neighborhood block	–	300–1,000	1,000–3,000

Source: The *Code GB 50180-93* revisions in 2002 and 2018.

meters for residential buildings, which would obviously prohibit the construction of super high-rise housing.

While the spatial organization of China's urban communities was slowly transformed under the guidance of new policies for quality development, the social management of communities also underwent transformations along with the practice of community theory and the awareness of private property ownership. A remarkable representation was the increase of bottom-up public participation in the efforts of improving the quality of the living environment. On the one hand, when there are more and more people becoming owners of private housing, there appears a strong initiative from the proprietors to participate in either property management or community renovation which concerns their basic interest. For example, in the new commodity housing communities, it is quite popular that the proprietors' committee plays an active role in the negotiation with the property management company and the local residents' committee to protect the value and quality of their properties. While in the old *Danwei* communities to be renovated, public voting by local residents is also adopted to decide the program of renovations, like the practice of the Jiuxianqiao Neighborhood in Beijing (Zhang et al., 2016). On the other hand, considering that urban renovation becomes an important task under the condition of inventory-based urbanization and housing privatization makes it difficult to conduct bull-dozer practice, local governments gradually recognize the necessity of involving the participation and contributions of the grassroots. Experiments of community building were conducted and the mechanism of community planners was implemented in various Chinese cities, including Beijing, Shanghai, Guangzhou, Qingdao and Hefei.

In recent years in Beijing, different modes of community building within the actual community administration system were experimented at both traditional Hutong neighborhoods in the Old City and in new commodity housing communities in the suburban areas (see Table 14.5). There were remarkable achievements, concerning both the improvement of the physical environment and the strengthening of the sense of belonging (Liu et al., 2017; Liang and Luo, 2018; Zhao, 2018). The community planner system was implemented in succession in East, Haidian,

TABLE 14.5 Practice of community building in Beijing

	Initiators	Participants	Objects	Platform
Qinghe, Haidian District	Sub-district office + trans-disciplinary professional team	Residents + property management company + enterprises	Governance innovation + space improvement + service enhancement	New Qinghe Experiment Project
Dashilar, West District	District government	Designers + planners + architects + residents	Heritage preservation + urban revival	Beijing International Design Week
Shijia Hutong, East District	NGO + sub-district office	Residents + agency representatives + planners	Historic preservation + urban renewal	Shijia Hutong Museum + courtyard self-governance

Source: Summarized by the author based on related references.

Chaoyang Districts, which designated a professional planner to each sub-district, who would work together with academic partners from universities and colleges to provide the local communities with necessary guidance and consultation on the issues and projects regarding the improvement of living environment. Although it may take time to witness the efficiency of this new system, workshops and competitions with the involvement of local residents have shown the enthusiasm of different parties, which will surely influence the transformation of communities.

Conclusions

In summary, from the past to the present, among the factors influencing the community development in China, planning has always played a critical role in community shaping in terms of scale, form and function. In the long history before China's modernization, the traditional Chinese city building principles formulated in the West Zhou Dynasty shaped the Chinese communities into the pattern of the gated *Li-Fang* system of residential neighborhoods, in correspondence to the regulations of social management, in spite of the terminological changes in different dynasties and the opening of gated communities during the Song Dynasty. In the 30 years of the planned economy since 1949 when China took industrialization as a national strategy, Chinese communities were shaped by urban planning, as a technical tool of planned socio-economic development, into various inward and self-contained *Danwei* communities of perimeter blocks, with the *Danwei* playing the role of "micro-government" for social management. In the next 30 years of economic transition toward a socialist market economy, the land reform to land use at compensation and the housing reform to commercialization and privatization, together with urban planning becoming oriented to market development, shaped Chinese communities into gated commodity housing communities of super blocks, with the *Shequ* taking the place of the *Danwei* to be in charge of the social management of communities under the instructions of local governments. Since 2011 when China became an urban society and issued the new policy of new urbanization, the quality-oriented urban planning led Chinese communities to new transformations, including the debatable *Jie-qu* system of dense grids, narrow streets and small blocks, with more public engagement in community building at both old and new communities. In particular, in the past four decades of transition, although Chinese communities witnessed a remarkable transformation from multi-function to mono-function and from low and multiple rise to high rise, the multi-leveled hierarchical community system originally set up in the West Zhou Dynasty never changed.

References

Bjorklund, E. M. (1986), "The Danwei: Socio-Spatial Characteristics of Work Units in China's Urban Society," *Economic Geography* 62: 19–29.

Bonino, M. and De Pieri F., eds. (2015), *Beijing Danwei: Industrial Heritage in the Contemporary City*. Berlin: Jovis Publisher.

Bray, D. (2005), *Social Space and Governance in Urban China: The Danwei System from Origins to Reform*. Stanford, CA: Stanford University Press.

Davis, D. S., Kraus, R., Naughton. B. and Perry, E. J. (1995), *Urban Spaces in Contemporary China: The Potential for Autonomy and Community in Post-Mao China*. Cambridge: The Press Syndicate of the University of Cambridge.

Deng, L., Shen, Q. and Wang, L. (2011), "The Emerging Housing Policy Framework in China," *Journal of Planning Literature* 26 (2): 168–83.

Dutton, M., ed. (1998), *Streetlife China*. Cambridge & New York: Cambridge University Press.

Hamama, B., Repellino, M. P., et al. (2019), "The Processes Behind Community Building and Place Making in Transitional Urban Moments: A Comparison between China and Italy," *China City Planning Review* 29 (2): 25–34.

He, Y. (1996), *Planning History of Ancient Chinese Cities*. Beijing: China Architecture & Building Press.

Heng, C. (1999), *Cities of Aristocrats and Bureaucrats: The Development of Medieval Chinese Cityscapes*. Honolulu: University of Hawaii Press.

Huang, Y. (2006), "Collectivism, Political Control, and Gating in Chinese Cities," *Urban Geography* 27 (6): 507–25.

Hui, X. (2009), *The Chinese Housing Reform and the Following New Urban Question*. Doctorate Thesis of Delft University of Technology.

Jiang, Z. and Hu, H. (2002), "A Short History for the Concept of Social Community," *Journal of China Youth College for Political Sciences* 21 (4): 121–4.

Li, X. and Ren, J. (2014), "The New Study on Development Characteristics of *Li-Fang* System," *Architecture & Culture* 3: 94–95.

Liang, X. and Luo, J. (2018), "A Study on Self-Organizing Process: Taking the Experiment in Dashilar District as an Example," *Urbanism and Architecture* 25 (9): 24–27.

Liao, K. and Cai, Y. (2018), "Reshaping the Publicity of Block Streets: The Conception, Practice and Inspirations of Barcelona's Superblocks Planning," *Urban Planning International* 33 (3): 98–104.

Lin, J. (2006), "Problems and Reflection on the Planning and Construction of "Mega-Community"," *Planners* 22 (12): 66–70.

Liu, J. (2014), "Interactions between China and West: Viewed from Urban Planning and Construction of Chinese Cities amid Modernization," in P. Servais and F. Mirguet, eds. *Transferts Artistiques Entre Orient et Occident du 17e au 21e Siècle*. Louvain-la-Neuve: Academia-L'Harmattan, pp. 275–89.

Liu, J. (2015), "Transformation of Industrial Layout in the Spatial Planning of Beijing," in M. Bonino and F. De Pieri, eds. *Beijing Danwei: Industrial Heritage in the Contemporary City*. Berlin: Jovis Publisher, pp. 56–73.

Liu, J., Tan, X. and Cheng, Q. (2017), "Practice and Reflection of Participatory Community Planning under the Background of Transformation: A Case Study of Y Community, Qinghe District in Beijing," *Shanghai Urban Planning Review* 2: 23–28.

Lu, J., Rowe, P. and Zhang, J. (2001), *Modern Urban Housing in China, 1840–2000*. Prestel: University of California.

Pow, C. P. (2009), *Gated Communities in China: Class, Privilege and the Moral Politics of the Good Life*. London: Routledge.

Rowe, P., Forsyth A. and Kan, Y. (2016), *China's Urban Communities: Concepts, Contexts, and Well-Being*. Berlin: Birkhäuser.

Salmenkari, T. (2011), "Community Building, Civil Society and Societal Service Production in China," *Journal of Civil Society* 7 (1): 101–18.

Tian, Y. and Lu, F. (2009), "The End of Danwei Society & Its Social Risks," *Jilin University Journal of Social Sciences Edition* 49 (6): 17–23.

Tong, X. and Zhao, X. (2006), "Community and Its Related Concept," *Journal of Nanjing University (Philosophy, Humanities and Social Sciences)* 2: 67–74.

Wang, X. and Wang, S. (2018), "Huilongguan: 20 Years' Evolution of a Community," *Archicreation* 5: 54–67.

Wang, Y. (2008), "A Livable Area for Low- and Medium-Income Families: A Brief Introduction on Huilongguan Cultural Residential Area," *Housing Industry* 2–3: 40–41.

Wang, Y. and Murie, A. (2000), "Social and Spatial Implications of Housing Reform in China," *International Journal of Urban and Regional Research* 24: 397–417.

Wu, C. (1987), "Planning of Fangzhuang New Area and Its Inspiration," *City Planning Review* 4: 35–39.

Wu, F. (1996), "Changes in the Structure of Public Housing Provision in Urban China," *Urban Studies* 33 (9): 1601–27.

Wu, F. (2018), "Housing Privatization and the Return of the State: Changing Governance in China," *Urban Geography* 39 (8): 1177–94.

Xu, B. (2013), "A Study on Status Quo and Countermeasures: Public Service Facilities in Fangzhuang Residential Area of Beijing," in: Urban Planning Society of China eds. (electronic version), *Proceedings of Annual National Planning Conference 2013 (7-Residential Areas Planning and Real Estate)*. Beijing, China Architecture & Building Press, pp. 19–30.

Zhang, L., Chen, J. and Tochen, R. (2016), "Shifts in Governance Modes in Urban Redevelopment: A Case Study of Beijing's Jiuxianqiao Area," *Cities* 53: 61–69.

Zhang, Y., Chai, Y. and Zhou, Q. (2009), "The Spatiality and Spatial Changes of Danwei Compound in Chinese Cities: Case Study of Beijing No. 2 Textile," *Urban Planning International* 254 (5): 20–27.

Zhao, X. (2018), "Public Participation and Community Building in Dongsi South Historic Block," *Human Settlements* 2: 34–37.

INDEX

Note: **Bold** page numbers refer to tables; *italic* page numbers refer to figures and page numbers followed by "n" denote endnotes.

Aarts, N. 18
adaptability 94
adaptive capacity 94
advocacy planning: described 3; *vs.* transformative planning 3
Agenda 2030 for Sustainable Development 155–7
Allmendinger, P. 18
alternative networks, UPE 111–13
Ansell, C. 125
Anthropocene 1
Asian Development Bank 104
Asian Planning Schools Association (APSA) 107
Assche, K. 18
Association for the Promotion of Learning and Research of Urban Planning (APERAU) 107, 111
Association of African Planning Schools (AAPS) 105–7, 110
Association of Canadian University Planning Program (ACUPP) 108
Association of Collegiate Schools of Planning (ACSP) 107
Association of European Schools of Planning (AESOP) 107
Association of Latin American Schools of Urbanism and Planning (ALEUP) 107, *113*
Association of Planning Schools of Turkey (TUPOB) 108

Association of Postgraduate Studies and Research in Urban and Regional Planning (ANPUR) 108, 110, 112, *113*
Association of Schools of Planning in Indonesia (ASPI) 108
Australian and New Zealand Association of Planning Schools (ANZAPS) 107
authoritarian environmentalism 221

Badan Pusat Statistik (BPS) 36
Baud, I. 95
Beard, C. 125
Beling, A. E. 4
Benedict, M. A. 198
Beunen, R. 18
Bevir, M. 25
Bhan, G. 104
Bitácora, Cuadernos de Geografía, Cuadernos de Vivienda y Urbanismo 110
blue-green infrastructure: changing management model 200–1; conceptualizing potential of 198–200; living with water 198–200; resilient city and disaster funding divide 196–7
blue infrastructure: components **199**; in recovery planning 204–5
Booher, D. E. 125
'branch method' 20
Bring New Orleans Back Commission 203
buildings: assessing relative importance 245–6; characteristics 243; commercial

286 Index

and multifamily buildings 252; common variables 247–52; conceptual framework and methodology 244–6; determinants for energy consumption 253–7; determinants for GHG emissions 253–7; examining determinants 246; occupancy and use 243–4; reducing energy use and greenhouse gas emissions of 238–59; related work on energy consumption of 241–4; relative importance of building characteristics, occupancy and use, and surroundings 252–3; surroundings 244
built environment 9, 177–8; Buikloterham's objectives **182**; circular economy in 178–80
Bylund, J. 47–8, 60
Byrne, E. T. 125

Callon, M. 62
case studies 181–7; Buiksloterham, Amsterdam 181–3; fair adaptation 70–80; Kera, Espoo 183–4; Les Groues, Nanterre 184–6; planning education 127–34, **129**, **131–2**; Saint-Vincent-de-Paul, Paris 186–7; transport planning 51–62
China: commodity housing communities shaped by market-oriented planning 273–9; comprehensive community improvement shaped by quality-oriented planning 279–82; *Danwei* communities shaped by planning for industrialization 270–3; economic transition period from 1980s to 2000s 273–9; environmental concerns in MMPs from 217–18; *Li-Fang* communities shaped by traditional city building principles 266–70; new urbanization period after 2010s 279–82; planned economy period from 1950s to 1970s 270–3; planning policies on community shaping in 265–83; pre-modernization period before 1900s 266–70
Chinese cities: ancient 268; community building of 280; feudalistic 268; and post-suburbanization 42; suburbanization of 31–2
Chinese Communist Party (CCP) 218, 221, 223, 231
'circular city' 178–80
circular economy (CE) 8; Buiksloterham, Amsterdam 181–3; in the built environment 178–80; case studies analysis 181–7; 'circular city' 178–80;

'circular neighbourhood' 178–80; cross-case comparison and discussion 187–90; implementation in urban projects 177–91; Kera, Espoo 183–4; Les Groues, Nanterre 184–6; methodology 180–1; overview 177–8; Saint-Vincent-de-Paul, Paris 186–7
circular neighbourhood 178–80
Classic Grounded Theory (CGT) 15
climate change 195–211; and elderly 83; fair adaptation 66–7, *67*; and fairness 68–73; and local government adaptation 68–73; and values 68–73; and vulnerability 82–5
Code for Urban Residential Areas Planning & Design (Code GB 50180-93) 275, 277–8, 280
collaborative planning 124–5
commercial buildings, variables specific to 252
commodity housing communities: property management of 275; self-governance organization in 274–5; shaped by market-oriented planning 273–9
Commonwealth Association of Planners (CAP) 107
community-minded business owners, and lived values 79
community shaping: and *Danwei* Communities 270–3; and planned economy period from 1950s to 1970s 270–3; and traditional city building principles 268
comparative perceptions **132–3**, 132–4
comprehensive community improvement shaped by quality-oriented planning 279–82
Comprehensive Impact Statement (CIS) 52, 54–5, 58–9
Confucianism 267
connectivity: networks 94; and smart cities 93–4
The Consensus Building Handbook: A Comprehensive Guide to Reaching Agreement (Susskind, McKearnen, and Thomas-Lamar) 124–5
'consensus politics' 49
Corner, A. 69
Crutzen, N. 91
Cruz, H. 158

Danwei communities 10; and community shaping 270–3; shaped by planning for industrialization 270–3
Davidson, M. 50

Deacon, R. 18
de-colonising planning 4
democratic environmentalism 221
Dewey, J. 62, 125
Dialogues in Urban and Regional Planning 106
disaster funding divide: resilient city and 196–7
diSP Planning Review 2018 106
distributive equality 104
distributive fairness 68, 85
divergence/convergence assessment 22
diversity: functional 92; and resilience 92–3; spatial 93
Duineveld, M. 18

Eastern Han Dynasty 268
East-West Link tunnel (Melbourne, Australia): Comprehensive Impact Statement (CIS) 52, 54–5; reaction, action and intersections 55–8
Eaton, S. 222
ecological resilience 91
economic transition period from 1980s to 2000s 273–9
"edgeless city" 29
educational associations, and UPE 116–17, *117*
education institutions, networking (higher) and UPE 114
effective leaders 20
energy/energy consumption 2; of buildings 241–4; significant determinants for 253–7; use and greenhouse gas emissions of buildings 238–9
environmental concerns: evaluating by word counting 218–20; and local leaders 216–34; in MMPs from China 217–18
environmentalism: authoritarian 221; democratic 221
EURE 111
evolutionary resilience 91
The Evolution of National Urban Policies: A Global Overview (UN-Habitat) 156

Faculty of Urban and Regional Planning (Autonomous University of the State of Mexico) 141; challenges for teaching at 146–8; training update from the field of planning theory 148–50
fair adaptation: case study Victoria, Australia 70–3, *71*; and climate change 68–73; and lived values 80–6

fairness 80–6; and climate change 68–73; dimensions of 68; distributive 68, 85; procedural 68
Faludi, A. 146
Federal disaster funding 203–4
Federal Emergency Management Agency (FEMA) 203–4, 209–10
Federal Emergency Management Agency Public Assistance (FEMA-PA) Grants 203
FEMA Hazard Mitigation Grant Program (HMGP) 203
Ferreira, A. 92
flood risk/flood resilience 8, 195–8, 208, 210
Forester, John 124–5
Fraser, N. 104
Friedmann, J. 18, 25
functional diversity 92
fundamental change, need for 1–3

Gash, A. 125
geographic density 108–10, *109*
GHG emissions: descriptive statistics for multifamily buildings **250**; descriptive statistics for office buildings **249**; estimation results of determinants of **255**; in office buildings **255**; relative impacts for energy consumption and **253**; significant determinants for 253–7
global challenges of Anthropocene 1
Global Planners Network 143
Global Planning Education Association Network (GPEAN) 107, 112
Global South: colonial legacies and planning networks 111–13; and UPE associations 107; and urban planning 103
good urban governance 50
good urban politics 50
governance 220; feudal 266; *Li-Fang* system 268; planning education 124–5; resilient 95; smart 91; urban 265
Graham, S. 69, 70, 73, 75
Greater New Orleans Urban Water Plan 208
greenhouse gases (GHGs) 2, 238–59; emissions, reductions in 9
green infrastructure: components **199**; defined 198; elements 199; as part of integrated flood management systems 199; in recovery planning 205–7
green roofs 240
greenway 8, 199, 204–11
Guadalajara, Mexico: alignment of planning instruments of 157–64; influence

area of mass public transit *167*; new urban agenda (NUA) and application in Mexico 155–7; priority polygons for densification *167*; university and professional participation and PPUD 2018 164–71; urban planning in 154–71
Guadalajara Metropolitan Area (GMA) 157, **159**; absolute variation of inhabitants *160*; built heritage protection perimeters *163*; built space area in **160**; commercial land value, 2016 162; concentration of employment *163*; mass public transport network of 162, *164*; valid PPUD at the time of analysis *161*
Guay, L. 155

Habitat International Coalition (HIC) 106
Habitat International Coalition— Latin America (HIC-AL) 116
Habitat Program: International Guidelines of Urban and Territorial Planning 143; UP under the scope of 142–5
Harvey, L.D.D. 243
Healey, P. 124
Hendriks, F. 50
higher education, networks in 105–6
housing privatization 274–5, 277, 281
Howard, Ebenezer: *To-morrow: A Peaceful Path to Real Reform* 3
Hurricane Katrina 8, 195–6, 204, 206; devastating impact of 200; flooding 202; recovery planning after 201–2
Hurricane Sandy Rebuilding Task Force 203

Inch, A. 60
incremental progress strategy 23
Independent Assessment Committee (IAC) 54
Indian Institute of Town Planners 114
industrial estate development: Jabodetabek 37–9
industrialization and *Danwei* communities 270–3
Innes, J. E. 125
innovation/innovative 141, 166, 210
innovation/innovative planning practice 2, 8–9; and resilience 96; socio-political 51
institutional landscapes: in NYC 240–1; in other cities 240–1
International Energy Agency 243
International Guidelines of Urban and Territorial Planning 143

International Society of City and Regional Planners (ISOCARP) 115
Iveson, K. 50

Jabodetabek: industrial estate development 37–9; land use conversion in 35–7; New Order period 33–4; new town residential development 39–41; population growth 35–7; privatization of metropolitan 29–42; role of public and private sectors 41; urban development in 32–5
Jakarta *see* Jabodetabek
Jiménez, E. R. 158
Journal of Planning Education and Research 106, 126
justice: climate 66, 68; social 95, 142; urban 104

Karlsson, M. 69
Kennedy, M. 3, 4, 10
Kolb, David 125
Kostka, G. 222
Kotval, Z. 136
Kummitha, R. K. R. 91

Lafitte Greenway 8; green-blue infrastructure in recovery planning 204–7; green infrastructure in recovery planning 205–7; "inside-outside" advocacy strategy 208; limitations 210; and social learning 207–9
Land Administration Law of the People's Republic of China 274
language and urban planning education 110–11
Latin American Council of Social Sciences (CLACSO) 112, *113*
Law of Urban Residents' Committee Organization of the People's Republic of China 274
leaders: by authority 18; effective 20; by influence 18; and power 18
learning from experience (EL) 125–6, *126*, 136–7
Leeuwis, C. 18
Levy, C. 111
Ley General de Asentamientos Humanos, Ordenamiento Territorial y Desarrollo Urbano (LGAHOTDU) 156–7, 166
Liberal-National Coalition 53
Li-Fang communities: hierarchical 265–70; shaped by traditional city building principles 266–70; traditional 271
Life Cycle Assessment (LCA) 184–5, 190

Lindblom, C. 25
lived values: case study 70–80, *71*; and fair adaptation 80–6; mail-out survey 74–5; people-centric 82–5; region- and place-specific 81–2; results 75–80, *76* , **77–8**; scoping interviews 73
local government adaptation: and climate change 68–73, 85–6; and values 85–6
local leaders and environmental concerns in master plans 216–34
long-term advocacy strategy development 22–3
The Louisiana Weekly 207

Major Transport Projects Facilitation Act 2009 53
Mario Molina Centre (*Centro Mario Molina*, CMM) 156
market-oriented planning 273–9
Marres, N. S. 62
Marubeni Group 38
Massive Open Online Courses (MOOCs) 113
master plans: defined 216; environmental-related words in 222; local leaders and environmental concerns in 216–34
McKearnen, S.: *The Consensus Building Handbook: A Comprehensive Guide to Reaching Agreement* 124–5
McMahon, E.T. 198
mega-urbanization 29
Melbourne, Australia: Comprehensive Impact Statement (CIS) 52, 54–5; urban transport planning case study 51–62
metropolitan turnaround 36
Mexican Institute for Competition (*Instituto Mexicano para la Competitividad*, IMCO) 156
Mexican Silicon Valley 158
Mexico: City Prosperity Initiative 140; new urban agenda (NUA) and its application in 155–7
Meyer, H. 200–1
microclimate 256, 258
Millennium Development Goals 2
Ming Dynasty 269
Modernism 144
modularity 93
Moncaster, A. 178
Mouffe, C. 47, 49
multifamily buildings 254–7; variables specific to 252
municipal master plans (MMPs): attributes of local leaders 223–4; city context 224–5, 231–2; environmental concerns in 217–18; evaluating environmental concerns by word counting 218–20; local leaders' attributes 231; local leaders' effects on environmental concerns 220–2; methods and data 222–6; planning consultants and public participation 225–6, 232

National Association of Educational Institutes for Territorial Planning, Urbanism and Urban Design (ANPUD, México) 152
Netherlands 195–6, 200–1, 207, 243
Newman, J. 51
New Order period 33–4
New Orleans: attempting to mobilize resilience 202–3; delta city in rising sea 201–2; Federal disaster funding 203–4; green and blue infrastructure in recovery planning 204–5; green infrastructure in recovery planning 205–7; Lafitte Greenway and social learning 207–9; Lafitte Greenway Project 204–7; New Orleans resiliency challenge 201–2; planning and policy implications 209–11; post-Katrina recovery planning 202–3
new town residential development 39–41
New Urban Agenda (NUA) 1, 2–3, 4, 141; Faculty of Urban and Regional Planning 146–8; and its application in Mexico 155–7; planners moving towards 140–52; planning theory and training challenges 145–6; Theory of Planning 150–2; training update from planning theory 148–50; UP under scope of Habitat Program 142–5
new urbanization period after 2010s 279–82
New York City (NYC): building codes 240; diverse institutional landscapes in 240–1; NYC Housing Authority 240; PlaNYC 240
'NIMBY' opposition 51

office buildings 253–4
Oosterlynck, S. 50
Open Working Group (OWG) 2
outcomes and transformative incrementalism 20–1

participatory planning: and transport planning 48–50; and urban transport planning 48–50

Paterson, R. G. 16
people-centric lived values 82–5
Perry, Clarence 271
Phelps, N. A. 31
planners: Dutch 207; moving towards New Urban Agenda 140–52; in New Orleans 196; US 207
planning education: case study 127–34, **129, 131–3**; and conventional studio education 123–6; learning from experience (EL) in 125–6, *126*; overview 121–2; transforming 121–38
planning policies on community shaping in China 265–83
planning practice 259, 280
planning theory 25, 125, 141; and training challenges 145–6; training update from the field of 148–50
policy environment assessment 22
political binaries 50–1
Pomponi, F. 178
Population Center Plan of Urban Development and the PPUD (2018) 164–71
post-Katrina recovery planning 202–3
post-suburbanization: in Asia 29–30; in developing world 29; Jabodetabek 32–5, 41–2; as world-wide phenomenon of urban development 30–2
"post-suburbia" phenomenon 29, 31; *vs.* traditional suburban phenomenon 31
power: assessment 22; and leaders 18; and transformative incrementalism 18–19
practice: planning 259, 280; and transformative incrementalism 19–20
private sector, role in Jabodetabek 41
privatization: described 32; housing 274–5, 277, 281; of metropolitan Jakarta's (Jabodetabek) urban fringes 29–42; and suburbanization 29–30
procedural fairness 68
professional accreditation, and UPE 114–16, *115*
professional associations, and UPE 116–17, *117*
PT Bumi Serpong Damai (BSD) 40
PT Jababeka Industrial Estate 38, 40
PT Plaza Indonesia Realty 40
public participation 220, 223, 225–6, 232, 233
public sector, role in Jabodetabek 41
Public Transport Not Traffic (PTNT) campaign 56–7, 60
Purcell, M. 51

Qin Dynasty 267
Qing Dynasty 268
quality-oriented planning 279–82

Ranciere, J. 47, 49
recovery planning: green and blue infrastructure in 204–5; green infrastructure in 205–7; post-Katrina 202–3
redundancy 93
regenerative development 96
regional retirees, and lived values 80
region- and place-specific lived values 81–2
Reilly, T. 125
resilience 91–2; and adaptability 94; attempting to mobilize 202–3; definitions 91; and diversity 92–3; ecological 91; evolutionary 91; and foresight 96; and learning 96; as non-normative concept 92; post-Katrina recovery planning 202–3; and sustainability 92
resilient city and disaster funding divide 196–7
resilient governance and smart cities 95
Revista INVI 111
'Revitalizing Planning Education in Africa' 106
Riverside Scene at Qingming Festival 268
Rockefeller Foundation 106

Sager, T. 125
Saha, D. 16
self-sufficient, middle-aged primary residents, and lived values 78–9
Shack/Slum Dwellers International (SDI) 106
Shang Dynasty 266
Siegel, D. 18, 25
Silver, C. 32–3
smart cities: adaptability 94; are for people 95; connectivity 93–4; diversity 92–3; foresight and learning 94; government for resilient 90–7; modularity 93; overview 90–1; planning for 6; principles of resilient governance in 95; redundancy 93; regenerative development 96; resilience 91–2; and social inclusion 95–6; and vulnerability 96–7
Smart City Agenda 187
smart governance 91
Smith, S. 125
social inclusion and smart cities 95–6
social learning 207–9

socially networked circumstantial seachangers, and lived values 79–80
socio-ecological systems (SES): cities as 90; urban 90
solar: insolation 244, 247–8, 251, 253–7; roofs 240
Song Dynasty 268
de Souza, M. L. 49
spatial diversity 93
spatial planning 33
'structural co-optation' 49
subject profiles **132–3**, 132–4
suburbanization: of Chinese cities 31–2; in the developed world 30–1
Sui Dynasty 268
superblock 40
Superstorm Sandy 195
Susskind, Larry: *The Consensus Building Handbook: A Comprehensive Guide to Reaching Agreement* 124–5
sustainability 142, 144, 157, 239, 241; normative 92; and regenerative development 96; and resilience 92; urban 178
Sustainable Development Goal (SDG) 11 2, 6, 103
Sustainable Development Goals (SDGs) 1–2
Sustainable Development Summit 2
Swyngedouw, E. 50

Tang Dynasty 268
"technoburbia" 29
Tee, Brian 53
Theory of Planning 150–2
Thomas-Lamar, J.: *The Consensus Building Handbook: A Comprehensive Guide to Reaching Agreement* 124–5
To-morrow: A Peaceful Path to Real Reform (Howard) 3
Town Planning and Architecture for Policy on Education 104
training update from field of planning theory 148–50
transformative change 16; and values 19
transformative incrementalism (TI) 5; analysis 17–21; applying 21–4; overview 15, 16; research approach for developing 15–16; roles and skills of people in 23–4; zones of divergence and convergence 16, *17*
transformative planning 3; *vs.* advocacy planning 3; described 3
transformative policy initiatives 8–10
transformative turn/practices 6–7

Transport Integration Act 54
transport planning: case study of Melbourne, Australia 51–62; intersections and interceptions 58–60; overview 47–8; and participatory planning 48–50; political binaries 50–1; subverting the political in 54–5; urban *see* urban transport planning

UNESCO World Heritage Sites 158
UN-Habitat 107, 152n1
United Nations (UN) 1
United Nations Conference on Housing and Sustainable Urban Development (Habitat III) 155
United Nations Organization (UNO) 155
United States: blue-green infrastructure 196–201; changing management model 200–1; living with water 198–200; resilient city and disaster funding divide 196–7
Unterhalter, E. 104
urban development: challenges in neoliberal era 124; in Jabodetabek 32–5; post-suburbanization as world-wide phenomenon of 30–2
urban entrepreneurialism 34
urban fringes: privatization of 29–42; privatization of Jabodetabek 29–42
urban planning (UP) 141; in Guadalajara, Mexico 154–71; with Habitat III 143–5; under scope of Habitat Program 142–5
urban planning education (UPE) 7; alternative networks 111–13; associations, geography of 107–8; and capital cities 110; de-colonising of current 103; distributional inequality in 105; geographic density and gaps 108–10, *109*; and language 110–11; networking (higher) education institutions 114; networks in 105–6; post-colonial networks 111; professional accreditation 114–16, *115*; and urban inequality 104
urban projects: circular economy implementation in 177–91
urban redevelopment 184
urban transport planning 47; case study of Melbourne, Australia 51–62; and participatory planning 48–50
US Department of HUD CDBG-DR 203

values 85–6; and climate change 68–73; and transformative change 19; and transformative incrementalism 19

Victoria, Australia: climate change adaptation 66–8, *67*; lived values 70–80
Victorian Integrated Transport Alliance (VITAL) 56
vulnerability: and climate change 82–5; and smart cities 96–7

Walker, M. 104
West Zhou Dynasty 282–3
Wilson, J. P. 125
Wolfe, D. E. 125

Women in Informal Employment — Globalizing and Organizing (WIEGO) 116
word counting: evaluating environmental concerns by 218–20
World Cities Report 2016 141
World Resources Institute (WRI) 156
Wu, F. 31

Zhang Zeduan 268
Zhou Dynasty 266–7
Žižek, S. 47, 49

Printed in the United States
by Baker & Taylor Publisher Services